Spanish
for
Educators

William C. Harvey

BARRON'S

All inquiries should be addressed to:
Barron's Educational Series, Inc.
250 Wireless Boulevard
Hauppauge, New York 11788
http://www.barronseduc.com

Library of Congress Catalog Card Number 98-72512

International Standard Book Number 0-7641-0496-9
International Standard Book Number (Book with cassettes) 0-7641-7272-7

PRINTED IN THE UNITED STATES OF AMERICA
19 18 17

TABLE OF CONTENTS

A NOTE FROM THE AUTHOR

Years ago, while teaching at a middle school in Southern California, I was frequently interrupted by other staff members who needed some quick Spanish instruction. All over campus, from the principal to the custodian, there was a demand for foreign language skills. I later discovered that the problem was nationwide. Spanish-speaking children were enrolling in schools, and English-speaking educators needed to talk to them.

This guidebook is designed for anyone involved in education who needs to communicate regularly with Spanish speakers. I have discovered that once the language and cultural barriers are removed between schools and the community, Hispanic students find greater success in the classroom. Moreover, learning Spanish often leads to exciting new experiences, as well as personal satisfaction and valuable professional growth. Trust me, fellow educators, reading through this guidebook will truly be worth your time and effort.

Good luck! **¡Buena suerte!** *('bweh-nah 'swehr-teh)*

Bill Harvey

HOW TO USE THIS GUIDEBOOK

Spanish for Educators teaches English-speaking educators, along with related professionals, how to understand and speak Spanish. This book provides readers with all the Spanish vocabulary and phrases needed to communicate key messages to Spanish-speaking students of all ages, as well as to converse socially with Hispanic visitors, co-workers, family members, and friends. To accelerate the learning process, all skills are taught gradually and are systematically reinforced through practice and review.

To get the most out of this book, either use the convenient specialized dictionary in the back, or try focusing on the icons provided below. They can be helpful when you are working on a specific skill or topic of interest. Simply scan the pages for the corresponding icon, and read up on whatever you need.

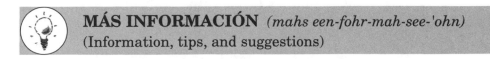 **MÁS INFORMACIÓN** *(mahs een-fohr-mah-see-'ohn)*
(Information, tips, and suggestions)

CONFLICTOS CULTURALES *(kohn-'fleek-tohs kool-too-'rahl-ehs)*
(Insights into Hispanic culture)

 ¡ÓRDENES! *('ohr-deh-nehs)*
(Spanish command words)

 ¡ACCIÓN! *(ahk-see-'ohn)*
(Basic Spanish verb tenses)

 ¿LISTOS PARA PRACTICAR? *('lee-stohs 'pah-rah prahk-tee-'kahr)*
(Review practice exercises)

GREAT NEWS!

If you're a little fearful about learning Spanish, here's some exciting news:

> ➤ Grammar and pronunciation don't have to be "perfect" in order to be understood.

> ➤ Thousands of words are similar in both English and Spanish, which makes it easier for you to remember vocabulary.

> ➤ Messages in Spanish can be communicated with only a few simple expressions.

Believe me. By following the proven suggestions mentioned in this guidebook, you can pick up lots of **español** *(eh-spah-'nyohl)* in no time at all!

CHAPTER ONE
Capítulo Uno
(kah-'pee-too-loh 'oo-noh)

BEFORE YOU BEGIN
Antes de que usted comience
('ahn-tes deh keh oo-'stehd koh-mee-'ehn-seh)

THE SOUNDS OF SPANISH
Los sonidos del español *(lohs soh-'nee-dohs dehl eh-spah-'nyohl)*

As a beginner in the language, your first step is to learn what Spanish sounds like. Fortunately, you don't have to pronounce everything correctly in order to be understood. Not only are people generally forgiving, but in reality there aren't that many differences between the two sound systems. In fact, you'll need to remember only *five* sounds to speak well enough to be understood. These are the vowels, and unlike their English equivalents, each one is pronounced the way it is written. Go ahead—read each letter aloud, and follow the corresponding pronunciation guide:

a *(ah)*   as in yacht
e *(eh)*   as in met
i *(ee)*   as in keep
o *(oh)*   as in open
u *(oo)*   as in tool

Now, let's learn how to pronounce all the other letters. And, remember—each letter has its own unique sound:

Spanish Letter	English Sound
c (after an **e** or **i**)	s as in sit (**cigarro**) *(see-'gah-rroh)*
g (after an **e** or **i**)	h as in hop (**general**) *(heh-neh-'rahl)*
h	silent, like k in knives (**hombre**) *('ohm-breh)*
j	h as in hat (**Julio**) *('hoo-lee·oh)*
ll	y as in yes (**pollo**) *('poh-yoh)*
ñ	ny as in canyon (**señor**) *(seh-'nyohr)*
qu	k as in kit (**tequila**) *(teh-'kee-lah)*
rr	the rolled r sound (**burro**) *('boo-rroh)*
v	v as in volt (**viva**) *('vee-vah)*
z	s as in son (**zapato**) *(sah-'pah-toh)*

Although some dialects may vary slightly, the rest of the letters in Spanish are similar to their equivalents in English:

b	**bueno** *('bweh-noh)*		**p**	**pronto** *('prohn-toh)*
d	**dinero** *(dee-'neh-roh)*		**r**	**tres** *(trehs)*
f	**flan** *(flahn)*		**s**	**sí** *(see)*
l	**loco** *('loh-koh)*		**t**	**taco** *('tah-koh)*
m	**mucho** *('moo-choh)*		**x**	**éxito** *('ehk-see-toh)*
n	**nada** *('nah-dah)*			

Now, read the following words aloud, and then guess at their meanings. Don't forget that each letter needs to be pronounced the way it was introduced earlier:

amigo	*(ah-'mee-goh)*
burro	*('boo-rroh)*
Cinco de Mayo	*('seen-koh deh 'mah-yoh)*
escuela	*(eh-'skweh-lah)*
español	*(eh-'spah-'nyohl)*
estudiante	*(eh-stoo-dee-'ahn-teh)*
excelente	*(ehk-seh-'lehn-teh)*
Feliz Navidad	*(feh-'lees nah-vee-'dahd)*
problema	*(proh-'bleh-mah)*
profesor	*(proh-feh-'sohr)*
televisión	*(teh-leh-vee-see-'ohn)*
tortilla	*(tohr-'tee-yah)*

MÁS INFORMACIÓN

➤ Any part of a word with an accent mark (') needs to be pronounced LOUDER and with more emphasis (i.e., **Ma**r**í**a) *(mah-'ree-ah)*. If there's no accent mark, say the last part of the word louder and with more emphasis (i.e., Bea**triz**) *(beh-ah-'trees)*. For words ending in a vowel, or in **n** or **s**, the next to the last syllable is stressed (i.e., Fer**nan**do) *(fehr-'nahn-doh)*.

➤ In some cases, the letter **u** doesn't make the "oo" sound (i.e., g**u**itarra *[gee-'tah-rrah]* or g**u**erra *['geh-rrah]*).

In the world of education, there are occasions when the best way to communicate is through the written word. In those cases, you may have to depend on your spelling skills in Spanish. Fortunately, the language is spelled the way it is pronounced. So, if you know your alphabet in Spanish, you are in pretty good shape. Try practicing these letters aloud:

a *(ah)*	**f** *('eh-feh)*
b *(beh 'grahn-deh)*	**g** *(heh)*
c *(seh)*	**h** *('ah-cheh)*
ch *(cheh)*	**i** *(ee)*
d *(deh)*	**j** *('hoh-tah)*
e *(eh)*	**k** *(kah)*

l *('eh-leh)*	**rr** *('eh-rreh)*
ll *('eh-yeh)*	**s** *('eh-seh)*
m *('eh-meh)*	**t** *(teh)*
n *('eh-neh)*	**u** *(oo)*
ñ *('eh-nyeh)*	**v** *('veh 'chee-kah)*
o *(oh)*	**w** *(veh 'doh-bleh)*
p *(peh)*	**x** *('eh-kees)*
q *(koo)*	**y** *(ee-gree-'eh-gah)*
r *('eh-reh)*	**z** *('seh-tah)*

¿LISTOS PARA PRACTICAR?

If you're having problems with the sounds of Spanish, try listening to the language for a few minutes each day. Spanish radio and TV stations or audio and video cassettes are fun yet effective ways to become familiar with your new pronunciation patterns.

KEY EXPRESSIONS
Las expresiones claves *(lahs ehk-spreh-see-'oh-nehs 'klah-vehs)*

The best way to get started in Spanish is to try out your new sounds in everyday conversations. Regardless of your situation, these basic expressions are a must for every Spanish student.

Excuse me!	¡Con permiso! *(kohn pehr-'mee-soh)*
Go ahead!	¡Pase! *('pah-seh)*
I'm sorry!	¡Lo siento! *(loh see-'ehn-toh)*
Thanks a lot!	¡Muchas gracias! *('moo-chahs 'grah-see·ahs)*
Please!	¡Por favor! *(pohr fah-'vohr)*
Yes!	¡Sí! *(see)*
You're welcome!	¡De nada! *(deh 'nah-dah)*
Hi!	¡Hola! *('oh-lah)*
Good morning!	¡Buenos días! *('bweh-nohs 'dee-ahs)*
Good afternoon!	¡Buenas tardes! *('bweh-nahs 'tahr-dehs)*
Good evening!/Good night!	¡Buenas noches! *('bweh-nahs 'noh-chehs)*
Good-bye!	¡Adiós! *(ah-dee-'ohs)*
See you later!	¡Hasta luego! *('ah-stah loo-'eh-goh)*
How are you!	¿Cómo está? *('koh-moh eh-'stah)*
What's happening?	¿Qué pasa? *('keh 'pah-sah)*
How's it going?	¿Qué tal? *(keh tahl)*
Nice to meet you!	¡Mucho gusto! *('moo-choh 'goo-stoh)*
Fine, thanks!	¡Bien, gracias! *('bee·ehn 'grah-see·ahs)*
And you?	¿Y usted? *(ee oo-'stehd)*
Very good!	¡Muy bien! *('moo·ee 'bee·ehn)*
Nothing much!	¡Sin novedad! *('seen noh-veh-'dahd)*
Same to you!	¡Igualmente! *(ee-gwahl-'mehn-teh)*

 ## MÁS INFORMACIÓN

➤ Several words in English are spelled the same in Spanish, and they usually have the same meaning. But, watch out! They are NOT pronounced the same!

chocolate *(choh-koh-'lah-teh)*
color *('koh-'lohr)*
final *(fee-'nahl)*
idea *(ee-'deh-ah)*
natural *(nah-too-'rahl)*
terror *(teh-'rrohr)*

➤ The upside down exclamation point (¡) and question mark (¿) are found at the beginning of sentences, and must be used when you write in Spanish.

➤ Scan these other "excuse me" phrases:

Excuse me! (if you cough or sneeze) **¡Perdón!** *(pehr-'dohn)*
Excuse me! (if you need someone's attention) **¡Disculpe!** *(dees-'kool-peh)*

➤ Look! Some words change meanings if you drop the accent mark:

yes	**sí** (see)	if	**si** (see)
how	**cómo** *('koh-moh)*	I eat	**como** *('koh-moh)*
give	**dé** *(deh)*	from	**de** *(deh)*
what?	**¿Qué?** *(keh)*	that	**que** *(keh)*

CONFLICTOS CULTURALES

Friendly greetings in Spanish are used all day long. Being courteous is the key to establishing trust with your students and their families. Throughout the Spanish-speaking world, a smile and a pleasant word can lead to respect and complete cooperation.

¿LISTOS PARA PRACTICAR?

Practice this dialogue with a friend:

Hola. *('oh-lah)*
¿Qué pasa? *('keh 'pah-sah)*
¿Cómo está? *('koh-moh eh-'stah)*

Muy bien. Hasta luego.
   *('moo·ee 'bee·ehn. 'ah-stah
   loo-'eh-goh)*

Buenas tardes. *('bweh-nahs 'tahr-dehs)*
Sin novedad. *(seen noh-veh-'dahd)*
Bien, gracias. ¿Y usted? *('bee·ehn,
   'grah-see·ahs. ee oo-'stehd)*
Adiós. *('ah-dee-'ohs)*

6

MORE ESSENTIAL PHRASES
Más frases esenciales *(mahs 'frah-sehs eh-sehn-see-'ah-lehs)*

Spanish is full of common expressions that are used regularly in normal conversations. A lot can be communicated simply by saying a few short phrases. Interject one of these whenever it is appropriate:

Don't worry.	**No se preocupe.** *(noh seh preh-oh-'koo-peh)*
Good idea.	**Buena idea.** *('bweh-nah ee-'deh-ah)*
I see.	**Ya veo.** *(yah 'veh-oh)*
I think so.	**Creo que sí.** *('kreh-oh keh see)*
Maybe.	**Quizás.** *(kee-'sahs)*
More or less.	**Más o menos.** *(mahs oh 'meh-nohs)*
Not yet.	**Todavía no.** *(toh-dah-'vee-ah noh)*
Ready?	**¿Listo?** *('lee-stoh)*
Sure.	**Claro.** *('klah-roh)*
That depends.	**Depende.** *(deh-'pehn-deh)*

Put a little more emotion into these!

Bless you!	**¡Salud!** *(sah-'lood)*
Congratulations!	**¡Felicitaciones!** *(feh-lee-see-tah-see-'oh-nehs)*
Good luck!	**¡Buena suerte!** *('bweh-nah 'swehr-teh)*
Happy Birthday!	**¡Feliz cumpleaños!** *(feh-'lees koom-pleh-'ah-nyohs)*
Welcome!	**¡Bienvenidos!** *('bee·ehn veh-'nee-dohs)*
Wow!	**¡Caramba!** *(kah-'rahm-bah)*
For heaven's sake!	**¡Dios mío!** *('dee-ohs 'mee-oh)*

Bear in mind that most idiomatic expressions cannot be translated word for word. Therefore, try to memorize each phrase as one long string of individual sounds.

MÁS INFORMACIÓN

➤ The word **Qué** (keh) is often part of an emotional comment:

What a shame!	**¡Qué lástima!** *(keh 'lah-stee-mah)*
That's great!	**¡Qué bueno!** *(keh 'bweh-noh)*
How funny!	**¡Qué chistoso!** *(keh chee-'stoh-soh)*

➤ And don't forget these holidays:

Merry Christmas!	**¡Feliz Navidad!** *(feh-'lees nah-vee-'dahd)*
Happy New Year!	**¡Feliz año nuevo!** *(feh-'lees 'ah-nyoh noo-'eh-voh)*
Happy Easter!	**¡Felices pascuas!** *(feh-'lee-sehs 'pah-skwahs)*

➤ There are several ways to say good-bye in Spanish, so continue to wave and shout:

Have a nice day!	**¡Que le vaya bien!** *(keh leh vah-yah bee-'ehn)*
We'll see you!	**¡Nos vemos!** *(nohs 'veh-mohs)*
Go with God!	**¡Vaya con Dios!** *('vah-yah kohn dee-'ohs)*

¿LISTOS PARA PRACTICAR?

Connect each phrase with its appropriate response:

Qué lástima. *(keh 'lah-stee-mah)*	**Todavía no.** *(toh-dah-'vee-ah noh)*
Mucho gusto. *('moo-choh 'goo-stoh)*	**Nos vemos.** *(nohs 'veh-mohs)*
¿Cómo está? *('koh-moh eh-'stah)*	**Salud.** *(sah-'lood)*
Gracias. *('grah-see·ahs)*	**De nada.** *(deh 'nah-dah)*
¡Ah-choo! *(ah-'choo)*	**Bien. ¿Y usted?** *('bee·ehn ee oo-'stehd)*
Hasta luego. *('ah-stah loo-'eh-goh)*	**Igualmente.** *(ee-gwahl-'mehn-teh)*
¿Listo? *('lee-stoh)*	**Lo siento.** *(loh see-'ehn-toh)*

DO YOU SPEAK SPANISH?
¿Habla usted español? *('ah-blah oo-'stehd eh-spah-'nyohl)*

Once you finish with the greetings and common courtesies, you will face the inevitable problem of not being able to understand one another. To make things easier, try to pronounce a few of these one-liners. They send the message that you are doing the best you can!

Again.	**Otra vez.** *('oh-trah vehs)*
Do you understand?	**¿Entiende?** *(ehn-tee-'ehn-deh)*
How do you say it?	**¿Cómo se dice?** *('koh-moh seh 'dee-seh)*
How do you spell it?	**¿Cómo se deletrea?** *('koh-moh seh deh-leh-'treh-ah)*

I don't understand!	**¡No entiendo!** *(noh ehn-tee-'ehn-doh)*
I'm learning Spanish.	**Estoy aprendiendo español.** *(eh-'stoh-ee ah-prehn-dee-'ehn-doh eh-spah-'nyohl)*
I speak a little Spanish.	**Hablo poquito español.** *('ah-bloh poh-'kee-toh eh-spah-'nyohl)*
More slowly!	**¡Más despacio!** *(mahs deh-'spah-see·oh)*
Thanks for your patience.	**Gracias por su paciencia.** *('grah-see·ahs pohr soo pah-see-'ehn-see·ah)*
What does it mean?	**¿Qué significa?** *(keh seeg-nee-'fee-kah)*
Word by word!	**¡Palabra por palabra!** *(pah-'lah-brah pohr pah-'lah-brah)*
Please repeat.	**Repita, por favor.** *(reh-'pee-tah, pohr fah-'vohr)*

Seriously consider posting these expressions nearby. They can help you out if you ever get into trouble!

NECESSARY VOCABULARY

El vocabulario necesario *(ehl voh-kah-boo-'lah-ree·oh neh-seh-'sah-ree·oh)*

It's impossible to carry on intelligent conversations in Spanish without the basic vocabulary words. To learn them quickly, let's list the terms under specific categories. And, as you read each series, try to pronounce everything correctly. Good luck!

Everyday Things	**Las cosas diarias** *(lahs 'koh-sahs dee-'ah-ree·ahs)*
bed	**la cama** *(lah 'kah-mah)*
book	**el libro** *(ehl 'lee-broh)*
car	**el carro** *(ehl 'kah-rroh)*
chair	**la silla** *(lah 'see-yah)*
classroom	**la clase** *(lah 'klah-seh)*
desk	**el escritorio** *(ehl ehs-kree-'toh-ree·oh)*
door	**la puerta** *(lah 'pwehr-tah)*
floor	**el piso** *(ehl 'pee-soh)*
food	**la comida** *(lah koh-'mee-dah)*
homework	**la tarea** *(lah tah-'reh-ah)*
house	**la casa** *(lah 'kah-sah)*
light	**la luz** *(lah loos)*
office	**la oficina** *(lah oh-fee-'see-nah)*
paper	**el papel** *(ehl pah-'pehl)*

pen	**el lapicero** (ehl lah-pee-'seh-roh)
pencil	**el lápiz** (ehl 'lah-pees)
restroom	**el servicio** (ehl sehr-'vee-see·oh)
room	**el cuarto** (ehl 'kwahr-toh)
school	**la escuela** (lah eh-'skweh-lah)
table	**la mesa** (lah 'meh-sah)
telephone	**el teléfono** (ehl teh-'leh-foh-noh)
trash	**la basura** (lah bah-'soo-rah)
water	**el agua** (ehl 'ah-gwah)
window	**la ventana** (lah vehn-'tah-nah)
work	**el trabajo** (ehl trah-'bah-hoh)

People — **La gente** (la 'hehn-teh)

baby	**el bebé** (ehl beh-'beh)
boy	**el niño** (ehl 'nee-nyoh)
brother	**el hermano** (ehl ehr-'mah-noh)
daughter	**la hija** (lah 'ee-hah)
father	**el padre** (ehl 'pah-dreh)
girl	**la niña** (lah 'nee-nyah)
man	**el hombre** (ehl 'ohm-breh)
mother	**la madre** (lah 'mah-dreh)
person	**la persona** (lah pehr-'soh-nah)
sister	**la hermana** (lah ehr-'mah-nah)
son	**el hijo** (ehl 'ee-hoh)
student	**el estudiante** (ehl eh-stoo-dee-'ahn-teh)
teacher	**el maestro** (ehl mah-'eh-stroh)
teenager (female)	**la muchacha** (lah moo-'chah-chah)
teenager (male)	**el muchacho** (ehl moo-'chah-choh)
woman	**la mujer** (lah moo-'hehr)

The Colors — **Los colores** (lohs koh-'loh-rehs)

black	**negro** ('neh-groh)
blue	**azul** (ah-'sool)
brown	**café** (kah-'feh)
green	**verde** ('vehr-deh)
orange	**anaranjado** (ah-nah-rahn-'hah-doh)
purple	**morado** (moh-'rah-doh)
red	**rojo** ('roh-hoh)
white	**blanco** ('blahn-koh)
yellow	**amarillo** (ah-mah-'ree-yoh)

More Important Words	Más palabras importantes *(mahs pah-'lah-brahs eem-pohr-'tahn-tehs)*
a few	**pocos** *('poh-kohs)*
a little	**poco** *('poh-koh)*
all	**todo** *('toh-doh)*
bad	**malo** *('mah-loh)*
big	**grande** *('grahn-deh)*
good	**bueno** *('bweh-noh)*
less	**menos** *('meh-nohs)*
many	**muchos** *('moo-chohs)*
more	**más** *(mahs)*
much	**mucho** *('moo-choh)*
small	**pequeño** *(peh-'keh-nyoh)*

MÁS INFORMACIÓN

➤ Notice that the names for people, places, and things are either masculine or feminine, and so have either **el** *(ehl)* or **la** *(lah)* in front. **El** and **la** mean "the." Generally, if the word ends in the letter **o** there's an **el** in front; i.e., **el cuarto** *(ehl 'kwahr-toh)*, **el niño** *(ehl 'nee-nyoh)*. Conversely, if the word ends in an **a** there's a **la** in front; i.e., **la mesa** *(lah 'meh-sah)*, **la persona** *(lah pehr-'soh-nah)*. Some Spanish words are exceptions: **el agua** *(ehl 'ah-gwah)*, **el sofá** *(ehl soh-'fah)*.

➤ Words not ending in either an **o** or **a** need to be memorized; i.e., **el amor** *(ehl ah-'mohr)*, **la luz** *(lah loos)*. In the case of single objects, use **el** and **la** much like the word "the" in English: The house is big **(la casa es grande)** *(lah 'kah-sah ehs 'grahn-deh)*.

➤ Remember, too, that **el** and **la** are used in Spanish to indicate a person's sex. **El maestro** *(ehl mah-'eh-stroh)* is a male teacher, while **la maestra** *(lah mah-'ehs-trah)* is a female teacher. Words ending in **e** usually do not change on account of sex: you usually identify them by putting **el** or **la** in front. **La estudiante** *(lah eh-stoo-dee-'ahn-teh)* is a female student, whereas **el estudiante** is a male student.

➤ One effective method to remember the names for things is to write their names on removable stickers and then place them on the objects you are trying to remember.

➤ Be aware that there are other names in Spanish for the items listed below. Here are a few synonyms you should know:

teacher	**el profesor** *(ehl proh-feh-'sohr)*
desk	**el pupitre** *(ehl poo-'peeh-treh)*
student	**el alumno** *(ehl ah-'loom-noh)*
young person	**el chico** *(ehl 'chee-koh)*
man	**el señor** *(ehl seh-'nyohr)*
woman	**la señora** *(lah seh-'nyoh-rah)*
pen	**la pluma** *(lah 'ploo-mah)*
car	**el coche** *(ehl 'koh-cheh)*

 ¿LISTOS PARA PRACTICAR?

Fill in the blank with an English translation:

el lápiz *(ehl 'lah-pees)*   _____

el libro *(ehl 'lee-broh)*   _____

la mesa *(lah 'meh-sah)*   _____

el trabajo *(ehl trah-'bah-hoh)*   _____

la escuela *(lah eh-'skweh-lah)*   _____

Now match the opposites:

padre *('pah-dreh)*   **maestro** *(mah-'eh-stroh)*
pequeño *(peh-'keh-nyoh)*   **mujer** *(moo-'hehr)*
hombre *('ohm-breh)*   **negro** *('neh-groh)*
blanco *('blahn-koh)*   **grande** *('grahn-deh)*
estudiante *(eh-stoo-dee-'ahn-teh)*   **madre** *('mah-dreh)*

NUMBERS

Los números *(lohs 'noo-meh-rohs)*

No one can survive in Spanish without the numbers, so say each of these words more than once:

0	**cero** *('seh-roh)*	14	**catorce** *(kah-'tohr-seh)*
1	**uno** *('oo-noh)*	15	**quince** *('keen-seh)*
2	**dos** *(dohs)*	16	**dieciséis** *(dee-ehs-ee-'seh·ees)*
3	**tres** *(trehs)*	17	**diecisiete** *(dee-ehs-ee-see-'eh-teh)*
4	**cuatro** *('kwa-troh)*	18	**dieciocho** *(dee-ehs-ee-'oh-choh)*
5	**cinco** *('seen-koh)*	19	**diecinueve** *(dee-ehs-ee-noo-'eh-veh)*
6	**seis** *('seh·ees)*	20	**veinte** *('veh·een-teh)*
7	**siete** *(see-'eh-teh)*	30	**treinta** *('treh·een-tah)*
8	**ocho** *('oh-choh)*	40	**cuarenta** *(kwah-'rehn-tah)*
9	**nueve** *(noo-'eh-veh)*	50	**cincuenta** *(seen-'kwehn-tah)*
10	**diez** *(dee-'ehs)*	60	**sesenta** *(seh-'sehn-tah)*
11	**once** *('ohn-seh)*	70	**setenta** *(seh-'tehn-tah)*
12	**doce** *('doh-seh)*	80	**ochenta** *(oh-'chehn-tah)*
13	**trece** *('treh-seh)*	90	**noventa** *(noh-'vehn-tah)*

For all the numbers in-between, just add **"y"** (ee), which means "and":

21   **veinte y uno** *('veh·een-teh ee 'oo-noh)*
22   **veinte y dos** *('veh·een-teh ee dohs)*
21   **veinte y tres** *('veh·een-teh ee trehs)*

Sooner or later, you'll also need to know how to say the larger numbers in Spanish. They aren't that difficult, so practice aloud:

100   **cien** *('see-ehn)*
200   **doscientos** *(dohs-see-'ehn-tohs)*
300   **trescientos** *(trehs-see-'ehn-tohs)*
400   **cuatrocientos** *(kwah-troh-see-'ehn-tohs)*
500   **quinientos** *(keen-ee-'ehn-tohs)*
600   **seiscientos** *(seh·ees-see-'en-tohs)*
700   **setecientos** *(seh-teh-see-'ehn-tohs)*
800   **ochocientos** *(oh-choh-see-'ehn-tohs)*
900   **novecientos** *(noh-veh-see-'ehn-tohs)*
1000   **mil** *(meel)*

➤ The cardinal numbers are valuable, too! Practice:

first	**primero** (*pree-'meh-roh*)
second	**segundo** (*seh-'goon-doh*)
third	**tercero** (*tehr-'seh-roh*)
fourth	**cuarto** (*'kwahr-toh*)
fifth	**quinto** (*'keen-toh*)
sixth	**sexto** (*'sehks-toh*)
seventh	**séptimo** (*'sehp-tee-moh*)
eighth	**octavo** (*ohk-'tah-voh*)
ninth	**noveno** (*noh-'veh-noh*)
tenth	**décimo** (*'deh-see-moh*)

➤ Look at what you can say now. By the way, "first" and "third" lose a letter when they go before a noun:

first grade	**primer grado** (*pree-'mehr 'grah-doh*)
second grade	**segundo grado** (*seh-'goon-doh 'grah-doh*)
third grade	**tercer grado** (*tehr-'sehr 'grah-doh*)

➤ Are you ready to form a few phrases? You'll need the following:

for	**para** (*'pah-rah*)	**para la clase** (*'pah-rah lah 'klah-seh*)
in, on, at	**en** (*ehn*)	**en el cuarto** (*ehn ehl 'kwahr-toh*)
of, from	**de** (*deh*)	**de la persona** (*deh lah pehr-'soh-nah*)
to	**a** (*ah*)	**a la oficina** (*ah lah oh-fee-'see-nah*)
with	**con** (*kohn*)	**con el agua** (*kohn ehl 'ah-gwah*)
without	**sin** (*seen*)	**sin el carro** (*seen ehl 'kah-rroh*)

➤ There are only two contractions in Spanish:

to the	**al** (*ahl*)	**al hombre** (*ahl 'ohm-breh*)
of the, from the	**del** (*dehl*)	**del libro** (*dehl 'lee-broh*)

➤ Use these words to link everything together:

and = **y** *(ee)*   or = **o** *(oh)*   but = **pero** *('peh-roh)*

Thank you and good-bye!
¡Gracias y adiós! *('grah-see·ahs ee ah-dee-'ohs)*

 CONFLICTOS CULTURALES

If you get stuck in the middle of a phrase or sentence, don't be afraid to send messages using hand gestures or facial expressions. Body signals are used frequently in conversations throughout the Spanish-speaking world. And remember, there's nothing wrong with repeating your message several times until you're understood!

FOLLOW THE RULES!
¡Siga las reglas! *('see-gah lahs 'reh-glahs)*

Certain grammatical rules must be followed. In Spanish, these two should always be taken seriously:

1) The Reverse Order Rule:

As you begin to link your Spanish words together, you will find that sometimes words are positioned in reverse order. This Reverse Rule is applied when you give a description. The descriptive word goes after the word being described. Study these examples.

The big house.   **La casa grande.** *(lah 'kah-sah 'grahn-deh)*
The green chair.   **La silla verde.** *(lah 'see-yah 'vehr-deh)*
The important teacher.   **El maestro importante.** *(ehl mah-'eh-stroh eem-pohr-'tahn-teh)*

2) The Agreement Rule:

Here's another rule that must be followed when you are referring to more than one item in Spanish. First, the words **el** *(ehl)* and **la** *(lah)* (see page 11), become **los** *(lohs)* and **las** *(lahs)*, respectively.

15

el estudiante *(ehl eh-stoo-dee-'ahn-teh)*
la mesa *(lah 'meh-sah)*
la silla *(lah 'see-yah)*
el servicio *(ehl sehr-'vee-see·oh)*

los estudiantes *(lohs eh-stoo-dee-'ahn-tehs)*
las mesas *(lahs 'meh-sahs)*
las sillas *(lahs 'see-yahs)*
los servicios *(lohs sehr-'vee-see·ohs)*

Second, not only do all nouns and adjectives need to end in **s** or **es** to make the sentence plural, but when they are used together, the genders (the **o** and **a** endings), must match as well.

two white doors	**dos puertas blancas** *(dohs 'pwehr-tahs 'blahn-kahs)*
many red cars	**muchos carros rojos** *('moo-chohs 'kah-rrohs 'roh-hohs)*
six little children	**seis niños pequeños** *('seh·ees 'nee-nyohs peh-'keh-nyohs)*

By the way, to say "a" or "an" in Spanish, use **un** *(oon)* or **una** *('oo-nah)*:

a student	**un estudiante** *(oon eh-stoo-dee-'ahn-teh)*
	un estudiante americano *(oon eh-stoo-dee-'ahn-teh ah-meh-ree-'kah-noh)*
a window	**una ventana** *('oo-nah vehn-'tah-nah)*
	una ventana blanca *('oo-nah vehn-'tah-nah 'blahn-kah)*

And to say "some" or "a few," use **unos** *('oo-nohs)* or **unas** *('oo-nahs)*:

some students	**unos estudiantes** *('oo-nohs eh-stoo-dee-'ahn-tehs)*
	unos estudiantes americanos *('oo-nohs eh-stoo-dee-'ahn-tehs ah-meh-ree-'kah-nohs)*
a few windows	**unas ventanas** *('oo-nahs vehn-'tah-nahs)*
	unas ventanas blancas *('oo-nahs vehn-'tah-nahs 'blahn-kahs)*

Fill in the missing number in each series:

treinta, cuarenta, _____, sesenta *('treh·een-tah, kwah-'rehn-tah,*

____, seh-'sehn-tah)

primero, segundo, tercero, _____, *(pree-'meh-roh, seh-'goon-*

doh, tehr-'seh-roh, _____)

_____, cinco, seis, siete *(_____, 'seen-koh,*

'seh·ees, see-'eh-teh)

Write the Spanish translation for these words:

with _____

on _____

to the _____

Follow the example. Change these from the singular to the plural:

el carro grande
(ehl 'kah-rroh 'grahn-deh)

los carros grandes
(lohs 'kah-rrohs 'grahn-dehs)

la silla roja
('lah 'see-yah 'roh-hah)

_____

un hombre importante
(oon 'ohm-breh eem-pohr-'tahn-teh)

_____

la oficina blanca
(lah oh-fee-'see-nah 'blahn-kah)

_____

una clase pequeña
('oo-nah 'klah-seh peh-'keh-nyah)

_____

THE QUESTIONS
Las preguntas *(lahs preh-'goon-tahs)*

The following set of Spanish questions should be memorized right away. See if you can recognize any of these from the expressions we learned earlier:

How many?	**¿Cuántos?** *('kwahn-tohs)*
How much?	**¿Cuánto?** *('kwahn-toh)*
How?	**¿Cómo?** *('koh-moh)*
What?	**¿Qué?** *(keh)*
When?	**¿Cuándo?** *('kwahn-doh)*
Where?	**¿Dónde?** *('dohn-deh)*
Which?	**¿Cuál?** *(kwahl)*
Who?	**¿Quién?** *(kee-'ehn)*
Whose?	**¿De quién?** *(deh kee-'ehn)*
Why?	**¿Por qué?** *(pohr keh)*

Now, cover up the right column and try to translate without looking. How many can you remember?

MÁS INFORMACIÓN

➤ A few questions are actually common one-liners used regularly in simple conversations. Notice how they are not literal translations.

How's it going?	**¿Qué tal?** *(keh tahl)*
What's your name?	**¿Cómo se llama?** *('koh-moh seh 'yah-mah)*
How old are you?	**¿Cuántos años tiene?** *('kwahn-tohs 'ah-nyohs tee-'eh-neh)*

POWERFUL PRONOUNS!
¡Los pronombres poderosos! *(lohs proh-'nohm-brehs poh-deh-'roh-sohs)*

Students and their families will ask who everybody is. This is the quickest way to respond:

I	**Yo** *(yoh)*
We	**Nosotros** *(noh-'soh-trohs)*
You	**Usted** *(oo-'stehd)*
You (plural)	**Ustedes** *(oo-'steh-dehs)*
She	**Ella** *('eh-yah)*
He	**El** *(ehl)*
They (feminine)	**Ellas** *('eh-yahs)*
They (masculine)	**Ellos** *('eh-yohs)*

Practice:

She's from Mexico.	**Ella es de Mexico.** *('eh-yah ehs deh 'meh-hee-koh)*
How are you?	**¿Cómo está usted?** *('koh-moh eh-'stah oo-'stehd)*
I am learning.	**Yo estoy aprendiendo.** *(yoh eh-'stoh-ee ah-prehn-dee-'ehn-doh)*

MÁS INFORMACIÓN

➤ **Nosotras** *(noh-'soh-trahs)* is "We" feminine:

¿Ustedes? *(oo-'steh-dehs)*   **¡Sí, nosotras!** *(see, noh-'soh-trahs)*

➤ Would any of the following words be helpful? Of course! Think of ways these can be used to answer school-related questions:

someone	**alguien** *('ahl-gee·ehn)*
something	**algo** *('ahl-goh)*
somewhere	**por alguna parte** *(pohr ahl-'goo-nah 'pahr-teh)*

anyone	**cualquiera** *(kwahl-kee-'eh-rah)*
anything	**cualquier cosa** *(kwahl-kee-'ehr 'koh-sah)*
anywhere	**en cualquier parte** *(ehn kwahl-kee-'ehr 'pahr-teh)*

everyone	**todos** *('toh-dohs)*
everything	**todo** *('toh-doh)*
everywhere	**por todas partes** *(pohr 'toh-dahs 'pahr-tehs)*

no one	**nadie** *('nah-dee·eh)*
nothing	**nada** *('nah-dah)*
nowhere	**por ninguna parte** *(pohr neen-'goo-nah 'pahr-teh)*

WHOSE IS IT?
¿De quién es? *(deh kee-'ehn ehs)*

A similar group of Spanish words is used to indicate possession. They tell us "whose" it is:

It's my desk.	**Es mi escritorio.** *(ehs mee eh-skree-'toh-ree·oh)*
It's your, his, her, or their desk.	**Es su escritorio.** *(ehs soo eh-skree-'toh-ree·oh)*
It's our desk.	**Es nuestro escritorio.** *(ehs noo-'eh-stroh eh-skree-'toh-ree·oh)*

Notice what happens to pronouns when you talk about more than one:

mi escritorio *(mee eh-skree-'toh-ree·oh)*

mis escritorios *(mees eh-skree-'toh-ree·ohs)*

su escritorio *(soo eh-skree-'toh-ree·oh)*

sus escritorios *(soos eh-skree-'toh-ree·ohs)*

nuestro escritorio *(noo-'eh-stroh eh-skree-'toh-ree·oh)*

nuestros escritorios *(noo-'eh-strohs eh-skree-'toh-ree·ohs)*

Now try these other possessive words. Are you able to translate the sentences?

mine   **mío** or **mía** *('mee-oh, 'mee-ah)*
           Es mío. *(ehs 'mee-oh)*

yours, his, hers, theirs   **suyo** or **suya**
           ('soo-yoh, 'soo-yah)
           Es suya. *(ehs 'soo-yah)*

By the way, if something belongs to someone else, use **de** to indicate possession:

It's Mary's.   **Es de María.**
          (ehs deh mah-'ree-ah)
It's the school's.   **Es de la escuela.**
          (ehs deh lah ehs-'kweh-lah)
It's his.   **Es de él.**
          (ehs deh ehl)

MÁS INFORMACIÓN

➤ Don't be afraid to answer simple questions with brief, effective responses. Notice these examples:

¿Cuántos? *('kwahn-tohs)* **Muchos.** *('moo-chohs)*
¿Quién? *(kee-'ehn)* **Ella.** *('eh-yah)*
¿Dónde? *('dohn-deh)* **San Antonio.** *(sahn ahn-'toh-nee·oh)*

¿LISTOS PARA PRACTICAR?

Connect the names with the corresponding pronouns:

Laura   **ustedes** *(oo-'steh-dehs)*
Francisco   **nosotros** *(noh-'soh-trohs)*
Carolina y yo   **ellos** *('eh-yohs)*

Raul y Paula   él (ehl)
Samuel y usted   ella ('eh-yah)

ESTÁ and ES
(eh-'stah) and (ehs)

Now that you can form short phrases on your own, it's time to join all of your words together. To accomplish this, you'll need to understand the difference between **está** (eh-'stah) and **es** (ehs). Both words mean "is," but they're used differently.

The word **está** (eh-'stah) expresses a temporary state, condition, or location:

The girl is fine.   **La niña está bien.**
                           (lah 'nee-nyah eh-'stah 'bee·ehn)
The girl is in the room.   **La niña está en el cuarto.**
                           (lah 'nee-nyah eh-'stah ehn ehl 'kwahr-toh)

The word **es** (ehs) expresses an inherent characteristic or quality, including origin and ownership.

The girl is small.   **La niña es pequeña.**
                           (lah 'nee-nyah ehs peh-'keh-nyah)
The girl is Maria.   **La niña es María.**
                           (lah 'nee-nyah ehs mah-'ree-ah)
The girl is American.   **La niña es americana.**
                           (lah 'nee-nyah ehs ah-meh-ree-'kah-nah)
The girl is my friend.   **La niña es mi amiga.**
                           (lah 'nee-nyah ehs mee ah-'mee-gah)

Can you see how helpful these two words can be? Countless comments can be made with only a minimum of vocabulary. You'll also need to talk about more than one person, place, or thing. To do so, replace **está** (eh-'stah) with **están** (eh-'stahn), and **es** (ehs) with **son** (sohn). And don't forget that words must agree when you change to plurals.

The book is on the table. **El libro está en la mesa.**
                           (ehl 'lee-broh eh-'stah ehn
                           lah 'meh-sah)

The books are on the table.	**Los libros están en la mesa.** *(lohs 'lee-brohs eh-'stahn ehn lah 'meh-sah)*
The book is important.	**El libro es importante.** *(ehl 'lee-broh ehs eem-pohr- 'tahn-teh)*
The books are important.	**Los libros son importantes.** *(lohs 'lee-brohs sohn eem- pohr-'tahn-tehs)*

Check out these other examples. Read them aloud as you focus on their structure and meaning:

The chairs are black.	**Las sillas son negras.** *(lahs 'see-yahs sohn 'neh-grahs)*
The papers are at my house.	**Los papeles están en mi casa.** *(lohs pah-'peh-lehs eh-'stahn ehn mee 'kah-sah)*
They are not friends.	**No son amigos.** *(noh sohn ah-'mee-gohs)*
Are they good?	**¿Están buenos?** *(eh-'stahn 'bweh-nohs)*

The best way to learn how to use these words correctly is to listen to Spanish speakers in real-life conversations. They constantly use **es** *(ehs)*, **está** *(eh-'stah)*, **son** *(sohn)*, and **están** *(eh-'stahn)* to communicate everyday messages.

MÁS INFORMACIÓN

➤ A lot more can be said when you learn these vocabulary terms. Remember that they change according to gender:

that	**ese** *('eh-seh)* or **esa** *('eh-sah)* **Ese muchacho está aquí.** *('eh-seh moo-'chah-choh ehs-'tah ah-'kee)*
these	**estos** *('eh-stohs)* or **estas** *('eh-stahs)* **Estos tacos están malos.** *('eh-stohs 'tah-kohs ehs-'tahn 'mah-lohs)*

this	**este** *('eh-steh)* or **esta** *('eh-stah)*
	Este es mi papel amarillo.
	('eh-steh ehs mee pah-'pehl ah-mah-'ree-yoh)
those	**esos** *('eh-sohs)* or **esas** *('eh-sahs)*
	Esos son hombres buenos.
	('eh-sohs sohn 'ohm-brehs 'bweh-nohs)

I AM and WE ARE

Estoy-Soy and Estamos-Somos *(eh-'stoh·ee / 'soh·ee and eh-'stah-mohs / 'soh-mohs)*

To say "I am" and "We are" in Spanish, you must also acquire their different forms. As with **está** *(eh-'stah)* and **están** *(eh-'stahn)*, the words **estoy** *(eh-'stoh·ee)* and **estamos** *(eh-'stah-mohs)* refer to the location or condition of a person, place, or thing. And just like **es** *(ehs)* and **son** *(sohn)*, the words **soy** *('soh·ee)* and **somos** *('soh-mohs)* are used with everything else.

I am fine.	**Estoy bien.**
	(eh-'stoh·ee 'bee·ehn)
We are in the room.	**Estamos en el cuarto.**
	(eh-'stah-mohs ehn ehl 'kwahr-toh)
I am Lupe.	**Soy Lupe.**
	('soh·ee 'loo-peh)
We are Cuban.	**Somos cubanos.**
	('soh-mohs koo-'bah-nohs)

Now let's group all of these forms together. Look at these present tense forms of the verbs **ESTAR** *(eh-'stahr)* and **SER** *(sehr)*:

To be	Estar	Ser
I'm	**estoy** *(eh-'stoh·ee)*	**soy** *('soh·ee)*
You're *(informal)*	**estás** *(eh-'stahs)*	**eres** *('eh-rehs)*
You're *(formal)*, He's, She's	**está** *(eh-'stah)*	**es** *(ehs)*
You're *(pl.)*, They're	**están** *(eh-'stahn)*	**son** *(sohn)*
We're	**estamos** *(eh-'stah-mohs)*	**somos** *('soh-mohs)*

MÁS INFORMACION

➤ Notice that Spanish has both formal and informal verb forms (check the verb **estar** on the previous page).

➤ You don't have to use the subject pronouns in every sentence. It's usually understood who's involved:

Nosotros somos *(noh-'soh-trohs 'soh-mohs)* and **Somos** *('soh-mohs)* both mean "We are."

➤ "There is" and "There are" are very easy in Spanish. In both cases you use the little word, **hay** *('ah·ee)* (pronounced "I").

There's one class.   **Hay una clase.** *('ah·ee 'oo-nah 'klah-seh)*
There are two classes.   **Hay dos clases.** *('ah·ee dohs 'klah-sehs)*

¿LISTOS PARA PRACTICAR?

Join the subject pronouns with their possessive forms:

Ella *('eh-yah)*   **mi** *(mee)*
Yo *(yoh)*   **nuestro** *(noo-'eh-stroh)*
Nosotros *(noh-'soh-trohs)*   **su** *(soo)*

Translate into English:

¿Quién? *(kee-'ehn)*   _____

¿Cuántos? *('kwahn-tohs)*   _____

¿Dónde? *('dohn-deh)*   _____

Fill in each blank with the appropriate verb form:

está, son, hay, estoy, somos *(eh-'stah, sohn, 'ah·ee, eh-'stoh·ee, 'soh-mohs)*

Estos _____ **muy buenos.** *('eh-stohs _____ 'moo·ee 'bweh-nohs)*

Pedro _____ **en la oficina.** *('peh-droh _____ ehn lah oh-fee-'see-nah)*

25

Ella y yo _____ **amigas.** *('eh-yah ee yoh* _____ *ah-'mee-gahs)*

No _____ **problema.** *(noh* _____ *proh-'bleh-mah)*

Yo _____ **bien.** *('yoh* _____ *'bee·ehn)*

TO HAVE
Tener *(teh-'nehr)*

Tener (to have) is another common linking word in Spanish, and its forms will become more necessary as you begin to create Spanish sentences on your own. Here are the basics to get you started:

I have	**tengo** *('tehn-goh)*
You *(informal)* have	**tienes** *(tee-'eh-nehs)*
You *(formal)* have, He has, She has	**tiene** *(tee-'eh-neh)*
You have (pl.), They have	**tienen** *(tee-'eh-nehn)*
We have	**tenemos** *(teh-'neh-mohs)*

Study these examples:

I have a pen.	**Tengo un lapicero.** *('tehn-goh oon lah-pee-'seh-roh)*
She has a white book.	**Tiene un libro blanco.** *(tee-'eh-neh oon 'lee-broh 'blahn-koh)*
They have twenty students.	**Tienen veinte estudiantes.** *(tee-'eh-nehn 'veh·een-teh eh-stoo-dee-'ahn-tehs)*
We have a big school.	**Tenemos una escuela grande.** *(teh-'neh-mohs 'oo-nah eh-'skweh-lah 'grahn-deh)*

➤ Even though **tener** literally means to "have," sometimes it is used instead of the verb **estar** to express a temporary condition. Review these expressions as often as you can:

(I am) afraid	**(tengo) miedo** *('tehn-goh mee-'eh-doh)*
(we are) at fault	**(tenemos) la culpa** *(teh-'neh-mohs lah 'kool-pah)*
(they are) cold	**(tienen) frío** *(tee-'eh-nehn 'free-oh)*
(she is) 15 years old	**(tiene) quince años** *(tee-'eh-neh 'keen-seh 'ah-nyohs)*
(I am) hot	**(tengo) calor** *('tehn-goh kah-'lohr)*
(They are) hungry	**(tienen) hambre** *(tee-'eh-nehn 'ahm-breh)*
(he is) sleepy	**(tiene) sueño** *(tee-'eh-neh 'sweh-nyoh)*
(we are) thirsty	**(tenemos) sed** *(teh-'neh-mohs sehd)*

➤ To say *not* in Spanish, interject the word **no** in front of the verb:

Mr. Smith is **not** my teacher.	**El Sr. Smith no es mi maestro.** *(ehl seh-'nyohr eh-'smeeth noh ehs mee mah-'eh-stroh)*
I do **not** have the paper.	**No tengo el papel.** *(noh 'tehn-goh ehl pah-'pehl)*
There are **no** more chairs.	**No hay más sillas.** *(noh 'ah·ee mahs 'see-yahs)*

➤ **Tienes** *(tee-'eh-nehs)* is the informal way to say "you have":

My friend, do you have a car?	**¿Amigo, tienes un carro?** *(ee-'mee-goh, tee-'eh-nehs oon 'kah-rroh)*

MORE SPANISH VERBS
Más verbos en español *(mahs 'vehr-bohs ehn eh-spah-'nyohl)*

Putting a few words together in a new language is a thrilling experience, but real communication begins once you start using verbs or action words. Although **estar**, **ser,** and **tener** *(eh-'stahr, sehr, teh-'nehr)* are extremely useful, they do not express action. Learning how to use Spanish verbs will allow us to talk about what's going on in the world around us.

Spend a few moments memorizing this brief list of helpful beginning verbs. Notice that Spanish action words end in the letters **-ar, -er,** or **-ir:**

to come	**venir** *(veh-'neer)*
to drink	**beber** *(beh-'behr)*
to drive	**manejar** *(mah-neh-'hahr)*
to eat	**comer** *(koh-'mehr)*
to follow	**seguir** *(seh-'geer)*
to go	**ir** *(eer)*
to learn	**aprender** *(ah-prehn-'dehr)*
to listen	**escuchar** *(eh-skoo-'chahr)*
to look	**mirar** *(mee-'rahr)*
to play	**jugar** *(hoo-'gahr)*
to read	**leer** *(leh-'ehr)*
to run	**correr** *(koh-'rrehr)*
to sleep	**dormir** *(dohr-'meer)*
to speak	**hablar** *(ah-'blahr)*
to study	**estudiar** *(ehs-too-dee-'ahr)*
to understand	**entender** *(ehn-tehn-'dehr)*
to wait	**esperar** *(eh-speh-'rahr)*
to walk	**caminar** *(kah-mee-'nahr)*
to work	**trabajar** *(trah-bah-'hahr)*
to write	**escribir** *(eh-skree-'beer)*

MÁS INFORMACIÓN

➤ You can never learn enough action words in Spanish. Over one hundred verbs are listed in the specialized dictionary at the end of this book, so use it as a reference tool. When you come across a verb as you study and practice, look it up in Spanish or English to learn its base form and meaning.

➤ Many Spanish verb infinitives that relate to education are similar to English. Look at these examples:

to communicate	**comunicar** *(koh-moo-nee-'kahr)*
to consult	**consultar** *(kohn-sool-'tahr)*
to converse	**conversar** *(kohn-vehr-'sahr)*
to observe	**observar** *(ohb-sehr-'vahr)*

to organize	**organizar** *(ohr-gah-nee-'sahr)*
to plan	**planear** *(plah-neh-'ahr)*
to practice	**practicar** *(prahk-tee-'kahr)*

THE SHORTCUTS
Los atajos *(lohs ah-'tah-hohs)*

Let's combine verbs with simple phrases to create complete sentences. For example, look what happens when you add these verb infinitives to **Favor de...** *(fah-'vohr deh)*, which implies, "Would you please...":

Please ...	**Favor de...** *(fah-'vohr deh)*
write everything.	**escribir todo.** *(eh-skree-'beer 'toh-doh)*
read the paper.	**leer el papel.** *(leh-'ehr ehl pah-'pehl)*
speak in English.	**hablar en inglés.** *(ah-'blahr ehn een-'glehs)*

Here are some other shortcuts. By adding these phrases to verb infinitives or vocabulary, you can make statements, ask questions, or give commands. First read the phrase, and then try out the sample sentence:

Don't	**No** *(noh)*
Don't run.	**No correr.** *(noh koh-'rrehr)*
You have to	**Tiene que** *(tee-'eh-neh keh)*
You have to study.	**Tiene que estudiar.** *(tee-'eh-neh keh eh-stoo-dee-'ahr)*
You should	**Debe** *('deh-beh)*
You should read.	**Debe leer.** *('deh-beh leh-'ehr)*
I'm going to	**Voy a** *('voh·ee ah)*
I'm going to eat.	**Voy a comer.** *('voh·ee ah koh-'mehr)*
You need	**Necesita** *(neh-seh-'see-tah)*
You need to learn.	**Necesita aprender.** *(neh-seh-'see-tah ah-prehn-'dehr)*

You're doing great! This time, work on a few question phrases:

Do you want	**Quiere** *(kee-'eh-reh)*
Do you want to come?	**¿Quiere venir?** *(kee-'eh-reh veh-'neer)*
Can you	**Puede** *('pweh-deh)*
Can you wait?	**¿Puede esperar?** *('pweh-deh eh-speh-'rahr)*
Do you like	**Le gusta** *(leh 'goo-stah)*
Do you like to play?	**¿Le gusta jugar?** *(leh 'goo-stah hoo-'gahr)*

MÁS INFORMACIÓN

➤ *Spanish For Educators* is full of these shortcut phrases, so jot them down now and start practicing right away!

➤ Check out these other one-liners. Add them to the verbs above if you need to:

One must	**Hay que** *('ah·ee keh)*
Do you prefer	**Prefiere** *(preh-fee-'eh-reh)*
I would like	**Quisiera** *(kee-see-'eh-rah)*
Let's	**Vamos a** *('vah-mohs ah)*
Could you	**Podría** *(poh-'dree-ah)*

¿LISTOS PARA PRACTICAR?

Use forms of **tener** *(teh-'nehr)* to translate the following:

They are cold. _____

I don't have the book. _____

We are hungry. _____

Insert the verb infinitive that best fits each sentence:

comer, hablar, escribir, leer, escuchar *(koh-'mehr, ah-'blahr, eh-skree-'beer, leh-'ehr, eh-skoo-'chahr)*

Favor de _____ **en el papel.** *(fah-'vohr deh* _____ *ehn ehl pah-'pehl)*

Tiene que _____ **el libro.** *(tee-'eh-neh keh* _____ *ehl 'lee-broh)*

Necesita _____ **inglés.** *(neh-seh-'see-tah* _____ *een-'glehs)*

¿Quiere _____ **en el restaurante?** *(kee-'eh-reh* _____ *ehn ehl reh-stah·oo-'rahn-teh)*

Voy a _____ **el radio.** *('voh·ee ah* _____ *ehl 'rah-dee·oh)*

¡ACCIÓN!

To express clearly your thoughts in Spanish, you'll need to learn as many verb tenses as possible. Throughout this book, in sections entitled **¡ACCIÓN!**, you will be introduced to a variety of conjugated verb forms. By practicing the patterns, you'll soon be able to discuss past, present, and future events.

Let's begin with one of the easiest verb forms to use. It's the present progressive tense, and it refers to actions that are taking place at this moment. It is similar to our "ing" form in English. Simply change the base verb ending slightly, and then combine the new form with the four forms of the verb **estar** *(eh-'stahr)*. The **-ar** verbs become **-ando** *('ahn-doh),* while the **-er** and **-ir** verbs become **-iendo** *('yehn-doh).* Study these examples closely:

work	**trabajar** *(trah-bah-'hahr)*
working	**trabajando** *(trah-bah-'hahn-doh)*
We're working.	**Estamos trabajando.** *(eh-'stah-mohs trah-bah-'hahn-doh)*
eat	**comer** *(koh-'mehr)*
eating	**comiendo** *(koh-mee-'ehn-doh)*
He is eating.	**Está comiendo.** *(eh-'stah koh-mee-'ehn-doh)*

| write | **escribir** *(eh-skree-'beer)* |
| writing | **escribiendo** *(eh-skree-bee-'ehn-doh)* |

| I'm writing. | **Estoy escribiendo.** *(eh-'stoh·ee eh-skree-bee-'ehn-doh)* |

MÁS INFORMACIÓN

➤ Some verbs change in spelling and pronunciation when you add the **-ndo** ending. Look at these examples:

| sleep | **dormir** *(dohr-'meer)* |
| sleeping | **durmiendo** *(duhr-mee-'ehn-doh)* |

| read | **leer** *(leh-'ehr)* |
| reading | **leyendo** *(leh-'yehn-doh)* |

¡ÓRDENES!

As long as we're talking about working with Spanish-speaking students, why not spend some time reviewing the following important command or request words. They are unique forms of verbs that can be used all by themselves. Try using them in work-related situations—and always say **por favor** *(pohr fah-'vohr)*:

Please...	**Por favor...** *(pohr fah-vohr)*
come	**venga** *('vehn-gah)*
follow	**siga** *('see-gah)*
go	**vaya** *('vah-yah)*
listen	**escuche** *(eh-'skoo-cheh)*
run	**corra** *('koh-rrah)*

wait	**espere** *(eh-'speh-reh)*
walk	**camine** *(kah-'mee-neh)*
watch	**mire** *('mee-reh)*

MÁS INFORMACIÓN

➤ Any vocabulary item can be learned quickly if it's practiced in conjunction with a command word. For example, to pick up the names for furniture, have a native Spanish speaker command you to touch, look at, or point to things throughout the home. This exercise really works, and more importantly, it can be fun:

Touch...	**Toque...** *('toh-keh)*	...the table	**...la mesa** *(lah 'meh-sah)*
Look at...	**Mire...** *('mee-reh)*	...the book	**...el libro** *(ehl 'lee-broh)*
Point to...	**Señale...** *(seh-'nyah-leh)*	...the chair	**...la silla** *(lah 'see-yah)*

➤ Several important command words have the word **se** at the end. Notice the pattern:

Hurry up!	**¡Apúrese!** *(ah-'poo-reh-seh)*
Sit down!	**¡Siéntese!** *(see-'ehn-teh-seh)*
Stand up!	**¡Levántese!** *(leh-'vahn-teh-seh)*
Stop!	**¡Párese!** *('pah-reh-seh)*
Stay!	**¡Quédese!** *('keh-deh-seh)*

➤ There's no better way to learn than by doing. That's why each chapter includes a section entitled **¡ÓRDENES!** where you receive new lists of command words, followed by tips on how to practice them with Spanish speakers.

CONFLICTOS CULTURALES

Commands are practical and easy to use, but try not to overdo it. Those teachers who tend to be overbearing have problems earning respect. Try to give your orders sparingly and always add **por favor** *(pohr fah-'vohr)*.

Follow the pattern as you practice:

caminar	caminando	Estoy caminando
(kah-mee-'nahr)	*(kah-mee-'nahn-doh)*	*(eh-'stoh·ee kah-mee-'nahn-doh)*
trabajar	_____	_____ *(trah-bah-hahr)*
hablar	_____	_____ *(ah-'blahr)*
estudiar	_____	_____ *(eh-stoo-dee-'ahr)*
comer	_____	_____ *(koh-'mehr)*
escribir	_____	_____ *(eh-skree-'beer)*
aprender	_____	_____ *(ah-prehn-'dehr)*
dormir	_____	_____ *(dohr-'meer)*

Connect the opposites:

Siéntese *(see-'ehn-teh-seh)*	**Vaya** *('vah-yah)*
Venga *('vehn-gah)*	**Camine** *(kah-'mee-neh)*
Corra *('koh-rrah)*	**Levántese** *(leh-'vahn-teh-seh)*

CHAPTER TWO
Capítulo Dos
(kah-'pee-too-loh dohs)

AT SCHOOL
En la escuela
(ehn lah eh-'skweh-lah)

WHERE DO YOU WORK?

¿Dónde trabaja usted? *('dohn-deh trah-'bah-hah oo-'stehd)*

Now that you've learned some of the fundamental skills in Spanish, it's time to tackle those words that relate to the workplace. This next list of terms should help to get you started. Use the opening phrase as you practice reading aloud:

Where's (the)...?	**¿Dónde está...?** *('dohn-deh eh-'stah...)*
academy	**la academia** *(ah-kah-'deh-mee·ah)*
agency	**la agencia** *(lah ah-'hehn-see·ah)*
branch	**la sucursal** *(lah soo-koor-'sahl)*
building	**el edificio** *(ehl eh-dee-'fee-see·oh)*
campus	**el campo** *(ehl 'kahm-poh)*
center	**el centro** *(ehl 'sehn-troh)*
class	**la clase** *(lah 'klah-seh)*
college	**la universidad** *(lah oo-nee-vehr-see-'dahd)*
department	**el departamento** *(ehl deh-pahr-tah-'mehn-toh)*
district	**el distrito** *(ehl dee-'stree-toh)*
division	**la división** *(lah dee-vee-see-'ohn)*
institute	**el instituto** *(ehl een-stee-'too-toh)*
institution	**la institución** *(lah een-stee-too-see-'ohn)*
large room	**el salón** *(ehl sah-'lohn)*
office	**la oficina** *(lah oh-fee-'see-nah)*
organization	**la organización** *(lah ohr-gah-nee-sah-see-'ohn)*
room	**el cuarto** *(ehl 'kwahr-toh)*
school	**la escuela** *(lah eh-'skweh-lah)*
site	**el sitio** *(ehl 'see-tee·oh)*
university	**la universidad** *(lah oo-nee-vehr-see-'dahd)*

Now, mention a few more key parts of the campus. Try out this new pattern while you review:

Go to (the)...	**Vaya a...** *('vah-yah ah...)*
auditorium	**el auditorio** *(ehl ow-dee-'toh-ree·oh)*
cafeteria	**la cafetería** *(lah kah-feh-teh-'ree-ah)*
courtyard	**la plaza** *(lah 'plah-sah)*
dormitory	**el dormitorio** *(ehl dohr-mee-'toh-ree·oh)*
gym	**el gimnasio** *(ehl heem-'nah-see·oh)*
hall	**el pasillo** *(ehl pah-'see-yoh)*

laboratory	**el laboratorio** *(ehl lah-boh-rah-'toh-ree·oh)*
library	**la biblioteca** *(lah bee-blee·oh-'teh-kah)*
lobby	**el vestíbulo** *(ehl veh-'stee-boo-loh)*
locker	**el armario** *(ehl ahr-'mah-ree·oh)*
mailbox	**el buzón** *(ehl boo-'sohn)*
parking lot	**el estacionamiento** *(ehl eh-stah-see·oh-nah-mee-'ehn-toh)*
playground	**el campo de recreo** *(ehl 'kahm-poh deh reh-'kreh·oh)*
restroom	**el servicio** *(ehl sehr-'vee-see·oh)*
theater	**el teatro** *(ehl teh-'ah-troh)*
warehouse	**el almacén** *(ehl ahl-mah-'sehn)*
workshop	**el taller** *(ehl tah-'yehr)*

The following vocabulary words will come in handy almost immediately. Notice how they fit into phrases:

It's in the _____ room.	**Está en el salón de _____ .** *(eh-'stah ehn ehl sah-'lohn deh _____)*
music	**la música** *(lah 'moo-see-kah)*
art	**el arte** *(ehl 'ahr-teh)*
study	**el estudio** *(ehl eh-'stoo-dee·oh)*
computer	**la computadora** *(lah kohm-poo-tah-'doh-rah)*
copy	**la copiadora** *(lah koh-pee·ah-'doh-rah)*
It's in the _____ office.	**Está en la oficina de _____ .** *(eh-'stah ehn lah oh-fee-'see-nah deh _____)*
administration	**la administración** *(lah ahd-mee-nee-strah-see-'ohn)*
health	**la salud** *(lah sah-'lood)*
attendance	**la asistencia** *(lah ah-see-'stehn-see·ah)*
athletic	**la educación física** *(lah eh-doo-kah-see-'ohn 'fee-see-kah)*
admissions	**las admisiones** *(lahs ahd-mee-see-'oh-nehs)*

It's in the _____ building.	**Está en el edificio de _____.** *(eh-'stah ehn ehl eh-dee-'fee-see·oh deh _____)*
conference	**las conferencias** *(lahs kohn-feh-'rehn-see·ahs)*
storage	**el depósito** *(ehl deh-'poh-see-toh)*
science	**las ciencias** *(lahs see-'ehn-see·ahs)*
humanities	**las humanidades** *(lahs oo-mah-nee-'dah-dehs)*
security	**la seguridad** *(lah seh-goo-ree-'dahd)*
It's in the _____ center.	**Está en el centro de _____.** *(eh-'stah ehn ehl 'sehn-troh deh _____)*
assessment	**la evaluación** *(lah eh-vah-loo-ah-see-'ohn)*
media	**los medios de comunicación** *(lohs 'meh-dee·ohs deh koh-moo-nee-kah-see-'ohn)*
training	**el entrenamiento** *(ehl ehn-treh-nah-mee-'ehn-toh)*
supplies	**las provisiones** *(lahs proh-vee-see-'oh-nehs)*
communications	**las comunicaciones** *(lahs koh-moo-nee-kah-see-'oh-nehs)*

MÁS INFORMACIÓN

➤ Words change meanings depending on where a student is from.

In most countries, "college" is **la universidad** *(lah oo-nee-vehr-see-'dahd)*, while **el colegio** *(ehl koh-'leh-hee·oh)* means "high school."

➤ There are all kinds of educational institutions:

monastery	**el monasterio** *(ehl moh-nah-'steh-ree·oh)*
convent	**el convento** *(ehl kohn-'vehn-toh)*
seminary	**el seminario** *(seh-mee-'nah-ree·oh)*

boarding school	**el internado** *(ehl een-tehr-'nah-doh)*
parochial school	**la escuela parroquial** *(lah eh-'skweh-lah pah-rroh-kee-'ahl)*

➤ Could these terms help you out in your situation? Notice the practice sentences:

zone	**la zona** *(lah 'soh-nah)*	**¿Dónde está la zona roja?** *('dohn-deh eh-'stah lah 'soh-nah 'roh-hah)*
area	**el área** *(f)* *(ehl 'ah-reh-ah)*	**Son áreas importantes.** *(sohn 'ah-reh-ahs eem-pohr-'tahn-tehs)*
place	**el lugar** *(ehl loo-'gahr)*	**Este es el lugar.** *('eh-steh ehs ehl loo-'gahr)*
property	**la propiedad** *(lah proh-pee·eh-'dahd)*	**La propiedad es grande.** *(lah proh-pee·eh-'dahd ehs 'grahn-deh)*
space	**el espacio** *(ehl eh-'spah-see·oh)*	**No hay espacio.** *(noh 'ah·ee eh-'spah-see·oh)*

WORDS THAT TELL *WHERE*
Palabras que expresan *dónde* *(pah-'lah-brahs keh ehk-'spreh-sahn 'dohn-deh)*

To find what you're looking for, these "where" words will be required. Pay attention to how they can be used:

It's…	**Está…** *(eh-'stah)*
above	**encima** *(ehn-'see-mah)*
at the bottom	**en el fondo** *(ehn ehl 'fohn-doh)*
behind	**detrás** *(deh-'trahs)*
down	**abajo** *(ah-'bah-hoh)*
far	**lejos** *('leh-hohs)*
here	**aquí** *(ah-'kee)*
in front of	**en frente de** *(ehn 'frehn-teh deh)*
inside	**adentro** *(ah-'dehn-troh)*
next to	**al lado de** *(ahl 'lah-doh deh)*
outside	**afuera** *(ah-'fweh-rah)*
over there	**allá** *(ah-'yah)*
straight ahead	**adelante** *(ah-deh-'lahn-teh)*
there	**allí** *(ah-'yee)*

to the left	**a la izquierda** *(ah lah ees-kee-'ehr-dah)*
near	**cerca** *('sehr-kah)*
to the right	**a la derecha** *(ah lah deh-'reh-chah)*
up	**arriba** *(ah-'rree-bah)*

If a map is required, send everybody this way:

east	**este** *('eh-steh)*
north	**norte** *('nohr-teh)*
south	**sur** *(soor)*
west	**oeste** *(oh-'eh-steh)*

MÁS INFORMACIÓN

➤ Be specific!

corner	**la esquina** *(lah eh-'skee-nah)*
side	**el lado** *(ehl 'lah-doh)*
on top	**encima** *(ehn-'see-mah)*
at the back	**detrás** *(deh-'trahs)*

La clase está en la esquina, al lado de la oficina. *(lah 'klah-seh eh-'stah ehn lah eh-'skee-nah, ahl 'lah-doh deh lah oh-fee-'see-nah)*

➤ You'll need these for larger facilities:

first floor	**primer piso** *(pree-'mehr 'pee-soh)*
second floor	**segundo piso** *(seh-'goon-doh 'pee-soh)*
third floor	**tercer piso** *(tehr-'sehr 'pee-soh)*

➤ By the way, **en** *(ehn)* (in, on, at) is one of the most commonly used words in Spanish. Watch:

She's in her office,
on the second floor,
at her desk.

Está en su oficina *(eh-'stah ehn soo oh-fee-'see-nah)*,
en el segundo piso *(ehn ehl seh-'goon-doh 'pee-soh)*.
en su escritorio. *(ehn soo eh-skree-'toh-ree-oh)*.

➤ And always use **estar** *(eh-'stahr)* instead of **ser** *(sehr)* to tell where someone is located:

The man is here. **El hombre está aquí.**
(ehl 'ohm-breh eh-'stah ah-'kee)

➤ Be familiar with as many location words as you can:

It's... **Está...** *(eh-'stah)*

face down **boca abajo** *('boh-kah ah-'bah-hoh)*
face up **boca arriba** *('boh-kah ah-'rree-bah)*
on its way **en camino** *(ehn kah-'mee-noh)*

backwards, inside out,
or upside down **al revés** *(ahl reh-'vehs)*
in back **atrás** *(ah-'trahs)*
in front **al frente** *(ahl 'frehn-teh)*
in the middle **al medio** *(ahl 'meh-dee·oh)*
underground **subterráneo** *(soob-teh-'rrah-neh-oh)*

 ¿LISTOS PARA PRACTICAR?

Can you name three important buildings on a school campus?

_____

_____

_____

41

Translate these sentences as fast as you can:

La clase está adelante y a la derecha. *(lah 'klah-seh eh-'stah ah-deh-'lahn-teh ah lah deh-'reh-chah)*

Los servicios están allí, arriba. *(lohs sehr-'vee-see·ohs eh-'stahn ah-'yee, ah-'rree-bah)*

El edificio no está muy lejos. *(ehl eh-dee-'fee-see·oh noh eh-'stah 'moo·ee 'leh-hohs)*

La oficina de asistencia está al sur del centro de comunicaciones. *(lah oh-fee-'see-nah deh ah-see-'stehn-see·ah eh-'stah ahl soor dehl 'sehn-troh deh koh-moo-nee-kah-see-'oh-nehs)*

El cuarto está en el tercer piso, al lado del salón de música. *(ehl 'kwahr-toh eh-'stah ehn ehl tehr-'sehr 'pee-soh ahl 'lah-doh dehl sah-'lohn deh 'moo-see-kah)*

This group of opposites should be simple. Just draw a line to connect each pair:

adentro *(ah-'dehn-troh)*	**derecha** *(deh-'reh-chah)*
abajo *(ah-'bah-hoh)*	**arriba** *(ah-'rree-bah)*
izquierda *(ees-kee-'ehr-dah)*	**norte** *('nohr-teh)*
sur *(soor)*	**cerca** *('sehr-kah)*
lejos *('leh-hohs)*	**afuera** *(ah-'fweh-rah)*
detrás *(deh-'trahs)*	**al frente** *(ahl 'frehn-teh)*

INSIDE THE BUILDING
Adentro del edificio *(ah-'dehn-troh dehl eh-dee-'fee-see·oh)*

Once you're inside the building, start to point out those things you recognize. By pointing at each item as you name it, your Spanish is acquired much faster:

It's near (the)...	**Está cerca de...** *(eh-'stah 'sehr-kah deh...)*
elevator	**el ascensor** *(ehl ah-sehn-'sohr)*
entrance	**la entrada** *(lah ehn-'trah-dah)*
escalator	**la escalera mecánica** *(lah eh-skah-'leh-rah meh-'kah-nee-kah)*
exit	**la salida** *(lah sah-'lee-dah)*
stairs	**las escaleras** *(lahs eh-skah-'leh-rahs)*
steps	**los escalones** *(lohs eh-skah-'loh-nehs)*

OK, now give details:

double doors	**las puertas dobles** *(lahs 'pwehr-tahs 'doh-blehs)*
front counter	**el mostrador principal** *(ehl moh-strah-'dohr preen-see-'pahl)*
It's in front of (the)...	**Está en frente de...** *(eh-'stah ehn 'frehn-teh deh...)*
public telephone	**el teléfono público** *(ehl teh-'leh-foh-noh 'poob-lee-koh)*
reception desk	**la recepción** *(lah reh-sehp-see-'ohn)*
trash can	**el bote de basura** *(ehl 'boh-teh deh bah-'soo-rah)*
water fountain	**la fuente de agua** *(lah 'fwehn-teh deh 'ah-gwah)*

Check all around the grounds. How many of these words can you put into practice?

Walk to (the)...	**Camine a...** *(kah-'mee-neh ah)*
balcony	**el balcón** *(ehl bahl-'kohn)*
bridge	**el puente** *(ehl 'pwehn-teh)*
deck	**la terraza** *(lah teh-'rrah-sah)*
driveway	**la entrada para carros** *(lah ehn-'trah-dah 'pah-rah 'kah-rrohs)*
fence	**la cerca** *(lah 'sehr-kah)*
garden	**el jardín** *(ehl hahr-'deen)*
gate	**el portón** *(ehl pohr-'tohn)*
lot	**el lote** *(ehl 'loh-teh)*
porch	**el portal** *(ehl pohr-'tahl)*
ramp	**la rampa** *(lah 'rahm-pah)*
sidewalk	**la acera** *(lah ah-'seh-rah)*
tower	**la torre** *(lah 'toh-rreh)*
wall	**la pared** *(lah pah-'rehd)*

➤ When giving instructions to younger students, be sure to tell them about the restroom:

Please use (the)... **Favor de usar...** *(fah-'vohr deh oo-'sahr)*
  dispenser   **el distribuidor** *(ehl dees-tree-boo-ee-'dohr)*

  mirror   **el espejo** *(ehl eh-'speh-hoh)*
  paper towel   **la toalla de papel** *(lah toh-'ah-yah deh pah-'pehl)*

  sink   **el lavamanos** *(ehl lah-vah-'mah-nohs)*
  soap   **el jabón** *(ehl hah-'bohn)*
  toilet   **el excusado** *(ehl ehk-skoo-'sah-doh)*
  toilet paper   **el papel higiénico** *(ehl pah-'pehl ee-hee-'eh-nee-koh)*

  urinal   **el orinal** *(ehl oh-ree-'nahl)*

¿LISTOS PARA PRACTICAR?

How would you say these in Spanish?

The stairs are next to the elevator.
There's no toilet paper in the restroom.
Where are the public telephones?

Connect the words that are related:

el jabón *(ehl hah-'bohn)*   **el portón** *(ehl pohr-'tohn)*
la terraza *(lah teh-'rrah-sah)*   **el lavamanos** *(ehl lah-vah-'mah-nohs)*
la cerca *(lah 'sehr-kah)*   **el portal** *(ehl pohr-'tahl)*

Trust is very important in the Hispanic culture, especially in student-teacher relationships. Throughout the education process, feel free to open up about yourself, your family, your work, and your home. Since language is a barrier, begin by showing your students where everything is located. Don't be shy, always be honest, and make them feel at home.

WORDS THAT TELL *WHEN*
Palabras que expresan *cuándo* (pah-'lah-brahs keh ehk-'spreh-sahn 'kwahn-doh)

One of the most frequently asked questions in the field of education is "when?" Be prepared when the time to answer in Spanish comes. Begin by learning a few of the most popular responses:

afterward	**después** (deh-'spwehs)
always	**siempre** (see-'ehm-preh)
before	**antes** ('ahn-tehs)
early	**temprano** (tehm-'prah-noh)
late	**tarde** ('tahr-deh)
later	**más tarde** (mahs 'tahr-deh)
lots of times	**muchas veces** ('moo-chahs 'veh-sehs)
never	**nunca** ('noon-kah)
now	**ahora** (ah-'oh-rah)
once	**una vez** ('oo-nah vehs)
sometimes	**a veces** (ah 'veh-sehs)
soon	**pronto** ('prohn-toh)
then	**entonces** (ehn-'tohn-sehs)
today	**hoy** ('oh·ee)
tomorrow	**mañana** (mah-'nyah-nah)
tonight	**esta noche** ('eh-stah 'noh-cheh)
yesterday	**ayer** (ah-'yehr)

➤ All sorts of time expressions are needed in a school setting. A good way to learn is to group your related phrases into sets of three:

last month	**el mes pasado** *(ehl mehs pah-'sah-doh)*
last night	**anoche** *(ah-'noh-cheh)*
last week	**la semana pasada** *(lah seh-'mah-nah pa-'sah-dah)*
next month	**el próximo mes** *(ehl 'prohk-see-moh mehs)*
next week	**la próxima semana** *(lah 'prohk-see-mah seh-'mah-nah)*
next year	**el próximo año** *(ehl 'prohk-see-moh 'ah-nyoh)*
tomorrow morning	**mañana por la mañana** *(mah-'nyah-nah pohr lah mah-'nyah-nah)*
the day before yesterday	**anteayer** *(ahn-teh-ah-'yehr)*
the day after tomorrow	**pasado mañana** *(pah-'sah-doh mah-'nyah-nah)*
in a moment	**en un momento** *(ehn oon moh-'mehn-toh)*
in a while	**en un rato** *(ehn oon 'rah-toh)*
in a minute	**en un minuto** *(ehn oon mee-'noo-toh)*
at dawn	**a la madrugada** *(ah lah mah-droo-'gah-dah)*
at dusk	**al anochecer** *(ahl ah-noh-cheh-'sehr)*
at sunset	**a la puesta del sol** *(ah lah 'pweh-stah dehl sohl)*
each day	**cada día** *('kah-dah 'dee-ah)*
every day	**todos los días** *('toh-dohs lohs 'dee-ahs)*
daily	**a diario** *(ah dee-'ah-ree-oh)*
yet	**todavía** *(toh-dah-'vee-ah)*
just	**apenas** *(ah-'peh-nahs)*
already	**ya** *(yah)*

➤ Understanding and using words like **dónde** *('dohn-deh)* and **cuándo** *('kwahn-doh)* is crucial in gathering information. The best way to learn how to use question words is to focus on the first word of each sentence and then try to get a general feel for what the person might be asking. Attempting to translate every word will only lead to frustration.

TIME TELLING!
¡Decir la hora! *(deh-'seer lah 'oh-rah)*

You can't discuss school activities without mentioning the clock. To read the clock in Spanish, simply give the hour, followed by the word **y** *(ee)* (and), and the minutes. For example, 8:15 is **ocho y quince** *('oh-choh ee 'keen-seh)*. Read through these other questions and answers:

What time is it?	**¿Qué hora es?** *(keh 'oh-rah ehs)*
At what time?	**¿A qué hora?** *(ah keh 'oh-rah)*
It's...	**Son las...** *(sohn lahs)*
At...	**A las...** *(ah lahs)*
10:40	**diez y cuarenta**
	(dee-'ehs ee kwah-'rehn-tah)
3:25	**tres y veinte y cinco**
	(trehs ee 'veh·een-teh ee 'seen-koh)
12:05 A.M.	**doce y cinco de la mañana**
	('doh-seh ee 'seen-koh deh lah mah-'nyah-nah)
4:00 P.M.	**cuatro de la tarde**
	('kwah-troh deh lah 'tahr-deh)
9:30 P.M.	**nueve y treinta de la noche**
	(noo-'eh-veh ee 'treh·een-tah deh lah 'noh-cheh)

➤ Are you picking up on everyday expressions as you review? Don't forget that "time" vocabulary can be practiced whenever you like:

on time	**a tiempo** *(ah tee-'ehm-poh)*
A.M.	**de la mañana** *(deh lah mah-'nyah-nah)*
P.M.	**de la tarde** *(deh lah 'tahr-deh)*

➤ For 1:00–1:59, use **Es la...** *(ehs lah)* instead of **Son las...** *(sohn lahs)*. For example:

It's one o' clock.	**Es la una.** *(ehs lah 'oo-nah)*
It's one-thirty.	**Es la una y treinta.** *(ehs lah 'oo-nah ee 'treh-een-tah)*

WHAT DAY?
¿Qué día? *(keh 'dee-ah)*

Spend a few minutes looking over the following Spanish words. They'll allow you to say things about the calendar and making schedules. Then stress each sound as you pronounce them aloud:

The days of the week	**Los días de la semana** *(lohs 'dee-ahs deh lah seh-'mah-nah)*
Monday	**lunes** *('loo-nehs)*
Tuesday	**martes** *('mahr-tehs)*
Wednesday	**miércoles** *(mee-'ehr-koh-lehs)*
Thursday	**jueves** *(hoo-'eh-vehs)*
Friday	**viernes** *(vee-'ehr-nehs)*
Saturday	**sábado** *('sah-bah-doh)*
Sunday	**domingo** *(doh-'meen-goh)*

Now, read these questions and answers. See how **los días** *(lohs 'dee-ahs)* function as one-word responses to "when" questions:

When is there school?	**¿Cuándo hay escuela?** *('kwahn-doh 'ah·ee eh-'skweh-lah)*
Tuesday and Thursday	**Martes y jueves** *('mahr-tehs ee hoo-'eh-vehs)*
When is the class?	**¿Cuándo es la clase?** *('kwahn-doh ehs lah 'klah-seh)*
Monday	**Lunes** *('loo-nehs)*
When are we going there?	**¿Cuándo vamos ahí?** *('kwahn-doh 'vah-mohs ah-'ee)*
Friday	**Viernes** *(vee-'ehr-nehs)*

MÁS INFORMACIÓN

➤ Most students of Spanish get confused when using the words **por** *(pohr)* and **para** *('pah-rah)* because they are similar in meaning. The differences between the two are not easy to explain, so it may be best to listen to Spanish speakers as they use them, and then try them out in short, practical phrases.

by Friday	**para el viernes** *('pah-rah ehl vee-'ehr-nehs)*
for two days	**por dos días** *(pohr dohs 'dee-ahs)*
in order to go	**para ir** *('pah-rah eer)*
throughout the afternoon	**por la tarde** *(pohr lah 'tahr-deh)*

➤ "On Friday" is **el viernes** *(ehl vee-'ehr-nehs)* but "on Fridays" is **los viernes** *(lohs vee-'ehr-nehs)*.

➤ If you want, you can interject the following expressions:

the next one	**el próximo** *(ehl 'prohk-see-moh)*
the past one	**el pasado** *(ehl pah-'sah-doh)*
the weekend	**el fin de semana** *(ehl feen deh-seh-'mah-nah)*

49

➤ Use **¿Hace cuánto?** *('ah-seh 'kwahn-toh)* for "How long ago?"

How long ago?	**¿Hace cuánto?** *('ah-seh 'kwahn-toh)*
Two weeks ago.	**Hace dos semanas.** *('ah-seh dohs seh-'mah-nahs)*

WHAT MONTH?
¿Qué mes? *(keh mehs)*

As far as the months are concerned, just remember that most words are similar in both Spanish and English.

The Months of the Year	**Los meses del año** *(lohs 'meh-sehs dehl 'ah-nyoh)*
January	**enero** *(eh-'neh-roh)*
February	**febrero** *(feh-'breh-roh)*
March	**marzo** *('mahr-soh)*
April	**abril** *(ah-'breel)*
May	**mayo** *('mah-yoh)*
June	**junio** *('hoo-nee·oh)*
July	**julio** *('hoo-lee·oh)*
August	**agosto** *(ah-'goh-stoh)*
September	**septiembre** *(sehp-tee-'ehm-breh)*
October	**octubre** *(ohk-'too-breh)*
November	**noviembre** *(noh-vee-'ehm-breh)*
December	**diciembre** *(dee-see-'ehm-breh)*

WHAT'S THE DATE?
¿Cuál es la fecha? *(kwahl ehs lah 'feh-chah)*

To give the date, reverse the order of your words. For example, February 2nd is **el dos de febrero** *(ehl dohs deh feh-'breh-roh)*.

And this is how you say "the first" in Spanish:

el primero *(ehl pree-'meh-roh)*
January 1st
el primero de enero *(ehl pree-'meh-roh deh eh-'neh-roh)*
The year is often read as one large number:

2005   **dos mil cinco** *(dos meel 'seen-koh)*

Can you give today's date in Spanish? Use a calendar to practice your new vocabulary!

 ¿LISTOS PARA PRACTICAR?

All set to translate? Good luck!

¿Está caminando a la escuela hoy? *(eh-'stah kah-mee-'nahn-doh ah lah eh-'skweh-lah 'oh·ee)*
¡Venga ahora! *('vehn-gah ah-'oh-rah)*
A veces tengo problemas con mi trabajo. *(ah 'veh-sehs 'tehn-goh proh-'bleh-mahs kohn mee trah-'bah-hoh)*

Choose the best word to complete each series:

mes   **ayer**   **a veces** *(mehs, ah-'yehr, ah 'veh-sehs)*

siempre, nunca, _____ *(see-'ehm-preh, 'noon-kah)*

hoy, mañana, _____ *('oh·ee, mah-'nyah-nah)*

día, semana, _____ *('dee-ah, seh-'mah-nah)*

Try to complete these lists, but without any help:

lunes, martes, miércoles, _____ *('loo-nehs, 'mahr-tehs,*

mee-'ehr-koh-lehs)

enero, febrero, marzo, _____ *(eh-'neh-roh, feh-'breh-roh,*

'mahr-soh)

Say these dates and times in Spanish:

At 6:00 A.M. _____

June 6, 1999 _____

It's 9:30 P.M. _____

 CONFLICTOS CULTURALES

Not all folks panic when it comes to tardiness—some cultures put less emphasis on beating the clock than others. Be direct and explain the importance of punctuality in school functions and activities.

You have to arrive early.
Tienes que llegar temprano.
(tee-'eh-nehs keh yeh-'gahr tehm-'prah-noh)

Don't be late!
¡No llegues tarde!
(noh 'yeh-gehs 'tahr-deh)

If you're late again, I'll have to call your home.
Si llegas tarde otra vez, tendré que llamar a tu casa.
(see 'yeh-gahs 'tahr-deh 'oh-trah vehs, tehn-'dreh keh yah-'mahr ah too 'kah-sah)

WHO IS IT?
¿Quién es? *(kee-'ehn ehs)*

Once you feel comfortable responding to "where" and "when" questions in Spanish, attempt to focus on "who" it is you're talking about. Perhaps the best place to start is among your fellow employees. Do any of these job titles sound familiar? Note that the "/a" indicates the feminine ending. Titles that do not have it are unisex.

Who's the...	¿Quién es el/la...? *(kee-'ehn ehs ehl/lah...)*
administrator	**administrador/a** *(ahd-mee-nee-strah-'dohr/ah)*
assistant	**asistente** *(ah-see-'stehn-teh)*
board member	**miembro/a de la junta directiva** *(mee-'ehm-broh/ah deh lah 'hoon-tah dee-rehk-'tee-vah)*
cashier	**cajero/a** *(kah-'heh-roh/ah)*
clerk	**dependiente** *(deh-pehn-dee-'ehn-teh)*
cook	**cocinero/a** *(koh-see-'neh-roh/ah)*
director	**director/a** *(dee-rehk-'tohr/ah)*
gardener	**jardinero/a** *(hahr-dee-'neh-roh/ah)*
instructor	**instructor/a** *(een-strook-'tohr/ah)*
janitor	**bedel** *(beh-'dehl)*
nurse	**enfermero/a** *(ehn-fehr-'meh-roh/ah)*
principal	**director/a** *(dee-rehk-'tohr/ah)*
secretary	**secretario/a** *(seh-kreh-'tah-ree·oh/ah)*
security guard	**guardia de seguridad** *('gwahr-dee·ah deh seh-goo-ree-'dahd)*
superintendent	**superintendente** *(soo-pehr-een-tehn-'dehn-teh)*
supervisor	**supervisor/a** *(soo-pehr-vee-'sohr/ah)*
teacher	**maestro/a** *(mah-'eh-stroh/ah)*
teacher's aide	**ayudante/a de maestro** *(ah-yoo-'dahn-teh/ah deh mah-'eh-stroh)*
trainer	**entrenador/a** *(ehn-treh-nah-'dohr/ah)*

You haven't mentioned everyone, so continue to practice:

Listen to (the)...	Escuche al/a la... *(eh-'skoo-cheh ahl/ah lah...)*
assistant superintendent	**asistente/a del superintendente** *(ah-see-'stehn-teh/ah dehl soo-pehr-een-tehn-'dehn-teh)*
bus driver	**chofer de autobús** *(choh-'fehr deh ow-toh-'boos)*
chairperson	**director/a del departamento** *(dee-rehk-'tohr/ah dehl deh-pahr-tah-'mehn-toh)*
consultant	**consultor/a** *(kohn-sool-'tohr/ah)*
counselor	**consejero/a** *(kohn-seh-'heh-roh/ah)*
crossing guard	**guardia del tráfico** *('gwahr-dee·ah dehl 'trah-fee-koh)*

educator	**educador/a** *(eh-doo-kah-'dohr/ah)*
helper	**ayudante/a** *(ah-yoo-'dahn-teh/ah)*
interpreter	**intérprete** *(een-'tehr-preh-teh)*
leader	**líder** *('lee-dehr)*
librarian	**bibliotecario/a** *(bee-blee·oh-teh-'kah-ree·oh / ah)*
official	**oficial** *(oh-fee-see-'ahl)*
operator	**operador/a** *(oh-peh-rah-'dohr/ah)*
psychologist	**psicólogo/a** *(see-'koh-loh-goh/ah)*
receptionist	**recepcionista** *(reh-sehp-see·oh-'nee-stah)*
specialist	**especialista** *(eh-speh-see·ah-'lee-stah)*
therapist	**terapista** *(teh-rah-'pee-stah)*
translator	**traductor/a** *(trah-dook-'tohr/ah)*
typist	**mecanógrafo/a** *(meh-kah-'noh-grah-foh/ah)*
vice-principal	**subdirector/a** *(soob-dee-rehk-'tohr/ah)*
volunteer	**voluntario/a** *(voh-loon-'tah-ree·oh/ah)*

For the sake of convenience, the masculine form will be used for generic titles in the remainder of this guidebook.

➤ Not every job title can be translated. Notice the shortcut method:

office professionals or clerical staff	=	**secretarios** *(seh-kreh-'tah-ree·ohs)*
instructional assistants	=	**ayudantes** *(ah-yoo-'dahn-tehs)*
campus caterers	=	**cocineros** *(koh-see-'neh-rohs)*

➤ In most cases, administrative positions are translated in reverse word order in Spanish. If you work as a specialist, learn how to give your unique title in Spanish:

Migrant Education Director
Director de educación para los inmigrantes *(dee-rehk-'tohr deh eh-doo-kah-see-'ohn 'pah-rah lohs een-mee-'grahn-tehs)*

Bilingual Education Specialist
Especialista de educación bilingüe *(eh-speh-see·ah-'lee-stah deh eh-doo-kah-see-'ohn bee-'leen-gweh)*

➤ And these are very general terms to define the people you work with:

staff	**los funcionarios** *(lohs foonk-see·oh-'nah-ree·ohs)*
personnel	**el personal** *(ehl pehr-soh-'nahl)*
employees	**los empleados** *(lohs ehm-pleh-'ah-dohs)*

MORE OCCUPATIONS
Más ocupaciones *(mahs oh-koo-pah-see-'oh-nehs)*

A variety of professionals are called to help out on campus, so learn the following job titles as well. Can you fill in the blank with a person's name? Don't forget to change these when you refer to a female:

_____ is (the)...   _____ **es...** *(ehs)*

architect	**el arquitecto** *(ehl ahr-kee-'tehk-toh)*
carpenter	**el carpintero** *(ehl kahr-peen-'teh-roh)*
dentist	**el dentista** *(ehl dehn-'tee-stah)*
doctor	**el doctor** *(ehl dohk-'tohr)*
engineer	**el ingeniero** *(ehl een-heh-nee-'eh-roh)*
firefighter	**el bombero** *(ehl bohm-'beh-roh)*
lawyer	**el abogado** *(ehl ah-boh-'gah-doh)*
mail carrier	**el cartero** *(ehl kahr-'teh-roh)*
mechanic	**el mecánico** *(ehl meh-'kah-nee-koh)*
painter	**el pintor** *(ehl peen-'tohr)*
plumber	**el plomero** *(ehl ploh-'meh-roh)*
police officer	**el policía** *(ehl poh-lee-'see-ah)*

HOW CAN I HELP YOU?
¿En qué puedo servirle? *(ehn keh 'pweh-doh sehr-'veer-leh)*

Do you know enough Spanish to ask questions by yourself? This first one is a classic, and usually follows an introduction or friendly greeting:

Are you...?   **¿Está...?** *(eh-'stah...)*

available	**disponible** *(dee-spoh-'nee-bleh)*
bored	**aburrido** *(ah-boo-'rree-doh)*
busy	**ocupado** *(oh-koo-'pah-doh)*
comfortable	**cómodo** *('koh-moh-doh)*
excited	**emocionado** *(eh-moh-see·oh-'nah-doh)*
fine	**bien** *('bee·ehn)*
happy	**contento** *(kohn-'tehn-toh)*
lost	**perdido** *(pehr-'dee-doh)*

nervous	**nervioso** *(nehr-vee-'oh-soh)*
OK	**regular** *(reh-goo-'lahr)*
prepared	**preparado** *(preh-pah-'rah-doh)*
ready	**listo** *('lee-stoh)*
relaxed	**relajado** *(reh-lah-'hah-doh)*
sad	**triste** *('tree-steh)*
sick	**enfermo** *(ehn-'fehr-moh)*
sure	**seguro** *(seh-'goo-roh)*
surprised	**sorprendido** *(sohr-prehn-'dee-doh)*
tired	**cansado** *(kahn-'sah-doh)*
upset	**enojado** *(eh-noh-'hah-doh)*
worried	**preocupado** *(preh-oh-koo-'pah-doh)*

Now, try one of these questions as you offer to help, and then focus on any key words that may sound familiar:

How can I help you?	**¿En qué puedo servirle?** *(ehn keh 'pweh-doh sehr-'veer-leh)*
What do you need?	**¿Qué necesita usted?** *(keh neh-seh-'see-tah oo-'stehd)*
Where are you going?	**¿Adónde va usted?** *(ah-'dohn-deh vah oo-'stehd)*
Who would you like to speak to?	**¿Con quién quisiera hablar?** *(kohn kee-'ehn kee-see-'eh-rah ah-'blahr)*
What is the problem?	**¿Cual es el problema?** *(kwahl ehs ehl proh-'bleh-mah)*

Keep going; however, this time find out who they are:

Are you (the) _____?	**¿Es usted _____?** *(ehs oo-'stehd ____)*

employee	**el empleado** *(ehl ehm-pleh-'ah-doh)*
guest	**el huésped** *(ehl 'weh-spehd)*
member	**el miembro** *(ehl mee-'ehm-broh)*
mother	**la madre** *(lah 'mah-dreh)*
neighbor	**el vecino** *(ehl veh-'see-noh)*

owner	**el dueño** *(ehl 'dweh-nyoh)*
parent	**el padre** *(ehl 'pah-dreh)*
relative	**el pariente** *(ehl pah-ree-'ehn-teh)*
salesperson	**el vendedor** *(ehl vehn-deh-'dohr)*
student	**el estudiante** *(ehl eh-stoo-dee-'ahn-teh)*
visitor	**el visitante** *(ehl vee-see-'tahn-teh)*

➤ Note that **padres** means "parents," whereas **parientes** means "relatives." This is a source of endless mistakes.

To find out what's going on, ask a simple question, and worry about the details later:

Do you have (the)...?	**¿Tiene...?** *(tee-'eh-neh)*
appointment	**la cita** *(lah 'see-tah)*
meeting	**la reunión** *(lah reh-oo-nee-'ohn)*
class	**la clase** *(lah 'klah-seh)*
conference	**la conferencia** *(lah kohn-feh-'rehn-see·ah)*
seminar	**el seminario** *(ehl seh-mee-'nah-ree·oh)*
Do you want (the)...?	**¿Quiere...?** *(kee-'eh-reh)*
schedule	**el horario** *(eh oh-'rah-ree·oh)*
map	**el mapa** *(ehl 'mah-pah)*
pass	**el permiso** *(ehl pehr-'mee-soh)*
application	**la solicitud** *(lah soh-lee-see-'tood)*
form	**el formulario** *(ehl fohr-moo-'lah-ree·oh)*
Do you need...?	**¿Necesita...?** *(neh-seh-'see-tah)*
to attend	**asistir** *(ah-see-'steer)*
to enroll	**matricularse** *(mah-tree-koo-'lahr-seh)*
to call	**llamar** *(yah-'mahr)*
to park	**estacionar** *(eh-stah-see·oh-'nahr)*
to deliver	**entregar** *(ehn-treh-'gahr)*
to visit	**visitar** *(vee-see-'tahr)*
to sign	**firmar** *(feer-'mahr)*

➤ Some things might require a little more explanation:

There's a...	**Hay un...** *('ah·ee oon...)*
plan	**plan** *(plahn)*
procedure	**procedimiento** *(proh-seh-dee-mee-'ehn-toh)*
process	**proceso** *(proh-'seh-soh)*

➤ Bear in mind that adjectives that are masculine often end in **o**. When the adjective is feminine, in most cases you delete the **o** and add an **a (aburrido— aburrida**, **contento—contenta**) *(ah-boo-'rree-doh, ah-boo-'rree-dah, kohn-'tehn-toh, kohn-'tehn-tah)*.

➤ These terms all refer to some kind of meeting. You'll run across them several times in this guidebook:

la reunión *(lah reh-oo-nee-'ohn)*
la junta *(lah 'hoon-tah)*
la conferencia *(lah kohn-feh-'rehn-see·ah)*

PERSONAL INFORMATION
La información personal *(lah een-fohr-mah-see-'ohn pehr-soh-'nahl)*

At times, it's necessary to gather personal information in order to assist others more efficiently. These next questions and answers are also useful for filling out documents or forms:

What is your...?	**¿Cuál es su...?** *(kwahl ehs soo....?)*
address	**dirección** *(dee-rehk-see-'ohn)*
age	**edad** *(eh-'dahd)*
date of birth	**fecha de nacimiento** *('feh-chah deh nah-see-mee-'ehn-toh)*
first language	**lengua materna** *('lehn-gwah mah-'tehr-nah)*
first name	**primer nombre** *(pree-'mehr 'nohm-breh)*

full name	**nombre y apellido** (*'nohm-breh ee ah-peh-'yee-doh*)
last name	**apellido** (*ah-peh-'yee-doh*)
maiden name	**nombre de soltera** (*'nohm-breh deh sohl-'teh-rah*)
middle initial	**segunda inicial** (*seh-'goon-dah een-nee-see-'ahl*)
nationality	**nacionalidad** (*nah-see·oh-nah-lee-'dahd*)
nickname	**apodo** (*ah-'poh-doh*)
place of birth	**lugar de nacimiento** (*loo-'gahr deh nah-see-mee-'ehn-toh*)
race	**raza** (*'rah-sah*)
relationship	**relación** (*reh-lah-see-'ohn*)
zip code	**zona postal** (*'soh-nah poh-'stahl*)

Here's another useful pattern:

What's the _____ number?	**¿Cuál es el número de _____ ?** (*kwahl ehs ehl 'noo-meh-roh deh...?*)
apartment	**apartamento** (*ah-pahr-tah-'mehn-toh*)
code	**código** (*'koh-dee-goh*)
I.D.	**identificación** (*ee-dehn-tee-fee-kah-see-'ohn*)
license	**licencia** (*lee-'sehn-see·ah*)
office	**oficina** (*oh-fee-'see-nah*)
room	**cuarto** (*'kwahr-toh*)
social security	**seguro social** (*seh-'goo-roh soh-see-'ahl*)
telephone	**teléfono** (*teh-'leh-foh-noh*)

MÁS INFORMACIÓN

➤ Take note:

male	**masculino** *(mah-skoo-'lee-noh)*
female	**femenino** *(feh-meh-'nee-noh)*

CONFLICTOS CULTURALES

When referring to others by name, it really helps if you are able to pronounce people's names correctly, as it makes them feel much more at ease. Always remember that Spanish is pronounced the way it is written. Also, it is not uncommon for someone in Spain or Latin America to have two last names. Don't get confused. Here's the order:

First name	Father's last name	Mother's last name
primer nombre	**apellido paterno**	**apellido materno**
(pree-'mehr	*(ah-peh-'yee-doh*	*(ah-'peh-'yee-doh*
'nohm-breh)	*pah-'tehr-noh)*	*mah-'tehr-noh)*
Juan Carlos	**Espinoza**	**García**
(wahn 'kahr-lohs)	*(eh-spee-'noh-sah)*	*(gahr-'see-ah)*

WHAT KIND OF SCHOOL?
¿Qué tipo de escuela? *(keh 'tee-poh deh eh-'skweh-lah)*

As the Spanish-speaking public begins to inquire about your educational program or facility, make sure you can give a description effectively.

It's a/an _____ school.	**Es una escuela** _____ . *(ehs 'oo-nah eh-'skweh-lah* _____ *)*
accelerated	**de estudiantes avanzados** *(deh eh-stoo-dee-'ahn-tehs ah-vahn-'sah-dohs)*
alternative	**alternativa** *(ahl-tehr-nah-'tee-vah)*
boys'	**para niños** *('pah-rah 'nee-nyohs)*

commuter	**para viajeros abonados** (*'pah-rah vee-ah-'heh-rohs ah-boh-'nah-dohs*)
continuation	**de continuación** (*deh kohn-tee-noo-ah-see-'ohn*)
correctional	**correccional** (*koh-rrehk-see·oh-'nahl*)
correspondence	**de correspondencia** (*deh koh-rreh-spohn-'dehn-see·ah*)
court	**de la corte** (*deh lah 'kohr-teh*)
day	**diurna** (*dee-'oor-nah*)
girls'	**para niñas** (*'pah-rah 'nee-nyahs*)
grammar	**primaria** (*pree-'mah-ree·ah*)
high	**secundaria** (*seh-koon-'dah-ree·ah*)
home	**domiciliaria** (*doh-mee-see-lee-'ah-ree·ah*)
military	**militar** (*mee-lee-'tahr*)
night	**nocturna** (*nohk-'toor-nah*)
nursery	**guardería** (*'gwahr-deh-'ree-ah*)
parochial	**parroquial** (*pah-rroh-kee-'ahl*)
preschool	**preescolar** (*preh-eh-skoh-'lahr*)
private	**privada** (*pree-'vah-dah*)
public	**pública** (*'poo-blee-kah*)
religious	**religiosa** (*reh-lee-hee-'oh-sah*)
trade	**de artes y oficios** (*deh 'ahr-tehs ee oh-'fee-see·ohs*)
training	**de entrenamiento** (*deh ehn-treh-nah-mee-'ehn-toh*)

MÁS INFORMACIÓN

➤ Acquire all the buzz words related to your professional field:

It's...	**Es...** (*ehs...*)
elementary education	**la enseñanza primaria** (*lah ehn-seh-'nyahn-sah pree-'mah-ree·ah*)
secondary education	**la enseñanza secundaria** (*lah ehn-seh-'nyahn-sah seh-koon-'dah-ree·ah*)
higher education	**la enseñanza superior** (*lah ehn-seh-'nyahn-sah soo-peh-ree-'ohr*)

It's a...	**Es un...** *(ehs oon...)*
magnet	**imán** *(ee-'mahn)*
model	**modelo** *(moh-'deh-loh)*
pilot	**piloto** *(pee-'loh-toh)*
satellite	**satélite** *(sah-'teh-lee-teh)*

CONFLICTOS CULTURALES

Grade levels seldom translate exactly from one country to the next, or from one U.S. school system to another. The following translations should provide a basic guide:

nursery school	**jardín infantil básico** *(hahr-'deen een-fahn-'teel 'bah-see-koh)*
kindergarten	**jardín infantil superior** *(hahr-'deen een-fahn-'teel soo-peh-ree-'ohr)*
grade school	**escuela primaria** *(eh-'skweh-lah pree-'mah-ree·ah)*
middle school intermediate school junior high school	**escuela intermedia** *(eh-'sweh-lah een-tehr-'meh-dee·ah)*
high school	**escuela superior, escuela de segunda enseñanza** *(eh-'skweh-lah soo-peh-ree-'ohr, eh-'skweh-lah deh seh-'goon-dah ehn-seh-'nyahn-sah)*
community college junior college	**universidad de dos años de estudios** *(oo-nee-vehr-see-'dahd deh dohs 'ah-nyohs deh eh-'stoo-dee·ohs)*
college university	**universidad de cuatro años de estudios o más** *(oo-nee-vehr-see-'dahd deh 'kwah-troh 'ah-nyohs deh eh-'stoo-dee·ohs oh mahs)*

DESCRIBE THINGS

Describa las cosas *(deh-'skree-bah lahs 'koh-sahs)*

Work on expanding your descriptive vocabulary by reading the list of opposites below:

| It's... | **Es...** *(ehs...)* |
| | **Está...** *(eh-'stah...)* |

cheap	**barato** *(bah-'rah-toh)*
expensive	**caro** *('kah-roh)*
clean	**limpio** *('leem-pee·oh)*
dirty	**sucio** *('soo-see·oh)*
deep	**profundo** *(proh-'foon-doh)*
shallow	**bajo** *('bah-hoh)*
difficult	**difícil** *(dee-'fee-seel)*
easy	**fácil** *('fah-seel)*
hard	**duro** *('doo-roh)*
soft	**blando** *('blahn-doh)*
long	**largo** *('lahr-goh)*
short (in length)	**corto** *('kohr-toh)*
narrow	**estrecho** *(eh-'streh-choh)*
wide	**ancho** *('ahn-choh)*
pretty	**bonito** *(boh-'nee-toh)*
ugly	**feo** *('feh-oh)*
rough	**áspero** *('ah-speh-roh)*
smooth	**liso** *('lee-soh)*
dry	**seco** *('seh-koh)*
wet	**mojado** *(moh-'hah-doh)*
thin	**delgado** *(dehl-'gah-doh)*
thick	**grueso** *(groo-'eh-soh)*

Keep in mind that in Spanish, the adjective (the word used to describe anything) usually goes after the noun. Here are some more vocabulary words:

It's an _____ class.   **Es una clase _____ .**
    (ehs 'oo-nah 'klah-seh)

excellent   **excelente** *(ehk-seh-'lehn-teh)*
important   **importante** *(eem-pohr-'tahn-teh)*
interesting   **interesante** *(een-teh-reh-'sahn-teh)*

He's a _____ teacher.   **Es un maestro _____ .**
    (ehs oon mah-'eh-stroh)

bald   **calvo** *('kahl-voh)*
blond   **rubio** *('roo-bee·oh)*
dark-haired   **moreno** *(moh-'reh-noh)*

She is a _____ principal.   **Es una directora _____ .**
    (ehs 'oo-nah dee-rehk-'toh-rah)

bad   **mala** *('mah-lah)*
good   **buena** *('bweh-nah)*
prepared   **preparada** *(preh-pah-'rah-dah)*

MÁS INFORMACIÓN

➤ Description words that begin with **no**, **in-**, or **des-** often refer to an opposite:

qualified (**calificado**) *(kah-lee-fee-'kah-doh)*
unqualified (**no calificado**) *(noh kah-lee-fee-'kah-doh)*

correct (**correcto**) *(koh-'rrehk-toh)*
incorrect (**incorrecto**) *(een-koh-'rrehk-toh)*

employed (**empleado**) *(ehm-pleh-'ah-doh)*
unemployed (**desempleado**) *(dehs-ehm-pleh-'ah-doh)*

➤ And use these little words to compare things:

a little big	**un poco grande** *(oon 'poh-koh 'grahn-deh)*
as big as	**tan grande como** *(tahn 'grahn-deh 'koh-moh)*
bigger than	**más grande que** *(mahs 'grahn-deh keh)*
biggest	**el más grande** *(ehl mahs 'grahn-deh)*
so big	**tan grande** *(tahn 'grahn-deh)*
too big	**demasiado grande** *(deh-mah-see-'ah-doh 'grahn-deh)*
very big	**muy grande** *('moo·ee 'grahn-deh)*

Can you translate the following sentences?

Carlos es más grande que Samuel.
('kahr-lohs ehs mahs 'grahn-deh keh sah-moo-'ehl)

Samuel es tan grande como una casa.
(sah-moo-'ehl ehs tahn 'grahn-deh 'koh-moh 'oo-nah 'kah-sah)

Felipe es el más grande.
(feh-'lee-peh ehs ehl mahs 'grahn-deh)

¿LISTOS PARA PRACTICAR?

Name three different kinds of schools in Spanish:

_____

_____

_____

Answer these questions about yourself in Spanish:

¿Cuál es su fecha de nacimiento? *(kwahl ehs soo 'feh-chah deh nah-see-mee-'ehn-toh)*

¿Cuál es su número de teléfono? *(kwahl ehs soo 'noo-meh-roh deh teh-'leh-foh-noh)*

¿Cuál es su nombre y apellido? *(kwahl ehs soo 'nohm-breh ee ah-peh-'yee-doh)*

Here are some more opposites to practice. You know what to do:

grueso *(groo-'eh-soh)*	**seco** *('seh-koh)*
moreno *(moh-'reh-noh)*	**rubio** *('roo-bee·oh)*
caro *('kah-roh)*	**fácil** *('fah-seel)*
limpio *('leem-pee·oh)*	**bonito** *(boh-'nee-toh)*
difícil *(dee-'fee-seel)*	**bajo** *('bah-hoh)*
feo *('feh-oh)*	**corto** *('kohr-toh)*
blando *('blahn-doh)*	**barato** *(bah-'rah-toh)*
largo *(bah-'rah-toh)*	**delgado** *(dehl-'gah-doh)*
profundo *(proh-'foon-doh)*	**sucio** *('soo-see·oh)*
mojado *(moh-'hah-doh)*	**duro** *('doo-roh)*

Fill in the blanks using the correct word:

la maestra, el cocinero, el bedel *(lah mah-'eh-strah, ehl koh-see-'neh-roh, ehl beh-'dehl)*

_____ **está esperando en la cafetería.** *(_____ eh-'stah eh-speh-'rahn-doh ehn lah kah-feh-teh-'ree-ah)*

_____ **está hablando en la clase.** *(_____ eh-'stah ah-'blahn-doh ehn lah 'klah-seh)*

_____ **está trabajando en el baño.** *(_____ eh-'stah trah-bah-'hahn-doh ehn ehl 'bah-nyoh)*

 ¡ACCIÓN!

To handle any encounter with a Spanish speaker, make sure you've set aside all the appropriate Spanish verbs. As you take on this new list of actions, utilize the shortcuts that you know:

to leave	**salir** *(sah-'leer)*	**Voy a salir a las tres.** *('voh·ee ah sah-'leer ah lahs trehs)*

to arrive	**llegar** *(yeh-'gahr)*	**Tiene que llegar temprano.** *(tee-'eh-neh keh yeh-'gahr tehm-'prah-noh)*
to enter	**entrar** *(ehn-'trahr)*	**Favor de entrar ahí.** *(fah-'vohr deh ehn-'trahr ah-'ee)*
to park	**estacionar** *(eh-stah-see·oh-'nahr)*	**No estacionar aquí.** *(noh eh-stah-see·oh-'nahr ah-'kee)*
to answer	**contestar** *(kohn-teh-'stahr)*	_____.
to ask	**preguntar** *(preh-goon-'tahr)*	_____.
to attend	**asistir** *(ah-see-'steer)*	_____.
to begin	**empezar** *(ehm-peh-'sahr)*	_____.
to bring	**traer** *(trah-'ehr)*	_____.
to call	**llamar** *(yah-'mahr)*	_____.
to close	**cerrar** *(seh-'rrahr)*	_____.
to deliver	**entregar** *(ehn-treh-'gahr)*	_____.
to do	**hacer** *(ah-'sehr)*	_____.
to end	**terminar** *(tehr-mee-'nahr)*	_____.
to find	**encontrar** *(ehn-kohn-'trahr)*	_____.
to look for	**buscar** *(boo-'skahr)*	_____.
to move	**mover** *(moh-'vehr)*	_____.
to open	**abrir** *(ah-'breer)*	_____.
to return	**regresar** *(reh-greh-'sahr)*	_____.
to sign	**firmar** *(feer-'mahr)*	_____.
to take	**tomar** *(toh-'mahr)*	_____.
to visit	**visitar** *(vee-see-'tahr)*	_____.

We have learned that our Spanish verbs change when we talk about current action:

To speak	**hablar** *(ah-'blahr)*
I'm speaking.	**Estoy hablando.** *(eh-'stoh·ee ah-'blahn-doh)*
To eat	**comer** *(koh-'mehr)*
We're eating.	**Estamos comiendo.**
	(eh-'stah-mohs koh-mee-'ehn-doh)
To write	**escribir** *(eh-skree-'beer)*
He's writing.	**Está escribiendo.** *(eh-'stah eh-skree-bee-'ehn-doh)*

The same thing happens consistently when we refer to everyday activities. However, this time the verbs shift according to who completes the action. This next pattern is the same for most action words:

To Speak	**Hablar** *(ah-'blahr)*
I speak	**hablo** *('ah-bloh)*
You speak (informal)	**hablas** *('ah-blahs)*
You speak (formal); he, she speaks	**habla** *('ah-blah)*
You (plural), they speak	**hablan** *('ah-blahn)*
We speak	**hablamos** *(ah-'blah-mohs)*

To Eat	**Comer** *(koh-'mehr)*
I eat	**como** *('koh-moh)*
You eat (informal)	**comes** *('koh-mehs)*
You eat (formal); he, she eats	**come** *('koh-meh)*
You (plural), they eat	**comen** *('koh-mehn)*
We eat	**comemos** *(koh-'meh-mohs)*

To Write	**Escribir** *(eh-skree-'beer)*
I write	**escribo** *(eh-'skree-boh)*
You write (informal)	**escribes** *(eh-'skree-behs)*
You write (formal); he, she writes	**escribe** *(eh-'skree-beh)*
You (plural), they write	**escriben** *(eh-'skree-behn)*
We write	**escribimos** *(eh-skree-'bee-mohs)*

Notice how the **-ar** verb, **hablar** *(ah-'blahr)*, doesn't change the same as the **-er** and **-ir** verbs! This tip will be helpful as you pick up more action forms later on. By the way, always be on the lookout for verbs that require **se**, which indicates that the action is undertaken personally: **él apura** *(ehl ah-'poo-rah)* — he hurries (somebody), **él se apura** *(ehl seh ah-'poo-rah)* — he hurries (himself).

to stay	**quedarse** *(keh-'dahr-seh)*	He stays in class.	**se queda en la clase.** *(seh 'keh-dah ehn lah 'klah-seh)*
to stop	**pararse** *(pah-'rahr-seh)*	He stops here.	**Se para aquí.** *(seh 'pah-rah ah-'kee)*
to hurry	**apurarse** *(ah-poo-'rahr -seh)*	He hurries a lot.	**Se apura mucho.** *(seh ah-'poo-rah 'moo-choh)*
to sit	**sentarse** *(sehn-'tahr-seh)*	He sits there.	**Se sienta ahí.** *(seh see-'ehn-tah ah-'ee)*
to get up	**levantarse** *(leh-vahn-'tahr-seh)*	He gets up at six.	**Se levanta a las seis.** *(seh leh-'vahn-tah ah lahs 'seh·ees)*
to enroll	**matricularse** *(mah-tree-koo-'lahr-seh)*	He enrolls late.	**Se matricula tarde.** *(seh mah-tree-'koo-lah 'tahr-deh)*
to meet	**reunirse** *(reh-oo-'neer-seh)*	He meets with her.	**Se reune con ella.** *(seh reh-'oo-neh kohn 'eh-yah)*

MÁS INFORMACIÓN

➤ Many Spanish verbs are irregular because they don't follow the pattern above. Look at the following:

to begin	**empezar** *(ehm-peh-'sahr)*
I begin	**Empiezo** *(ehm-pee-'eh-soh)*
to think	**pensar** *(pehn-'sahr)*
I think	**Pienso** *(pee-'ehn-soh)*
to leave	**salir** *(sah-'leer)*
I leave	**Salgo** *('sahl-goh)*

to tell	**decir** *(deh-'seer)*
I tell	**Digo** *('dee-goh)*
to see	**ver** *(vehr)*
I see	**Veo** *('veh-oh)*
to give	**dar** *(dahr)*
I give	**Doy** *(doh·ee)*
to find	**encontrar** *(ehn-kohn-'trahr)*
I find	**Encuentro** *(ehn-'kwehn-troh)*
to offer	**ofrecer** *(oh-freh-'sehr)*
I offer	**Ofrezco** *(oh-'freh-skoh)*
to do	**hacer** *(ah-'sehr)*
I do	**Hago** *('ah-goh)*
to bring	**traer** *(trah-'ehr)*
I bring	**Traigo** *('trah-ee-goh)*
to understand	**entender** *(ehn-tehn-'dehr)*
I understand	**Entiendo** *(ehn-tee-'ehn-doh)*

➤ An additional Spanish verb form may be added, especially if you consistently talk to small children. In general, all you do is add **-s** to the "you" singular word form:

¿Habla español? *('ah-blah eh-spah-'nyohl)*	**¿Hablas español?** *('ah-blahs eh-spah-'nyohl)*
¿Escribe mucho? *(eh-'skree-beh 'moo-choh)*	**¿Escribes mucho?** *(eh-'skree-behs 'moo-choh)*
¿Entiende inglés? *(ehn-tee-'ehn-deh een-'glehs)*	**¿Entiendes inglés?** *(ehn-tee-'ehn-dehs een-'glehs)*

➤ To describe an action word in Spanish, try one of these. Do you note any pattern?

completely	**completamente** *(kohm-pleh-tah-'mehn-teh)*
quickly	**rápidamente** *(rah-pee-dah-'mehn-teh)*
slowly	**lentamente** *(lehn-tah-'mehn-teh)*

➤ And this is how you ask a question in the present tense:

Are they working?
¿Están trabajando?
(eh-'stahn trah-bah-'hahn-doh)

Do they work?
¿Trabajan?
(trah-'bah-hahn)

 ¡ÓRDENES!

Although we've learned several valuable command words already, let's work on a few more. This group relates to general activities around the school site:

bring	**traiga** *('trah·ee-gah)*
call	**llame** *('yah-meh)*
close	**cierre** *(see-'eh-rreh)*
enter	**entre** *('ehn-treh)*
leave	**salga** *('sahl-gah)*
move	**mueva** *('mweh-vah)*
open	**abra** *('ah-brah)*
read	**lea** *('leh-ah)*
return	**regrese** *(reh-'greh-seh)*
sign	**firme** *('feer-meh)*
take	**tome** *('toh-meh)*
write	**escriba** *(eh-'skree-bah)*

Enter through the large gate.
Entre por el portón grande. *('ehn-treh pohr ehl pohr-'tohn 'grahn-deh)*

Return tomorrow at eight o'clock.
Regrese mañana a las ocho. *(reh-'greh-seh mah-'nyah-nah ah lahs 'oh-choh)*

➤ A simple approach to forming a command in Spanish requires knowledge of the three different action word (verb) endings. As you know, the endings are:

-ar as in **hablar** *(ah-'blahr)*   to speak
-er as in **comer** *(koh-'mehr)*   to eat
-ir as in **escribir** *(eh-skree-'beer)*   to write

To make a formal command word, drop the last two letters of the infinitive ("to") form and replace them as follows:

-ar	=	**-e**	
hablar	=	**¡Hable!** *('ah-bleh)*	Speak!
-er	=	**-a**	
comer	=	**¡Coma!** *('koh-mah)*	Eat!
-ir	=	**-a**	
escribir	=	**¡Escriba!** *(eh-'skree-bah)*	Write!

But beware! Some verbs are special and simply have to be memorized:

ir	=	**¡Vaya!** *('vah-yah)*	Go!
venir	=	**¡Venga!** *('vehn-gah)*	Come!
decir	=	**¡Diga!** *('dee-gah)*	Speak!

¿LISTOS PARA PRACTICAR?

Now choose the best command word!

Lea, Llame, Conteste, Firme, Traiga
('leh-ah, 'yah-meh, kohn-'teh-steh, 'feer-meh, 'trah·ee-gah)

_____ **la pregunta.** *(lah preh-'goon-tah)*

_____ **el libro.** *(ehl 'lee-broh)*

_____ **su nombre.** *(soo 'nohm-breh)*

_____ **a su casa.** *(ah soo 'kah-sah)*

_____ **la silla.** *(lah 'see-yah)*

Connect the opposites:

contestar *(kohn-teh-'stahr)*	**encontrar** *(ehn-kohn-'trahr)*
abrir *(ah-'breer)*	**terminar** *(tehr-mee-'nahr)*
empezar *(ehm-peh-'sahr)*	**cerrar** *(seh-'rrahr)*
entrar *(ehn-'trahr)*	**salir** *(sah-'leer)*
buscar *(boo-'skahr)*	**preguntar** *(preh-goon-'tahr)*

Shift from one tense to the next. Follow the example given:

Están visitando. *(eh-'stahn vee-see-'tahn-doh)*   <u>**Visitan.**</u> *(vee-'see-tahn)*

Están llamando. *(eh-'stahn yah-'mahn-doh)*   _____

Están regresando. *(eh-'stahn reh-greh-'sahn-doh)*   _____

Están llegando. *(eh-'stahn yeh-'gahn-doh)*   _____

CHAPTER THREE
Capítulo Tres
(kah-'pee-too-loh trehs)

THE YOUNGER STUDENTS

Los estudiantes menores
(lohs eh-stoo-dee-'ahn-tehs meh-'noh-rehs)

HOW ARE YOU, SWEETHEART?

¿Cómo estás tú, querido? *('koh-moh eh-'stahs too, keh-'ree-doh)*

Let's begin our classroom experiences in Spanish by exploring the world of early education. As you have seen, some of the words in Spanish change slightly when you address loved ones or young children. Here are a few examples of casual or informal Spanish:

You are my friend.	**Tú eres mi amigo.** *(too 'eh-rehs mee ah-'mee-goh)*
Do you speak Spanish?	**¿Tú hablas español?** *(too 'ah-blahs eh-spah-'nyohl)*
You don't have a pencil.	**Tú no tienes un lápiz.** *(too noh tee-'eh-nehs oon 'lah-pees)*

Can you tell that **tú** *(too)* means "you"? Note that the word "your" is **tu**, which is the same as "you" but without the written accent:

Where's your family?	**¿Dónde está tu familia?** *('dohn-deh eh-'stah too fah-'mee-lee·ah)*

All informal verb forms require changes when you talk in casual settings, and most can be recognized because they end in the letter **-s**.

Do you have...?	**¿Tienes...?** *(tee-'eh-nehs)*
Do you want...?	**¿Quieres...?** *(kee-'eh-rehs)*
Do you need...?	**¿Necesitas...?** *(neh-seh-'see-tahs)*

OK, picture a group of children as you practice:

How many do you have?	**¿Cuántos tienes?** *('kwahn-tohs tee-'eh-nehs)*
Which one do you want?	**¿Cuál quieres?** *(kwahl kee-'eh-rehs)*
What do you need?	**¿Qué necesitas?** *(keh neh-seh-'see-tahs)*

These comments are common around the very young:

How cute!	**¡Qué precioso!** *(keh pre-see-'oh-soh)*
How funny!	**¡Qué cómico!** *(keh 'koh-mee-koh)*
How pretty!	**¡Qué bonito!** *(keh boh-'nee-toh)*
What a beautiful face!	**¡Qué linda cara!** *(keh 'leen-dah 'kah-rah)*

What a beautiful outfit!	**¡Qué linda ropa!**
	(keh 'leen-dah 'roh-pah)
What a beautiful smile!	**¡Qué linda sonrisa!**
	(keh 'leen-dah sohn-'ree-sah)
What a beautiful voice!	**¡Qué linda voz!**
	(keh 'leen-dah vohs)
What beautiful hair!	**¡Qué lindo pelo!**
	(keh 'leen-doh 'peh-loh)

CONFLICTOS CULTURALES

Hispanics also use the informal **tú** form whenever they tell children what to do. It sends a message of closeness and intimacy. We'll study these verb conjugations soon:

Come here, my darling.	**Ven acá, mi querido.**
	(vehn ah-'kah, mee keh-'ree-doh)
Come here, my love.	**Ven acá, mi amor.**
	(vehn ah-'kah, mee ah-'mohr)
Don't be afraid.	**No tengas miedo.**
	(noh 'tehn-gahs mee-'eh-doh)
Don't cry.	**No llores.**
	(noh 'yoh-rehs)
Give me a hug.	**Dame un abrazo.**
	('dah-meh oon ah-'brah-soh)
It's lots of fun.	**Es muy divertido.**
	(ehs 'moo·ee dee-vehr-'tee-doh)
It's for you.	**Es para ti.**
	(ehs 'pah-rah tee)

THE LITTLE ONES
Los niñitos *(lohs nee-'nyee-tohs)*

Many parents today get a jump start on their child's formal education by enrolling them into nurseries, preschools, and child-care facilities. For those educators who teach Spanish-speaking infants and toddlers, here are some key words that can make early instruction a whole lot easier:

Let's go to (the)...	**Vamos a...** *('vah-mohs ah...)*
bassinet	**el bacinete** *(ehl bah-see-'neh-teh)*
cradle	**la cuna mecedora** *(lah 'koo-nah meh-seh-'doh-rah)*
crib	**la cuna** *(lah 'koo-nah)*
doll house	**la casa de muñecas** *(lah 'kah-sah deh moo-'nyeh-kahs)*
game	**el juego** *(ehl 'hweh-goh)*
playpen	**el corral de juego** *(ehl koh-'rrahl deh 'hweh-goh)*
potty	**la vasinica** *(lah vah-see-'nee-kah)*
stroller	**el carrito de bebé** *(ehl kah-'rree-toh deh beh-'beh)*
stuffed animal	**el animal de peluche** *(ehl ah-nee-'mahl deh peh-'loo-cheh)*
toy	**el juguete** *(ehl hoo-'geh-teh)*
Take (the)...	**Toma...** *('toh-mah)*
bib	**el babero** *(ehl bah-'beh-roh)*
blanket	**la cobija** *(lah koh-'bee-hah)*
nursing bottle	**el biberón** *(ehl bee-beh-'rohn)*
pacifier	**el chupete** *(ehl choo-'peh-teh)*
rattle	**el sonajero** *(ehl soh-nah-'heh-roh)*

THE TOY CHEST

El baúl de juguetes *(ehl bah-'ool deh hoo-'geh-tehs)*

Bring (the)...	**Trae...** *('trah-eh...)*
ball	**la pelota** *(lah peh-'loh-tah)*
balloon	**el globo** *(ehl 'gloh-boh)*
blocks	**los cubitos** *(lohs koo-'bee-tohs)*
coloring book	**el librito de dibujos** *(ehl lee-'bree-toh deh dee-'boo-hohs)*
crayons	**los lápices para pintar** *(lohs 'lah-pee-sehs 'pah-rah peen-'tahr)*
doll	**la muñeca** *(lah moo-'nyeh-kah)*
jump rope	**la cuerda para brincar** *(lah 'kwehr-dah 'pah-rah breen-'kahr)*
kite	**la cometa** *(lah koh-'meh-tah)*

little car	**el carrito** *(ehl kah-'rree-toh)*
marbles	**las canicas** *(lahs kah-'nee-kahs)*
mobile	**el móvil** *(ehl 'moh-veel)*
model	**el modelo** *(ehl moh-'deh-loh)*
monster	**el monstruo** *(ehl 'mohn-stroo-oh)*
puppets	**los títeres** *(lohs 'tee-teh-rehs)*
puzzle	**el rompecabezas** *(ehl rohm-peh-kah-'beh-sahs)*
skates	**los patines** *(lohs pah-'tee-nehs)*
sled	**el trineo** *(ehl tree-'neh-oh)*
spaceship	**la nave espacial** *(lah 'nah-veh eh-spah-see-'ahl)*
storybook	**el libro de cuentos** *(ehl 'lee-broh deh 'kwehn-tohs)*
top	**el trompo** *(ehl 'trohm-poh)*
tricycle	**el triciclo** *(ehl tree-'see-kloh)*
video	**el vídeo** *(ehl 'vee-deh-oh)*
wagon	**el vagón** *(ehl vah-'gohn)*
whistle	**el silbato** *(ehl seel-'bah-toh)*

The toy _____   _____ **de juguete** *(_____ deh hoo-'geh-teh)*

airplane	**el avión** *(ehl ah-vee-'ohn)*
boat	**el barco** *(ehl 'bahr-koh)*
horn	**la trompeta** *(lah trohm-'peh-tah)*
soldier	**el soldado** *(ehl sohl-'dah-doh)*
truck	**el camión** *(ehl kah-mee-'ohn)*

It's...   **Es de...** *(ehs deh ...)*

cardboard	**cartón** *(kahr-'tohn)*
cloth	**tela** *('teh-lah)*
modeling clay	**plastilina** *(plah-stee-'lee-nah)*
plastic	**plástico** *('plah-stee-koh)*
wood	**madera** *(mah-'deh-rah)*

MÁS INFORMACIÓN

➤ Most Spanish speakers have learned to use English brand names to specify their favorite plaything:

78

el Nintendo *(ehl neen-'tehn-doh)*
la Barbie *(lah 'bahr-bee)*
los Legos *(lohs 'leh-gohs)*

➤ There are plenty of words that relate to child's play—try these out as part of your instruction:

Do you like...?	**¿Te gustan...?** *(teh 'goo-stahn)*
cartoons	**los dibujos animados** *(lohs dee-'boo-hohs ah-nee-'mah-dohs)*
jokes	**los chistes** *(lohs 'chee-stehs)*
rhymes	**las rimas** *(lahs 'ree-mahs)*
skits	**los dramas cortos** *(lohs 'drah-mahs 'kohr-tohs)*
songs	**las canciones** *(lahs kahn-see-'oh-nehs)*
tricks	**los trucos** *(lohs 'troo-kohs)*

➤ A few games have their own special names in Spanish:

chess	**el ajedrez** *(ehl ah-heh-'drehs)*
checkers	**el juego de damas** *(ehl 'hweh-goh deh 'dah-mahs)*
playing cards	**la baraja de juguete** *(lah bah-'rah-hah deh hoo-'geh-teh)*

THE LESSONS
Las lecciones *(lahs lehk-see-'oh-nehs)*

In addition to playtime, preschool-aged children also need academic instruction. See if you can figure out what to say about these popular classroom items:

toy dishes	**la vajilla de juguete** *(lah vah-'hee-yah deh hoo-'geh-teh)*
small boxes	**las cajas chicas** *(lahs 'kah-hahs 'chee-kahs)*
plastic scissors	**las tijeras de plástico** *(lahs tee-'heh-rahs deh 'plah-stee-koh)*
work tables	**las mesas de trabajo** *(lahs 'meh-sahs deh trah-'bah-hoh)*
large pictures	**los dibujos grandes** *(lohs dee-'boo-hohs 'grahn-dehs)*
music tapes	**los casetes de música** *(lohs kah-'seh-tehs deh 'moo-see-kah)*

And, what about the curriculum? Most schools for the very young teach basic skills in the following areas:

Let's study...	**Vamos a estudiar...** *('vah-mohs ah eh-stoo-dee-'ahr)*
art	**el arte** *(ehl 'ahr-teh)*
language	**el lenguaje** *(ehl lehn-'gwah-heh)*
math	**las matemáticas** *(lahs mah-teh-'mah-tee-kahs)*
music	**la música** *(lah 'moo-see-kah)*
physical education	**la educación física** *(lah eh-doo-kah-see-'ohn 'fee-see-kah)*
science	**la ciencia** *(lah see-'ehn-see·ah)*
social studies	**los estudios sociales** *(lohs eh-'stoo-dee·ohs soh-see-'ah-lehs)*

These topics should be covered, too:

behavior	**el comportamiento** *(ehl kohm-pohr-tah-mee-'ehn-toh)*
health	**la salud** *(lah sah-'lood)*
safety	**la seguridad** *(lah seh-goo-ree-'dahd)*

MÁS INFORMACIÓN

➤ If stuffed animals are being used for either instruction or play, learn the proper names for each one:

elephant	**el elefante** *(ehl eh-leh-'fahn-teh)*
giraffe	**la jirafa** *(lah hee-'rah-fah)*
lion	**el león** *(ehl leh-'ohn)*
monkey	**el mono** *(ehl 'moh-noh)*
tiger	**el tigre** *(ehl 'tee-greh)*

VOCABULARY LIST
Lista de vocabulario *('lee-stah deh voh-kah-boo-'lah-ree·oh)*

Besides grammar and pronunciation practice, preschool teachers teach vocabulary words to enhance language development. Look at this selection.

Let's learn about...	**Aprendamos sobre...** *(ah-prehn-'dah-mohs 'soh-breh...)*
actions	**las acciones** *(lahs ahk-see-'oh-nehs)*
animals	**los animales** *(lohs ah-nee-'mah-lehs)*
body parts	**las partes del cuerpo** *(lahs 'pahr-tehs dehl 'kwehr-poh)*
calendar	**el calendario** *(ehl kah-lehn-'dah-ree·oh)*
city	**la ciudad** *(lah see-oo-'dahd)*
clock	**el reloj** *(ehl reh-'loh)*
clothing	**la ropa** *(lah 'roh-pah)*
colors	**los colores** *(lohs koh-'loh-rehs)*
descriptions	**las descripciones** *(lahs deh-skreep-see-'oh-nehs)*
family	**la familia** *(lah fah-'mee-lee·ah)*
foods	**las comidas** *(lahs koh-'mee-dahs)*
home	**la casa** *(lah 'kah-sah)*
instruments	**los instrumentos musicales** *(lohs een-stroo-'mehn-tohs moo-see-'kah-lehs)*
numbers	**los números** *(lohs 'noo-meh-rohs)*
occupations	**las ocupaciones** *(lahs oh-koo-pah-see-'oh-nehs)*
outdoors	**las afueras** *(lahs ah-'fweh-rahs)*
school	**la escuela** *(lah eh-'skweh-lah)*
sports	**los deportes** *(lohs deh-'pohr-tehs)*
transportation	**el transporte** *(ehl trahns-'pohr-teh)*
weather	**el clima** *(ehl 'klee-mah)*

MÁS INFORMACIÓN

➤ To be more specific, break your word groups into detailed selections. For example, here's what you can share about **la casa** *(lah 'kah-sah)*:

They are...	**Son...** *(sohn...)*
appliances	**los electrodomésticos** *(lohs eh-lehk-troh-doh-'meh-stee-kohs)*
furniture	**los muebles** *(lohs 'mweh-blehs)*
rooms	**los cuartos** *(lohs 'kwahr-tohs)*

➤ Check out these other visual aids:

films	**las películas** *(lahs peh-'lee-koo-lahs)*
paintings	**los cuadros** *(lohs 'kwah-drohs)*
photos	**las fotos** *(lahs 'foh-tohs)*
picture books	**los libros ilustrados** *(lohs 'lee-brohs ee-loo-'strah-dohs)*
portraits	**los retratos** *(lohs reh-'trah-tohs)*

CONFLICTOS CULTURALES

What do you know about children's games from other countries? You may have to ask around for the equivalents to activities such as hopscotch, dodgeball, or tag. Their names generally differ from one country to the next.

LET'S CLEAN UP!
¡Vamos a limpiar! *('vah-mohs ah leem-pee-'ahr)*

When the lesson is over and it's time to clean their mess, many youngsters may not know what they're supposed to do. You can help:

Pick up...	**Recoge...** *(reh-'koh-heh)*
Move... (the)	**Mueve...** *('mweh-veh)*
Take...	**Toma...** *('toh-mah)*
basket	**la canasta** *(lah kah-'nah-stah)*
broom	**la escoba** *(lah eh-'skoh-bah)*
bucket	**el balde** *(ehl 'bahl-deh)*
duster	**el limpiador** *(ehl leem-pee·ah-'dohr)*
dustpan	**el recogedor de basura** *(ehl reh-koh-heh-'dohr deh bah-'soo-rah)*
mop	**el trapeador** *(ehl trah-peh-ah-'dohr)*
sponge	**la esponja** *(lah eh-'spohn-hah)*
towel	**la toalla** *(lah toh-'ah-yah)*

While working alongside little children during cleanup, mention a few of these common action words:

to dust	**sacudir** *(sah-koo-'deer)*	**Estamos sacudiendo el escritorio.** *(eh-'stah-mohs sah-koo-dee-'ehn-doh ehl eh-skree-'toh-ree·oh)*
to mop	**trapear** *(trah-peh-'ahr)*	**Estamos trapeando el baño.** *(eh-'stah-mohs trah-peh-'ahn-doh ehl 'bah-nyoh)*
to sweep	**barrer** *(bah-'rrehr)*	**Estamos barriendo la basura.** *(eh-'stah-mohs bah-rree-'ehn-doh lah bah-'soo-rah)*

¿LISTOS PARA PRACTICAR?

What's going on here? Go ahead and translate these command phrases.

Escribe los números en el pizarrón. *(eh-'skree-beh lohs 'noo-meh-rohs ehn ehl pee-sah-'rrohn)*
Trae las fotos de tu familia. *('trah-eh lahs 'foh-tohs deh too fah-'mee-lee·ah)*
Toma la esponja y mueve el balde. *('toh-mah lah eh-'spohn-hah ee 'mweh-veh ehl 'bahl-deh)*

Can you name three different toys in Spanish?

_____   _____   _____

THE GRADE SCHOOL
La escuela primaria *(lah eh-'skweh-lah pree-'mah-ree·ah)*

Many children don't receive formal instruction until they enter elementary or grammar school. The traditional classroom is full of new terminology for the Spanish speaker, so consider labeling the following items in both languages:

Look at the...	**Mira...** *('mee-rah)*
alarm	**la alarma** *(lah ah-'lahr-mah)*
bell	**la campana** *(lah kahm-'pah-nah)*
bench	**el banco** *(ehl 'bahn-koh)*

bulletin board	**el tablero de anuncios** *(ehl tah-'bleh-roh deh ah-'noon-see·ohs)*
cabinet	**el gabinete** *(ehl gah-bee-'neh-teh)*
chalkboard	**el pizarrón** *(ehl pee-sah-'rrohn)*
clock	**el reloj** *(ehl reh-'loh)*
computer	**la computadora** *(lah kohm-poo-tah-'doh-rah)*
flag	**la bandera** *(lah bahn-'deh-rah)*
loudspeaker	**el altoparlante** *(ehl ahl-toh-pahr-'lahn-teh)*
projector	**el proyector** *(ehl proh-yehk-'tohr)*
pencil sharpener	**el sacapuntas** *(ehl sah-kah-'poon-tahs)*
teacher's desk	**el escritorio del maestro** *(ehl eh-skree-'toh-ree·oh dehl mah-'eh-stroh)*
television	**el televisor** *(ehl teh-leh-vee-'sohr)*
typewriter	**la máquina de escribir** *(lah 'mah-kee-nah deh eh-skree-'beer)*
VCR	**la videocasetera** *(lah vee-deh-oh-kah-seh-'teh-rah)*
wastebasket	**el cesto de basura** *(ehl 'seh-stoh deh bah-'soo-rah)*

As the children move through the grade school level, a variety of classroom materials will be put to use during instruction. To learn these objects quickly, try moving them around. Watch:

Bring...	**Trae...** *('trah-eh)*
Use... (the)	**Usa...** *('oo-sah)*
Pick up...	**Recoge...** *(reh-'koh-heh)*
book	**el libro** *(ehl 'lee-broh)*
brush	**la brocha** *(lah 'broh-chah)*
card	**la tarjeta** *(lah tahr-'heh-tah)*
chalk	**el gis** *(ehl hees)*
envelope	**el sobre** *(ehl 'soh-breh)*
eraser	**el borrador** *(ehl boh-rrah-'dohr)*
folder	**la libreta** *(lah lee-'breh-tah)*
glue	**el pegamento** *(ehl peh-gah-'mehn-toh)*
marker	**el marcador** *(ehl mahr-kah-'dohr)*
notebook	**el cuaderno** *(ehl kwah-'dehr-noh)*
paint	**la pintura** *(lah peen-'too-rah)*
paper	**el papel** *(ehl pah-'pehl)*
paper clip	**el clip** *(ehl kleep)*
pen	**el lapicero** *(ehl lah-pee-'seh-roh)*
pencil	**el lápiz** *(ehl 'lah-pees)*

pin	**el alfiler** *(ehl ahl-fee-'lehr)*
ruler	**la regla** *(lah 'reh-glah)*
stapler	**la engrapadora** *(lah ehn-grah-pah-'doh-rah)*
string	**el hilo** *(ehl 'ee-loh)*
thumbtack	**la tachuela** *(lah tah-choo-'eh-lah)*

Continue to give directions. Most of the time, all that's needed is a one-liner or two:

This way.	**De esta manera.** *(deh 'eh-stah mah-'neh-rah)*
Like this.	**Así.** *(ah-'see)*
Keep going.	**Sigue.** *('see-geh)*

MÁS INFORMACIÓN

➤ Here's more complex vocabulary:

national anthem	**el himno nacional** *(ehl 'eem-noh nah-see·oh-'nahl)*
pledge of allegiance	**la promesa patriótica** *(lah proh-'meh-sah pah-tree-'oh-tee-kah)*
textbook	**el libro de texto** *(ehl 'lee-broh deh 'tehk-stoh)*
sheet of paper	**la hoja de papel** *(lah 'oh-hah deh pah-'pehl)*

➤ Be on the lookout for other Spanish words that refer to the objects mentioned here. Not all Spanish-speaking countries use the same vocabulary!

pen	**la pluma** *(lah 'ploo-mah)* instead of **lapicero** *(lah-pee-'seh-roh)*
notebook	**la carpeta** *(lah kahr-'peh-tah)* instead of **cuaderno** *(kwah-'dehr-noh)*

➤ Spanglish is OK with some trademarks:

el Whiteout®
el Gluestick®
el Post-it®
el Scotch® tape

MORE IMPORTANT WORDS

Más palabras importantes *(mahs pah-'lah-brahs eem-pohr-'tahn-tehs)*

All sorts of valuable phrases will be exchanged at this level, so grab hold of the most popular terms right away. Here's an easy pattern:

What's (the)...?	**¿Cuál es... ?** *(kwahl ehs...?)*
chapter	**el capítulo** *(ehl kah-'pee-too-loh)*
date	**la fecha** *(lah 'feh-chah)*
grade (academic)	**la nota** *(lah 'noh-tah)*
grade (level)	**el grado** *(ehl 'grah-doh)*
letter	**la letra** *(lah 'leh-trah)*
number	**el número** *(ehl 'noo-meh-roh)*
page	**la página** *(lah 'pah-hee-nah)*
story	**el cuento** *(ehl 'kwehn-toh)*
title	**el título** *(ehl 'tee-too-loh)*
word	**la palabra** *(lah pah-'lah-brah)*

Throughout each lesson, feel free to stimulate responses using key Spanish words:

Let's do...	**Vamos a hacer...** *('vah-mohs ah ah-'sehr...)*
activity	**la actividad** *(lah ahk-tee-vee-'dahd)*
assignment	**la tarea** *(lah tah-'reh-ah)*
course	**el curso** *(ehl 'koor-soh)*
exercise	**el ejercicio** *(ehl eh-hehr-'see-see·oh)*

lesson	**la lección** *(lah lehk-see 'ohn)*
program	**el programa** *(ehl proh-'grah-mah)*

Do all of you understand (the)...?	**¿Todos entienden...?** *('toh-dohs ehn-tee-'ehn-dehn...?)*

answer	**la respuesta** *(lah reh-'spweh-stah)*
concept	**el concepto** *(ehl kohn-'sehp-toh)*
idea	**la idea** *(lah ee-'deh-ah)*
principle	**el principio** *(ehl preen-'see-pee·oh)*
problem	**el problema** *(el proh-'bleh-mah)*
question	**la pregunta** *(lah preh-'goon-tah)*
reason	**la razón** *(lah rah-'sohn)*
result	**el resultado** *(ehl reh-sool-'tah-doh)*
secret	**el secreto** *(ehl seh-'kreh-toh)*
solution	**la solución** *(lah soh-loo-see-'ohn)*
theme	**el tema** *(ehl 'teh-mah)*
theory	**la teoría** *(lah teh-oh-'ree-ah)*
topic	**el asunto** *(ehl ah-'soon-toh)*

MÁS INFORMACIÓN

➤ As lessons are being presented, you'll emphasize the importance of learning English. Here are a few beginning skills:

We study (the)...	**Estudiamos...** *(eh-stoo-dee-'ah-mohs)*
alphabet	**el alfabeto** *(ehl ahl-fah-'beh-toh)*
handwriting	**la caligrafía** *(lah kah-lee-grah-'fee-ah)*
printing	**la imprenta** *(lah eem-'prehn-tah)*
pronunciation	**la pronunciación** *(lah proh-noon-see-ah-see-'ohn)*
reading	**la lectura** *(lah lehk-'too-rah)*
spelling	**la ortografía** *(lah ohr-toh-grah-'fee-ah)*

THE PLAYGROUND

El campo de recreo *(ehl 'kahm-poh deh reh-'kreh-oh)*

There's a break between classes, so the kids are dashing outside to play with their friends. Younger students will often talk about these things on the playground:

Let's run to (the)...	**Corramos a...** *(koh-'rrah-mohs ah...)*
bars	**las barras** *(lahs 'bah-rrahs)*
benches	**las bancas** *(lahs 'bahn-kahs)*
jungle gym	**los juegos infantiles** *(lohs 'hweh-gohs een-fahn-'tee-lehs)*
merry-go-round	**los caballitos** *(lohs kah-bah-'yee-tohs)*
poles	**los postes** *(lohs 'poh-stehs)*
rings	**los anillos** *(lohs ah-'nee-yohs)*
rope	**la soga** *(lah 'soh-gah)*
sandbox	**el cajón de arena** *(ehl kah-'hohn deh ah-'reh-nah)*
seesaw	**el subibaja** *(ehl soo-bee-'bah-hah)*
slide	**el tobogán** *(ehl toh-boh-'gahn)*
swing	**el columpio** *(ehl koh-'loom-pee·oh)*
water fountain	**el bebedero** *(ehl beh-beh-'deh-roh)*

Whenever children get together to play, there are disagreements. Practice these verbs by writing full sentences:

to argue	**discutir** *(dee-skoo-'teer)* _____
to beat up	**golpear** *(gohl-peh-'ahr)* _____
to bite	**morder** *(mohr-'dehr)* _____
to bother	**molestar** *(moh-leh-'stahr)* _____
to bounce	**rebotar** *(reh-boh-'tahr)* _____
to break	**romper** *(rohm-'pehr)* _____
to climb	**subir** *(soo-'beer)* _____
to cry	**llorar** *(yoh-'rahr)* _____
to complain	**quejarse** *(keh-'hahr-seh)* _____
to curse	**decir groserías** *(deh-'seer groh-seh-'ree-ahs)* _____
to fall	**caerse** *(kah-'ehr-seh)* _____
to fight	**pelear** *(peh-leh-'ahr)* _____
to grab	**agarrar** *(ah-gah-'rrahr)* _____
to hide	**esconder** *(eh-skohn-'dehr)* _____
to hit	**pegar** *(peh-'gahr)* _____

to jump	**saltar** *(sahl-'tahr)*	_____
to kick	**patear** *(pah-teh-'ahr)*	_____
to lose	**perder** *(pehr-'dehr)*	_____
to pull	**jalar** *(hah-'lahr)*	_____
to push	**empujar** *(ehm-poo-'hahr)*	_____
to roll	**rodar** *(roh-'dahr)*	_____
to shake	**sacudir** *(sah-koo-'deer)*	_____
to skip	**dar brincos** *('dahr 'breen-kohs)*	_____
	¿Quiere dar brincos? *Kee-'eh-reh 'dahr 'breen-kohs)*	_____
to spit	**escupir** *(eh-skoo-'peer)*	_____
to throw	**tirar** *(tee-'rahr)*	_____
to trip	**tropezar** *(troh-peh-'sahr)*	
	Están tropezando. *(eh-'stahn troh-peh-'sahn-doh)* _____	
to win	**ganar** *(gah-'nahr)*	_____
to wrestle	**luchar** *(loo-'chahr)*	_____
to yell	**gritar** *(gree-'tahr)*	_____

 ## MÁS INFORMACIÓN

➤ For a more extensive list of Spanish verbs, check the specialized selection at the end of the book!

➤ Do not forget this shortcut that was presented earlier:

Please don't...	**Favor de no...** *(fah-'vohr deh noh...)*
fight	**pelear** *(peh-leh-'ahr)*
push	**empujar** *(ehm-poo-'hahr)*
yell	**gritar** *(gree-'tahr)*

➤ Become familiar with any Spanish word that relates to playground activity:

You guys need (the)...	**Necesitan...** *(neh-seh-'see-tahn)*
ball	**la pelota** *(peh-'loh-tah)*
basket	**la canasta** *(kah-'nah-stah)*
bat	**el bate** *(ehl 'bah-teh)*
captain	**el capitán** *(ehl kah-pee-'tahn)*
coach	**el entrenador** *(ehl ehn-treh-nah-'dohr)*

equipment	**el equipaje** *(ehl eh-kee-'pah-heh)*
glove	**el guante** *(ehl 'gwahn-teh)*
player	**el jugador** *(ehl hoo-gah-'dohr)*
racket	**la raqueta** *(lah rah-'keh-tah)*
rules	**los reglamentos** *(lohs reh-glah-'mehn-tohs)*
score	**la cuenta** *(lah 'kwehn-tah)*
stick	**el palo** *(ehl 'pah-loh)*
team	**el equipo** *(ehl eh-'kee-poh)*
tournament	**el torneo** *(ehl tohr-'neh-oh)*
uniforms	**los uniformes** *(lohs oo-nee-'fohr-mehs)*

➤ The names for major sports are very similar to English. Can you guess at the meanings of these?

el béisbol *(ehl 'beh·ees-bohl)*
el básquetbol *(ehl 'bah-skeht-bohl)*
el vólibol *(ehl 'voh-lee-bohl)*

➤ The following playtimes may vary depending on where you work:

snack time	**el descanso para comer** *(ehl deh-'skahn-soh 'pah-rah koh-'mehr)*
recess	**el recreo** *(ehl reh-'kreh-oh)*
lunchtime	**la hora de almuerzo** *(lah 'oh-rah dehl ahl-moo-'ehr-soh)*

 ¿LISTOS PARA PRACTICAR?

Connect the terms that belong together:

la alarma *(lah ah-'lahr-mah)*   **la brocha** *(lah 'broh-chah)*
el televisor *(ehl teh-leh-vee-'sohr)*   **el pizarrón** *(ehl pee-sah-'rrohn)*
la pintura *(lah peen-'too-rah)*   **la videocasetera** *(lah vee-deh-oh-kah-seh-'teh-rah)*

el gis *(ehl hees)*   **la campana** *(lah kahm-'pah-nah)*
el cuaderno *(ehl kwah-'dehr-noh)*   **la libreta** *(lah lee-'breh-tah)*

Translate into English:

The question is on page 5. _____

What is the title of the story? _____

The chapter has an important theme. _____

Name three things in Spanish that kids like to play during recess:

_____   _____   _____

Change these actions from one tense to the other. Then, go back and translate. See example:

Pateamos. *(pah-teh-'ah-mohs)*   **Estamos pateando.**
(We kick)   (We're kicking)

Saltamos. *(sahl-'tah-mohs)*   _____

Empujamos. *(ehm-poo-'hah-mohs)*   _____

Gritamos. *(gree-'tah-mohs)*   _____

Jugamos. *(hoo-'gah-mohs)*   _____

HEALTH CARE
El cuidado de la salud *(ehl kwee-'dah-doh deh lah sah-'lood)*

Educators need plenty of energy to keep up with the demands of young children, especially when it comes to emergency health care. At the preschool level, for example, treatment is often part of the daily routine. Look through this first list if you take care of the very little ones:

Do you want (the)...?   **¿Quieres...?** *(kee-'eh-rehs)*

Band Aid®   **la curita** *(lah koo-'ree-tah)*
cotton   **el algodón** *(ehl ahl-goh-'dohn)*
cream   **la crema** *(lah 'kreh-mah)*
diaper   **el pañal** *(ehl pah-'nyahl)*
formula   **la fórmula** *(lah 'fohr-moo-lah)*
lotion   **la loción** *(lah loh-see-'ohn)*

pin	**el alfiler** (ehl ahl-fee-'lehr)
powder	**el talco** (ehl 'tahl-koh)
towelette	**la toallita** (lah toh-ah-'yee-tah)

You have (the)...	**Tienes...** (tee-'eh-nehs)
cold	**resfrío** (rehs-'free-oh)
colic	**cólico** ('koh-lee-koh)
rash	**erupciones** (eh-roop-see-'oh-nehs)

Now help out the students who are a little older. Talk to them in private:

Is/Are there...?	**¿Hay...?** ('ah·ee...)
bleeding	**sangramiento** (sahn-grah-mee-'ehn-toh)
fever	**fiebre** (fee-'eh-breh)
pain	**dolor** (doh-'lohr)

It's a...	**Es un/una...** (ehs 'oon / 'oo-nah...)
blister	**ampolla** (ahm-'poh-yah)
break	**quebradura** (keh-'brah-dah)
bruise	**contusión** (kohn-too-see-'ohn)
burn	**quemadura** (keh-mah-'doo-rah)
cut	**cortadura** (kohr-tah-'doo-rah)
scrape	**rasguño** (rahs-'goo-nyoh)
sprain	**torcedura** (tohr-seh-'doo-rah)

Here's (the)...	**Aquí tienes...** (ah-'kee tee-'eh-nehs...)
bandage	**el vendaje** (ehl vehn-'dah-heh)
blanket	**la cobija** (lah koh-'bee-hah)
ice	**el hielo** (ehl 'yeh-loh)
medicine	**la medicina** (lah meh-dee-'see-nah)
water	**el agua** (ehl 'ah-gwah)

MÁS INFORMACIÓN

➤ Don't fret if you didn't find what you're looking for. We'll talk more about health care in Chapter Eight when we discuss the school nurse.

➤ By the way, these terms are always good to know:

blind	**ciego** *(see-'eh-goh)*
deaf	**sordo** *('sohr-doh)*
handicapped	**incapacitado** *(een-kah-pah-see-'tah-doh)*

➤ Bodily functions have names in Spanish, also. Read on:

burp	**el eructo** *(ehl eh-'rook-toh)*
cough	**la tos** *(lah tohs)*
hiccup	**el hipo** *(ehl 'ee-poh)*
sneeze	**el estornudo** *(ehl eh-stohr-'noo-doh)*

CONFLICTOS CULTURALES

Throughout history, we have discovered that certain herbs and spices work wonders on common ailments. In Latin America, the practice of home remedies—**los remedios caseros** *(lohs reh-'meh-dee-ohs kah-'seh-rohs)*—is quite popular, so don't be surprised if your Hispanic students offer to prepare something when a fellow pupil gets sick or injured.

WHERE DOES IT HURT?
¿Dónde te duele? *('dohn-deh teh 'dweh-leh)*

Assisting Spanish-speaking kids is a breeze once you determine what's troubling them. The fastest way is to use "yes-no" questions. Ask them to point as you move through the list below:

Does (the) _____ hurt?　　**¿Te duele _____ ?** *(teh 'dweh-leh)*

ankle	**el tobillo** *(ehl toh-'bee-yoh)*
arm	**el brazo** *(ehl 'brah-soh)*
back	**la espalda** *(lah eh-'spahl-dah)*
body	**el cuerpo** *(ehl 'kwehr-poh)*
cheek	**la mejilla** *(lah meh-'hee-yah)*
chest	**el pecho** *(ehl 'peh-choh)*
chin	**la barbilla** *(lah bahr-'bee-yah)*
ear	**la oreja** *(lah oh-'reh-hah)*
elbow	**el codo** *(ehl 'koh-doh)*
eye	**el ojo** *(ehl 'oh-hoh)*
face	**la cara** *(lah 'kah-rah)*
finger	**el dedo** *(ehl 'deh-doh)*
foot	**el pie** *(ehl 'pee-eh)*
hand	**la mano** *(lah 'mah-noh)*
head	**la cabeza** *(lah kah-'beh-sah)*
hip	**la cadera** *(lah kah-'deh-rah)*
knee	**la rodilla** *(lah roh-'dee-yah)*
leg	**la pierna** *(lah pee-'ehr-nah)*
lip	**el labio** *(ehl 'lah-bee·oh)*
mouth	**la boca** *(lah 'boh-kah)*
neck	**el cuello** *(ehl 'kweh-yoh)*
nose	**la nariz** *(lah nah-'rees)*
shoulder	**el hombro** *(ehl 'ohm-broh)*
stomach	**el estómago** *(ehl eh-'stoh-mah-goh)*
throat	**la garganta** *(lah gahr-'gahn-tah)*
toe	**el dedo del pie** *(ehl 'deh-doh dehl pee-'eh)*
tongue	**la lengua** *(lah 'lehn-gwah)*
wrist	**la muñeca** *(lah moo-'nyeh-kah)*

➤ Add these one-liners to your collection:

Be careful!	**¡Ten cuidado!** *(tehn kwee-'dah-doh)*
Call your mother!	**¡Llama a tu mamá!** *('yah-mah ah too mah-'mah)*
Danger!	**¡Peligro!** *(peh-'lee-groh)*
It's an emergency!	**¡Es una emergencia!** *(ehs 'oo-nah eh-mehr-'hehn-see·ah)*
Go to the nurse!	**¡Ve a la enfermera!** *(veh ah lah ehn-fehr-'meh-rah)*

➤ You'll probably hear these terms mentioned, too:

brain	**el cerebro** *(ehl seh-'reh-broh)*
hair	**el pelo** *(ehl 'peh-loh)*
heart	**el corazón** *(ehl koh-rah-'sohn)*
lungs	**los pulmones** *(lohs pool-'moh-nehs)*
skin	**la piel** *(lah pee-'ehl)*
teeth	**los dientes** *(lohs dee-'ehn-tehs)*

HOW'S THE WEATHER?

¿Cómo está el tiempo? *('koh-moh eh-'stah ehl tee-'ehm-poh)*

Some things in life we can't control. They often are the cause of our physical problems. Here's how we comment on the current weather conditions:

It's...	**Hace...** *('ah-seh...)*
cold	**frío** *('free-oh)*
hot	**calor** *(kah-'lohr)*
nice weather	**buen tiempo** *('bwehn tee-'ehm-poh)*
sunny	**sol** *(sohl)*
windy	**viento** *(vee-'ehn-toh)*
It's...	**Está...** *(eh-'stah...)*
clear	**despejado** *(dehs-'peh-'hah-doh)*
cloudy	**nublado** *(noo-'blah-doh)*

drizzling	**lloviznando** *(yoh-vees-'nahn-doh)*
raining	**lloviendo** *(yoh-vee-'ehn-doh)*
snowing	**nevando** *(neh-'vahn-doh)*

Throughout the year, spend time with your students discussing health and safety concerns related to changes in the weather. If you like, consider teaching units based on the four seasons or **estaciones** *(eh-stah-see-'oh-nehs)*:

It's...	**Es...** *(ehs...)*
winter	**el invierno** *(ehl een-vee-'ehr-noh)*
spring	**la primavera** *(lah pree-mah-'veh-rah)*
summer	**el verano** *(ehl veh-'rah-noh)*
fall	**el otoño** *(ehl oh-'toh-nyoh)*

SAFETY FIRST!
¡Primero, la seguridad! *(pree-'meh-roh, lah seh-goo-ree-'dahd)*

The safety of all children is of tremendous importance, so continue to acquire all the Spanish words and phrases that you can.

You shouldn't...	**No debes...** *(noh 'deh-behs...)*
use drugs	**usar drogas** *(oo-'sahr 'droh-gahs)*
talk to strangers	**hablar con extraños** *(ah-'blahr kohn eh-'strah-nyohs)*
smoke cigarettes	**fumar cigarillos** *(foo-'mahr see-gah-'ree-yohs)*
Let's talk about...	**Hablemos de...** *(ah-'bleh-mohs deh...)*
abandoned buildings	**los edificios abandonados** *(lohs eh-dee-'fee-see·ohs ah-bahn-doh-'nah-dohs)*
natural disasters	**los desastres naturales** *(lohs deh-'sah-strehs nah-too-'rah-lehs)*
good health	**la buena salud** *(lah 'bweh-nah sah-'lood)*

96

➤ Outline these important topics and present them in full detail:

attendance procedures **los procedimientos de asistencia** *(lohs proh-seh-dee-mee-'ehn-tohs deh ah-see-'stehn-see·ah)*

fire drill **el simulacro de incendio** *(ehl see-moo-'lah-kroh deh een-'sehn-dee·oh)*

safety rules **las reglas de seguridad** *(lahs 'reh-glahs deh seh-goo-ree-'dahd)*

telephone use **el uso del teléfono** *(ehl 'oo-soh dehl teh-'leh-foh-noh)*

➤ In an emergency, you might have to use several actions at once:

to breathe **respirar** *(reh-spee-'rahr)*
to chew **masticar** *(mah-stee-'kahr)*
to swallow **tragar** *(trah-'gahr)*

➤ In order to disseminate information, most schools issue the following items:

Take (the)... **Toma...** *('toh-mah)*

brochure **el folleto** *(ehl foh-'yeh-toh)*

coupon **el cupón** *(ehl koo-'pohn)*
envelope **el sobre** *(ehl 'soh-breh)*
flyer **la hoja** *(lah 'oh-hah)*
notice **el anuncio** *(ehl ah-'noon-see·oh)*
ticket **el boleto** *(ehl boh-'leh-toh)*

➤ A variety of school events cannot be translated easily, so you may want to announce them in English only:

Back-to-School Night
Open House
Parent Conference Day

MORE VERBS FOR TEACHERS
Más verbos para los maestros *(mahs 'vehr-bohs 'pah-rah lohs mah-'eh-strohs)*

If you're involved in elementary education, you're going to need a lot more action words in Spanish. Say each word as you practice the present tense:

to arrange **arreglar** *(ah-rreh-'glahr)* **Arreglamos las sillas.** *(ah-rreh-'glah-mohs lahs 'see-yahs)*

to ask for	**pedir** *(peh-'deer)*	**Pedimos la engrapadora.** *(peh-'dee-mohs lah ehn-grah-pah-'doh-rah)*
to check	**revisar** *(reh-vee-'sahr)*	**Revisamos los problemas.** *(reh-vee-'sah-mohs lohs proh-'bleh-mahs)*
to choose	**escoger** *(eh-skoh-'hehr)*	**Escogemos las pinturas.** *(eh-skoh-'heh-mohs lahs peen-'too-rahs)*
to correct	**corregir** *(koh-rreh-'heer)*	**Corregimos los papeles.** *(koh-rreh-'hee-mohs lohs pah-'peh-lehs)*
to erase	**borrar** *(boh-'rrahr)*	**Borramos el pizarrón.** *(boh-'rrah-mohs ehl pee-sah-'rrohn)*
to fill out	**llenar** *(yeh-'nahr)*	**Llenamos la página.** *(yeh-'nah-mohs lah 'pah-hee-nah)*
to pass out	**repartir** *(reh-pahr-'teer)*	**Repartimos los libros.** *(reh-pahr-'tee-mohs lohs 'lee-brohs)*
to pronounce	**pronunciar** *(proh-noon-see-'ahr)*	**Pronunciamos las letras.** *(proh-noon-see-'ah-mohs lahs 'leh-trahs)*
to remember	**recordar** *(reh-kohr-'dahr)*	**Recordamos el número.** *(reh-kohr-'dah-mohs ehl 'noo-meh-roh)*
to repeat	**repetir** *(reh-peh-'teer)*	**Repetimos las palabras.** *(reh-peh-'tee-mohs lahs pah-'lah-brahs)*
to ride	**montar** *(mohn-'tahr)*	**Montamos las bicicletas.** *(mohn-'tah-mohs lahs bee-see-'kleh-tahs)*
to see	**ver** *(vehr)*	**Vemos los dibujos.** *('veh-mohs lohs dee-'boo-hohs)*
to spell	**deletrear** *(deh-leh-treh-'ahr)*	**Deletreamos los nombres.** *(deh-leh-treh-'ah-mohs lohs 'nohm-brehs)*
to stack	**amontonar** *(ah-mohn-toh-'nahr)*	**Amontonamos los cuadernos.** *(ah-mohn-toh-'nah-mohs lohs kwah-'dehr-nohs)*
to teach	**enseñar** *(ehn-seh-'nyahr)*	**Enseñamos a los amigos.** *(ehn-seh-'nyah-mohs ah lohs ah-'mee-gohs)*

You still need more action words. Fill in the blanks by following the pattern shown.

to give	**dar** *(dahr)*	**<u>Damos el papel a los niños.</u>** *('dah-mohs ehl pah-'pehl ah lohs 'nee-nyohs)*
to help	**ayudar** *(ah-yoo-'dahr)*	**<u>Ayudamos a los estudiantes.</u>** *(ah-yoo-'dah-mohs ah lohs eh-stoo-dee-'ahn-tehs)*
to use	**usar** *(oo-'sahr)*	**<u>Usamos los libros rojos.</u>** *(oo-'sah-mohs lohs 'lee-brohs 'roh-hohs)*
to carry	**llevar** *(yeh-'vahr)*	_____.
to clean	**limpiar** *(leem-pee-'ahr)*	_____.
to count	**contar** *(kohn-'tahr)*	_____.
to cut	**cortar** *(kohr-'tahr)*	_____.
to draw	**dibujar** *(dee-boo-'hahr)*	_____.
to fold	**doblar** *(doh-'blahr)*	_____.
to paint	**pintar** *(peen-'tahr)*	_____.
to point	**señalar** *(seh-nyah-'lahr)*	_____.
to put	**poner** *(poh-'nehr)*	_____.
to put in	**meter** *(meh-'tehr)*	_____.
to show	**mostrar** *(moh-'strahr)*	_____.
to sing	**cantar** *(kahn-'tahr)*	_____.
to take out	**sacar** *(sah-'kahr)*	_____.
to tie	**amarrar** *(ah-mah-'rrahr)*	_____.
to touch	**tocar** *(toh-'kahr)*	_____.

➤ Teachers ought to remember a few verbs with **se** as well:

to bathe	**bañarse** *(bah-'nyahr-seh)*
to behave	**portarse** *(pohr-'tahr-seh)*
to comb one's hair	**peinarse** *(peh·ee-'nahr-seh)*
to complain	**quejarse** *(keh-'hahr-seh)*
to fall	**caerse** *(kah-'ehr-seh)*
to get dressed	**vestirse** *(veh-'steer-seh)*
to get lost	**perderse** *(pehr-'dehr-seh)*
to turn around	**darse vuelta** *('dahr-seh 'vwehl-tah)*
to wash	**lavarse** *(lah-'vahr-seh)*

➤ Here's a common way to recognize opposites in Spanish. Notice the prefix **des-** in these examples:

to dress	**vestirse** *(veh-'steer-seh)*
to undress	**desvestirse** *(dehs-veh-'steer-seh)*
to tie	**amarrar** *(ah-mah-'rrahr)*
to untie	**desamarrar** *(dehs-ah-mah-'rrahr)*
to fold	**doblar** *(doh-'blahr)*
to unfold	**desdoblar** *(dehs-doh-'blahr)*

Bear in mind that all action words can be altered to communicate time-referenced messages. For example, you know that the -**ndo** ending indicates that actions are taking place right now:

to drive	**manejar** *(mah-neh-'hahr)*
I am driving	**Estoy manejando** *(eh-'stoh-ee mah-neh-'han-doh)*

And you know that there are at least four consistent changes that occur when action words refer to everyday activities:

I drive	**Manejo** (mah-'neh-hoh)
You (informal) drive	**Manejas** (mah-'neh-hahs)
You (formal) drive; He, She drives	**Maneja** (mah-'neh-hah)
You (pl.), They drive	**Manejan** (mah-'neh-hahn)
We drive	**Manejamos** (mah-neh-'hah-mohs)

You've also probably realized that not all action words like to follow the rules. Look at these three familiar irregular verbs. Can you tell which person these forms are referring to?

Ir (to go)	**Tener (to have)**	**Ser (to be)**
(eer)	(teh-'nehr)	('sehr)
voy ('voh-ee)	**tengo** ('tehn-goh)	**soy** ('soh-ee)
vas (informal) (vahs)	**tienes** (informal)(tee-'eh-nehs)	**eres** (informal) ('eh-rehs)
va (vah)	**tiene** (tee-'eh-neh)	**es** (ehs)
van (vahn)	**tienen** (tee-'eh-nehn)	**son** (sohn)
vamos	**tenemos**	**somos**
('vah-mohs)	(teh-'neh-mohs)	('soh-mohs)

See how they don't follow the regular-verb patterns? Notice the other unusual patterns below. These two verbs are used daily by teachers everywhere, so spend as much time as you need to review:

Poder (to be able) (poh-'dehr)

puedo ('pweh-doh)	I can read.	**Puedo leer.** ('pweh-doh leh-'ehr)
puedes (informal) (pweh-dehs)	You can ski.	**Puedes esquiar.** ('pweh-dehs eh-skee-'ahr)

puede *('pweh-deh)*	He can go.	**Puede ir.** *('pweh-deh eer)*
pueden *('pweh-dehn)*	They can play.	**Pueden jugar.** *('pweh-dehn hoo-'gahr)*
podemos *(poh-'deh-mohs)*	We can study.	**Podemos estudiar.** *(poh-'deh-mohs eh-stoo-dee-'ahr)*

Querer (to want) *(keh-'rehr)*

quiero *(kee-'eh-roh)*	I want to leave.	**Quiero salir.** *(kee-'eh-roh sah-'leer)*
quieres (informal) *(kee-'eh-rehs)*	You want to drive.	**Quieres manejar.** *(kee-'eh-rehs mah-neh-'hahr)*
quiere *(kee-'eh-reh)*	She wants to walk.	**Quiere caminar.** *(kee-'eh-reh kah-mee-'nahr)*
quieren *(kee-'eh-rehn)*	They want to eat.	**Quieren comer.** *(kee-'eh-rehn koh-'mehr)*
queremos *(keh-'reh-mohs)*	We want to see.	**Queremos ver.** *(keh-'reh-mohs vehr)*

Many irregular verbs follow a **-ue** or **-ie** pattern that becomes familiar with practice:

Dormir (to sleep) *(dohr-'meer)*	**Entender (to understand)** *(ehn-tehn-'dehr)*
duermo *('dwehr-moh)*	**entiendo** *(ehn-tee-'ehn-doh)*
duermes (informal) *('dwehr-mehs)*	**entiendes** (informal) *(ehn-tee-'ehn-dehs)*
duerme *('dwehr-meh)*	**entiende** *(ehn-tee-'ehn-deh)*
duermen *('dwehr-mehn)*	**entienden** *(ehn-tee-'ehn-dehn)*
dormimos *(dohr-'mee-mohs)*	**entendemos** *(ehn-tehn-'deh-mohs)*

MÁS INFORMACIÓN

➤ Here are three other ways to discuss one's likes and dislikes. Note how unique each form is:

Do you like...?	**¿Te gusta...?** *(teh 'goo-stah...)*
Yes, I like...	**Sí, me gusta...** *(see, meh-'goo-stah...)*

Would you like...?	**¿Quisieras...?** *(kee-see-'eh-rahs...)*
Yes, I'd like...	**Sí, quisiera...** *(see, kee-see-'eh-rah...)*

| Do you wish...? | **¿Deseas...?** *(deh-'seh-ahs...)* |
| Yes, I wish... | **Sí, deseo...** *(see, deh-'seh-oh...)* |

➤ In Spanish, there are two primary ways to say "to know".

<u>To know something</u> requires the verb **saber** *(sah-'behr),* while <u>to know someone</u> requires the verb **conocer** *(koh-noh-'sehr).* Instead of working on all the conjugated forms of these new verbs, why not put them to practical use. Next time you need to know, pull a line from the sentences below:

I don't know.	**No sé.**
	(noh seh)
I don't know him.	**No le conozco.**
	(noh leh koh-'noh-skoh)
Do you know English?	**¿Sabes inglés?**
	('sah-behs een-'glehs)
Do they know her?	**¿La conocen a ella?**
	(lah koh-'noh-sehn ah 'eh-yah)

Obviously, **saber** *(sah-'behr)* works wonders in the classroom. Ask your students about anything:

Do you know how to speak English?
¿Sabe hablar inglés? *('sah-beh ah-'blahr een-'glehs)*

Do you know how to read and write?
¿Sabe leer y escribir? *('sah-beh leh-'ehr ee eh-skree-'beer)*

Do you know how to do it?
¿Sabe hacerlo? *('sah-beh ah-'sehr-loh)*

 ¡ÓRDENES!

A good part of teaching involves giving commands, so don't hold back as you direct these verb forms at your students. See how the forms are informal, which means they are addressed to children, family, or friends. The form is the same as the third person singular in the present tense. Can you translate?

Arrange	**Arregla** las sillas. *(ah-'rreh-glah lahs 'see-yahs)*
Ask for	**Pide** mi ayuda. *('pee-deh mee ah-'yoo-dah)*
Check	**Revisa** los problemas. *(reh-'vee-sah lohs proh-'bleh-mahs)*
Choose	**Escoge** el color. *(eh-'skoh-heh ehl koh-'lohr)*
Erase	**Borra** el pizarrón. *('boh-rrah ehl pee-sah-'rrohn)*
Fill out	**Llena** los papeles. *('yeh-nah lohs pah-'peh-lehs)*
Pass out	**Reparte** los lápices. *(reh-'pahr-teh lohs 'lah-pee-sehs)*
Remember	**Recuerda** el número. *(reh-'kwehr-dah ehl 'noo-meh-roh)*
Repeat	**Repite** la palabra. *(reh-'pee-teh lah pah-'lah-brah)*
Spell	**Deletrea** tu nombre. *(deh-leh-'treh-ah too 'nohm-breh)*
Stack	**Amontona** los libros. *(ah-mohn-'toh-nah lohs 'lee-brohs)*

Now, utilize these commands on the playground:

Catch!	**¡Agarra!** *(ah-'gah-rrah)*
Climb!	**¡Sube!** *('soo-beh)*
Hit!	**¡Pega!** *('peh-gah)*
Jump!	**¡Salta!** *('sahl-tah)*
Throw!	**¡Tira!** *('tee-rah)*
Win!	**¡Gana!** *('gah-nah)*

Note the changes below in the personal **tú** form for both the singular and plural. You'll have to do your own translating. Be careful—a few of them are irregular!

Singular	**Plural**	
ayuda	**ayuden**	*(ah-'yoo-dah, ah-'yoo-dehn)*
canta	**canten**	*('kahn-tah, 'kahn-tehn)*
corta	**corten**	*('kohr-tah, 'kohr-tehn)*
cuenta	**cuenten**	*('kwehn-tah, 'kwehn-tehn)*
da	**den**	*(dah, dehn)*
dibuja	**dibujen**	*(dee-'boo-hah, dee-'boo-hehn)*
empuja	**empujen**	*(ehm-'poo-hah, ehm-'poo-hehn)*
limpia	**limpien**	*('leem-pee·ah, 'leem-pee·ehn)*
lleva	**lleven**	*('yeh-vah, 'yeh-vehn)*
muestra	**muestren**	*('mweh-strah, 'mweh-strehn)*

pinta	pinten	*('peen-tah, 'peen-tehn)*
señala	señalen	*(seh-'nyah-lah, seh-'nyah-lehn)*
toca	toquen	*('toh-kah, 'toh-kehn)*
usa	usen	*('oo-sah, 'oo-sehn)*

¡Antonio, empuja la puerta! *(ahn-'toh-nee·oh, ehm-'poo-hah lah 'pwehr-tah)*

¡Marcos y Antonio, empujen la puerta! *('mahr-kohs ee ahn-'toh-nee·oh, ehm-'poo-hehn lah 'pwehr-tah)*

 ## MÁS INFORMACIÓN

➤ A handful of informal commands are irregular and may have to be memorized:

Leave!	**¡Sal!** *(sahl)*	
Put!	**¡Pon!** *(pohn)*	
Do!	**¡Haz!** *(ahs)*	

➤ Also remember that some verbs have more than one meaning in Spanish. Look at these examples:

tocar *(toh-'kahr)*	to touch or to play a musical instrument
contar *(kohn-'tahr)*	to count or to tell a story
hacer *(ah-'sehr)*	to do or to make
tomar *(toh-'mahr)*	to take or to drink
esperar *(eh-speh-'rahr)*	to wait or to hope for
llevar *(yeh-'vahr)*	to carry or to wear

➤ Sometimes action words are actually more like phrases or expressions. Try out these one-liners today!

Behave!	**¡Pórtate bien!** *('pohr-tah-teh 'bee·ehn)*
Pay attention!	**¡Presta atención!** *('preh-stah ah-tehn-see-'ohn)*
Line up!	**¡Pónganse en fila!** *('pohn-gahn-seh ehn 'fee-lah)*
Turn around!	**¡Date vuelta!** *('dah-teh 'vwehl-tah)*
Be quiet!	**¡Silencio!** *(see-'lehn-see·oh)*
Ask permission!	**¡Pidan permiso!** *('pee-dahn pehr-'mee-soh)*

➤ When the class gets noisy, utilize key phrases to keep things in order:

Only one person speaks at a time. **Solo una persona hable a la vez.** *('soh-loh 'oo-nah pehr-'soh-nah 'ah-bleh ah lah vehs)*

Please raise your hand.	**Levanta la mano, por favor.** *(leh-'vahn-tah lah 'mah-noh, pohr fah-'vohr)*
You have to wait your turn.	**Tienes que esperar tu turno.** *(tee-'eh-nehs keh eh-speh-'rahr too 'toor-noh)*

 ¿LISTOS PARA PRACTICAR?

Name five body parts in Spanish:

_____ _____ _____ _____ _____

Look outside and answer these questions:

¿En qué estación estás ahora? *(ehn keh eh-stah-see-'ohn eh-'stahs ah-'oh-rah)*
¿Cómo está el tiempo? *('koh-moh eh-'stah ehl tee-'ehm-poh)*
¿Hace frío hoy? *('ah-seh 'free-oh 'oh·ee)*

Which words best relate to each other?

cortadura *(kohr-tah-'doo-rah)*	**el hielo** *(ehl 'yeh-loh)*
torcedura *(tohr-seh-'doo-rah)*	**la aspirina** *(lah ah-spee-'ree-nah)*
fiebre *(fee-'eh-breh)*	**la curita** *(lah koo-'ree-tah)*

Study the examples, and then make the changes:

ir (yo) *(eer, yoh)*   <u>**voy**</u> *('voh·ee)*

tener (nosotros) *(teh-'nehr, noh-'soh-trohs)* _____

tenemos *(teh-'neh-mohs)* _____

ser (ellos) *(sehr, 'eh-yohs)* _____

poder (él) *(poh-'dehr, ehl)* _____

querer (usted) *(keh-'rehr, oo-'stehd)* _____

entender (ella) *(ehn-tehn-'dehr, 'eh-yah)* _____

Alter these formal commands slightly to create informal ones:

cante *('kahn-teh)*   <u>**canta**</u> *('kahn-tah)*

ayude *(ah-'yoo-deh)*   _____

empuje *(ehm-'poo-heh)*   _____

limpie *('leem-pee·eh)*   _____

use *('oo-seh)*   _____

 CONFLICTOS CULTURALES

Notice how in some cultures, male and female roles are extremely different. From childhood, many Hispanic students are raised to perform some tasks, while leaving others to the opposite sex. Over time children will learn to make their own choices, so try not to force boys and girls to participate in some events when they adamantly refuse.

CHAPTER FOUR
Capítulo Cuatro
(kah-'pee-too-loh 'kwah-troh)

THE OLDER STUDENTS

Los estudiantes mayores
(lohs eh-stoo-dee-'ahn-tehs mah-'yoh-rehs)

COURSE OF STUDY

El plan de estudios *(ehl plahn deh eh-'stoo-dee·ohs)*

At middle schools and high schools across the country, young people move quickly from classroom to classroom, taking courses in a variety of subjects. Many of their class titles are listed below. Can you identify them in Spanish?

It's a course in...	**Es un curso de...** *(ehs oon 'koor-soh deh...)*
algebra	**el álgebra** *(ehl 'ahl-heh-brah)*
art	**el arte** *(ehl 'ahr-teh)*
astronomy	**la astronomía** *(lah ah-stroh-noh-'mee-ah)*
biology	**la biología** *(lah bee·oh-loh-'hee-ah)*
calculus	**el cálculo** *(ehl 'kahl-koo-loh)*
chemistry	**la química** *(lah 'kee-mee-kah)*
civics	**el civismo** *(ehl see-'vees-moh)*
competitive athletics	**los deportes competitivos** *(lohs deh-'pohr-tehs kohm-peh-tee-'tee-vohs)*
computers	**las computadoras** *(lahs kohm-poo-tah-'doh-rahs)*
drama	**el drama** *(ehl 'drah-mah)*
driver's education	**la enseñanza de conducir** *(lah ehn-seh-'nyahn-sah deh kohn-doo-'seer)*
earth science	**la ciencia del mundo** *(lah see-'ehn-see·ah dehl 'moon-doh)*
economics	**la economía** *(lah eh-koh-noh-'mee-ah)*
English as a second language	**el inglés como segundo idioma** *(ehl een-'glehs 'koh-moh seh-'goon-doh ee-dee-'oh-mah)*
English literature	**la literatura inglesa** *(lah lee-teh-rah-'too-rah een-'gleh-sah)*
European history	**la historia de Europa** *(lah ee-'stoh-ree·ah deh eh-oo-'roh-pah)*
foreign language	**los idiomas extranjeros** *(lohs ee-dee-'oh-mahs eks-trahn-'heh-rohs)*
geography	**la geografía** *(lah heh-oh-grah-'fee-ah)*
geometry	**la geometría** *(lah heh-oh-meh-'tree-ah)*
health	**la salud** *(lah sah-'lood)*
industrial arts	**las artes industriales** *(lahs 'ahr-tehs een-doo-stree-'ah-lehs)*
journalism	**el periodismo** *(ehl peh-ree·oh-'dees-moh)*

language arts	**el lenguaje** *(ehl lehn-'gwah-heh)*
Latin	**el latín** *(ehl lah-'teen)*
mathematics	**las matemáticas** *(lahs mah-teh-'mah-tee-kahs)*
music	**la música** *(lah 'moo-see-kah)*
philosophy	**la filosofía** *(lah fee-loh-soh-'fee-ah)*
physical education	**la educación física** *(lah eh-doo-kah-see-'ohn 'fee-see-kah)*
physics	**la física** *(lah 'fee-see-kah)*
psychology	**la psicología** *(lah see-koh-loh-'hee-ah)*
reading	**la lectura** *(lah lehk-'too-rah)*
social studies	**los estudios sociales** *(lohs eh-'stoo-dee·ohs soh-see-'ah-lehs)*
special education	**la educación especial** *(lah eh-doo-kah-see-'ohn eh-speh-see-'ahl)*
speech	**el discurso** *(ehl dee-'skoor-soh)*
trigonometry	**la trigonometría** *(lah tree-goh-noh-meh-'tree-ah)*
typing	**la escritura a máquina** *(lah eh-skree-'too-rah ah 'mah-kee-nah)*
U.S. history	**la historia de los Estados Unidos** *(lah ee-'stoh-ree·ah deh lohs eh-'stah-dohs oo-'nee-dohs)*
Western civilization	**la civilización del Occidente** *(lah see-vee-lee-sah-see·'ohn dehl ohk-see-'dehn-teh)*
world history	**la historia mundial** *(lah ee-'stoh-ree·ah moon-dee-'ahl)*
writing	**la escritura** *(lah eh-skree-'too-rah)*

Using what we've already learned in Spanish, let's create a few practical sentences that can help us communicate better with our Spanish-speaking students. Think of situations where these comments would be considered appropriate:

You need to take a <u>math</u> class.
Necesitas tomar una clase de matemáticas. *(neh-seh-'see-tahs toh-'mahr 'oo-nah 'klah-seh deh mah-teh-'mah-tee-kahs)*

There is no <u>P.E.</u> today.
No hay clase de educación física hoy. *(noh 'ah·ee 'klah-seh deh eh-doo-kah-see-'ohn 'fee-see-kah 'oh·ee)*

Does your <u>English </u>class have a lot of students?
¿Hay muchos estudiantes en tu clase de inglés? *('ah·ee 'moo-chohs eh-stoo-dee-'ahn-tehs ehn too 'klah-se deh een-'glehs)*

You have to read your <u>history</u> book.
Tienes que leer tu libro de historia. *(tee-'eh-nehs keh leh-'ehr too 'lee-broh deh ee-'stoh-ree·ah)*

Are you studying <u>geography</u>?
¿Estás estudiando geografía? *(eh-'stahs eh-stoo-dee-'ahn-doh heh-oh-grah-'fee-ah)*

Now, go back and substitute the underlined word with a different class title. Continue to read aloud in Spanish.

MORE THINGS IN THE CLASSROOM
Más cosas en la clase *(mahs 'koh-sahs ehn lah 'klah-seh)*

You already know the names in Spanish for several objects in the classroom. Those words were introduced earlier when we learned about the elementary school. However, at the middle and high school levels, a number of other items need to be identified. Again, use bilingual labels whenever possible:

We have (the)...

Tenemos...*(teh-'neh-mohs)*

atlas	**el atlas** *(ehl 'aht-lahs)*
binder	**el encuadernador** *(ehl ehn-kwah-dehr-nah-'dohr)*
calculator	**la calculadora** *(lah kahl-koo-lah-'doh-rah)*
cassette player	**el tocador de casetes** *(ehl toh-kah-'dohr deh kah-'seh-tehs)*
chalk tray	**la bandeja del gis** *(lah bahn-'deh-hah dehl hees)*
chart	**el diagrama** *(ehl dee-ah-'grah-mah)*
dictionary	**el diccionario** *(ehl deek-see-oh-'nah-ree·oh)*
easel	**el caballete** *(ehl kah-bah-'yeh-teh)*
encyclopedia	**la enciclopedia** *(lah ehn-see-kloh-'peh-dee·ah)*
globe	**el mundo** *(ehl 'moon-doh)*
graph	**el gráfico** *(ehl 'grah-fee-koh)*
headphones	**los audífonos** *(lohs ow-'dee-foh-nohs)*
intercom	**el interfono** *(ehl een-tehr-'foh-noh)*
labels	**las etiquetas** *(lahs eh-tee-'keh-tahs)*

laminations	**las hojas laminadas** *(lahs 'oh-hahs lah-mee-'nah-dahs)*
map	**el mapa** *(ehl 'mah-pah)*
model	**el modelo** *(ehl moh-'deh-loh)*
screen	**la pantalla** *(lah pahn-'tah-yah)*
stationery	**los objetos de escritorio** *(lohs ohb-'heh-tohs dehl eh-skree-'toh-ree·oh)*
stool	**el banquillo** *(ehl bahn-'kee-yoh)*
transparency	**la hoja transparente** *(lah 'oh-hah trahns-'pah-'rehn-teh)*

Outside the classroom, children should be informed about school activities, policy changes, and upcoming events. Tell the Spanish speakers where they can find the information they need:

Everyone look at (the)...	**Todos miren...** *('toh-dohs 'mee-rehn)*
announcement	**el anuncio** *(ehl ah-'noon-see·oh)*
bulletin	**el boletín** *(ehl boh-leh-'teen)*
bulletin board	**el tablón de anuncios** *(ehl tah-'blohn deh ah-'noon-see·ohs)*
calendar	**el calendario** *(ehl kah-lehn-'dah-ree·oh)*
film	**la película** *(lah peh-'lee-koo-lah)*
flyer	**el papel** *(ehl pah-'pehl)*
letter	**la carta** *(lah 'kahr-tah)*
memo	**el memorándum** *(ehl meh-moh-'rahn-doom)*
note	**la nota** *(lah 'noh-tah)*
notice	**el anuncio** *(ehl ah-'noon-see·oh)*
page	**la página** *(lah 'pah-hee-nah)*
poster	**el cartel** *(ehl kahr-'tehl)*
report	**el reporte** *(ehl reh-'pohr-teh)*
schedule	**el horario** *(ehl oh-'rah-ree·oh)*
sheet	**la hoja** *(lah 'oh-hah)*
sign	**el letrero** *(ehl leh-'treh-roh)*
video	**el vídeo** *(ehl 'vee-deh-oh)*

If things are filed away, make sure all students can find them:

Look in (the)...	**Busquen en...** *('boo-skehn ehn)*
bag	**la bolsa** *(lah 'bohl-sah)*
box	**la caja** *(lah 'kah-hah)*

cabinet	**el gabinete** *(ehl gah-bee-'neh-teh)*
cupboard	**el armario** *(ehl ahr-'mah-ree·oh)*
drawer	**el cajón** *(ehl kah-'hohn)*
file	**el archivo** *(ehl ahr-'chee-voh)*
It's in (the)...	**Está en...** *(eh-'stah ehn...)*
aisle	**el pasillo** *(ehl pah-'see-yoh)*
group	**el grupo** *(ehl 'groo-poh)*
line	**la línea** *(lah 'lee-neh-ah)*
pack	**el paquete** *(ehl pah-'keh-teh)*
row	**la fila** *(lah 'fee-lah)*
set	**el conjunto** *(ehl kohn-'hoon-toh)*

For those educators who keep all they can in the classroom, here's a set of words just for you:

armchair	**el sillón** *(ehl see-'yohn)*
bin	**el depósito** *(ehl deh-'poh-see-toh)*
chest	**el baúl** *(ehl bah-'ool)*
flower	**la flor** *(lah flohr)*
hanger	**el gancho** *(ehl 'gahn-choh)*
key	**la llave** *(lah 'yah-veh)*
lock	**el candado** *(ehl kahn-'dah-doh)*
mat	**el tapete** *(ehl tah-'peh-teh)*
photos	**las fotos** *(lahs 'foh-tohs)*
picture frame	**el marco** *(ehl 'mahr-koh)*
plant	**la planta** *(lah 'plahn-tah)*
rack	**el estante** *(ehl eh-'stahn-teh)*
rug	**la alfombra** *(lah ahl-'fohm-brah)*
shelf	**la repisa** *(lah reh-'pee-sah)*
sofa	**el sofá** *(ehl soh-'fah)*
stereo	**el estéreo** *(ehl eh-'steh-reh-oh)*
vase	**el florero** *(ehl floh-'reh-roh)*

Does anything need to be plugged in?

air conditioner	**el acondicionador de aire** *(ehl ah-kohn-dee-see·oh-nah-'dohr deh 'ah·ee-reh)*
electrical outlet	**el enchufe** *(ehl ehn-'choo-feh)*

fan	**el ventilador** *(ehl vehn-tee-lah-'dohr)*
heater	**el calentador** *(ehl kah-lehn-tah-'dohr)*
lamp	**la lámpara** *(lah 'lahm-pah-rah)*
light switch	**el interruptor** *(ehl een-teh-rroop-'tohr)*
thermostat	**el termostato** *(ehl tehr-moh-'stah-toh)*

THE LABORATORY
El laboratorio *(ehl lah-boh-rah-'toh-ree·oh)*

Science class has its own vocabulary list. For starters, why not point to these items on the counters and shelves:

We'll use (the)...	**Vamos a usar...** *('vah-mohs ah oo-'sahr...)*
beaker	**la cubeta** *(lah koo-'beh-tah)*
burner	**el quemador** *(ehl keh-mah-'dohr)*
candle	**la vela** *(lah 'veh-lah)*
clamp	**la abrazadera** *(lah ah-brah-sah-'deh-rah)*
faucet	**el grifo** *(ehl 'gree-foh)*
feather	**la pluma** *(lah 'ploo-mah)*
filter paper	**el papel filtro** *(ehl pah-'pehl 'feel-troh)*
fishbowl	**la pecera** *(lah peh-'seh-rah)*
flask	**el frasco** *(ehl 'frah-skoh)*
forceps	**las tenazas** *(lahs teh-'nah-sahs)*
funnel	**el embudo** *(ehl ehm-'boo-doh)*
lens	**el lente** *(ehl 'lehn-teh)*
magnet	**el imán** *(ehl ee-'mahn)*
magnifying glass	**la lupa** *(lah 'loo-pah)*
match	**el fósforo** *(ehl 'fohs-foh-roh)*
microscope	**el microscopio** *(ehl mee-kroh-'skoh-pee·oh)*
prism	**el prisma** *(ehl 'prees-mah)*
petri dish	**el platito de muestras** *(ehl plah-'tee-toh deh 'mweh-strahs)*
safety glasses	**los lentes de seguridad** *(lohs 'lehn-tehs deh seh-goo-ree-'dahd)*
scale	**la balanza** *(lah bah-'lahn-sah)*
slide	**la muestra en transparencia** *(lah 'mweh-strah ehn trahns-pah-'rehn-see·ah)*

stand	**el soporte** *(ehl soh-'pohr-teh)*
telescope	**el telescopio** *(ehl teh-leh-'skoh-pee·oh)*
test tube	**el tubo de ensayo** *(ehl 'too-boh deh ehn-'sah-yoh)*
tube	**el tubo** *(ehl 'too-boh)*

MÁS INFORMACIÓN

➤ Each new word will help:

electricity	**la electricidad** *(lah eh-lehk-tree-see-'dahd)*
heating	**la calefacción** *(lah kah-leh-fahk-see-'ohn)*
plumbing	**las tuberías** *(lahs too-beh-'ree-ahs)*

➤ And, how about those appliances that may be required during scientific experiments?

Use (the)...	**Usa...** *('oo-sah...)*
dishwasher	**el lavaplatos** *(ehl lah-vah-'plah-tohs)*
dryer	**la secadora** *(lah seh-kah-'doh-rah)*
freezer	**el congelador** *(ehl kohn-heh-lah-'dohr)*
hot water heater	**el calentador de agua** *(ehl kah-lehn-tah-'dohr deh 'ah-gwah)*
microwave	**el microonda** *(ehl mee-kroh-'ohn-dah)*
oven	**el horno** *(ehl 'ohr-noh)*
refrigerator	**el refrigerador** *(ehl reh-free-heh-rah-'dohr)*
sewing machine	**la máquina de coser** *(lah 'mah-kee-nah deh koh-'sehr)*
stove	**la estufa** *(lah eh-'stoo-fah)*
washer	**la lavadora** *(lah lah-vah-'doh-rah)*

¿LISTOS PARA PRACTICAR?

Name five popular high school subjects:

_____   _____   _____   _____   _____

Translate into Spanish:

Where's the lamp?

_____

We need a heater.

_____

The light switch is over there.

_____

Can you list three common items found in a science lab?

_____   _____   _____

Use the sample sentence as you fill in the blanks:

mapa (estudiar) *('mah-pah, eh-stoo-dee-'ahr)*   **Estudias el mapa.** *(eh-'stoo-dee-ahs ehl 'mah-pah)*

paquete (abrir) *(pah-'keh-teh, ah-'breer)*   _____

anuncio (leer) *(ah-'noon-see·oh, leh-'ehr)*   _____

álgebra (entender) *('ahl-heh-brah, ehn-tehn-'dehr)* _____

THE COMPUTER
La computadora *(lah kohm-poo-tah-'doh-rah)*

The classroom computer is now a common sight at schools everywhere. Assist the Spanish speakers by using the words below:

byte	**el octeto, el byte** *(ehl ohk-'teh-toh, ehl 'bee-teh)*
cable	**el cable** *(ehl 'kah-bleh)*
database	**la base de datos** *(lah 'bah-seh deh 'dah-tohs)*
disc	**el disco** *(ehl 'dee-skoh)*
drive	**el impulsor** *(ehl eem-pool-'sohr)*
hardware	**los elementos físicos** *(lohs eh-leh-'mehn-tohs 'fee-see-kohs)*
input	**la entrada de información** *(lah ehn-'trah-dah deh een-fohr-mah-see-'ohn)*
keyboard	**el teclado** *(ehl teh-'klah-doh)*
language	**el lenguaje** *(ehl lehn-'gwah-heh)*
memory	**la memoria** *(lah meh-'moh-ree·ah)*
microchip	**la microficha** *(lah mee-kroh-'fee-chah)*

116

microprocessor	**el microprocesador** *(ehl mee-kroh-proh-seh-sah-'dohr)*
monitor	**el monitor** *(ehl moh-nee-'tohr)*
mouse	**el ratón** *(ehl rah-'tohn)*
output	**la salida de información** *(lah sah-'lee-dah deh een-fohr-mah-see-'ohn)*
printer	**la impresora** *(lah eem-preh-'soh-rah)*
program	**el programa** *(ehl proh-'grah-mah)*
programming	**la programación** *(lah proh-grah-mah-see-'ohn)*
scanner	**el escáner** *(ehl eh-'skah-nehr)*
screen	**la pantalla** *(lah pahn-'tah-yah)*
software	**el programa** *(ehl proh-'grah-mah)*
system	**el sistema** *(ehl see-'steh-mah)*
terminal	**el terminal** *(ehl tehr-mee-'nahl)*
tower	**la torre** *(lah 'toh-rreh)*

SCIENCE CLASS
La clase de ciencias *(lah 'klah-seh deh see-'ehn-see·ahs)*

Obviously, you are unable to teach complex scientific concepts in Spanish, but you may explain general areas:

We study (the)...	**Estudiamos...** *(eh-stoo-dee-'ah-mohs)*
animals	**los animales** *(lohs ah-nee-'mah-lehs)*
engines	**los motores** *(lohs moh-'toh-rehs)*
environment	**el ambiente** *(ehl ahm-bee-'ehn-teh)*

heat	**el calor** *(ehl kah-'lohr)*
human body	**el cuerpo humano** *(ehl 'kwehr-poh oo-'mah-noh)*
machines	**las máquinas** *(lahs 'mah-kee-nahs)*
motion	**el movimiento** *(ehl moh-vee-mee-'ehn-toh)*
plants	**las plantas** *(lahs 'plahn-tahs)*
sound	**el sonido** *(ehl soh-'nee-doh)*
universe	**el universo** *(ehl oo-nee-'vehr-soh)*
weather	**el clima** *(ehl 'klee-mah)*

Some concepts or principles, however, cannot be defined in simple terms. Here are a few examples:

Do you understand...?	**¿Entiendes...?** *(ehn-tee-'ehn-dehs)*
centrifugal force	**la fuerza centrífuga** *(lah 'fwehr-sah sehn-'tree-foo-gah)*
energy	**la energía** *(lah eh-nehr-'hee-ah)*
gravity	**la gravedad** *(lah grah-veh-'dahd)*
inertia	**la inercia** *(lah ee-'nehr-see·ah)*
matter	**la materia** *(lah mah-'teh-ree·ah)*
power	**la potencia** *(lah poh-'tehn-see·ah)*

By the way, can you define the object you're working with?

It's a...	**Es un...** *(ehs oon)*
gas	**gas** *(gahs)*
grain	**grano** *('grah-noh)*
liquid	**líquido** *('lee-kee-doh)*
powder	**polvo** *('pohl-voh)*
solid	**sólido** *('soh-lee-doh)*

 MÁS INFORMACIÓN

➤ Next time, ask a Spanish-speaking pupil what everyone is shouting about. Here's what to say when there's a problem in the lab:

Something's wrong!	**¡Algo está mal!** *('ahl-goh eh-'stah mahl)*
It looks strange!	**¡Se ve raro!** *(seh veh 'rah-roh)*

Let's clean it up!	**¡Vamos a limpiarlo!** *('vah-mohs ah leem-pee-'ahr-loh)*
Check the...!	**¡Verifique...!** *(veh-ree-'fee-keh...)*

control	**el control** *(ehl kohn-'trohl)*
cycle	**el ciclo** *(ehl 'see-kloh)*
level	**el nivel** *(ehl nee-'vehl)*
light	**la luz** *(lah loos)*
power	**la potencia** *(lah poh-'tehn-see·ah)*
speed	**la velocidad** *(lah veh-loh-see-'dahd)*
temperature	**la temperatura** *(lah tehm-peh-rah-'too-rah)*
time	**la hora** *(lah 'oh-rah)*
tune	**el tono** *(ehl 'toh-noh)*
weight	**el peso** *(ehl 'peh-soh)*

I'm going to...!	**¡Voy a...!** *('voh·ee ah...)*

cancel it	**cancelarlo** *(kahn-seh-'lahr-loh)*
deactivate it	**desactivarlo** *(dehs-ahk-tee-'vahr-loh)*
pause it	**pausarlo** *(pow-'sahr-loh)*
stop it	**pararlo** *(pah-'rahr-loh)*
turn it off	**apagarlo** *(ah-pah-'gahr-loh)*

➤ Astronomy, **la astronomía** *(lah ah-stroh-noh-'mee-ah)*, is generally part of the science curriculum:

I want to study (the)...	**Quiero estudiar...** *(kee-'eh-roh eh-stoo-dee-'ahr)*

moon	**la luna** *(lah 'loo-nah)*
planet	**el planeta** *(ehl plah-'neh-tah)*
solar system	**el sistema solar** *(ehl see-'steh-mah soh-'lahr)*
star	**la estrella** *(lah eh-'streh-yah)*
sun	**el sol** *(ehl sohl)*

MATH CLASS
La clase de matemáticas *(lah 'klah-seh deh mah-teh-'mah-tee-kahs)*

Math is full of details that need to be explained, so do what you can with this next list of words and phrases. Bear in mind that attempting to use Spanish to teach tougher material often accelerates the learning process:

area	**el área** *(ehl 'ah-reh-ah)*
average	**el promedio** *(ehl proh-'meh-dee·oh)*
bar	**la barra** *(lah 'bah-rrah)*
circumference	**la circunferencia** *(lah seer-koon-feh-'rehn-see·ah)*
computation	**la computación** *(lah kohm-poo-tah-see-'ohn)*
cost	**el coste** *(ehl 'koh-steh)*
decimal	**el decimal** *(ehl deh-see-'mahl)*
degree	**el grado** *(ehl 'grah-doh)*
denominator	**el denominador** *(ehl deh-noh-mee-nah-'dohr)*
diagram	**el diagrama** *(ehl dee-ah-'grah-mah)*
diameter	**el diámetro** *(ehl dee-'ah-meh-troh)*
difference	**la diferencia** *(lah dee-feh-'rehn-see·ah)*
digit	**el dígito** *(ehl 'dee-hee-toh)*
dimension	**la dimensión** *(lah dee-mehn-see-'ohn)*
distance	**la distancia** *(lah dee-'stahn-see·ah)*
equal	**la igualdad** *(lah ee-gwahl-'dahd)*
equation	**la ecuación** *(lah eh-kwah-see-'ohn)*
equivalent	**el equivalente** *(ehl eh-kee-vah-'lehn-teh)*
exponent	**el exponente** *(ehl ehks-poh-'nehn-teh)*
figure	**la figura** *(lah fee-'goo-rah)*
formula	**la fórmula** *(lah 'fohr-moo-lah)*
fraction	**la fracción** *(lah frahk-see-'ohn)*
height	**la altura** *(lah ahl-'too-rah)*
length	**el largo** *(ehl 'lahr-goh)*
line	**la línea** *(lah 'lee-neh-ah)*
logic	**la lógica** *(lah 'loh-hee-kah)*
mode	**el modo** *(ehl 'moh-doh)*
numeral	**el numeral** *(ehl noo-meh-'rahl)*
numerator	**el numerador** *(ehl noo-meh-rah-'dohr)*
operation	**la operación** *(lah oh-peh-rah-see-'ohn)*
percent	**el porcentaje** *(ehl pohr-sehn-'tah-heh)*
perimeter	**el perímetro** *(ehl peh-'ree-meh-troh)*
point	**el punto** *(ehl 'poon-toh)*
probability	**la probabilidad** *(lah proh-bah-bee-lee-'dahd)*
product	**el producto** *(ehl proh-'dook-toh)*
quadrant	**el cuadrante** *(ehl kwah-'drahn-teh)*
quantity	**la cantidad** *(lah kahn-tee-'dahd)*
quotient	**el cociente** *(ehl koh-see-'ehn-teh)*
radius	**el radio** *(ehl 'rah-dee·oh)*
rate	**la tasa** *(lah 'tah-sah)*
ratio	**la proporción** *(lah proh-pohr-see-'ohn)*

remainder	**el residuo** *(ehl reh-'see-doo·oh)*
result	**el resultado** *(ehl reh-sool-'tah-doh)*
solution	**la solución** *(lah soh-loo-see-'ohn)*
speed	**la velocidad** *(lah veh-loh-see-'dahd)*
square	**el cuadro** *(ehl 'kwah-droh)*
statistic	**la estadística** *(lah eh-stah-'dee-stee-kah)*
sum	**la suma** *(lah 'soo-mah)*
surface	**la superficie** *(lah soo-pehr-'fee-see·eh)*
term	**el término** *(ehl 'tehr-mee-noh)*
time	**el tiempo** *(ehl tee-'ehm-poh)*
total	**el total** *(ehl toh-'tahl)*
triangle	**el triángulo** *(ehl tree-'ahn-goo-loh)*
unit	**la unidad** *(lah oo-nee-'dahd)*
value	**el valor** *(ehl vah-'lohr)*
weight	**el peso** *(ehl 'peh-soh)*

Continue to copy the words you need, but this time, focus on "mathematic" verbs:

to add	**sumar** *(soo-'mahr)*	**Estamos sumando las fracciones** *(eh-'stah-mohs soo-'mahn-doh lahs frahk-see-'oh-nehs)*
to calculate	**calcular** *(kahl-koo-'lahr)*	_____
to change	**cambiar** *(kahm-bee-'ahr)*	_____
to compare	**comparar** *(kohm-pah-'rahr)*	_____
to divide	**dividir** *(dee-vee-'deer)*	_____
to factor	**factorar** *(fahk-toh-'rahr)*	_____
to guess	**adivinar** *(ah-dee-vee-'nahr)*	_____
to measure	**medir** *(meh-'deer)*	_____
to multiply	**multiplicar** *(mool-tee-plee-'kahr)*	_____
to omit	**omitir** *(oh-mee-'teer)*	_____
to practice	**practicar** *(prahk-tee-'kahr)*	_____
to reduce	**reducir** *(reh-doo-'seer)*	_____
to round off	**redondear** *(reh-dohn-deh-'ahr)*	_____

to simplify	**simplificar** (seem-plee-fee-'kahr)	_____
to solve	**resolver** (reh-sohl-'vehr)	_____
to subtract	**restar** (reh-'stahr)	_____

MÁS INFORMACIÓN

➤ Use the vocabulary from the right column to create sentences:

_____ number   **el número** _____ (ehl 'noo-meh-roh)

whole	**entero** (ehn-'teh-roh)
negative	**negativo** (neh-gah-'tee-voh)
mixed	**mixto** ('meeks-toh)
like	**mismo** ('mees-moh)
unlike	**diferente** (dee-feh-'rehn-teh)
real	**real** (reh-'ahl)
rational	**racional** (rah-see·oh-'nahl)

➤ Learn faster by grouping key words into pairs:

| sample | **la muestra** (lah 'mweh-strah) |
| example | **el ejemplo** (ehl eh-'hehm-ploh) |

| parallel | **paralelo** (pah-rah-'leh-loh) |
| perpendicular | **perpendicular** (pehr-pehn-dee-koo-'lahr) |

| plus | **más** (mahs) |
| minus | **menos** ('meh-nohs) |

| times | **por** (pohr) |
| divided by | **dividido por** (dee-vee-'dee-doh pohr) |

| center | **el centro** (ehl 'sehn-troh) |
| side | **el lado** (ehl 'lah-doh) |

| cone | **el cono** (ehl 'koh-noh) |
| cylinder | **el cilindro** (ehl see-'leen-droh) |

¡Los <u>lados</u> del <u>ejemplo</u> son <u>paralelos</u>! *(lohs 'lah-dohs dehl eh-'hehm-ploh sohn pah-rah-'leh-lohs)*

MEASUREMENT
Las medidas *(lahs meh-'dee-dahs)*

Discussing measurements is a daily routine in math or science, so learn these powerful words and phrases in Spanish as soon as you can:

It's a/an...	**Es...** *(ehs)*
double	**un doble** *(oon 'doh-bleh)*
dozen	**una docena** *('oo-nah doh-'seh-nah)*
drop	**una gota** *('oo-nah 'goh-tah)*
gross	**una gruesa** *('oo-nah groo-'eh-sah)*
half	**una mitad** *('oo-nah mee-'tahd)*
pair	**un par** *(oon pahr)*
portion	**una porción** *('oo-nah pohr-see-'ohn)*
quarter	**un cuarto** *(oon 'kwahr-toh)*
third	**un tercio** *(oon 'tehr-see·oh)*
ton	**una tonelada** *('oo-nah toh-neh-'lah-dah)*
unit	**una unidad** *('oo-nah oo-nee-'dahd)*

Take a/an...	**Tome...** *('toh-meh)*
centimeter	**un centímetro** *(oon sehn-'tee-meh-troh)*
foot	**un pie** *(oon 'pee-eh)*
gallon	**un galón** *(oon gah-'lohn)*
gram	**un gramo** *(oon 'grah-moh)*
kilogram	**un kilogramo** *(oon kee-loh-'grah-moh)*
inch	**una pulgada** *('oo-nah pool-'gah-dah)*
meter	**un metro** *(oon 'meh-troh)*
millimeter	**un milímetro** *(oon mee-'lee-meh-troh)*
ounce	**una onza** *('oo-nah 'ohn-sah)*
pound	**una libra** *('oo-nah 'lee-brah)*
quart	**un cuarto** *(oon 'kwahr-toh)*
yard	**una yarda** *('oo-nah 'yahr-dah)*

➤ Stick in a word that helps describe:

only   **solamente** *(soh-lah-'mehn-teh)*   **Solamente tres pulgadas.**
                                                       (soh-lah-'mehn-teh trehs pool-
                                                       'gah-dahs)

none   **ninguno** *(neen-'goo-noh)*   **Ninguno de los dos números.**
                                                 (neen-'goo-noh deh lohs dohs
                                                 'noo-meh-rohs)

the rest   **los demás** *(lohs deh-'mahs)*   **Los demás problemas.** *(lohs*
                                                     deh-'mahs proh-'bleh-mahs)

CONFLICTOS CULTURALES

What do you know about the metric system? You may need to post a conversion table if your class makeup is international.

5/8 mi.	=	**un kilómetro** *(oon kee-'loh-meh-troh)*
2.2 lbs.	=	**un kilógramo** *(oon kee-'loh-grah-moh)*
32° Fahrenheit	=	**0° Celsius** *('seh-roh 'sehl-see-oos)*

GLOBAL STUDIES
Los Estudios Globales *(lohs eh-'stoo-dee·ohs gloh-'bah-lehs)*

Why not set aside those vocabulary items that specifically focus on lessons in humanities. Here's a beginner's list in Spanish. Learn it and create full sentences.

politics	**la política** *(lah poh-'lee-tee-kah)*	**¿Qué sabes tú de la política de Cuba?** *(keh 'sah-behs too deh deh 'koo-bah)*

agriculture	**la agricultura** *(lah ah-gree-kool-'too-rah)*
ancestor	**el antepasado** *(ehl ahn-teh-pah-'sah-doh)*
army	**el ejército** *(ehl eh-'hehr-see-toh)*
battle	**la batalla** *(lah bah-'tah-yah)*
border	**la frontera** *(lah frohn-'teh-rah)*
century	**el siglo** *(ehl 'see-gloh)*
civilization	**la civilización** *(lah see-vee-lee-sah-see-'ohn)*
colony	**la colonia** *(lah koh-'loh-nee·ah)*
conquest	**la conquista** *(lah kohn-'kee-stah)*
continent	**el continente** *(ehl kohn-tee-'nehn-teh)*
country	**el país** *(ehl pah-'ees)*
culture	**la cultura** *(lah kool-'too-rah)*
custom	**la costumbre** *(lah koh-'stoom-breh)*
development	**el desarrollo** *(ehl dehs-ah-'rroh-yoh)*
discovery	**el descubrimiento** *(ehl deh-skoo-bree-mee-'ehn-toh)*
dynasty	**la dinastía** *(lah dee-nah-'stee-ah)*
economy	**la economía** *(lah eh-koh-noh-'mee-ah)*
election	**la elección** *(lah eh-lehk-see-'ohn)*
empire	**el imperio** *(ehl eem-'peh-ree·oh)*
evolution	**la evolución** *(lah eh-voh-loo-see-'ohn)*
expansion	**la expansión** *(lah ehk-spahn-see-'ohn)*
exploration	**la exploración** *(lah ehks-ploh-rah-see-'ohn)*
exportation	**la exportación** *(lah ehks-pohr-tah-see-'ohn)*
freedom	**la libertad** *(lah lee-behr-'tahd)*
government	**el gobierno** *(ehl goh-bee-'ehr-noh)*
growth	**el crecimiento** *(ehl kreh-see-mee-'ehn-toh)*
hunger	**el hambre** *(ehl 'ahm-breh)*
immigration	**la inmigración** *(lah een-mee-grah-see-'ohn)*
importation	**la importación** *(lah eem-pohr-tah-see-'ohn)*

independence	**la independencia** *(lah een-deh-pehn-'dehn-see·ah)*
industry	**la industria** *(lah een-'doo-stree·ah)*
invasion	**la invasión** *(lah een-vah-see-'ohn)*
law	**la ley** *(lah 'leh·ee)*
mining	**la minería** *(lah mee-neh-'ree-ah)*
monarchy	**la monarquía** *(lah moh-nahr-'kee-ah)*
nation	**la nación** *(lah nah-see-'ohn)*
origin	**el origen** *(ehl oh-'ree-hehn)*
peace	**la paz** *(lah pahs)*
pollution	**la contaminación** *(lah kohn-tah-mee-nah-see-'ohn)*
population	**la población** *(lah poh-blah-see-'ohn)*
poverty	**la pobreza** *(lah poh-'breh-sah)*
race	**la raza** *(lah 'rah-sah)*
reign	**el reino** *(ehl 'reh·ee-noh)*
religion	**la religión** *(lah reh-lee-hee-'ohn)*
republic	**la república** *(lah reh-'poo-blee-kah)*
reunification	**la reunificación** *(lah reh-oo-nee-fee-kah-see-'ohn)*
revolution	**la revolución** *(lah reh-voh-loo-see-'ohn)*
state	**el estado** *(ehl eh-'stah-doh)*
territory	**el territorio** *(ehl teh-rree-'toh-ree·oh)*
trade	**el comercio** *(ehl koh-'mehr-see·oh)*
voyage	**el viaje** *(ehl vee-'ah-heh)*
war	**la guerra** *(lah 'geh-rrah)*
wealth	**la riqueza** *(lah ree-'keh-sah)*
world	**el mundo** *(ehl 'moon-doh)*

MÁS INFORMACIÓN

➤ Memorize strategic times in world history:

Industrial Revolution	**La Revolución industrial** *(lah reh-voh-loo-see-'ohn een-doo-stree-'ahl)*
Reformation	**La Reforma** *(lah reh-'fohr-mah)*
Renaissance	**El Renacimiento** *(ehl reh-nah-see-mee-'ehn-toh)*

➤ Start a list of meaningful descriptive words. Study these examples:

ancient	**antiguo** *(ahn-'tee-gwoh)*
modern	**moderno** *(moh-'dehr-noh)*
prehistoric	**prehistórico** *(preh-ee-'stoh-ree-koh)*

➤ Use magazines or newspapers to discuss any important issue:

civil rights	**los derechos humanos** *(lohs deh-'reh-chohs oo-'mah-nohs)*
political parties	**los partidos políticos** *(lohs pahr-'tee-dohs poh-'lee-tee-kohs)*
pollution	**la contaminación** *(lah kohn-tah-mee-nah-see-'ohn)*

➤ Deeper concepts should be translated, so memorize these words, too:

hatred	**el odio** *(ehl 'oh-dee·oh)*
hope	**la esperanza** *(lah eh-speh-'rahn-sah)*
injustice	**la injusticia** *(lah een-hoo-'stee-see·ah)*
justice	**la justicia** *(lah hoo-'stee-see·ah)*
kindness	**la bondad** *(lah bohn-'dahd)*
love	**el amor** *(ehl ah-'mohr)*
racism	**el racismo** *(ehl rah-'sees-moh)*
respect	**el respeto** *(ehl reh-'speh-toh)*
trust	**la confianza** *(lah kohn-fee-'ahn-sah)*

RACE AND NATIONALITY
Raza y nacionalidad *('rah-sah ee nah-see·oh-nah-lee-'dahd)*

Identify the folks around you by race and nationality. Use these words to describe:

She's...	**Ella es...** *('eh-yah ehs...)*
Asian	**asiática** *(ah-see-'ah-tee-kah)*
black	**negra** *('neh-grah)*
Hispanic	**hispana** *(ee-'spah-nah)*
Latin	**latina** *(lah-'tee-nah)*
Middle Eastern	**del Oriente Medio** *(dehl oh-ree-'ehn-teh 'meh-dee·oh)*
Native American	**amerindia** *(ah-mehr-'een-dee·ah)*
Polynesian	**polinesia** *(poh-lee-'neh-see·ah)*
white	**blanca** *('blahn-kah)*

He's...	Él es... *(ehl ehs...)*
African-American	**afroamericano** *(ah-froh-ah-meh-ree-'kah-noh)*
Anglo-Saxon	**anglosajón** *(ahn-gloh-sah-'hohn)*
Asian-American	**asiáticoamericano** *(ah-see-'ah-tee-koh-ah-meh-ree-'kah-noh)*
Latin-American	**latinoamericano** *(lah-tee-noh-ah-meh-ree-'kah-noh)*

Here's another pattern. Just insert the appropriate word:

The boy is...	El niño es... *(ehl 'nee-nyoh ehs...)*
African	**africano** *(ah-free-'kah-noh)*
Arab	**árabe** *('ah-rah-beh)*
Australian	**australiano** *(ow-strah-lee-'ah-noh)*
Canadian	**canadiense** *(kah-nah-dee-'ehn-seh)*
Chinese	**chino** *('chee-noh)*
Dutch	**holandés** *(oh-lahn-'dehs)*
English	**inglés** *(een-'glehs)*
French	**francés** *(frahn-'sehs)*
German	**alemán** *(ah-leh-'mahn)*
Greek	**griego** *(gree-'eh-goh)*
Irish	**irlandés** *(eer-lahn-'dehs)*
Italian	**italiano** *(ee-tah-lee-'ah-noh)*
Japanese	**japonés** *(hah-poh-'nehs)*
Portuguese	**portugués** *(pohr-too-'gehs)*
Russian	**ruso** *('roo-soh)*
Scottish	**escocés** *(ehs-koh-'sehs)*
Spanish	**español** *(eh-spah-'nyohl)*
Swedish	**sueco** *('sweh-koh)*
Swiss	**suizo** *('swee-soh)*
U.S.	**norteamericano** *(nohr-teh-ah-meh-ree-'kah-noh)*
Vietnamese	**vietnamita** *(vee-eht-nah-'mee-tah)*

And, how about south of the border? Allow your students to share:

I'm _____	Soy _____ *('soh·ee...)*
Argentinean	**argentino** *(ahr-hehn-'tee-noh)*
Bolivian	**boliviano** *(boh-lee-vee-'ah-noh)*

Brazilian	**brasileño** *(brah-see-'leh-nyoh)*
Chilean	**chileno** *(chee-'leh-noh)*
Costa Rican	**costarricense** *(koh-stah-rree-'sehn-seh)*
Cuban	**cubano** *(koo-'bah-noh)*
Dominican	**dominicano** *(doh-mee-nee-'kah-noh)*
Ecuadorian	**ecuatoriano** *(eh-kwah-'toh-ree-'ah-noh)*
Guatemalan	**guatemalteco** *(gwah-teh-mahl-'teh-koh)*
Haitian	**haitiano** *(ah·ee-tee-'ah-noh)*
Honduran	**hondureño** *(ohn-doo-'reh-nyoh)*
Mexican	**mexicano** *(meh-hee-'kah-noh)*
Nicaraguan	**nicaragüense** *(nee-kah-rah-'gwehn-seh)*
Panamanian	**panameño** *(pah-nah-'meh-nyoh)*
Paraguayan	**paraguayo** *(pah-rah-'gwah-yoh)*
Peruvian	**peruano** *(peh-roo-'ah-noh)*
Puerto Rican	**puertorriqueño** *(pwehr-toh-rree-'keh-nyoh)*
Salvadoran	**salvadoreño** *(sahl-vah-doh-'reh-nyoh)*
Uruguayan	**uruguayo** *(oo-roo-'gwah-yoh)*
Venezuelan	**venezolano** *(veh-neh-soh-'lah-noh)*

MÁS INFORMACIÓN

➤ What about political titles?

dictator	**el dictador** *(ehl deek-tah-'dohr)*
king	**el rey** *(ehl 'reh·ee)*
president	**el presidente** *(ehl preh-see-'dehn-teh)*
queen	**la reina** *(lah 'reh·ee-nah)*
ruler	**el gobernante** *(ehl goh-behr-'nahn-teh)*

➤ Now, look at these religious believers:

Buddhist	**budista** *(boo-'dee-stah)*
Catholic	**católico** *(kah-'toh-lee-koh)*
Christian	**cristiano** *(kree-stee-'ah-noh)*
Islamic	**islámita** *(ees-'lah-mee-tah)*
Jewish	**judío** *(hoo-'dee-oh)*
Mormon	**mormón** *(mohr-'mohn)*
Muslim	**musulmán** *(moo-sool-'mahn)*

Most of Latin America is Roman Catholic, and you may notice the religious influence during your association with some Hispanics during a crisis. Using the word God, **Dios** *('dee-ohs)* in the conversation, attending daily mass, **la misa** *(lah 'mee-sah)*, or observing Catholic traditions are common signs of their faith. Remember that respect and sensitivity are always in demand when topics center around cultural and religious beliefs.

¿LISTOS PARA PRACTICAR?

Choose the best word to fit in the blank:

continente, país, estado *(kohn-tee-'nehn-teh, pah-'ees, eh-'stah-doh)*

Los Estados Unidos es un _____. *(lohs eh-'stah-dohs oo-'nee-dohs*

ehs oon _____)

Africa es un _____. *('ah-free-kah ehs oon _____)*

California es un _____. *(kah-lee-'fohr-nee·ah ehs oon)*

Connect the math terms that closely relate to each other:

triángulo *(tree-'ahn-goo-loh)*	**mixto** *('meeks-toh)*
peso *('peh-soh)*	**restar** *(reh-'stahr)*
simplificar *(seem-plee-fee-'kahr)*	**estatura** *(eh-stah-'too-rah)*
ecuación *(eh-kwah-see-'ohn)*	**reducir** *(reh-doo-'seer)*
entero *(ehn-'teh-roh)*	**cuadrado** *(kwah-'drah-doh)*
sumar *(soo-'mahr)*	**operación** *(oh-peh-rah-see-'ohn)*

Translate:

el poder *(ehl poh-'dehr)* _____

la energía *(lah eh-nehr-'hee-ah)* _____

el calor *(ehl kah-'lohr)* _____

Write in Spanish:

1/2 _____

3 ft. _____

1/3 _____

12 oz. _____

1 in. _____

List three countries and the languages spoken there:

Italia *(ee-'tah-lee-ah)*   **italiano** *(ee-tah-lee-'ah-noh)*

_____   _____

_____   _____

_____   _____

ENGLISH CLASS
La clase de inglés *(lah 'klah-seh deh een-'glehs)*

Due to the high numbers of non-English and limited-English-speaking children in schools across the U.S., educators are struggling to find the best methods to teach English as a second language. Older learners require plenty of explanation and practice, so be sure to present these terms to all your native Spanish speakers. They can be useful when questions arise about English:

character	**el personaje** *(ehl pehr-soh-'nah-heh)*
composition	**la composición** *(lah kohm-poh-see-see-'ohn)*
novel	**la novela** *(lah noh-'veh-lah)*
plot	**el argumento** *(ehl ahr-goo-'mehn-toh)*
poetry	**la poesía** *(lah poh-eh-'see-ah)*
prose	**la prosa** *(lah 'proh-sah)*
short story	**el cuento** *(ehl 'kwehn-toh)*
table of contents	**el contenido** *(ehl kohn-teh-'nee-doh)*

In English class, teachers communicate using grammar words found in textbooks. They're a bore, but any student of languages needs to know them. Fortunately, many of these look like English:

adjective	**el adjetivo** *(ehl ahd-heh-'tee-voh)*
adverb	**el adverbio** *(ehl ahd-'vehr-bee·oh)*
capital letter	**la mayúscula** *(lah mah-'yoo-skoo-lah)*
cognate	**la palabra afín** *(lah pah-'lah-brah ah-'feen)*
comma	**la coma** *(lah 'koh-mah)*
conditional	**el condicional** *(ehl kohn-dee-see·oh-'nahl)*
conjugation	**la conjugación** *(lah kohn-hoo-gah-see-'ohn)*
consonant	**la consonante** *(lah kohn-soh-'nahn-teh)*
dialog	**el diálogo** *(ehl dee-'ah-loh-goh)*
ending	**el final** *(ehl fee-'nahl)*
exercise	**el ejercicio** *(ehl eh-hehr-'see-see·oh)*
feminine	**femenino** *(feh-meh-'nee-noh)*
form	**la forma** *(lah 'fohr-mah)*
future	**el futuro** *(ehl foo-'too-roh)*
gerund	**el gerundio** *(ehl heh-'roon-dee·oh)*
grammar	**la gramática** *(lah grah-'mah-tee-kah)*
imperative	**el imperativo** *(ehl eem-peh-rah-'tee-voh)*
imperfect	**el imperfecto** *(ehl eem-pehr-'fehk-toh)*
infinitive	**el infinitivo** *(ehl een-fee-nee-'tee-voh)*
language	**el idioma** *(ehl ee-dee-'oh-mah)*
letter	**la letra** *(lah 'leh-trah)*
lower case letter	**la minúscula** *(lah mee-'noo-skoo-lah)*
masculine	**masculino** *(mah-skoo-'lee-noh)*
meaning	**el significado** *(ehl seeg-nee-fee-'kah-doh)*
noun	**el sustantivo** *(ehl soo-stahn-'tee-voh)*
object	**el objetivo** *(ehl ohb-heh-'tee-voh)*
participle	**el participio** *(ehl pahr-tee-'see-pee·oh)*
passive voice	**la voz pasiva** *(lah vohs pah-'see-vah)*
past	**el pasado** *(ehl pah-'sah-doh)*
perfect	**el perfecto** *(ehl pehr-'fehk-toh)*
period	**el punto** *(ehl 'poon-toh)*
person	**la persona** *(lah pehr-'soh-nah)*
possessive	**el posesivo** *(ehl poh-seh-'see-voh)*

present	**el presente** *(ehl preh-'sehn-teh)*
preterit	**el pretérito** *(ehl preh-'teh-ree-toh)*
progressive	**el progresivo** *(ehl proh-greh-'see-voh)*
pronoun	**el pronombre** *(ehl proh-'nohm-breh)*
pronunciation	**la pronunciación** *(lah proh-noon-see-ah-see-'ohn)*
radical	**el radical** *(ehl rah-dee-'kahl)*
reflexive	**el reflexivo** *(ehl reh-flehk-'see-voh)*
regular	**regular** *(reh-goo-'lahr)*
sentence	**la frase** *(lah 'frah-seh)*
singular	**el singular** *(ehl seen-goo-'lahr)*
sound	**el sonido** *(ehl soh-'nee-doh)*
speech	**el habla** *(ehl 'ah-blah)*
structure	**la estructura** *(lah eh-strook-'too-rah)*
subject	**el sujeto** *(ehl soo-'heh-toh)*
subjunctive	**el subjuntivo** *(ehl soob-hoon-'tee-voh)*
syllable	**la sílaba** *(lah 'see-lah-bah)*
symbol	**el símbolo** *(ehl 'seem-boh-loh)*
synonym	**el sinónimo** *(ehl see-'noh-nee-moh)*
the reading	**la lectura** *(lah lehk-'too-rah)*
tense	**el tiempo** *(ehl tee-'ehm-poh)*
test	**el examen** *(ehl ehk-'sah-mehn)*
theme	**el tema** *(ehl 'teh-mah)*
verb	**el verbo** *(ehl 'vehr-boh)*
vocabulary	**el vocabulario** *(ehl voh-kah-boo-'lah-ree·oh)*
vowel	**la vocal** *(lah voh-'kahl)*
word	**la palabra** *(lah pah-'lah-brah)*
writing	**la escritura** *(lah eh-skree-'too-rah)*

Now, create a few sentences:

La frase no tiene una coma. *(lah 'frah-seh noh tee-'eh-neh 'oo-nah 'koh-mah)*
Escriba el verbo en el tiempo pasado. *(eh-'skree-bah ehl 'vehr-boh ehn ehl tee-'ehm-poh pah-'sah-doh)*

_____

_____

_____

THE FINE ARTS
Las bellas artes *(lahs 'beh-yahs 'ahr-tehs)*

Young people take classes in other areas besides the basics. Let's review a few subjects that help students develop their unique talents and abilities:

Art **(el arte)** *(ehl 'ahr-teh)*

Look at (the)...	**Mira...** *('mee-rah)*
design	**el diseño** *(dee-'seh-nyoh)*
drawing	**el dibujo** *(ehl dee-'boo-hoh)*
illustration	**la ilustración** *(lah ee-loo-strah-see-'ohn)*
painting	**la pintura** *(lah peen-'too-rah)*
photography	**la fotografía** *(lah foh-toh-grah-'fee-ah)*
pottery	**la cerámica** *(lah seh-'rah-mee-kah)*
sculpture	**la escultura** *(lah eh-skool-'too-rah)*

Theater **(el teatro)** *(ehl teh-'ah-troh)*

actor	**el actor** *(ehl ahk-'tohr)*
actress	**la actriz** *(lah ahk-'trees)*
director	**el director** *(ehl dee-rehk-'tohr)*
playwright	**el dramaturgo** *(ehl drah-mah-'toor-goh)*

We study (the)...	**Estudiamos...** *(eh-stoo-dee-'ah-mohs...)*
acting	**la actuación** *(lah ahk-too-ah-see-'ohn)*
audience	**el auditorio** *(ehl ow-dee-'toh-ree·oh)*
ballet	**el balet** *(ehl bah-'leh)*
choreography	**la coreografía** *(lah koh-reh-oh-grah-'fee-ah)*
comedy	**la comedia** *(lah koh-'meh-dee·ah)*
costume	**el disfraz** *(ehl dees-'frahs)*
dance	**el baile** *(ehl 'bah·ee-leh)*
improvisation	**la improvisación** *(lah eem-proh-vee-sah-see-'ohn)*
play	**el drama** *(ehl 'drah-mah)*
production	**la producción** *(lah proh-dook-see-'ohn)*
scene	**la escena** *(lah eh-'seh-nah)*
stage	**el escenario** *(ehl eh-seh-'nah-ree·oh)*
tragedy	**la tragedia** *(lah trah-'heh-dee·ah)*

Music **(la música)** *(lah 'moo-see-kah)*

I like (the)...	**Me gusta...** *(meh 'goo-stah)*
band	**la banda** *(lah 'bahn-dah)*
choir	**el coro** *(ehl 'koh-roh)*
instrument	**el instrumento** *(ehl een-stroo-'mehn-toh)*
note	**la nota** *(lah 'noh-tah)*
opera	**la ópera** *(lah 'oh-peh-rah)*
orchestra	**la orquesta** *(lah ohr-'keh-stah)*
scale	**la escala** *(lah eh-'skah-lah)*
song	**la canción** *(lah kahn-see-'ohn)*

I play (the)...	**Toco...** *('toh-koh)*
clarinet	**el clarinete** *(ehl klah-ree-'neh-teh)*
drum	**el tambor** *(ehl tahm-'bohr)*
guitar	**la guitarra** *(lah gee-'tah-rrah)*
organ	**el órgano** *(ehl 'ohr-gah-noh)*
piano	**el piano** *(ehl pee-'ah-noh)*
saxophone	**el saxófono** *(ehl sahk-'soh-foh-noh)*
trombone	**el trombón** *(ehl trohm-'bohn)*
trumpet	**la trompeta** *(lah trohm-'peh-tah)*
violin	**el violín** *(ehl vee-oh-'leen)*

Physical Education **(la educación física)** *(lah eh-doo-kah-see-'ohn 'fee-see-kah)*

We are...	**Estamos...** *(eh-'stah-mohs...)*
doing exercise	**haciendo ejercicio** *(ah-see-'ehn-doh eh-hehr-'see-see·oh)*
jumping	**saltando** *(sahl-'tahn-doh)*
lifting weights	**levantando pesos** *(leh-vahn-'tahn-doh 'peh-sohs)*
running	**corriendo** *(koh-rree-'ehn-doh)*
swimming	**nadando** *(nah-'dahn-doh)*

Let's...	Vamos a... *('vah-mohs ah...)*
bounce	**rebotar** *(reh-boh-'tahr)*
catch	**agarrar** *(ah-gah-'rrahr)*
hit	**pegar** *(peh-'gahr)*
kick	**patear** *(pah-teh-'ahr)*
pass	**pasar** *(pah-'sahr)*
pitch	**lanzar** *(lahn-'sahr)*
serve	**servir** *(sehr-'veer)*
shoot	**disparar** *(dee-spah-'rahr)*
throw	**tirar** *(tee-'rahr)*

MÁS INFORMACIÓN

➤ P.E. teachers should label some of these items in Spanish with removable stickers:

I need (the)...	Necesito... *(neh-seh-'see-toh...)*
ball	**la pelota** *(lah peh-'loh-tah)*
basket	**la canasta** *(lah kah-'nah-stah)*
bat	**el bate** *(ehl 'bah-teh)*
mitt	**el guante** *(ehl 'gwahn-teh)*
net	**la red** *(lah rehd)*
racket	**la raqueta** *(lah rah-'keh-tah)*
treadmill	**el molino** *(ehl moh-'lee-noh)*
weights	**las pesas** *(lahs 'peh-sahs)*

➤ When exercise is the topic, be sure to explain the benefits:

You need...	Necesitas... *(neh-seh-'see-tahs...)*
fitness	**el buen estado físico** *(ehl bwehn eh-'stah-doh 'fee-see-koh)*
strength	**la fuerza** *(lah 'fwehr-sah)*
weight loss	**la pérdida de peso** *(lah 'pehr-dee-dah deh 'peh-soh)*

TIME TO STUDY

La hora de estudiar *(lah 'oh-rah deh eh-stoo-dee-'ahr)*

Help out any student who is lacking those vital study skills. First, get them to the right location, and then explain all the procedures that you can:

We're going to (the)...	**Vamos a...** *('vah-mohs ah...)*
library	**la biblioteca** *(lah beeb-lee·oh-'teh-kah)*
resource room	**el salón de recursos** *(ehl sah-'lohn deh reh-'koor-sohs)*
study hall	**el salón de estudio** *(ehl sah-'lohn deh eh-'stoo-dee·oh)*
Please finish (the)...	**Favor de terminar...** *(fah-'vohr deh tehr-'mee-'nahr)*
assignment	**la tarea** *(lah tah-'reh-ah)*
essay	**el ensayo** *(ehl ehn-'sah-yoh)*
exam	**el examen** *(ehl ehk-'sah-mehn)*
project	**el proyecto** *(ehl proh-'yehk-'toh)*
quiz	**el cuestionario** *(ehl kweh-stee·oh-'nah-ree·oh)*
report	**el reporte** *(ehl reh-'pohr-teh)*
research	**la investigación** *(lah een-veh-stee-gah-see-'ohn)*
summary	**el resumen** *(ehl reh-'soo-mehn)*
test	**la prueba** *(lah proo-'eh-bah)*
You need to read (the)...	**Necesitas leer...** *(neh-seh-'see-tahs leh-'ehr...)*
chapter	**el capítulo** *(ehl kah-'pee-too-loh)*
section	**la sección** *(lah sehk-see-'ohn)*
unit	**la unidad** *(lah oo-nee-'dahd)*
Take out (the)...	**Saca...** *('sah-kah...)*
copies	**las copias** *(lahs 'koh-pee·ahs)*
notes	**las anotaciones** *(lahs ah-noh-tah-see-'oh-nehs)*
outlines	**los resúmenes** *(lohs reh-'soo-meh-nehs)*

We're looking for...	Buscamos... *(boo-'skah-mohs...)*
appendix	**el apéndice** *(ehl ah-'pehn-dee-seh)*
article	**el artículo** *(ehl ahr-'tee-koo-loh)*
author	**el autor** *(ehl ow-'tohr)*
bibliography	**la bibliografía** *(lah bee-blee·oh-grah-'fee-ah)*
biography	**la biografía** *(lah bee·oh-grah-'fee-ah)*
call number	**el número de clasificación** *(ehl 'noo-meh-roh deh klah-see-fee-kah-see-'ohn)*
catalog	**el catálogo** *(ehl kah-'tah-loh-goh)*
dictionary	**el diccionario** *(ehl deek-see·oh-'nah-ree·oh)*
encyclopedia	**la enciclopedia** *(lah ehn-see-kloh-'peh-dee·ah)*
fiction	**la ficción** *(lah feek-see-'ohn)*
glossary	**el glosario** *(ehl gloh-'sah-ree·oh)*
index	**el índice** *(ehl 'een-dee-seh)*
librarian	**el bibliotecario** *(ehl bee-blee·oh-teh-'kah-ree·oh)*
library card	**la tarjeta de la biblioteca** *(lah tahr-'heh-tah deh lah beeb-lee·oh-'teh-kah)*
magazine	**la revista** *(lah reh-'vee-stah)*
microfilm	**el microfilm** *(ehl mee-kroh-'feelm)*
newspaper	**el periódico** *(ehl peh-ree-'oh-dee-koh)*
reference	**la referencia** *(lah reh-feh-'rehn-see·ah)*
subject	**el tema** *(ehl 'teh-mah)*
title	**el título** *(ehl 'tee-too-loh)*
yearbook	**el anuario** *(ehl ah-noo-'ah-ree·oh)*

This group will help you explain valuable study skills:

Do you understand (the)..?	¿Entiendes..? *(ehn-tee-'ehn-dehs)*
approach	**el enfoque** *(ehl ehn-'foh-keh)*
concept	**el concepto** *(ehl kohn-'sehp-toh)*
content	**el contenido** *(ehl kohn-teh- 'nee-doh)*
data	**los datos** *(lohs 'dah-tohs)*
evidence	**la evidencia** *(lah eh-vee-'dehn-see·ah)*
example	**el ejemplo** *(ehl eh-'hehm-ploh)*
fact	**el hecho** *(ehl 'eh-choh)*
information	**la información** *(lah een-fohr-mah-see-'ohn)*

material	**la materia** *(lah mah-'teh-ree·ah)*
method	**el método** *(ehl 'meh-toh-doh)*
model	**el modelo** *(ehl moh-'deh-loh)*
opinion	**la opinión** *(lah oh-pee-nee-'ohn)*
principle	**el principio** *(ehl preen-'see-pee·oh)*
reason	**la razón** *(lah rah-'sohn)*
step	**el paso** *(ehl 'pah-soh)*
strategy	**la estrategia** *(lah eh-strah-'teh-hee·ah)*
technique	**la técnica** *(lah 'tehk-nee-kah)*
theory	**la teoría** *(lah teh-oh-'ree-ah)*
topic	**el tema** *(ehl 'teh-mah)*

MÁS INFORMACIÓN

➤ During test-taking, teachers need to be sure students understand the instructions. These expressions will come in handy:

You have to...	**Tienes que...** *(tee-'eh-nehs keh...)*
write definitions	**escribir las definiciones** *(eh-skree-'beer lahs deh-fee-nee-see-'oh-nehs)*
listen to dictation	**escuchar el dictado** *(eh-skoo-'chahr ehl deek-'tah-doh)*
say true or false	**decir verdadero o falso** *(deh-'seer vehr-dah-'deh-roh oh 'fahl-soh)*
do multiple choice	**hacer elección múltiple** *(ah-'sehr eh-lehk-see-'ohn 'mool-tee-pleh)*
fill in the blank	**llenar el espacio vacío** *(yeh-'nahr ehl eh-'spah-see·oh vah-'see·oh)*
find the opposite	**encontrar lo opuesto** *(ehn-kohn-'trahr loh oh-'pweh-stoh)*
match the words	**poner en pareja las palabras** *(poh-'nehr ehn pah-'reh-hah lahs pah-'lah-brahs)*
answer the questions	**contestar las preguntas** *(kohn-teh-'stahr lahs preh-'goon-tahs)*

EXTRACURRICULAR ACTIVITIES
Las actividades extracurriculares
(lahs ahk-tee-vee-'dah-dehs ehks-trah-koo-ree-koo-'lah-rehs)

Not all learning takes place in the classroom. Students have the opportunity to join clubs, teams, or similar youth-oriented organizations. Several terms may be needed as you share information with Spanish-speaking students and their families.

Would you like to join?   **¿Quisieras inscribirte?** *(kee-see-'eh-rahs een-skree-'beer-teh)*

There's a _____ club.   **Hay un club de _____.** *('ah·ee oon kloob deh _____)*

bicycle	**ciclismo** *(see-'klees-moh)*
business	**negocios** *(neh-'goh-see·ohs)*
chess	**ajedrez** *(ah-heh-'drehs)*
computer	**computadoras** *(kohm-poo-tah-'doh-rahs)*
cooking	**cocina** *(koh-'see-nah)*
culture	**cultura** *(kool-'too-rah)*
dance	**baile** *('bah·ee-leh)*
debate	**debate** *(deh-'bah-teh)*
drama	**drama** *('drah-mah)*
ecology	**ecología** *(eh-koh-loh-'hee-ah)*
film	**películas** *(peh-'lee-koo-lahs)*
nature	**naturaleza** *(nah-too-rah-'leh-sah)*
religion	**religión** *(reh-lee-hee-'ohn)*
sewing	**costura** *(koh-'stoo-rah)*
ski	**esquí** *(eh-'skee)*
travel	**viajes** *(vee-'ah-hehs)*
yearbook	**anuario** *(ah-noo-'ah-ree·oh)*

It's a/an...   **Es un/una...** *(ehs oon / 'oo-nah...)*

club	**club** *(kloob)*
group	**grupo** *('groo-poh)*
league	**liga** *('lee-gah)*
organization	**organización** *(ohr-gah-nee-sah-see-'ohn)*
team	**equipo** *(eh-'kee-poh)*

They have (the)...	Tienen... *(tee-'eh-nehn)*
auction	**la subasta** *(soo-'bah-stah)*
banquet	**el banquete** *(ehl bahn-'keh-teh)*
carnival	**el carnaval** *(ehl kahr-nah-'vahl)*
ceremony	**la ceremonia** *(lah seh-reh-'moh-nee·ah)*
conference	**la conferencia** *(lah kohn-feh-'rehn-see·ah)*
contest	**el concurso** *(ehl kohn-'koor-soh)*
dance	**el baile** *(ehl 'bah·ee-leh)*
event	**el evento** *(ehl eh-'vehn-toh)*
fair	**la feria** *(lah 'feh-ree·ah)*
festival	**el festival** *(ehl feh-stee-'vahl)*
game	**el juego** *(ehl hoo-'eh-goh)*
meeting	**la reunión** *(lah reh-oo-nee-'ohn)*
parade	**el desfile** *(ehl dehs-'fee-leh)*
party	**la fiesta** *(lah fee-'eh-stah)*
performance	**la función** *(lah foon-see-'ohn)*
picnic	**el picnic** *(ehl peek-'neek)*
program	**el programa** *(ehl proh-'grah-mah)*
raffle	**el sorteo** *(ehl sohr-'teh-oh)*
show	**el espectáculo** *(ehl eh-spehk-'tah-koo-loh)*
trip	**el viaje** *(ehl vee-'ah-heh)*

SPORTS
Los deportes *(lohs deh-'pohr-tehs)*

Throughout the U.S., many extracurricular student events and activities include the world of sports. As you read through the following set of vocabulary items, notice how many Spanish words resemble their equivalents in English.

I really like...	Me gusta mucho... *(meh 'goo-stah 'moo-choh...)*
badminton	**el badminton** *(ehl bahd-'meen-tohn)*
baseball	**el béisbol** *(ehl 'beh·ees-bohl)*
basketball	**el básquetbol** *(ehl 'bah-skeht-bohl)*
boxing	**el boxeo** *(ehl bohk-'seh-oh)*

cross country	**la carrera a campo traviesa** *(lah kah-'rreh-rah ah 'kahm-poh trah-vee-'eh-sah)*
football	**el fútbol americano** *(ehl 'foot-bohl ah-meh-ree-'kah-noh)*
golf	**el golf** *(ehl gohlf)*
gymnastics	**la gimnasia** *(lah heem-'nah-see·ah)*
handball	**el frontón de mano** *(ehl frohn-'tohn deh 'mah-noh)*
ice hockey	**el hockey sobre hielo** *(ehl 'hoh-kee 'soh-breh 'yeh-loh)*
lacrosse	**el lacrosse** *(ehl lah-'kroh-seh)*
ping pong	**el pin-pon** *(ehl peen-pohn)*
racquetball	**el frontón con raqueta** *(ehl frohn-'tohn kohn rah-'keh-tah)*
roller hockey	**el hockey en patines** *(ehl 'hoh-kee ehn pah-'tee-nehs)*
soccer	**el fútbol** *(ehl 'foot-bohl)*
softball	**el sófbol** *(ehl 'sohf-bohl)*
tennis	**el tenis** *(ehl 'teh-nees)*
track and field	**el atletisno** *(ehl aht-leh-'tees-moh)*
volleyball	**el vóleibol** *(ehl voh-'leh·ee-bohl)*
water polo	**el polo acuático** *(ehl 'poh-loh ah-'kwah-tee-koh)*
wrestling	**la lucha libre** *(lah 'loo-chah 'lee-breh)*

Not all sporting activities are considered competitive athletics. Many groups meet simply for exercise and fun.

Do you like to...?	**¿Le gusta...?** *(leh 'goo-stah...)*
dance	**bailar** *(bah·ee-'lahr)*
dive	**zambullirse** *(sahm-boo-'yeer-seh)*

fish	**pescar** *(peh-'skahr)*
skate	**patinar** *(pah-tee-'nahr)*
ski	**esquiar** *(eh-skee-'ahr)*
swim	**nadar** *(nah-'dahr)*

Some activities consist of more than one word in Spanish:

Do you want to...?	**¿Quieres...?** *(kee-'eh-rehs...)*
do aerobics	**hacer ejercicios aeróbicos** *(ah-'sehr eh-hehr-'see-see·ohs ah·eh-'roh-bee-kohs)*
go camping	**ir a acampar** *(eer ah ah-kahm-'pahr)*
ride bikes	**montar bicicletas** *(mohn-'tahr bee-see-kleh-tahs)*
sail	**navegar a vela** *(nah-veh-'gahr ah 'veh-lah)*
surf	**correr tabla** *(koh-'rrehr tah-'blah)*

And these sports have their our special word in Spanish:

bowling	**el boliche** *(ehl boh-lee-cheh)*
hiking	**la caminata** *(lah kah-mee-'nah-tah)*
horseback riding	**la equitación** *(lah eh-kee-tah-see-'ohn)*
jogging	**el trote** *(ehl 'troh-teh)*
skin diving	**el buceo** *(ehl boo-'seh-oh)*

MÁS INFORMACIÓN

➤ If you're into sports, learn those words that relate to what you do:

I go to (the)...	**Voy a...** *('voh·ee ah...)*
arena	**el anfiteatro** *(ehl ahn-fee-teh-'ah-troh)*
bowling alley	**la bolera** *(lah boh-'leh-rah)*
court	**la cancha** *(lah 'kahn-chah)*
field	**el campo** *(ehl 'kahm-poh)*
game	**el juego** *(ehl hoo-'eh-goh)*
golf course	**el campo de golf** *(ehl 'kahm-poh deh gohlf)*
gym	**el gimnasio** *(ehl heem-'nah-see·oh)*
match	**el partido** *(ehl pahr-'tee-doh)*
pool	**la piscina** *(lah pee-'see-nah)*

practice	**la práctica** *(lah 'prahk-tee-kah)*
skating rink	**el patinadero** *(ehl pah-tee-nah-'deh-roh)*
stadium	**el estadio** *(ehl eh-'stah-dee·oh)*

➤ This selection helps out every high school educator:

I'm a _____   **Estoy en el** _____ . *(eh-'stoh·ee ehn ehl* _____ *)*

freshman	**primer año** *(pree-'mehr 'ah-nyoh)*
sophomore	**segundo año** *(seh-'goon-doh 'ah-nyoh)*
junior	**tercer año** *(tehr-'sehr 'ah-nyoh)*
senior	**cuarto año** *('kwahr-toh 'ah-nyoh)*

 ## ¿LISTOS PARA PRACTICAR?

Translate and then use in a sentence. Notice the sample:

word	**la palabra** *(lah pah-'lah-brah)*	**Estoy estudiando la lista de palabras.** *(eh-'stoh·ee eh-stoo-dee-'ahn-doh lah 'lee-stah deh pah-'lah-brahs)*
language	_____	_____
sentence	_____	_____
essay	_____	_____

Connect the related vocabulary:

el diseño *(ehl dee-'seh-nyoh)*	**la banda** *(lah 'bahn-dah)*
el balet *(ehl bah-'leh)*	**el dibujo** *(ehl dee-'boo-hoh)*
el tambor *(ehl tahm-'bohr)*	**el baile** *(ehl 'bah·ee-leh)*

List three things you can find in a library:

_____   _____   _____

List three different sports facilities:

_____   _____   _____

List three major sports:

_____ _____ _____

THE FIELD TRIP
El paseo educativo *(ehl pah-'seh-oh eh-doo-kah-'tee-voh)*

One of the most effective ways to instruct students is to actually visit those places that are being discussed in the classroom. If you're filling out permission slips for Spanish-speaking students, be sure everyone knows where they are going.

We're going to visit (the)...   **Vamos a visitar...** *('vah-mohs ah vee-see-'tahr...)*

airport	**el aeropuerto** *(ehl ah·eh-roh-'pwehr-toh)*
bank	**el banco** *(ehl 'bahn-koh)*
bookstore	**la librería** *(lah lee-breh-'ree-ah)*
bus station	**la estación de autobuses** *(lah eh-stah-see-'ohn deh ow-toh-'boo-sehs)*
church	**la iglesia** *(lah ee-'gleh-see·ah)*
college	**la universidad** *(lah oo-nee-vehr-see-'dahd)*
factory	**la fábrica** *(lah 'fah-bree-kah)*
fire department	**el departamento de bomberos** *(ehl deh-pahr-tah-'mehn-toh deh bohm-'beh-rohs)*
hospital	**el hospital** *(ehl oh-spee-'tahl)*
library	**la biblioteca** *(lah bee-blee·oh-'teh-kah)*
market	**el mercado** *(ehl mehr-'kah-doh)*
museum	**el museo** *(ehl moo-'seh-oh)*
office	**la oficina** *(lah oh-fee-'see-nah)*
park	**el parque** *(ehl 'pahr-keh)*
police station	**la estación de policía** *(lah eh-stah-see-'ohn deh poh-lee-'see-ah)*
post office	**el correo** *(ehl koh-'rreh-oh)*
school	**la escuela** *(lah eh-'skweh-lah)*
store	**la tienda** *(lah tee-'ehn-dah)*
theater	**el teatro** *(ehl teh-'ah-troh)*
university	**la universidad** *(lah oo-nee-vehr-see-'dahd)*

Keep practicing. Have you ever taken a group to one of these special places?

We will see (the)...   **Vamos a ver...** *('vah-mohs ah vehr...)*

campgrounds	**el campamento** *(ehl kahm-pah-'mehn-toh)*
cemetery	**el cementerio** *(ehl seh-mehn-'teh-ree·oh)*
city hall	**el municipio** *(ehl moo-nee-'see-pee·oh)*
jail	**la cárcel** *(lah 'kahr-sehl)*
warehouse	**el almacén** *(ehl ahl-mah-'sehn)*
zoo	**el zoológico** *(ehl soh-oh-'loh-hee-koh)*

Now, how about those key words needed to share your travel plans with the parents:

It's...   **Es...** *(ehs...)*

for one night	**para una noche** *('pah-rah 'oo-nah 'noh-cheh)*
for one day	**para un día** *('pah-rah oon 'dee-ah)*
for the whole class	**para toda la clase** *('pah-rah 'toh-dah lah 'klah-seh)*

We need (the)...   **Necesitamos...** *(neh-seh-see-'tah-mohs...)*

bus	**el autobús** *(ehl ow-toh-'boos)*
insurance	**el seguro** *(ehl seh-'goo-roh)*
money	**el dinero** *(ehl dee-'neh-roh)*
permit	**el permiso** *(ehl pehr-'mee-soh)*
signature	**la firma** *(lah 'feer-mah)*
volunteers	**los voluntarios** *(lohs voh-loon-'tah-ree·ohs)*

You can pick up the students tomorrow in front of the bus.

Usted puede recoger a los estudiantes mañana en frente del autobús. *(oo-'stehd 'pweh-deh reh-koh-'hehr ah lohs eh-stoo-dee-'ahn-tehs mah-'nyah-nah ehn 'frehn-teh dehl ow-toh-'boos)*

 MÁS INFORMACIÓN

➤ Head to the outdoors **las afueras** *(lahs ah-'fweh-rahs)*, and your students can learn all kinds of important lessons.

I enjoy (the)...	**Me gusta...** *(meh 'goo-stah)*
beach	**la playa** *(lah 'plah-yah)*
cave	**la cueva** *(lah 'kweh-vah)*
coast	**la costa** *(lah 'koh-stah)*
desert	**el desierto** *(ehl deh-see-'ehr-toh)*
forest	**el bosque** *(ehl 'boh-skeh)*
hill	**el cerro** *(ehl 'seh-rroh)*
jungle	**la selva** *(lah 'sehl-vah)*
lagoon	**la laguna** *(lah lah-'goo-nah)*
lake	**el lago** *(ehl 'lah-goh)*
mountain	**la montaña** *(lah mohn-'tah-nyah)*
ocean	**el océano** *(ehl oh-'seh-ah-noh)*
pond	**la charca** *(lah 'chahr-kah)*
river	**el río** *(ehl 'ree-oh)*
sea	**el mar** *(ehl mahr)*
stream	**el arroyo** *(ehl ah-'rroh-yoh)*
valley	**el valle** *(ehl 'vah-yeh)*

CONFLICTOS CULTURALES

Many cultures are somewhat suspicious about after-school activities. If you have new immigrants in school, they may refuse to participate in extracurricular events, or their parents may deny them permission to do so. Not only do many youngsters have responsibilities at home, but many families worry about their children's safety in a foreign land. Be prepared to face parental and student fears and lack of trust.

THE 4-H CLUB
El Club de 4-H *(ehl kloob deh 'kwah-troh 'ah-cheh)*

4-H Clubs and similar community organizations sometimes offer programs or events involving the care and preservation of local domestic animals. Not only do the following words help out club leaders, but they're also valuable to any educator in a science program. Here's a tip—instead of practicing each word you see, first focus on those items that you generally use the most:

They feed (the)...	**Alimentan...** *(ah-lee-'mehn-tahn...)*
They raise (the)...	**Crian...** *('kree-ahn)*
They have (the)...	**Tienen...** *(tee-'eh-nehn)*

bird	**el pájaro** *(ehl 'pah-hah-roh)*
cat	**el gato** *(ehl 'gah-toh)*
chicken	**la gallina** *(lah gah-'yee-nah)*
cow	**la vaca** *(lah 'vah-kah)*
dog	**el perro** *(ehl 'peh-rroh)*
duck	**el pato** *(ehl 'pah-toh)*
fish	**el pez** *(ehl pehs)*
goat	**el chivo** *(ehl 'chee-voh)*
hamster	**el hámster** *(ehl 'ahm-stehr)*
horse	**el caballo** *(ehl kah-'bah-yoh)*
pig	**el cerdo** *(ehl 'sehr-doh)*
rabbit	**el conejo** *(ehl koh-'neh-hoh)*
sheep	**la oveja** *(lah oh-'veh-hah)*
turtle	**la tortuga** *(lah tohr-'too-gah)*

MÁS INFORMACIÓN

➤ Students in rural areas often hold activities at one of these locations:

Let's go to (the)...	**Vamos a...** *('vah-mohs ah...)*

barn	**el establo** *(ehl eh-'stah-bloh)*
dairy	**la lechería** *(lah leh-cheh-'ree-ah)*
farm	**la granja** *(lah 'grahn-hoh)*
ranch	**el rancho** *(ehl 'rahn-choh)*

➤ Watch out for these animals who live in the wild:

beaver	**el castor** *(ehl kah-'stohr)*
fox	**el zorro** *(ehl 'soh-rroh)*
lizard	**la lagartija** *(lah lah-gahr-'tee-hah)*
raccoon	**el mapache** *(ehl mah-'pah-cheh)*
skunk	**el zorrino** *(ehl soh-'rree-noh)*
snake	**la culebra** *(lah koo-'leh-brah)*
wolf	**el lobo** *(ehl 'loh-boh)*

So far we have discovered that in order to converse about educational activities, it was necessary to make changes to the basic verb. Notice the difference in meanings here:

to work	**Trabajar** *(trah-bah-'hahr)*
I'm working.	**Estoy trabajando.**
	(eh-'stoh·ee trah-bah-'hahn-doh)
I work.	**Trabajo.** *(trah-'bah-hoh)*
I'm going to work.	**Voy a trabajar.** *('voh·ee ah trah-bah-'hahr)*

Now, check out this new way to refer to future actions. Just add new endings to the infinitive, as shown. Look at this regular **-ar** verb:

I will work	**Trabajaré** *(trah-bah-hah-'reh)*
You (informal) will work	**Trabajarás** *(trah-bah-hah-'rahs)*
You, He, She will work	**Trabajará** *(trah-bah-hah-'rah)*
You (pl.), They will work	**Trabajarán** *(trah-bah-hah-'rahn)*
We will work	**Trabajaremos** *(trah-bah-hah-'reh-mohs)*

The same patterns hold true for the **-er** and **-ir** verbs:

to eat (**comer**) *(koh-'mehr)*	I'll eat.	**Comeré** *(koh-meh-'reh)*
to live (**vivir**) *(vee-'veer)*	He'll live.	**Vivirá** *(vee-vee-'rah)*
to run (**correr**) *(koh-'rrehr)*	We'll run.	**Correremos**
		(koh-rreh-'reh-mohs)

➤ Beware of those irregular verbs in the future tense! Here are a few examples:

I'll have a job.	**Tendré un trabajo.**
	(tehn-'dreh oon trah-'bah-hoh)
They'll come soon.	**Vendrán luego.**
	(vehn-'drahn 'lweh-goh)

She'll leave at two.	**Saldrá a las dos.** *(sahl-'drah ah lahs dohs)*	

➤ Since you already know how to say "going to" in Spanish, there are actually two ways to talk about the future:

to eat **comer** *(koh-'mehr)*	I'm going to eat. **Voy a comer.** *('voh-ee ah koh-'mehr)*	I will eat. **Comeré.** *(koh-meh-'reh)*
to wait **esperar** *(eh-speh-'rahr)*	They're going to wait. **Van a esperar.** *('vahn ah eh-speh-'rahr)*	They will wait. **Esperarán.** *(eh-speh-rah-'rahn)*

¡ÓRDENES!

Negative formal commands are easy. Just say **no**:

Come!	**¡Venga!** *('vehn-gah)*
Don't come!	**¡No venga!** *('noh 'vehn-gah)*
Write, you guys!	**¡Escriban!** *(eh-'skree-bahn)*
Don't write, you guys!	**¡No escriban!** *(noh eh-'skree-bahn)*

And notice how the verbs with **se** change in word order:

Get up!	**¡Levántese!** *(leh-'vahn-teh-seh)*
Don't get up!	**¡No se levante!** *(noh seh leh-'vahn-teh)*
Sit down, you guys!	**¡Siéntense!** *(see-'ehn-tehn-seh)*
Don't sit down, you guys!	**¡No se sienten!** *(noh seh see-'ehn-tehn)*

As for the informal (**tú**) commands, here's what happens. Both the regular and irregular forms shift to a formal-looking command, but with an **-s** at the end:

Read!	**¡Lee!** *('leh-eh)*
Don't read!	**¡No leas!** *(noh 'leh-ahs)*

Go!	**¡Ve!** *(veh)*
Don't go!	**¡No vayas!** *(noh 'vah-yahs)*
Stay!	**¡Quédate!** *('keh-dah-teh)*
Don't stay!	**¡No te quedes!** *(noh teh 'keh-dehs)*

¿LISTOS PARA PRACTICAR?

Follow this sample set, change the other verbs in the same manner, and add some vocabulary:

llegar *(yeh-'gahr)*

Está llegando ahora.
(eh-'stah yeh-'gahn-doh ah-'oh-rah)
Llega todos los días.
('yeh-gah 'toh-dohs lohs 'dee-ahs)
Llegará mañana.
(yeh-gah-'rah mah-'nyah-nah)

estudiar *(eh-stoo-dee-'ahr)*

Está estudiando ahora. *(eh-'stah eh-stoo-dee-'ahn-doh ah-'oh-rah)*

_____

_____

correr *(koh-'rrehr)*

_____

_____

_____

explicar *(ehks-plee-'kahr)*

_____

_____

_____

Select the word that fits best:

el gato, el caballo, el pollo *(ehl 'gah-toh, ehl kah-'bah-yoh, ehl 'poh-yoh)*

_____ **es un pájaro.** *(_____ ehs oon 'pah-hah-roh)*

_____ **no le gusta al perro.** *(_____ noh leh 'goo-stah ahl 'peh-rroh)*

_____ **está comiendo en el establo.** *(_____ eh-'stah koh-mee-'ehn-*
doh ehn ehl eh-'stah-bloh)

Connect the words that relate:

la policía *(lah poh-lee-'see-ah)*   **la costa** *(lah 'koh-stah)*
la playa *(lah 'plah-yah)*   **la cárcel** *(lah 'kahr-sehl)*
el almacén *(ehl ahl-mah-'sehn)*   **la fábrica** *(lah 'fah-bree-kah)*

 ## CONFLICTOS CULTURALES

Students from Spanish-speaking countries are often familiar with those extracurricular activities that are offered at schools in their homeland. As a class assignment, ask them to share with other classmates any details about their favorite hobbies, sports, and student organizations.

CHAPTER FIVE
Capítulo Cinco
(kah-'pee-too-loh 'seen-koh)

DISCIPLINE
La disciplina
(lah dee-see-'plee-nah)

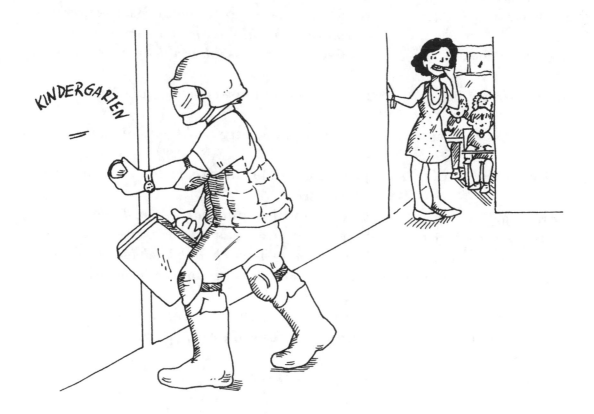

SCHOOL RULES

Las reglas de la escuela *(lahs 'reh-glahs deh lah eh-'skweh-lah)*

Regarding student discipline, some settings may require nothing more than personal contracts, while others may demand strictly enforced regulations. For younger students, school rules should be clear and concise, so that they can remember the words more easily. Here are a few general guidelines for conduct that can be presented at the grammar school to Spanish-speaking students and their parents:

Students need to...	**Los estudiantes necesitan...** *(lohs eh-stoo-dee-'ahn-tehs neh-seh-'see-tahn...)*
attend school	**asistir a la escuela** *(ah-see-'steer ah lah eh-'skweh-lah)*
arrive on time	**llegar a tiempo** *(yeh-'gahr ah tee-'ehm-poh)*
behave well	**portarse bien** *(pohr-'tahr-seh 'bee·ehn)*
do their assignments	**hacer sus tareas** *(ah-'sehr soos tah-'reh-ahs)*
study for tests	**estudiar para los exámenes** *(eh-stoo-dee-'ahr 'pah-rah lohs ehk-'sah-meh-nehs)*
obey the rules	**obedecer las reglas** *(oh-beh-deh-'sehr lahs 'reh-glahs)*
raise their hands	**levantar las manos** *(leh-vahn-'tahr lahs 'mah-nohs)*
listen to the teacher	**escuchar al maestro** *(eh-skoo-'chahr ahl mah-'eh-stroh)*
participate in class	**participar en la clase** *(pahr-tee-see-'pahr ehn lah 'klah-seh)*
bring supplies	**traer sus útiles** *(trah-'ehr soos 'oo-tee-lehs)*
respect school property	**respetar la propiedad de la escuela** *(reh-speh-'tahr lah proh-pee-eh-'dahd deh lah eh-'skweh-lah)*
wear appropriate clothing	**ponerse ropa apropiada** *(poh-'nehr-seh 'roh-pah ah-proh-pee-'ah-dah)*
clean up their mess	**limpiar su basura** *(leem-pee-'ahr soo bah-'soo-rah)*
take care of their things	**cuidar sus cosas** *(kwee-'dahr soos 'koh-sahs)*

Now, let everyone know what they're <u>not</u> allowed to do:

No...	No...
bothering others	**molestar a los demás** *(moh-leh-'stahr ah lohs deh-'mahs)*
cursing	**decir groserías** *(deh-'seer groh-seh-'ree-ahs)*
cutting class	**faltar a la clase** *(fahl-'tahr ah lah 'klah-seh)*
forgetting pencil and paper	**olvidar lápiz y papel** *(ohl-vee-'dahr 'lah-pees ee pah-'pehl)*
gum chewing	**masticar chicle** *(mah-stee-'kahr 'chee-kleh)*
littering	**tirar basura** *(tee-'rahr bah-'soo-rah)*
loitering	**holgazanear** *(ohl-gah-sah-neh-'ahr)*
losing books	**perder los libros** *(pehr-'dehr lohs 'lee-brohs)*
making obscene gestures	**hacer señales groseras** *(ah-'sehr seh-'nyah-lehs groh-'seh-rahs)*
smoking	**fumar** *(foo-'mahr)*
threatening	**amenazar** *(ah-meh-nah-'sahr)*
throwing things	**tirar cosas** *(tee-'rahr 'koh-sahs)*
whistling	**silbar** *(seel-'bahr)*

MÁS INFORMACIÓN

➤ Remember these commands from grammar school?

No...	No...
fighting	**pelear** *(peh-leh-'ahr)*
grabbing	**agarrar** *(ah-gah-'rrahr)*
hitting	**pegar** *(peh-'gahr)*
kicking	**patear** *(pah-teh-'ahr)*
pulling	**jalar** *(hah-'lahr)*
pushing	**empujar** *(ehm-poo-'hahr)*
spitting	**escupir** *(eh-skoo-'peer)*
tripping	**tropezar** *(troh-peh-'sahr)*
wrestling	**luchar** *(loo-'chahr)*
yelling	**gritar** *(gree-'tahr)*

DISCIPLINE FOR TEENS
La disciplina para los adolescentes
(lah dee-see-'plee-nah 'pah-rah lohs ah-doh-leh-'sehn-tehs)

For older students, you may want to consider using some of the following terms to explain the rules and regulations:

Let's talk about (the)...	**Vamos a hablar de...** *('vah-mohs ah ah-'blahr deh...)*
conduct	**la conducta** *(lah kohn-'dook-tah)*
consequences	**las consecuencias** *(lahs kohn-seh-'kwehn-see·ahs)*
control	**el control** *(ehl kohn-'trohl)*
responsibility	**la responsabilidad** *(lah reh-spohn-sah-bee-lee-'dahd)*
right	**el derecho** *(ehl deh-'reh-choh)*
maturity	**la madurez** *(lah mah-doo-'rehs)*
Please do not bring...	**Favor de no traer...** *(fah-'vohr deh noh trah-'ehr)*
audiocassettes	**los audiocasetes** *(lohs ow-dee-oh-kah-'seh-tehs)*
CDs	**los discos compactos** *(lohs 'dee-skohs kohm-'pahk-tohs)*
cell phones	**los teléfonos celulares** *(lohs teh-'leh-foh-nohs seh-loo-'lah-rehs)*
chains	**las cadenas** *(lahs kah-'deh-nahs)*
fireworks	**los fuegos artificiales** *(lohs 'fweh-gohs ahr-tee-fee-see-'ah-lehs)*
knives	**los cuchillos** *(lohs koo-'chee-yohs)*
lighters	**los encendedores** *(lohs ehn-sehn-deh-'doh-rehs)*
magazines	**las revistas** *(lahs reh-'vee-stahs)*
pets	**las mascotas** *(lahs mah-'skoh-tahs)*
radios	**los radios** *(lohs 'rah-dee·ohs)*
razors	**las navajas** *(lahs nah-'vah-hahs)*
stereos	**los estéreos** *(lohs eh-'steh-reh-ohs)*
tobacco	**el tabaco** *(ehl tah-'bah-koh)*
toys	**los juguetes** *(lohs hoo-'geh-tehs)*

They are...	**Son...** *(sohn...)*
dangerous	**peligrosos** *(peh-lee-'groh-sohs)*
disruptive	**desordenadores** *(deh-'sohr-deh-nah-doh-rehs)*
illegal	**ilegales** *(ee-leh-'gah-lehs)*

They are not...	**No son...** *(noh sohn...)*
appropriate	**apropiados** *(ah-proh-pee-'ah-dohs)*
legal	**legales** *(leh-'gah-lehs)*
necessary	**necesarios** *(neh-seh-'sah-ree·ohs)*
permitted	**permitidos** *(pehr-mee-'tee-dohs)*
safe	**seguros** *(seh-'goo-rohs)*

For many schools, even these things are considered disruptive:

Give me (the)...	**Dame...** *('dah-meh...)*
badges	**las chapas** *(lahs 'chah-pahs)*
hats	**los sombreros** *(lohs sohm-'breh-rohs)*
jewelry	**las joyas** *(lahs 'hoh-yahs)*
makeup	**el maquillaje** *(ehl mah-kee-'yah-heh)*
markers	**los marcadores** *(lohs mahr-kah-'doh-rehs)*
skateboards	**las patinetas** *(lahs pah-tee-'neh-tahs)*
skates	**los patines** *(lohs pah-'tee-nehs)*
sunglasses	**los lentes del sol** *(lohs 'lehn-tehs dehl sohl)*

MÁS INFORMACIÓN

➤ This is what you say when things get out of hand:

We are going to...	**Vamos a...** *('vah-mohs ah...)*
call the police	**llamar a la policía** *(yah-'mahr ah lah poh-lee-'see-ah)*
search your locker	**registrar tu armario** *(reh-hee-'strahr too ahr-'mah-ree·oh)*
talk to the witnesses	**hablar con los testigos** *(ah-'blahr kohn lohs teh-'stee-gohs)*

➤ And always give reminders to students who speak only Spanish:

Do not forget (the)...	**No olvidar...** *(noh ohl-vee-'dahr...)*
application	**la solicitud** *(lah soh-lee-see-'tood)*
assignment	**la tarea** *(lah tah-'reh-ah)*
card	**la tarjeta** *(lah tahr-'heh-tah)*
form	**el formulario** *(ehl fohr-moo-'lah-ree·oh)*
lock	**el candado** *(ehl kahn-'dah-doh)*
pass	**el pase** *(ehl 'pah-seh)*
signed note	**la notificación firmada** *(lah noh-tee-fee-kah-see-'ohn feer-'mah-dah)*
ticket	**el boleto** *(ehl boh-'leh-toh)*
written excuse	**la excusa escrita** *(lah ehk-'skoo-sah eh-'skree-tah)*

➤ Pick up on new terms that relate to your concern:

curfew	**el toque de queda** *(ehl 'toh-keh deh 'keh-dah)*
truant	**el estudiante que no va a sus clases** *(ehl eh-stoo-dee-'ahn-teh keh noh vah ah soos 'klah-sehs)*

IT'S A PROBLEM
Es un problema *(ehs oon proh-'bleh-mah)*

More and more educational institutions face kids with severe behavior problems. Do any of these words sound familiar?

He has (the)...	**Tiene...** *(tee-'eh-neh...)*
alcohol	**el alcohol** *(ehl ahl-koh-'ohl)*
contraband	**el contrabando** *(ehl kohn-trah-'bahn-doh)*
drug	**la droga** *(lah 'droh-gah)*
explosive	**el explosivo** *(ehl ehk-sploh-'see-voh)*
firearm	**el arma de fuego** *(ehl 'ahr-mah deh 'fweh-goh)*

It's...	**Es...** *(ehs...)*
cheating	**el fraude** *(ehl 'frow-deh)*
extortion	**la extorsión** *(lah ehk-stohr-see-'ohn)*

gambling	**el juego por dinero** *(ehl 'hweh-goh pohr dee-'neh-roh)*
graffiti	**el grafiti** *(ehl grah-'fee-tee)*
harassment	**el acosamiento** *(ehl ah-koh-sah-mee-'ehn-toh)*
trespassing	**la intrusión** *(ah een-troo-see-'ohn)*
They are...each other!	**¡Se están...!** *(seh eh-'stahn...)*
hugging	**abrazando** *(ah-brah-'sahn-doh)*
kissing	**besando** *(beh-'sahn-doh)*
touching	**tocando** *(toh-'kahn-doh)*
She is...!	**¡Ella está...!** *('eh-yah eh-'stah...)*
carrying a dangerous object	**llevando un objeto peligroso** *(yeh-'vahn-doh oon ohb-'heh-toh peh-lee-'groh-soh)*
flashing gang signs	**mostrando las señas de la pandilla** *(moh-'strahn-doh lahs 'seh-nyahs deh lah pahn-'dee-yah)*
threatening the teacher	**amenazando al maestro** *(ah-meh-nah-'sahn-doh ahl mah-'eh-stroh)*

MÁS INFORMACIÓN

➤ Be extra careful about discussing some activities:

to gossip	**chismear** *(chees-meh-'ahr)*
to lie	**mentir** *(mehn-'teer)*
to steal	**robar** *(roh-'bahr)*

➤ Not all disruptive items have to be translated:

el Walkman
el Nintendo
el beeper

CITIZENSHIP GRADES

Las notas de comportamiento *(lahs 'noh-tahs deh kohm-pohr-tah-mee-'ehn-toh)*

Classroom regulations differ from place to place, but these lists deal with the basics:

You have a problem with...	**Tiene problema con...** *(tee-'eh-neh proh-'bleh-mah kohn...)*
defiance of authority	**oposición a la autoridad** *(oh-poh-see-see-'ohn ah lah ow-toh-ree-'dahd)*
disruptive behavior	**desorden** *(dehs-'ohr-dehn)*
incomplete assignments	**tareas incompletas** *(tah-'reh-ahs een-kohm-'pleh-tahs)*
poor work habits	**malos hábitos de estudio** *('mah-lohs 'ah-bee-tohs deh eh-'stoo-dee·oh)*
tardiness and attendance	**tardanza y asistencia** *(tahr-'dahn-sah ee ah-see-'stehn-see·ah)*
His/Her behavior is...	**Su comportamiento es...** *(soo kohm-pohr-tah-mee-'ehn-toh ehs...)*
average	**promedio** *(proh-'meh-dee·oh)*
better	**mejor** *(meh-'hohr)*
outstanding	**destacado** *(deh-stah-'kah-doh)*
satisfactory	**satisfactorio** *(sah-tees-fahk-'toh-ree·oh)*
unsatisfactory	**malo** *('mah-loh)*
worse	**peor** *(peh-'ohr)*

Having Spanish-speaking students, rules should be posted in both languages for everyone to see:

No...in class.	**No...en la clase.** *(noh...ehn lah 'klah-seh)*
drinking	**beber** *(beh-'behr)*
eating	**comer** *(koh-'mehr)*
playing	**jugar** *(hoo-'gahr)*
running	**correr** *(koh-'rrehr)*
sleeping	**dormir** *(dohr-'meer)*
Please do not...	**Favor de no...** *(fah-'vohr deh noh...)*
leave your desk	**dejar su escritorio** *(deh-'hahr soo eh-skree-'toh-ree·oh)*
pass notes	**pasar notas** *(pah-'sahr 'noh-tahs)*
copy someone else's assignment	**copiar la tarea de otra persona** *(koh-pee-'ahr lah tah-'reh-ah deh 'oh-trah pehr-'soh-nah)*
speak without permission	**hablar sin permiso** *(ah-'blahr seen pehr-'mee-soh)*
write in the textbook	**escribir en el libro de texto** *(eh-skree-'beer ehn ehl 'lee-broh deh 'tehks-toh)*
play with the lights	**jugar con las luces** *(hoo-'gahr kohn lahs 'loo-sehs)*
touch the fire alarm	**tocar la alarma de fuego** *(toh-'kahr lah ah-'lahr-mah deh 'fweh-goh)*
Use the _____, please.	**Por favor, use _____.** *(pohr fah-'vohr, 'oo-seh_____)*
trash can	**el bote de basura** *(ehl 'boh-teh deh bah-'soo-rah)*
pencil sharpener	**el sacapuntas** *(ehl sah-kah-'poon-tahs)*
stapler	**la engrapadora** *(lah ehn-grah-pah-'doh-rah)*

MÁS INFORMACIÓN

➤ You need to...	**Necesitas...** *(neh-seh-'see-tahs...)*
call your home	**llamar a tu casa** *(yah-'mahr ah too 'kah-sah)*
talk to the nurse	**hablar con la enfermera** *(ah-'blahr kohn lah ehn-fehr-'meh-rah)*

go to the bathroom	**ir al baño** (eer ahl 'bah-nyoh)
buy a meal ticket	**comprar un boleto de comida** (kohm-'prahr oon boh-'leh-toh deh koh-'mee-dah)
wear the uniform	**ponerte el uniforme** (poh-'nehr-teh ehl oo-nee-'fohr-meh)
use a locker	**usar un armario** (oo-'sahr oon ahr-'mah-ree·oh)

➤ Now ask your students about their homework. Notice the past tense verb form:

Did you turn it in?	**¿Lo entregaste?** (loh ehn-treh-'gah-steh)
Did you lose it?	**¿Lo pediste?** (loh peh-'dee-steh)
Did you finish it?	**¿Lo terminaste?** (loh tehr-mee-'nah-steh)
Did you do it?	**¿Lo hiciste?** (loh loh ee-'see-steh)
Did you understand it?	**¿Lo entendiste?** (loh ehn-tehn-'dee-steh)

➤ Speaking of homework, listen closely as the student tries to explain:

It's...	**Está...** (eh-'stah...)
lost	**perdido** (pehr-'dee-doh)
at home	**en casa** (ehn 'kah-sah)
incomplete	**incompleto** (een-kohm-'pleh-toh)

THE CONTRACT
El contrato (ehl kohn-'trah-toh)

It's time to set up disciplinary contracts with some of the students. Parent or guardian signatures are required, so you explain each procedure in Spanish:

This is for the safety of the student.
Esto es para la seguridad del estudiante. ('eh-stoh ehs 'pah-rah lah seh-goo-ree-'dahd dehl eh-stoo-dee-'ahn-teh)

The student must follow the code of behavior.
El estudiante tiene que cumplir con el código de comportamiento. (ehl eh-stoo-dee-'ahn-teh tee-'eh-neh keh koom-'pleer kohn ehl 'koh-dee-goh deh kohm-pohr-tah-mee-'ehn-toh)

They are responsible for their actions.
Son responsables de sus acciones. *(sohn reh-spohn-'sah-blehs deh soos ahk-see-'oh-nehs)*

It is a school-wide progressive discipline plan.
Es un plan de disciplina progresiva para toda la escuela. *(ehs oon plahn deh dee-see-'plee-nah proh-greh-'see-vah 'pah-rah 'toh-dah lah eh-'skweh-lah)*

Please read the contract and sign your name.
Favor de leer el contrato y firmar su nombre. *(fah-'vohr deh leh-'ehr ehl kohn-'trah-toh ee feer-'mahr soo 'nohm-breh)*

Make a comment or two about the agreement:

It's...   **Es...** *(ehs...)*

confidential   **confidencial** *(kohn-fee-dehn-see-'ahl)*
effective now   **efectivo ahora** *(eh-fehk-'tee-voh ah-'oh-rah)*
serious   **serio** *('seh-ree·oh)*

It includes...   **Este incluye...** *('eh-steh een-'kloo-yeh...)*

before and after school activities   **actividades antes y después de la escuela**
                                           (lahs ahk-tee-vee-'dah-dehs 'ahn-tehs ee deh-'spwehs deh lah eh-'skweh-lah)
all school events   **todos los eventos escolares** *('toh-dohs lohs eh-'vehn-tohs eh-skoh-'lah-rehs)*
the rest of the year   **el resto del año** *(ehl 'reh-stoh dehl 'ah-nyoh)*

MÁS INFORMACIÓN

➤ Check out this important pattern:

It's a _____ slip.   **Es un formulario de _____ .** *(ehs oon fohr-moo-'lah-ree·oh deh _____)*

attendance   **asistencia** *(ah-see-'stehn-see·ah)*
call   **llamadas** *(yah-'mah-dahs)*

163

discipline	**disciplina** *(dee-see-'plee-nah)*
health	**salud** *(sah-'lood)*
permission	**permiso** *(pehr-'mee-soh)*
tardiness	**tardanza** *(tahr-'dahn-sah)*
transfer	**transferencia** *(trahns-feh-'rehn-see·ah)*
visitors	**visitantes** *(vee-see-'tahn-tehs)*

➤ Has every concern been addressed?

What do you know about (the) ...?	**¿Qué sabes tú de ...?** *(keh 'sah-behs too deh...)*
insubordination	**la insubordinación** *(lah een-soob-ohr-dee-nah-see-'ohn)*
lack of cooperation	**la falta de cooperación** *(lah 'fahl-tah deh koh-oh-peh-rah-see-'ohn)*
misconduct	**la mala conducta** *(lah 'mah-lah kohn-'dook-tah)*
procrastination	**el incumplimiento a tiempo** *(ehl een-koom-plee-mee-'ehn-toh ah tee-'ehm-poh)*
disturbance	**el tumulto** *(ehl too-'mool-toh)*
confrontation	**la confrontación** *(lah kohn-frohn-tah-see-'ohn)*

¿LISTOS PARA PRACTICAR?

Name in Spanish five student actions that would be considered unacceptable at most high schools:

_____ _____ _____ _____ _____

Name three items that would be considered illegal on a school campus:

_____ _____ _____

Finish the sentences with the best words that fit:

los formularios, los sombreros, las consecuencias *(lohs fohr-moo-'lah-ree·ohs, lohs sohm-'breh-rohs, lahs kohn-seh-'kwehn-see·ahs)*

No traigan _____ *(noh 'trah·ee-gahn _____)*
Escribe en _____ *(eh-skree-beh ehn _____)*

¿Entiendes _____ ? *(ehn-tee-'ehn-dehs _____)*

Translate:

outstanding   _____

better   _____

worse   _____

THE CONSEQUENCES

Las consecuencias *(lahs kohn-seh-'kwehn-see·ahs)*

Along with student rights and responsibilities come well-defined consequences for bad behavior. Each situation varies, so why not make statements using this vocabulary based upon your specific situation:

He is...	**El es...** *(ehl ehs)*
careless	**descuidado** *(dehs-kwee-'dah-doh)*
critical	**crítico** *('kree-tee-koh)*
cruel	**cruel** *(kroo-'ehl)*
dishonest	**deshonesto** *(dehs-oh-'neh-stoh)*
disrespectful	**irrespetuoso** *(ee-reh-speh-too-'oh-soh)*
incompetent	**incompetente** *(een-kohm-peh-'tehn-teh)*
negligent	**negligente** *(nehg-lee-'hehn-teh)*
rude	**grosero** *(groh-'seh-roh)*
sarcastic	**sarcástico** *(sahr-'kah-stee-koh)*

He needs...	**Necesita...** *(neh-seh-'see-tah...)*
detention	**la detención** *(lah deh-tehn-see-'ohn)*
discipline	**la disciplina** *(lah dee-see-'plee-nah)*
expulsion	**la expulsión** *(lah ehk-spool-see-'ohn)*
formal report	**el reporte formal** *(ehl reh-'pohr-teh fohr-'mahl)*
home phone call	**la llamada a la casa** *(lah yah-'mah-dah ah lah 'kah-sah)*
juvenile court	**el tribunal de menores** *(ehl tree-boo-'nahl deh meh-'noh-rehs)*

legal contract	**el contrato legal** *(ehl kohn-'trah-toh leh-'gahl)*
official transfer	**la transferencia oficial** *(lah trahns-feh-'rehn-see·ah oh-fee-see-'ahl)*
parent conference	**la conferencia con los padres** *(lah kohn-feh-'rehn-see·ah kohn lohs 'pah-drehs)*
personal intervention	**la intervención personal** *(lah een-tehr-vehn-see-'ohn pehr-soh-'nahl)*
punishment	**el castigo** *(ehl kah-'stee-goh)*
reprimand	**la reprensión** *(lah reh-prehn-see-'ohn)*
suspension	**la suspensión** *(lah soo-spehn-see-'ohn)*
teacher referral	**la referencia del maestro** *(lah reh-feh-'rehn-see·ah dehl mah-'eh-stroh)*
warning	**la advertencia** *(lah ahd-vehr-'tehn-see·ah)*

While you're talking, interject a couple of these terms, also:

| It's (the)... | **Es...** *(ehs...)* |

attitude	**la actitud** *(lah ahk-tee-'tood)*
care	**el cuidado** *(ehl kwee-'dah-doh)*
change	**el cambio** *(ehl 'kahm-bee·oh)*
conflict	**el conflicto** *(ehl kohn-'fleek-toh)*
consent	**el consentimiento** *(ehl kohn-sehn-tee-mee-'ehn-toh)*
notice	**el aviso** *(ehl ah-'vee-soh)*
privilege	**el privilegio** *(ehl pree-vee-'leh-hee·oh)*
supervision	**la supervisión** *(lah soo-pehr-vee-see-'ohn)*
violation	**la violación** *(lah vee-oh-lah-see-'ohn)*
violence	**la violencia** *(lah vee-oh-'lehn-see·ah)*

MÁS INFORMACIÓN

➤ Discipline demands action. You may want to learn these verbs soon:

confiscate	**confiscar**	<u>**Confiscamos las drogas.**</u> *(kohn-fee-'skah-mohs lahs 'droh-gahs)*
expel	**expulsar** *(ehks-pool-'sahr)*	_____
assign	**asignar** *(ah-seeg-'nahr)*	_____

| protect | **proteger** (proh-teh-'hehr) | _____ |
| deserve | **merecer** (meh-reh-'sehr) | _____ |

HOME PHONE CALLS
Las llamadas a la casa (lahs yah-'mah-dahs ah lah 'kah-sah)

To maintain discipline, keep in touch with each student's family. Begin with questions about their telephone system:

Do you have (the)...?	**¿Tienes...?** (tee-'eh-nehs)
answering machine	**el contestador telefónico** (ehl kohn-teh-stah-'dohr teh-leh-'foh-nee-koh)
answering service	**el servicio de respuesta telefónica** (ehl sehr-'vee-see·oh deh reh-'spweh-stah teh-leh-'foh-nee-kah)
area code	**el código de área** (ehl 'koh-dee-goh deh 'ah-reh-ah)
beeper	**el bíper** (ehl 'bee-pehr)
cellular phone	**el teléfono celular** (ehl teh-'leh-foh-noh seh-loo-'lahr)
e-mail	**el correo electrónico** (ehl koh-'rreh-oh eh-lehk-'troh-nee-koh)
extension	**la extensión** (lah ehks-tehn-see-'ohn)
fax	**el fax** (ehl fahks)

Now, practice the following phrases. Making phone calls in Spanish is a tough task, but with the proper one-liners in hand, you at least will have a chance of getting or giving basic information to parents who only speak Spanish.

Hello, is _____ there?
¿Aló, está _____ ?
(ah-'loh, eh-'stah _____)

May I speak to _____ ?
¿Puedo hablar con _____ ?
(pweh-doh ah-'blahr kohn _____)

I'm calling about _____ .
Estoy llamando acerca de _____ .
(eh-'stoh-ee yah-'mahn-doh ah-'sehr-kah deh _____)

I'll transfer you to _____ .
Le voy a transferir a _____ .
(leh 'voh·ee ah trahns-feh-'reer ah _____)

Tell him/her that _____ .
Dígale que _____ .
('dee-gah-leh keh _____)

More slowly, please.
Más despacio, por favor.
(mahs deh-'spah-see·oh, pohr fah-'vohr)

Wait a moment, please.
Espere un momento, por favor.
(eh-'speh-reh oon moh-'mehn-toh, pohr fah-'vohr)

Please, it's very urgent.
Por favor, es muy urgente.
(pohr fah-'vohr, ehs 'moo·ee oor-'hehn-teh)

Your number, please.
Su número, por favor.
(soo 'noo-meh-'roh, pohr fah-'vohr)

Could you please repeat that?
¿Puede repetirlo, por favor?
('pweh-deh reh-peh-'teer-loh, pohr fah-'vohr)

One method is to break your one-liners into vocabulary-specific sets:

Can you call later?
¿Puede llamar más tarde?
('pweh-deh yah-'mahr mahs 'tahr-deh)

He/She will call you later.
El/ella llamará más tarde.
(ehl/'eh-yah yah-mah-'rah mahs 'tahr-deh)

Do you want to leave a message?
¿Quiere dejar un recado?
(kee-'eh-reh deh-'hahr oon reh-'kah-doh)

I'd like to leave a message
Quisiera dejar un recado.
(kee-see-'eh-rah deh-'hahr oon reh-'kah-doh)

I will give him/her your message.
Le voy a dejar su mensaje.
(leh 'voh·ee ah deh-'hahr soo mehn-'sah-heh)

Is it long distance?
¿Es de larga distancia?
(ehs deh 'lahr-gah dee-'stahn-see·ah)

Is it a local call?
¿Es una llamada local?
(ehs 'oo-nah yah-'mah-dah loh-'kahl)

Is it a collect call?
¿Es una llamada a cobro revertido?
(ehs 'oo-nah yah-'mah-dah ah 'koh-broh reh-vehr-'tee-doh)

In any language, using the phone can be frustrating. Here are a few examples:

He isn't here.
No está aquí.
(noh eh-'stah ah-'kee)

She can't come to the phone.
No puede contestar la llamada.
(noh 'pweh-deh kohn-teh-'stahr lah yah-'mah-dah)

He is busy.
Está ocupado.
(eh-'stah oh-koo-'pah-doh)

Is this the correct number?
¿Es el número correcto?
(ehs ehl 'noo-meh-roh koh-'rrehk-toh)

I have the wrong number.
Tengo el número equivocado.
('tehn-goh ehl 'noo-meh-roh eh-kee-voh-'kah-doh)

You have the wrong number.
Tiene el número equivocado.
(tee-'eh-neh ehl 'noo-meh-roh eh-kee-voh-'kah-doh)

The number has been changed.
Se ha cambiado el número.
(seh ah kahm-bee-'ah-doh ehl 'noo-meh-roh)

The line is bad.
La línea está mala.
(lah 'lee-neh-ah eh-'stah 'mah-lah)

The line is busy.
La línea está ocupada.
(lah 'lee-neh-ah eh-'stah oh-koo-'pah-dah)

The line is disconnected.
La línea está desconectada.
(lah 'lee-neh-ah eh-'stah dehs-koh-nehk-'tah-dah)

Now direct others how to handle the calls:

Dial this number.
Marque este número.
('mahr-keh 'eh-steh 'noo-meh-roh)

Press this number.
Oprima este número.
(oh-'pree-mah 'eh-steh 'noo-meh-roh)

Ask for this number.
Pida este número.
('pee-dah 'eh-steh 'noo-meh-roh)

Wait for the tone.
Espere por el tono.
(eh-'speh-reh pohr ehl 'toh-noh)

Hang up the phone.
Cuelgue el teléfono.
('kwehl-geh ehl teh-'leh-foh-noh)

BICYCLE RULES
Las reglas para montar bicicleta
(lahs 'reh-glahs 'pah-rah mohn-'tahr bee-see-'kleh-tah)

Let's read through some of the key Spanish words and phrases needed to discuss bicycle regulations on campus.

Do not ride your bike here.
No montes tu bicicleta aquí. *(noh 'mohn-tehs too bee-see-'kleh-tah ah-'kee)*

Lock your bike in the bike rack.
Asegura tu bicicleta en el sujetador de bicicletas. *(ah-seh-'goo-rah too bee-see-'kleh-tah ehn ehl soo-heh-tah-'dohr deh bee-see-'kleh-tahs)*

Your bike must be registered with the Police Department.
Tu bicicleta tiene que ser registrada en el departamento de policía. *(too bee-see-'kleh-tah tee-'eh-neh keh sehr reh-hee-'strah-dah ehn ehl deh-pahr-tah-'mehn-toh deh poh-lee-'see-ah)*

Bikes are kept in the bicycle area.
Se guardan las bicicletas en la zona de bicicletas. *(seh 'gwahr-dahn lahs bee-see-'kleh-tahs ehn lah 'soh-nah deh bee-see-'kleh-tahs)*

The bike area is not for motorized bicycles.
La zona de bicicletas no es para bicicletas motorizadas. *(lah 'soh-nah deh bee-see-'kleh-tahs noh ehs 'pah-rah bee-see-'kleh-tahs moh-toh-ree-'sah-dahs)*

The school is not responsible for robbery or damage to bikes.
La escuela no es responsable por el robo o daño a las bicicletas. *(lah eh-'skweh-lah noh ehs reh-spohn-'sah-bleh pohr ehl 'roh-boh o 'dah-nyoh ah lahs bee-see-'kleh-tahs)*

You cannot carry passengers on a bike.
No puedes llevar pasajeros en una bicicleta. *(noh 'pweh-dehs yeh-'vahr pah-sah-'heh-rohs ehn 'oo-nah bee-see-'kleh-tah)*

You need to wear a helmet.
Necesitas usar un casco. *(neh-seh-'see-tahs oo-'sahr oon 'kah-skoh)*

You must follow the same rules as automobile drivers.
Tienes que seguir las mismas reglas que los choferes de autos. *(tee-'eh-nehs keh seh-'geer lahs 'mees-mahs 'reh-glahs keh lohs choh-'feh-rehs deh 'ow-tohs)*

Walk your bike!
¡Camina con tu bicicleta! *(kah-'mee-nah kohn too bee-see-'kleh-tah)*

THE PARKING LOT
El lote de estacionamiento *(ehl 'loh-teh deh eh-stah-see·oh-nah-mee-'ehn-toh)*

Knowing how to talk about cars in Spanish will not only help out the teachers in auto shop and driver's education, but it will also assist anyone who needs to explain campus parking procedures.

You need (the)...	**Ustedes necesitan...** *(oo-'steh-dehs neh-seh-'see-tahn...)*
handicapped parking	**estacionamiento para incapacitadaos** *(eh-stah-see·oh-nah-mee-'ehn-toh 'pah-rah een-kah-pah-see-'tah-dohs)*
permit	**el permiso** *(ehl pehr-'mee-soh)*
sticker	**la etiqueta** *(lah eh-tee-'keh-tah)*
ticket	**el boleto** *(ehl boh-'leh-toh)*
This is...	**Este está...** *('eh-steh eh-'stah...)*
parked poorly	**mal estacionado** *(mahl eh-stah-see·oh-'nah-doh)*
double parked	**estacionado en doble hilera** *(eh-stah-see·oh-'nah-doh ehn 'doh-bleh ee-'leh-rah)*

Look at (the)...	**Mira...** *('mee-rah...)*
arrow	**la flecha** *(lah 'fleh-chah)*
color	**el color** *(ehl koh-'lohr)*
cone	**el cono** *(ehl 'koh-noh)*
hydrant	**la llave de incendios** *(lah 'yah-veh deh een-'sehn-dee·ohs)*
line	**la línea** *(lah 'lee-neh-ah)*
meter	**el parquímetro** *(ehl pahr-'kee-meh-troh)*
sign	**la señal** *(lah seh-'nyahl)*
space	**el espacio** *(ehl eh-'spah-see·oh)*
zone	**la zona** *(lah 'soh-nah)*

MÁS INFORMACIÓN

➤ You may have to stop a vehicle and ask these key questions:

Show me your...	**Muéstrame tu...** *('mweh-strah-meh too...)*
insurance	**seguro** *(seh-'goo-roh)*
license	**licencia** *(lee-'sehn-see·ah)*
registration	**registro** *(reh-'hee-stroh)*

➤ It may be a good idea to learn the names in Spanish for various auto parts. They could be useful in an emergency setting.

➤ How about some other ways to travel? Students often get to school by means of one of these:

I come by...	**Vengo por...** *('vehn-gah pohr...)*
bus	**el autobús** *(ehl ow-toh-'boos)*
moped	**la bicicleta motorizada** *(lah beh-see-'kleh-tah moh-toh-ree-'sah-dah)*
motorcycle	**la motocicleta** *(lah moh-toh-see-'kleh-tah)*
school bus	**el autobús escolar** *(ehl ow-toh-'boos eh-skoh-'lahr)*
streetcar	**el tranvía** *(ehl trah-'vee-ah)*
subway	**el metro** *(ehl 'meh-troh)*
train	**el tren** *(ehl trehn)*
truck	**el camión** *(ehl kah-mee-'ohn)*

173

 ## ¿LISTOS PARA PRACTICAR?

Name three forms of discipline at a typical public high school:

_____   _____   _____

Practice this phone conversation. It will help get you started:

¿Aló, está el Sr. Sánchez?
(ah-'loh, eh-'stah ehl seh-'nyohr 'sahn-chehs)

¿Es usted la Sra. Sánchez?
(ehs oo-'stehd lah seh-'nyoh-rah 'sahn-chehs)

Soy (your name) *('soh·ee _____)*

de la escuela (your school) *(deh lah eh-'skweh-lah)*

y estoy llamando acerca de *(ee eh-'stoh·ee yah-'mahn-doh ah-'sehr-kah deh)*

su hijo/hija (student's name). *(soo 'hee-hoh)*

No, no está aquí. Está trabajando.
(noh, noh eh-'stah ah-'kee. eh-'stah trah-bah-'hahn-doh)

Sí. ¿Quién habla? *(see, kee-'ehn 'ah-blah)*

How do you say these words in Spanish?

helmet   _____

permit   _____

sign   _____

THE CAFETERIA
La cafetería (lah kah-feh-teh-'ree-ah)

School rules also extend into the local dining area, so be sure you know what to say in Spanish when everyone is hungry. Use your hands as you give commands:

Get in line!	**¡Ponte en fila!** *('pohn-teh ehn 'fee-lah)*
Sit over there!	**¡Siéntate allí!** *(see-'ehn-tah-teh ah-'yee)*
Wait for your turn!	**¡Espera tu turno!** *(eh-'speh-rah too 'toor-noh)*
Give me your lunch ticket.	**Dame tu boleto de almuerzo.** *('dah-meh too boh-'leh-toh deh ahl-moo-'ehr-soh)*
Go to (the)...	**Ve a...** *(veh ah...)*
benches	**las bancas** *(lahs 'bahn-kahs)*
cafeteria	**la cafetería** *(lah kah-feh-teh-'ree-ah)*
lunch room	**el comedor** *(ehl koh-meh-'dohr)*
tables	**las mesas** *(lahs 'meh-sahs)*
Use (the)...	**Usa...** *('oo-sah...)*
glass	**el vaso** *(ehl 'vah-soh)*
machine	**la máquina** *(lah 'mah-kee-nah)*
napkin	**la servilleta** *(lah sehr-vee-'yeh-tah)*
plate	**el plato** *(ehl 'plah-toh)*
silverware	**los cubiertos** *(lohs koo-bee-'ehr-tohs)*
trash can	**el bote para basura** *(ehl 'boh-teh 'pah-rah bah-'soo-rah)*
tray	**la bandeja** *(lah bahn-'deh-hah)*

Continue to use command phrases to control unruly students. These words should look familiar:

Don't...	**No...** *(noh...)*
grab	**agarrar** *(ah-gah-'rrahr)*
push	**empujar** *(ehm-poo-'hahr)*
run	**correr** *(koh-'rrehr)*
shout	**gritar** *(gree-'tahr)*
throw	**tirar** *(tee-'rahr)*

Now, let's talk about the food!

They sell...	**Venden...** *('vehn-dehn...)*
breakfast	**el desayuno** *(ehl deh-sah-'yoo-noh)*
lunch	**el almuerzo** *(ehl ahl-moo-'ehr-soh)*
dinner	**la cena** *(lah 'seh-nah)*

They serve...	**Sirven...** *('seer-vehn)*
bacon	**el tocino** *(ehl toh-'see-noh)*
cereal	**el cereal** *(ehl seh-reh-'ahl)*
chicken	**el pollo** *(ehl 'poh-yoh)*
eggs	**los huevos** *(lohs 'weh-vohs)*
fish	**el pescado** *(ehl peh-'skah-doh)*
french fries	**las papas fritas** *(lahs 'pah-pahs 'free-tahs)*
ham	**el jamón** *(ehl hah-'mohn)*
hamburgers	**las hamburguesas** *(lahs ahm-boor-'geh-sahs)*
hot dogs	**los perros calientes** *(lohs 'peh-rrohs kah-lee-'ehn-tehs)*
meat	**la carne** *(lah 'kahr-neh)*
noodles	**los fideos** *(lohs fee-'deh-ohs)*
pork	**el cerdo** *(ehl 'sehr-doh)*
potato chips	**las papitas** *(lahs pah-'pee-tahs)*
rice	**el arroz** *(ehl ah-'rrohs)*
roast beef	**el rósbif** *(ehl rohs-'beef)*
rolls	**los panecillos** *(lohs pah-neh-'see-yohs)*
salad	**la ensalada** *(lah ehn-sah-'lah-dah)*
sandwiches	**los sandwiches** *(lohs 'sahnd-wee-chehs)*
sausage	**la salchicha** *(lah sahl-'chee-chah)*
seafood	**el marisco** *(ehl mah-'ree-skoh)*
soup	**la sopa** *(lah 'soh-pah)*
steak	**el bistec** *(ehl bee-'stehk)*
toast	**el pan tostado** *(ehl pahn toh-'stah-doh)*
tuna	**el atún** *(ehl ah-'toon)*
turkey	**el pavo** *(ehl 'pah-voh)*

Vegetables
Los vegetales *(lohs veh-heh-'tah-lehs)*

They have...   **Tienen...** *(tee-'eh-nehn)*

beans   **los frijoles** *(lohs free-'hoh-lehs)*
beet   **la remolacha** *(lah reh-moh-'lah-chah)*
cabbage   **el repollo** *(ehl reh-'poh-yoh)*
carrot   **la zanahoria** *(lah sah-nah-'oh-ree·ah)*
celery   **el apio** *(ehl 'ah-pee·oh)*
corn   **el maíz** *(ehl mah-'ees)*
cucumber   **el pepino** *(ehl peh-'pee-noh)*
lettuce   **la lechuga** *(lah leh-'choo-gah)*
mushrooms   **los champiñones** *(lohs chahm-pee-'nyoh-nehs)*
onion   **la cebolla** *(lah seh-'boh-yah)*
peas   **las arvejitas** *(lahs ahr-veh-'hee-tahs)*
potato   **la papa** *(lah 'pah-pah)*
radish   **el rábano** *(ehl 'rah-bah-noh)*
spinach   **la espinaca** *(lah eh-spee-'nah-kah)*
tomato   **el tomate** *(ehl toh-'mah-teh)*

Fruit
La fruta *(lah 'froo-tah)*

Do you like...?   **¿Te gusta...?** *(teh 'goo-stah)*

apple   **la manzana** *(lah mahn-'sah-nah)*
apricot   **el albaricoque** *(ehl ahl-bah-ree-'koh-keh)*
banana   **el plátano** *(ehl 'plah-tah-noh)*
cantaloupe   **el melón** *(ehl meh-'lohn)*
cherry   **la cereza** *(lah seh-'reh-sah)*
coconut   **el coco** *(ehl 'koh-koh)*
grape   **la uva** *(lah 'oo-vah)*
grapefruit   **la toronja** *(lah toh-'rohn-hah)*
lemon   **el limón** *(ehl lee-'mohn)*
orange   **la naranja** *(lah nah-'rahn-hah)*
peach   **el melocotón** *(ehl meh-loh-koh-'tohn)*
pear   **la pera** *(lah 'peh-rah)*
strawberry   **la fresa** *(lah 'freh-sah)*

Dessert and snacks
El postre y las meriendas *(ehl 'poh-streh ee lahs meh-ree-'ehn-dahs)*

You can buy...   **Pueden comprar...** *('pweh-dehn kohm-'prahr...)*

cake	**la torta** *(lah 'tohr-tah)*
candy	**los dulces** *(lohs 'dool-sehs)*
cookie	**la galleta** *(lah gah-'yeh-tah)*
gum	**el chicle** *(ehl 'chee-kleh)*
ice cream	**el helado** *(ehl eh-'lah-doh)*
jello	**la gelatina** *(lah heh-lah-'tee-nah)*
pie	**el pastel** *(ehl pah-'stehl)*
yogurt	**el yogur** *(ehl yoh-'goor)*

How are you doing with the drinks? Quench everyone's thirst with this group of vocabulary:

I'd like...   **Quisiera...** *(kee-see-'eh-rah...)*

coffee	**el café** *(ehl kah-'feh)*
decaffeinated coffee	**el café descafeinado** *(ehl kah-'feh dehs-kah-feh·ee-'nah-doh)*
diet soda	**la soda dietética** *(lah 'soh-dah dee-eh-'teh-tee-kah)*
hot chocolate	**el chocolate caliente** *(ehl choh-koh-'lah-teh kah-lee-'ehn-teh)*
iced tea	**el té helado** *(ehl teh eh-'lah-doh)*
juice	**el jugo** *(ehl 'hoo-goh)*
lemonade	**la limonada** *(lah lee-moh-'nah-dah)*
milk	**la leche** *(lah 'leh-cheh)*
shake	**el batido** *(ehl bah-'tee-doh)*
skim milk	**la leche descremada** *(lah 'leh-cheh dehs-kreh-'mah-dah)*
soft drink	**el refresco** *(ehl reh-'frehs-koh)*
tea	**el té** *(ehl teh)*
water	**el agua** *(ehl 'ah-gwah)*

➤ How many one-liners can you come up with for use during the lunch hour?

Are you going home for lunch?
¿Vas a tu casa para el almuerzo? *(vahs ah too 'kah-sah 'pah-rah ehl ahl-moo-'ehr-soh)*

Do you have an off-campus pass?
¿Tienes un pase para salir de la escuela? *(tee-'eh-nehs oon 'pah-seh 'pah-rah sah-'leer deh lah eh-'skweh-lah)*

You may sit where you want.
Puedes sentarte dónde quieras.
('pweh-dehs sehn-'tahr-teh 'dohn-deh kee-'eh-rahs)

These are the hours of service.
Estas son las horas de servicio.
('eh-stahs sohn lahs 'oh-rahs deh sehr-'vee-see·oh)

You don't have much time to eat.
No tienes mucho tiempo para comer.
(noh tee-'eh-nehs 'moo-choh tee-'ehm-poh 'pah-rah koh-'mehr)

The food is very good.
La comida es muy buena.
(lah koh-'mee-dah ehs 'moo·ee 'bweh-nah)

You have to pay over there.
Tienes que pagar ahí.
(tee-'eh-nehs keh pah-'gahr ah-'ee)

It's free.
Es gratis. *(ehs 'grah-tees)*

Here's your ticket
Aquí tienes el boleto. *(ah-'kee tee-'eh-nehs ehl boh-'leh-toh)*

You need exact change.
Necesitas el cambio exacto. *(neh-seh-'see-tahs ehl 'kahm-bee·oh ehk-'sahk-toh)*

CONFLICTOS CULTURALES

Traditional American foods don't always appeal to a multiethnic student body. Many Hispanics, for example, simply prefer to bring their homemade foods for lunch. To raise campus morale, have an "International Food Day," or consider asking students about the foods they enjoy most, and then add them to the current cafeteria menu.

CLOTHING
La ropa *(lah 'roh-pah)*

One of the toughest areas to control at many schools is the dress code. Open up with a few useful phrases, and then specify which article of clothing is causing the problem. Take as much time as you need—these are important!

You're not supposed to wear that.
No debes ponerte eso. *(noh 'deh-behs poh-'nehr-teh 'eh-soh)*

It's against the district regulations.
Es contra los reglamentos del distrito. *(ehs 'kohn-trah lohs reh-glah-'mehn-tohs dehl dee-'stree-toh)*

It distracts others from learning.
Distrae la atención de los otros. *(dee-'strah-eh lah ah-tehn-see-'ohn deh lohs 'oh-trohs)*

It isn't appropriate.
No es apropiada. *(noh ehs ah-proh-pee-'ah-dah)*

What seems to be the problem? It could be just about anything:

Look at (the)...	Mira... (*'mee-rah*)
bathing suit	**el traje de baño** (*ehl 'trah-heh deh 'bah-nyoh*)
bathrobe	**la bata de baño** (*lah 'bah-tah deh 'bah-nyoh*)
belt	**el cinturón** (*ehl seen-too-'rohn*)
blouse	**la blusa** (*lah 'bloo-sah*)
boots	**las botas** (*lahs 'boh-tahs*)
brassiere	**el sostén** (*ehl soh-'stehn*)
cap	**la gorra** (*lah 'goh-rrah*)
dress	**el vestido** (*ehl veh-'stee-doh*)
gloves	**los guantes** (*lohs 'gwahn-tehs*)
jacket	**la chaqueta** (*lah chah-'keh-tah*)
mittens	**los mitones** (*lohs mee-'toh-nehs*)
overcoat	**el abrigo** (*ehl ah-'bree-goh*)
panties	**las bragas** (*lahs 'brah-gahs*)
pants	**los pantalones** (*lohs pahn-tah-'loh-nehs*)
raincoat	**el impermeable** (*ehl eem-pehr-meh-'ah-bleh*)
sandals	**las sandalias** (*lahs sahn-'dah-lee·ahs*)
scarf	**la bufanda** (*lah boo-'fahn-dah*)
shirt	**la camisa** (*lah kah-'mee-sah*)
shoes	**los zapatos** (*lohs sah-'pah-tohs*)
shorts	**los calzoncillos** (*lohs kahl-sohn-'see-yohs*)
skirt	**la falda** (*lah 'fahl-dah*)
slip	**la combinación** (*lah kohm-bee-nah-see-'ohn*)
slippers	**las zapatillas** (*lahs sah-pah-'tee-yahs*)
socks	**los calcetines** (*lohs kahl-seh-'tee-nehs*)
sportcoat	**el saco** (*ehl 'sah-koh*)
stockings	**las medias** (*lahs 'meh-dee·ahs*)
suit	**el traje** (*ehl 'trah-heh*)
sweater	**el suéter** (*ehl 'sweh-tehr*)
sweatsuit	**la sudadera** (*lah soo-dah-'deh-rah*)
T-shirt	**la camiseta** (*lah kah-mee-'seh-tah*)
tennis shoes	**los tenis** (*lohs 'teh-nees*)
tie	**la corbata** (*lah kohr-'bah-tah*)
underwear	**la ropa interior** (*lah 'roh-pah een-teh-ree-'ohr*)
vest	**el chaleco** (*ehl chah-'leh-koh*)

➤ Keep naming items that disrupt activity in the classroom:

Don't bring (the)...   **No traigas...** *(noh 'trah·ee-gahs)*

comb	**el peine** *(ehl 'peh·ee-neh)*
hairbrush	**el cepillo** *(ehl seh-'pee-yoh)*
handkerchief	**el pañuelo** *(ehl pah-nyoo-'eh-loh)*
suntan lotion	**el bronceador** *(ehl brohn-seh-ah-'dohr)*
umbrella	**el paraguas** *(ehl pah-'rah-gwahs)*

➤ And there's always the jewelry:

Don't wear (the)...   **No uses...** *(noh 'oo-sehs)*

bracelet	**el brazalete** *(ehl brah-sah-'leh-teh)*
chain	**la cadena** *(lah kah-'deh-nah)*
earring	**el arete** *(ehl ah-'reh-teh)*
jewel	**la joya** *(lah 'hoh-yah)*
necklace	**el collar** *(ehl koh-'yahr)*
ring	**el anillo** *(ehl ah-'nee-yoh)*
watch	**el reloj** *(ehl reh-'loh)*

List ten popular food items in Spanish:

_____ _____ _____ _____

_____ _____ _____ _____

List ten articles of clothing in Spanish:

_____ _____ _____ _____

_____ _____ _____ _____

GOOD BEHAVIOR!

¡Buen comportamiento! *(bwehn kohm-pohr-tah-mee-'ehn-toh)*

Not all students have discipline problems. One of the chief reasons why students succeed in school is that they feel the support of their educators. Praise and encouragement can be tremendous motivators, even for the most troubled youth. Try out some of these powerful expressions today!

How...!	¡Qué...! *(keh)*
excellent	**excelente** *(ehk-seh-'lehn-teh)*
exceptional	**excepcional** *(ehk-sehp-see·oh-'nahl)*
fabulous	**fabuloso** *(fah-boo-'loh-soh)*
fantastic	**fantástico** *(fahn-'tah-stee-koh)*
great	**bueno** *('bweh-noh)*
incredible	**increíble** *(een-kreh-'ee-bleh)*
marvelous	**maravilloso** *(mah-rah-vee-'yoh-soh)*
outstanding	**destacado** *(dehs-tah-'kah-doh)*
remarkable	**extraordinario** *(ehks-trah-ohr-dee-'nah-ree·oh)*
stupendous	**estupendo** *(eh-stoo-'pehn-doh)*
tremendous	**magnífico** *(mahg-'nee-fee-koh)*

Nothing works better than encouraging remarks, so keep it up!

What a great job!	**¡Qué buen trabajo!** *(keh bweh trah-'bah-hoh)*
Very good!	**¡Muy bien!** *('moo·ee 'bee·ehn)*
Good work!	**¡Bien hecho!** *('bee·ehn 'eh-choh)*
You could do it!	**¡Pudiste hacerlo!** *(pooh-'dee-steh ah-'sehr-loh)*
You're important!	**¡Tú eres importante!** *(too 'eh-rehs eem-pohr-'tahn-teh)*
You learn quickly!	**¡Aprendes rápido!** *(ah-'prehn-dehs 'rah-pee-doh)*
We need you!	**¡Te necesitamos!** *(teh neh-seh-see-'tah-mohs)*
We can't do it without you!	**¡No podemos hacerlo sin tí!** *(noh poh-'deh-mohs ah-'sehr-loh seen tee)*
I trust you!	**¡Confío en ti!** *(kohn-'fee-oh ehn tee)*

I respect you!	**¡Te respeto!**
	(teh reh-'speh-toh)
You're valuable!	**¡Tú eres valioso!**
	(too 'eh-rehs vah-lee-'oh-soh)
I like what you did!	**¡Me gusta lo que hiciste!**
	(meh 'goo-stah loh keh ee-'sees-teh)

Keep passing out the compliments. Their behavior is improving:

I like the...	**Me gusta...** *(meh 'goo-stah)*
attitude	**la actitud** *(lah ahk-tee-'tood)*
mood	**el humor** *(ehl oo-'mohr)*
spirit	**el espíritu** *(ehl eh-'spee-ree-'too)*
I have seen...	**He visto...** *(eh 'vee-stoh)*
appreciation	**aprecio** *(ah-'preh-see·oh)*
commitment	**compromiso** *(kohm-proh-'mee-soh)*
confidence	**confianza** *(kohn-fee-'ahn-sah)*
creativity	**creatividad** *(kreh-ah-tee-vee-'dahd)*
dialogue	**diálogo** *(dee-'ah-loh-goh)*
enthusiasm	**entusiasmo** *(ehn-too-see-'ahs-moh)*
friendship	**amistad** *(ah-mee-'stahd)*
harmony	**armonía** *(ahr-moh-'nee-ah)*
honesty	**honradez** *(ohn-rah-'dehs)*
initiative	**iniciativa** *(ee-nee-see·ah-'tee-vah)*
patience	**paciencia** *(pah-see-'ehn-see·ah)*
responsibility	**responsabilidad** *(reh-spohn-sah-bee-lee-'dahd)*
safety	**seguridad** *(seh-goo-ree-'dahd)*
value	**valor** *(vah-'lohr)*

This shows me that you are...
Esto me muestra que tú eres...
('eh-stoh meh 'mweh-strah keh too 'eh-rehs...)

ambitious	**ambicioso** *(ahm-bee-see-'oh-soh)*
competent	**competente** *(kohm-peh-'tehn-teh)*
efficient	**eficiente** *(eh-fee-see-'ehn-teh)*
independent	**independiente** *(een-deh-pehn-dee-'ehn-teh)*

| organized | **organizado** *(ohr-gah-nee-'sah-doh)* |
| punctual | **puntual** *(poon-too-'ahl)* |

O.K. Now go back and change all these one-liners so that they refer to your female students!

¡ACCIÓN!

Up to now, you've been given the skills to converse about current, everyday, and future activities around the school site.

Now take a look at the past tense in Spanish. You can start by learning the more commonly used form. Read the following examples and, just as you did with present and future actions, make the changes in your verbs. You won't be perfect at first, but Spanish speakers will know what you're trying to say.

-ar Verbs: *To Speak*	**hablar** *(ah-'blahr)*
I spoke with the child.	**Hablé con el niño.** *(ah-'bleh kohn ehl 'nee-nyoh)*
You (informal) spoke slowly.	**Hablaste lentamente.** *(ah-'blah-steh lehn-tah-'mehn-teh)*
You (formal), He, She spoke a lot.	**Habló mucho.** *(ah-'bloh 'moo-choh)*
You (pl.), They spoke English.	**Hablaron inglés.** *(ah-'blah-rohn een-'glehs)*
We spoke a little.	**Hablamos un poco.** *(ah-'blah-mohs oon 'poh-koh)*

-er/ir Verbs: *To Leave*	**salir** *(sah-'leer)*
I left at eight	**Salí a las ocho.** *(sah-'lee ah lahs 'oh-choh)*
You (informal) left quickly.	**Saliste rápidamente.** *(sah-'lee-steh 'rah-pee-dah-'mehn-teh)*
You (formal), He, She left late.	**Salió tarde.** *(sah-lee-'oh 'tahr-deh)*

185

You (pl.), They left.	**Salieron.**
	(sah-lee-'eh-rohn)
We left in a car.	**Salimos en el carro.**
	(sah-'lee-mohs ehn ehl 'kah-rroh)

As usual, some common verbs have irregular past tenses, so be on the lookout for new patterns.

To Go: ir *(eer)*

I went	**Fui** *(fwee)*	<u>**Fui a la casa.**</u>
		(fwee ah lah 'kah-sah)
You (informal) went	**Fuiste** *('fwee-steh)*	_____
You (formal), He, She went	**Fue** *(fweh)*	_____
You (pl.), They went	**Fueron** *('fweh-rohn)*	_____
We went	**Fuimos** *('fwee-mohs)*	_____

To Have: tener *(teh-'nehr)*

I had	**Tuve** *('too-veh)*	<u>**Tuve la fiesta.**</u>
		('too-veh lah fee-'eh-stah)
You (informal) had	**Tuviste** *('too-vee-steh)*	_____
You (formal), He, She had	**Tuvo** *('too-voh)*	_____
You (pl.), They had	**Tuvieron** *(too-vee-'eh-rohn)*	_____
We had	**Tuvimos** *(too-'vee-mohs)*	_____

To Say: decir *(deh-'seer)*

I said	**Dije** *('dee-heh)*	<u>**Dije la verdad.**</u>
		('dee-heh lah vehr-'dahd)
You (informal) said	**Dijiste** *(dee-'hee-steh)*	_____
You (formal), He, She said	**Dijo** *('dee-hoh)*	_____
You (pl.), They said	**Dijeron** *(dee-'heh-rohn)*	_____
We said	**Dijimos** *(dee-'hee-mohs)*	_____

➤ This verb form is called the preterit, and it isn't the only past tense you're going to need. Although these phrases won't be discussed in detail, check out the spellings and meanings of the examples below:

I used to have	**tenía** *(teh-'nee-ah)*
I would have	**tendría** *(tehn-'dree-ah)*
I was having	**estaba teniendo**
	(eh-'stah-bah teh-nee-'ehn-doh)
I have had	**he tenido** *(eh teh-'nee-doh)*

➤ The verb **ser** *(sehr)* (to be) has the same preterit forms as the verb **ir** *(eer)* (to go). Take note:

I was	**Fui** *(fwee)*
You (informal) were	**Fuiste** *('fwee-steh)*
You (formal), He, She was	**Fue** *(fweh)*
You (pl.), They were	**Fueron** *('fweh-rohn)*
We were	**Fuimos** *('fwee-mohs)*

While learning Spanish commands, you're going to come across the following object pronouns that refer to people. Notice what they can mean in English:

le	you, to you, for you, him, to him, for him, her, to her, for her
les	you, to you, for you (plural), them, to them, for them

See how they fit at the end of an affirmative command. Look out for the accent marks:

Talk to him	**Háblele** *('ah-bleh-leh)*
Look at them	**Míreles** *('mee-reh-lehs)*
Tell her	**Dígale** *('dee-gah-leh)*
Ask them	**Pregúnteles** *(preh-'goon-teh-lehs)*

MÁS INFORMACIÓN

➤ Note that, in most sentences, **le** and **les** go in front of the verb:

I understand you.	**Le entiendo.** *(leh ehn-tee-'ehn-doh)*
We're going to tell them.	**Les vamos a decir.** *(lehs 'vah-mohs ah deh-'seer)*
She hit him.	**Le pegó.** *(leh peh-'goh)*

➤ Read through the other pronouns that are used to refer to people:

He talks to me.	**Me habla.** *(meh 'ah-blah)*
He talks to you (informal).	**Te habla.** *(teh 'ah-blah)*
He talks to us.	**Nos habla.** *(nohs 'ah-blah)*

¿LISTOS PARA PRACTICAR?

Saying nice things in Spanish is easy, since most of the words are similar to their English equivalents. Guess at the meanings of these:

fantástico *(fahn-'tah-stee-koh)*　＿＿＿＿＿＿＿＿＿＿＿＿

paciente *(pah-see-'ehn-teh)*　＿＿＿＿＿＿＿＿＿＿＿＿

creativo *(kreh-ah-'tee-voh)*　＿＿＿＿＿＿＿＿＿＿＿＿

puntual *(poon-too-'ahl)* _____

fabuloso *(fah-boo-'loh-soh)* _____

Follow the example:

I speak.	**Hablo.** *('ah-bloh)*	I spoke.	**Hablé.** *(ah-'bleh)*
I walk.	_____	_____	_____
I study.	_____	_____	_____
I work.	_____	_____	_____

CHAPTER SIX
Capítulo Seis
(kah-'pee-too-loh 'seh·ees)

THE COUNSELORS
Los consejeros
(lohs kohn-seh-'heh-rohs)

THERE'S A LOT TO DO!

¡Hay mucho que hacer! *('ah·ee 'moo-choh keh ah-'sehr)*

Share these tasks with a Spanish-speaking student or parent. They outline some of the responsibilities of a school counselor:

Talk to me about...	**Háblame acerca de...** *('ah-blah-meh ah-'sehr-kah deh...)*
assemblies	**las asambleas** *(lahs ah-sahm-'bleh-ahs)*
career planning	**la planificación de trabajo** *(lah plah-nee-fee-kah-see-'ohn deh trah-'bah-hoh)*
counseling	**el asesoramiento** *(ehl ah-seh-soh-rah-mee-'ehn-toh)*
discipline	**la disciplina** *(lah dee-see-'plee-nah)*
enrollment	**la matrícula** *(lah mah-'tree-koo-lah)*
evaluations	**las evaluaciones** *(lahs eh-vah-loo-ah-see-'oh-nehs)*
fund-raising	**la recolección de fondos** *(lah reh-koh-lehk-see-'ohn deh 'fohn-dohs)*
graduation	**la graduación** *(lah grah-doo-ah-see-'ohn)*
health problems	**los problemas de salud** *(lohs proh-'bleh-mahs deh sah-'lood)*
personal needs	**los requisitos personales** *(lohs reh-kee-'see-tohs pehr-soh-'nah-lehs)*
promotion	**la promoción** *(lah proh-moh-see-'ohn)*
registration	**la inscripción** *(lah een-skreep-see-'ohn)*
schedules	**los horarios** *(lohs oh-'rah-ree·ohs)*
special programs	**los programas especiales** *(lohs proh-'grah-mahs eh-speh-see-'ah-lehs)*
summer school	**la escuela del verano** *(lah eh-'skweh-lah dehl veh-'rah-noh)*
transfers	**las transferencias** *(lahs trahns-feh-'rehn-see·ahs)*
transportation	**el transporte** *(ehl trahns-'pohr-teh)*
I have meetings with...	**Tengo reuniones con...** *('tehn-goh reh-oo-nee-'oh-nehs kohn...)*
administrators	**los administradores** *(lohs ahd-mee-nee-strah-'doh-rehs)*
other counselors	**los otros consejeros** *(lohs 'oh-trohs kohn-seh-'heh-rohs)*

191

parents	**los padres** *(lohs 'pah-drehs)*
students	**los estudiantes** *(lohs eh-stoo-dee-'ahn-tehs)*
teachers	**los maestros** *(lohs mah-'eh-strohs)*

Before you help anyone, make sure you have the correct general information:

| I need to know (the)... | **Necesito saber...** *(neh-seh-'see-toh sah-'behr...)* |

average	**el promedio** *(ehl proh-'meh-dee·oh)*
class	**la clase** *(lah 'klah-seh)*
grade	**el grado** *(ehl 'grah-doh)*
level	**el nivel** *(ehl nee-'vehl)*
mark	**la nota** *(lah 'noh-tah)*
name	**el nombre** *(ehl 'nohm-breh)*
number	**el número** *(ehl 'noo-meh-roh)*
score	**la calificación** *(lah kah-lee-fee-kah-see-'ohn)*
title	**el título** *(ehl 'tee-too-loh)*
year	**el año** *(ehl 'ah-nyoh)*

 ## CONFLICTOS CULTURALES

As you have learned, a number of high school events simply don't exist in Spanish-speaking countries. Get an interpreter to help you explain these activities to non-English speakers:

Grad night	Class photos
Homecoming	Cap and gown
The prom	Commencement exercises
Yearbooks	Class rings

ATTENDANCE
La asistencia *(lah ah-see-'stehn-see·ah)*

Counselors can't do their job if the students don't attend school, so you may use these examples to get your message across:

Why are you late?	**¿Por qué llegas tarde?** *(pohr keh'yeh-gahs'tahr-deh)*
Why were you absent?	**¿Por qué estabas ausente?** *(pohr keh eh-'stah-bahs ow-'sehn-teh)*
Why didn't you go to class?	**¿Por qué no fuiste a la clase?** *(pohr keh noh'fwee-steh ah lah'klah-seh)*
Why didn't you come?	**¿Por qué no viniste?** *(pohr keh noh vee-'nee-steh)*
Where is (the)...?	**¿Dónde está...?** *('dohn-deh eh-'stah...)*
tardy slip	**la nota de tardanzas** *(lah'noh-tah deh tahr-'dahn-sahs)*
doctor's note	**la nota del médico** *(lah'noh-tah dehl'meh-dee-koh)*
letter from home	**la carta de tu casa** *(lah'kahr-tah deh too'kah-sah)*
parent signature	**la firma de los padres** *(lah'feer-mah deh lohs'pah-drehs)*
work phone number	**el número de teléfono del trabajo** *(ehl'noo-meh-roh deh teh-'leh-foh-noh dehl trah-'bah-hoh)*
What...?	**¿Qué...?** *(keh...)*
class	**clase** *('klah-seh)*
day	**día** *('dee-ah)*
hour	**hora** *('oh-rah)*
month	**mes** *(mehs)*
quarter	**trimestre** *(tree-'meh-streh)*
semester	**semestre** *(seh-'meh-streh)*
term	**período de estudios** *(peh-'ree-oh-doh deh eh-'stoo-dee·ohs)*
week	**semana** *(seh-'mah-nah)*
year	**año** *('ah-nyoh)*

You may have to pull the student aside, and discuss your concern in detail:

You are missing school a lot.
Faltas mucho a la escuela. *('fahl-tahs'moo-choh ah lah eh-'skweh-lah)*

You always arrive late.
Siempre llegas tarde. *(see-'ehm-preh'yeh-gahs'tahr-deh)*

You can't learn if you're not here.
No puedes aprender si no estás aquí. *(noh'pweh-dehs ah-prehn-'dehr see noh eh-'stahs ah-'kee)*

Now, explain the situation in simple terms:

This is your last chance.	**Esta es tu última oportunidad.** *('eh-stah ehs too 'ool-tee-mah oh-pohr-too-nee-'dahd)*
This is a serious problem.	**Este problema es muy serio.** *('eh-steh proh-'bleh-mah ehs'moo·ee'seh-ree·oh)*
This is the rule.	**Esta es la regla.** *('eh-stah ehs lah'reh-glah)*

If things get worse, lay down the law:

You will stay after school.	**Te quedarás después de clases.** *(teh keh-dah-'rahs deh-'spwehs deh'klah-sehs)*
We'll suspend you.	**Te vamos a suspender.** *(teh'vah-mohs ah soo-spehn-'dehr)*
I'll call your parents.	**Voy a llamar a tus padres.** *('voh·ee ah yah-'mahr ah toos'pah-drehs)*

MÁS INFORMACIÓN

➤ Find out why the student has trouble getting to school:

Do you live...?	**¿Vives...?** *('vee-vehs)*
in this city	**en esta ciudad** *(ehn'eh-stah see-oo-'dahd)*
near the school	**cerca de la escuela** *('sehr-kah deh lah eh-'skweh-lah)*
far from here	**lejos de aquí** *('leh-hohs deh ah-'kee)*
outside the district	**fuera del distrito** *('fweh-rah dehl dee-'stree-toh)*

Is/Are there...?	¿Hay...? (*'ah·ee...*)
a major illness	**una enfermedad grave** (*'oo-nah ehn-fehr-meh-'dahd'grah-veh*)
family problems	**problemas familiares** (*proh-'bleh-mahs fah-mee-lee-'ah-rehs*)
transportation to school	**transporte a la escuela** (*trahns-'pohr-teh ah lah eh-'skweh-lah*)

➤ Keep acquiring questions related to student attendance:

Are you going to miss school?
¿Vas a faltar a la escuela?
(*vahs ah fahl-'tahr ah lah ehs-'kweh-lah*)

Are you going to be late?
¿Vas a llegar tarde?
(*vahs ah yeh-'gahr'tahr-deh*)

Did you call the office?
¿Llamaste a la oficina?
(*yah-'mah-steh ah lah oh-fee-'see-nah*)

Do you have an excuse?
¿Tienes una excusa?
(*tee-'eh-nehs'oo-nah ehk-'skoo-sah*)

What's the reason?
¿Cuál es la razón?
(*kwahl ehs lah rah-'sohn*)

And, here's what you can say about their make-up work:

The work is late.
La tarea está atrasada. (*lah tah-'reh-ah eh-'stah ah-trah-'sah-dah*)
You have to make up the work.
Tiene que completar el trabajo. (*tee-'eh-neh keh kohm-pleh-'tahr ehl trah-'bah-hoh*)
You will get a lower grade.
Recibirás una nota más baja. (*reh-see-bee-'rahs'oo-nah'noh-tah mahs'bah-hah*)

Absences are often due to family-related events that require the attendance of all family members. Here's a brief list of common excuses for missing class:

anniversary	**el aniversario** *(ehl ah-nee-vehr-'sah-ree·oh)*
birth	**el nacimiento** *(ehl nah-see-mee-'ehn-toh)*
birthday	**el cumpleaños** *(ehl koom-pleh-'ah-nyohs)*
engagement	**el compromiso** *(ehl kohm-proh-'mee-soh)*
funeral	**el funeral** *(ehl foo-neh-'rahl)*
shower	**el shower** *(ehl 'shah-wehr)*
15-year-old daughter's "coming out" party	**la quinceañera** *(lah keen-seh-ah-'nyeh-rah)*
wedding	**el casamiento** *(ehl kah-sah-mee-'ehn-toh)*

¿LISTOS PARA PRACTICAR?

Practice this dialog about school attendance:

¿Por qué estabas ausente?
(pohr keh eh-'stah-bahs ow-'sehn-teh)

Porque estaba enfermo. *('pohr-keh eh-'stah-bah ehn-'fehr-moh)*

¿Dónde está la nota del doctor?
('dohn-deh eh-'stah lah 'noh-tah dehl dohk-'tohr)

No la tengo. *(noh lah 'tehn-goh)*

Muy bien. Voy a llamar a tus padres. *('moo·ee 'bee·ehn. 'voh·ee ah yah-'mahr ah toos 'pah-drehs)*

PERSONAL PROBLEMS
Los problemes personales *(lohs proh-'bleh-mahs pehr-soh-'nah-lehs)*

Students often talk to counselors, teachers, and administrators about issues related to their personal lives. Pay attention to some of the topics listed below—you'll probably need an interpreter to handle these discussions in detail:

I need (the)...	**Necesito...** *(neh-seh-'see-toh...)*
clothing	**la ropa** *(lah'roh-pah)*
food	**la comida** *(lah koh-'mee-dah)*
help	**la ayuda** *(lah ah-'yoo-dah)*
medicine	**la medicina** *(lah meh-dee-'see-nah)*
money	**el dinero** *(ehl dee-'neh-roh)*
Someone is.... me.	**Alguien me está....** *('ahl-gee·ehn meh eh-'stah...)*
beating	**golpeando** *(gohl-peh-'ahn-doh)*
following	**persiguiendo** *(pehr-see-gee-'ehn-doh)*
grabbing	**agarrando** *(ah-gah-'rrahn-doh)*
looking at	**mirando** *(mee-'rahn-doh)*
threatening	**amenazando** *(ah-meh-nah-'sahn-doh)*

Stay with simple patterns. Some of these words you've seen before:

Let's talk about (the)...	**Vamos a hablar de...** *('vah-mohs ah ah-'blahr deh...)*
absences	**las ausencias** *(lahs ow-'sehn-see·ahs)*
alcohol	**el alcohol** *(ehl ahl-koh-'ohl)*
attitude	**la actitud** *(lah ahk-tee-'tood)*
cigarettes	**los cigarrillos** *(lohs see-gah-'rree-yohs)*
conflict	**el conflicto** *(ehl kohn-'fleek-toh)*
drugs	**las drogas** *(lahs'droh-gahs)*
harassment	**el acosamiento** *(ehl ah-koh-sah-mee-'ehn-toh)*
illness	**la enfermedad** *(lah ehn-fehr-meh-'dahd)*
injury	**la lesión** *(lah leh-see-'ohn)*
tardiness	**las tardanzas** *(lahs tahr-'dahn-sahs)*
I heard about (the)...	**Escuché de...** *(eh-skoo-'cheh deh...)*
accident	**el accidente** *(ehl ahk-see-'dehn-teh)*
argument	**la discusión** *(lah dees-koo-see-'ohn)*
confrontation	**la confrontación** *(lah kohn-frohn-tah-see-'ohn)*
disturbance	**el tumulto** *(ehl too-'mool-toh)*
fight	**la pelea** *(lah peh-'leh-ah)*
interruption	**la interrupción** *(lah een-teh-roop-see-'ohn)*
threat	**la amenaza** *(lah ah-meh-'nah-sah)*

Create more clusters for each concern:

There's a problem with (the)...

Hay un problema con...
('ah·ee oon proh-'bleh-mah kohn...)

lack of support
la falta de apoyo
(lah'fahl-tah deh ah-'poh-yoh)

language proficiency
la competencia en el lenguaje
(lah kohm-peh-'tehn-see·ah ehn ehl lehn-'gwah-heh)

personality differences
las diferencias de personalidad
(lahs dee-feh-'rehn-see·ahs deh pehr-soh-nah-lee-'dahd)

personal hygiene
la higiene personal
(lah ee-hee-'eh-neh pehr-soh-'nahl)

style of clothing
el estilo de ropa
(ehl eh-'stee-loh deh'roh-pah)

MÁS INFORMACIÓN

➤ Personal concerns often involve serious matters, so learn the following terms:

abuse	**el abuso** *(ehl ah-'boo-soh)*
addiction	**la adicción** *(lah ah-deek-see-'ohn)*
crime	**el crimen** *(ehl'kree-mehn)*
discrimination	**la discriminación** *(lah dee-skree-mee-nah-see-'ohn)*
pregnancy	**el embarazo** *(ehl ehm-bah-'rah-soh)*
sex relations	**las relaciones sexuales** *(lahs reh-lah-see-'oh-nehs sehk-soo-'ah-lehs)*
violence	**la violencia** *(lah vee-oh-'lehn-see·ah)*

TELL ME EVERYTHING!

¡Dime todo! *('dee-meh'toh-doh)*

When there's trouble, make sure the student speaks to the proper authorities. Do any of these words look familiar?

Tell (the)...	**Dígale a...** *('dee-gah-leh ah...)*
administrator	**el administrador** *(ehl ahd-mee-nee-strah-'dohr)*
counselor	**el consejero** *(ehl kohn-seh-'heh-roh)*
doctor	**el médico** *(ehl'meh-dee-koh)*
family	**la familia** *(lah fah-'mee-lee·ah)*
nurse	**la enfermera** *(lah ehn-fehr-'meh-rah)*
officer	**el oficial** *(ehl oh-fee-see-'ahl)*
police	**la policía** *(lah poh-lee-'see-ah)*
principal	**el director** *(ehl dee-rehk-'tohr)*
psychiatrist	**el psiquiatra** *(ehl see-kee-'ah-trah)*
psychologist	**el psicólogo** *(ehl see-'koh-loh-goh)*
secretary	**el secretario** *(ehl seh-kreh-'tah-ree·oh)*
social worker	**el trabajador social** *(ehl trah-bah-hah-'dohr soh-see-'ahl)*
specialist	**el especialista** *(ehl eh-speh-see·ah-'lee-stah)*
supervisor	**el supervisor** *(ehl soo-pehr-vee-'sohr)*
teacher	**el maestro** *(ehl mah-'eh-stroh)*
therapist	**el terapeuta** *(ehl teh-rah-peh-'oo-tah)*

Now, ask the right questions. Keep things brief:

Are you OK?
¿Estás bien? *(eh-'stahs'bee·ehn)*
Are you sick?
¿Estás enfermo? *(eh-'stahs ehn-'fehr-moh)*
Are you injured?
¿Estás lastimado? *(eh-'stahs lah-stee-'mah-doh)*
What's the trouble?
¿Cuál es el problema? *(kwahl ehs ehl proh-'bleh-mah)*
Do you need help?
¿Necesitas ayuda? *(neh-seh-'see-tahs ah-'yoo-dah)*

Do you wish to talk to me?
¿Deseas hablarme? *(deh-'seh-ahs ah-'blahr-meh)*
Can you tell me?
¿Puedes decirme? *('pweh-dehs deh-'seer-meh)*
Do you have information?
¿Tienes información? *(tee-'eh-nehs een-fohr-mah-see-'ohn)*
Who is the person?
¿Quién es la persona? *(kee-'ehn ehs lah pehr-'soh-nah)*
How can I help you?
¿Cómo puedo ayudarte? *('koh-moh 'pweh-doh ah-yoo-'dahr-teh)*
What do you want to do?
¿Qué quieres hacer? *(keh kee-'eh-rehs ah-'sehr)*
Do you know the procedure?
¿Sabes el procedimiento?
('sah-behs ehl proh-seh-dee-mee-'ehn-toh)

 MÁS INFORMACIÓN

➤ Notice how these new verb forms below refer to past actions. We'll talk more about this verb tense later on in this chapter:

What happened?
¿Qué pasó? *(keh pah-'soh)*
Where did it happen?
¿Dónde pasó eso? *('dohn-deh pah-'soh 'eh-soh)*
Who saw what happened?
¿Quién vio lo que pasó? *(kee-'ehn vee-'oh loh keh pah-'soh)*
When did it happen?
¿Cuándo pasó eso? *('kwahn-doh pah-'soh 'eh-soh)*
How did it happen?
¿Cómo pasó eso? *('koh-moh pah-'soh 'eh-soh)*

➤ And why was the student sent to the office? Memorize this pattern:

Did you argue?
¿Discutiste? *(dees-koo-'tee-steh)*

Did you refuse?

¿Te negaste? *(teh neh-'gahs-teh)*

Did you disobey?

¿Desobedeciste? *(des-oh-beh-deh-'see-steh)*

Did you steal?

¿Robaste? *(roh-'bah-steh)*

Did you break it?

¿Lo quebraste? *(loh keh-'brah-steh)*

Did you lie?

¿Mentiste? *(men-'tee-steh)*

Did you lose it?

¿Lo perdiste? *(loh pehr-'dee-steh)*

Did you forget it?

¿Lo olvidaste? *(loh ohl-vee-'dah-steh)*

HOW DO YOU FEEL?

¿Cómo te sientes? *('koh-moh teh see-'ehn-tehs)*

A good part of counseling involves getting the other person to talk. This is especially true in an educational setting. Even though you'll probably end up asking for an interpreter, there's still a lot you can say all by yourself.

It seems you are...	**Parece que estás...** *(pah-'reh-seh keh eh-'stahs)*
afraid	**asustado** *(ah-soo-'stah-doh)*
angry	**enojado** *(eh-noh-'hah-doh)*
apathetic	**apático** *(ah-'pah-tee-koh)*
bitter	**amargado** *(ah-mahr-'gah-doh)*
distracted	**distraído** *(dee-strah-'ee-doh)*
frustrated	**frustrado** *(froo-'strah-doh)*
hostile	**hostil** *(oh-'steel)*
in mourning	**de luto** *(deh 'loo-toh)*
nervous	**nervioso** *(nehr-vee-'oh-soh)*
sad	**triste** *('tree-steh)*
tense	**tenso** *('tehn-soh)*

Don't stop talking about how the person feels. One method is to hold up a list of feelings in Spanish, and then ask the student to point to the word that best describes his or her emotions:

Do you feel...?	**¿Te sientes..?** *(teh see-'ehn-tehs)*
I feel...	**Me siento...** *(meh see-'ehn-toh)*

abused	**abusado** *(ah-boo-'sah-doh)*
anxious	**ansioso** *(ahn-see-'oh-soh)*
ashamed	**avergonzado** *(ah-vehr-gohn-'sah-doh)*
bored	**aburrido** *(ah-boo-'rree-doh)*
bothered	**molesto** *(moh-'leh-stoh)*
burned out	**agotado** *(ah-goh-'tah-doh)*
confused	**confundido** *(kohn-foon-'dee-doh)*
depressed	**deprimido** *(deh-pree-'mee-doh)*
desperate	**desesperado** *(dehs-eh-speh-'rah-doh)*
embarrassed	**turbado** *(toor-'bah-doh)*
fed up	**harto** *('ahr-toh)*
furious	**furioso** *(foo-ree-'oh-soh)*
guilty	**culpable** *(kool-'pah-bleh)*
hated	**odiado** *(oh-dee-'ah-doh)*
impatient	**impaciente** *(eem-pah-see-'ehn-teh)*
inferior	**inferior** *(een-feh-ree-'ohr)*
insecure	**inseguro** *(een-seh-'goo-roh)*
jealous	**celoso** *(seh-'loh-soh)*
resentful	**resentido** *(reh-sehn-'tee-doh)*
restless	**inquieto** *(een-kee-'eh-toh)*

sensitive	**sensible** *(sehn-'see-bleh)*
strange	**raro** *('rah-roh)*
trapped	**atrapado** *(ah-trah-'pah-doh)*
uncomfortable	**incómodo** *(een-'koh-moh-doh)*
unhappy	**descontento** *(dehs-kohn-'tehn-toh)*
worried	**preocupado** *(preh-oh-koo-'pah-doh)*

MÁS INFORMACIÓN

➤ Keep altering your descriptive words to reflect the feelings of female students:

La muchacha está <u>preocupada</u> y <u>confundida</u>. *(lah moo-'chah-chah eh-'stah pre-oh-koo-'pah-dah ee kohn-foon-'dee-dah)*

➤ Deeper emotions are a little tougher to describe:

suicidal tendencies	**tendencias suicidas** *(teh-'dehn-see·ahs soo-ee-'see-dahs)*
emotional instability	**inestabilidad emocional** *(een-eh-stah-bee-lee-'dahd eh-moh-see·oh-'nahl)*
violent behavior	**comportamiento violento** *(kohm-pohr-tah-mee-'ehn-toh vee-oh-'lehn-toh)*

¿LISTOS PARA PRACTICAR?

Connect the words that have similar meanings:

triste *('tree-steh)*	**relajado** *(reh-lah-'hah-doh)*
enojado *(eh-noh-'hah-doh)*	**ansioso** *(ahn-see-'oh-soh)*
nervioso *(nehr-vee-'oh-soh)*	**descontento** *(dehs-kohn-'tehn-toh)*
cómodo *('koh-moh-doh)*	**furioso** *(foo-ree-'oh-soh)*

Are you able to name three professionals who help out when students are in trouble?

_____   _____   _____

EMOTIONAL PROBLEMS
Los problemas emocionales *(lohs proh-'bleh-mahs eh-moh-see·oh-'nah-lehs)*

There's no need to elaborate on body parts and health problems since they were covered in an earlier chapter. However, some emotions may be health-related. Here are a few more phrases you may be exposed to during a counseling session:

I feel...	**Me siento...** *(meh see-'ehn-toh...)*
dizzy	**mareado** *(mah-reh-'ah-doh)*
faint	**débil** *('deh-beel)*
poorly	**mal** *(mahl)*
sleepy	**soñoliento** *(soh-nyoh-lee-'ehn-toh)*
sore	**dolorido** *(doh-loh-'ree-doh)*
I have problems with (the)...	**Tengo problemas con...** *('tehn-goh proh-'bleh-mahs kohn...)*
balance	**el equilibrio** *(ehl eh-kee-'lee-bree·oh)*
breathing	**la respiración** *(lah reh-spee-rah-see-'ohn)*
hearing	**el oído** *(ehl oh-'ee-doh)*
nerves	**los nervios** *(lohs 'nehr-vee·ohs)*
sight	**la vista** *(lah 'vee-stah)*
speech	**el habla** *(ehl 'ah-blah)*
There is/are...	**Hay...** *('ah·ee...)*
bad dreams	**sueños malos** *('sweh-nyohs 'mah-lohs)*
convulsions	**convulsiones** *(kohn-vool-see-'oh-nehs)*
headaches	**dolores de cabeza** *(doh-'loh-rehs deh kah-'beh-sah)*
insomnia	**insomnio** *(een-'sohm-nee·oh)*
loss of memory	**falta de memoria** *('fahl-tah deh meh-'moh-ree·ah)*
numbness	**adormecimiento** *(ah-dohr-meh-see-mee-'ehn-toh)*
seizures	**ataques** *(ah-'tah-kehs)*

Check the medical file on the student. Are there any causes for special attention or alarm?

It's (the)...	**Es...** *(ehs...)*
abnormality	**la anormalidad** *(lah ah-nohr-mah-lee-'dahd)*
disability	**la minusvalía** *(lah mee-noos-vah-'lee-ah)*
disease	**la enfermedad** *(lah ehn-fehr-meh-'dahd)*
disorder	**el desorden** *(ehl dehs-'ohr-dehn)*
handicap	**la incapacidad** *(lah een-kah-pah-see-'dahd)*
syndrome	**el síndrome** *(ehl 'seen-droh-meh)*

MÁS INFORMACIÓN

➤ When it comes to concerns about emotional health, make an effort to ask questions carefully. Practice with these:

Are you eating and sleeping OK?
¿Estás comiendo y durmiendo bien?
(eh-'stahs koh-mee-'ehn-doh ee door-mee-'ehn-doh 'bee·ehn)

Are you worried about anything?
¿Estás preocupado por algo?
(Eh-'stahs preh-oh-koo-'pah-doh pohr 'ahl-goh)

Did you have problems when you were a child?
¿Tuviste problemas de niño?
(too-'vees-teh proh-'bleh-mahs deh 'nee-nyoh)

Do you have good relations with your relatives and friends?
¿Tienes buenas relaciones con sus parientes y amigos?
(tee-'eh-nehs 'bweh-nahs reh-lah-see-'oh-ehs kohn soos pah-ree-'ehn-tehs ee ah-'mee-gohs)

Do you have many responsibilities?
¿Tienes muchas responsabilidades?
(tee-'eh-nehs 'moo-chahs reh-spohn-sah-bee-lee-'dah-dehs)

What illnesses and operations have you had?
¿Qué enfermedades y operaciones has tenido?
('keh ehn-fehr-meh-'dah-dehs ee oh-peh-rah-see-'oh-nehs ahs teh-'nee-doh)

When did the problem start?
¿Cuándo empezó el problema?
('kwahn-doh ehm-peh-'soh ehl proh-'bleh-mah)

SENSITIVE ISSUES
Los temas delicados *(lohs 'teh-mahs deh-lee-'kah-dohs)*

Learn to discuss any sensitive issue, but be sure that a fluent Spanish-speaking professional is there to assist you:

Would you like to talk about (the)...?
¿Quisieras hablar sobre...?
(kee-see-'eh-rahs ah-'blahr 'soh-breh)

abandonment	**el abandono** *(ehl ah-bahn-'doh-noh)*
abortion	**el aborto** *(ehl ah-'bohr-toh)*
death	**la muerte** *(lah 'mwehr-teh)*
depression	**la depresión** *(lah deh-preh-see-'ohn)*
divorce	**el divorcio** *(ehl dee-'vohr-see·oh)*
failure	**el fracaso** *(ehl frah-'kah-soh)*
incest	**el incesto** *(ehl een-'seh-stoh)*
loneliness	**la soledad** *(lah soh-leh-'dahd)*
molestation	**el acoso sexual** *(ehl ah-'koh-soh sehk-soo-'ahl)*
obesity	**la obesidad** *(lah oh-beh-see-'dahd)*
phobia	**la fobia** *(lah 'foh-bee·ah)*
rape	**la violación** *(lah vee-oh-lah-see-'ohn)*
tragedy	**la tragedia** *(lah trah-'heh-dee·ah)*
trauma	**el trauma** *(ehl 'trah-ooh-mah)*
It's (the)...	**Es...** *(ehs)*
belief	**la creencia** *(lah kreh-'ehn-see·ah)*
dream	**el sueño** *(ehl 'sweh-nyoh)*

feeling	**el sentimiento** *(ehl sehn-tee-mee-'ehn-toh)*
personality	**la personalidad** *(lah pehr-soh-nah-lee-'dahd)*
thought	**el pensamiento** *(ehl-pehn-sah-mee-'ehn-toh)*

To provide a few words of support:

| There's no... | **No hay...** *(noh'ah·ee...)* |

danger	**peligro** *(peh-'lee-groh)*
harm	**daño** *('dah-nyoh)*
obstacle	**obstáculo** *(ohb-'stah-koo-loh)*
pain	**dolor** *(doh-'lohr)*
risk	**riesgo** *(ree-'ehs-goh)*

MÁS INFORMACIÓN

➤ The topic of sex can get delicate, but don't hesitate to probe if there's a concern. Here are some words you may hear:

birth control	**la anticoncepción** *(lah ahn-tee-kohn-sehp-see-'ohn)*
condom	**el condón** *(ehl kohn-'dohn)*
family planning	**la planificación familiar** *(lah plah-nee-fee-kah-see-'ohn fah-mee-lee-'ahr)*
homosexuality	**la homosexualidad** *(lah oh-moh-sehk-soo-ah-lee-'dahd)*
hormones	**las hormonas** *(lahs ohr-'moh-nahs)*
intercourse	**el coito** *(ehl koh-'ee-toh)*
masturbation	**la masturbación** *(lah mah-stoor-bah-see-'ohn)*
menstrual period	**la regla** *(lah'reh-glah)*
pregnancy test	**el examen de embarazo** *(ehl ehk-'sah-mehn deh ehm-bah-'rah-soh)*
sexual relations	**las relaciones sexuales** *(lahs reh-lah-see-'oh-nehs sehk-soo-'ah-lehs)*

THE SPECIAL STUDENT

El estudiante especial *(ehl eh-stoo-dee-'ahn-teh eh-speh-see-'ahl)*

As the young people wander in and out for assistance, be sure that all who speak Spanish receive the attention they need. In some cases, students with very special needs are mainstreamed into regular programs, which puts unique demands on the counseling staff.

It's a case of...	**Es un caso de...** *(ehs oon'kah-soh deh...)*
cerebral palsy	**parálisis cerebral** *(pah-'rah-lee-sees seh-reh-'brahl)*
cystic fibrosis	**fibrosis quística** *(fee-'broh-sees'kee-stee-kah)*
Down's syndrome	**síndrome de Down** *('seen-droh-meh deh'dowhn)*
epilepsy	**epilepsia** *(eh-pee-'lehp-see·ah)*
multiple sclerosis	**esclerosis múltiple** *(eh-skleh-'roh-sees'mool-tee-pleh)*
muscular dystrophy	**distrofia muscular** *(dees-'troh-fee·ah moo-skoo-'lahr)*
osteoarthritis	**osteoartritis** *(oh-steh-oh-ahr-'tree-tees)*
paralysis	**parálisis** *(pah-'rah-lee-sees)*
polio	**polio** *('poh-lee·oh)*
retardation	**retraso** *(reh-'trah-soh)*
It's...	**Es...** *(ehs...)*
AIDS	**SIDA** *('see-dah)*
cancer	**cáncer** *('kahn-sehr)*
leukemia	**leucemia** *(leh-oo-'seh-mee·ah)*

MORE DISABILITIES

Más incapacidades *(mahs een-kah-pah-see-'dah-dehs)*

In addition to the severely handicapped students, there are others who have been diagnosed with lesser concerns. Sometimes, simple physical disabilities can affect academic success in the classroom.

Do you have...	¿Tienes...? *(tee-'eh-nehs...)*
allergies	**alergias** *(ah-'lehr-hee·ahs)*
asthma	**asma** *('ahs-mah)*
astigmatism	**astigmatismo** *(ah-steeg-mah-'tees-moh)*
attention deficit disorder	**dificultades a prestar atención** *(dee-fee-kool-'tah-dehs ah preh-'stahr ah-tehn-see-'ohn)*
diabetes	**diabetes** *(dee-ah-'beh-tehs)*
hay fever	**fiebre del heno** *(fee-'eh-breh dehl'eh-noh)*
high blood pressure	**presión de sangre alta** *(preh-see-'ohn deh'sahn-greh'ahl-tah)*
limp	**cojera** *(koh-'heh-rah)*
myopia	**miopía** *(mee-oh-'pee-ah)*
stutter	**tartamudeo** *(tahr-tah-moo-'deh-oh)*
He is...	**Es...** *(ehs...)*
hyperactive	**hiperactivo** *(ee-pehr-ahk-'tee-voh)*
impaired	**debilitado** *(deh-bee-lee-'tah-doh)*
slow	**lento** *('lehn-toh)*

MÁS INFORMACIÓN

➤ You may also hear about items that special students bring to school. Utilize the phrases below:

He needs (the)...	**Necesita...** *(neh-seh-'see-tah...)*
She uses (the)...	**Usa...** *('oo-sah...)*
cane	**el bastón** *(ehl bah-'stohn)*
contact lenses	**los lentes de contacto** *(lohs'lehn-tehs deh kohn-'tahk-toh)*
crutches	**las muletas** *(lahs moo-'leh-tahs)*
glasses	**los lentes** *(lohs'lehn-tehs)*
guide dog	**el perro lazarillo** *(ehl'peh-rroh lah-sah-'ree-yoh)*
hearing aids	**los audífonos** *(lohs ow-'dee-foh-nohs)*
wheelchair	**la silla de ruedas** *(lah'see-yah deh roo-'eh-dahs)*

➤ Don't forget surgery. Notice this key phrase:

He had _____ surgery.   **Tuvo cirugía en _____ .** *('too-voh see-roo-'hee-ah ehn _____)*

arm	**el brazo** *(ehl 'brah-soh)*
brain	**el cerebro** *(ehl seh-'reh-broh)*
heart	**el corazón** *(ehl koh-rah-'sohn)*
leg	**la pierna** *(lah pee-'ehr-nah)*
lungs	**los pulmones** *(lohs pool-'moh-nehs)*
stomach	**el estómago** *(ehl eh-'stoh-mah-goh)*

It's not difficult to guess the meanings of these Spanish words:

anemia *(ah-'neh-mee·ah)*
anorexia *(ah-noh-'rehk-see·ah)*
bulimia *(boo-'lee-mee·ah)*

SOME ADVICE
Unos consejos *('oo-nohs kohn-'seh-hohs)*

Now that you've heard what's troubling the student, how about offering a little advice. Of course, if the problem is serious, contact the family along with anyone else who can help. Next, request an interpreter. Open with one-liners that get everyone to settle down.

You should...	Debe... *('deh-beh...)*
calm down	**calmarse** *(kahl-'mahr-seh)*
relax	**relajarse** *(reh-lah-'hahr-seh)*
rest	**descansar** *(deh-skahn-'sahr)*
breathe deeply	**respirar profundamente** *(reh-spee-'rahr proh-foon-dah-'mehn-teh)*
leave this office	**salir de esta oficina** *(sah-'leer deh'eh-stah oh-fee-'see-nah)*
lower your voice	**bajar la voz** *(bah-'hahr lah vohs)*
come back later	**regresar más tarde** *(reh-greh-'sahr mahs'tahr-deh)*
pay attention	**prestar atención** *(preh-'stahr ah-tehn-see-'ohn)*

Are you all set to counsel? Keep your comments short as you create the phrases that you'll need:

You need to...	Necesitas... *(neh-seh-'see-tahs...)*
call your doctor	**llamar a tu doctor** *(yah-'mahr ah too dohk-'tohr)*
get more sleep	**dormir más** *(dohr-'meer mahs)*
see a specialist	**ver a un especialista** *(vehr ah oon eh-speh-see·ah-'lee-stah)*
take your medication	**tomar tu medicamento** *(toh-'mahr too meh-dee-kah-'mehn-toh)*
tell your family	**decirle a tu familia** *(deh-'seer-leh ah too fah-'mee-lee·ah)*
go to class	**ir a tu clase** *(eer ah too'klah-seh)*
stay away from them	**apartarte de ellos** *(ah-pahr-'tahr-teh deh 'eh-yohs)*
change your class schedule	**cambiar tu horario de clases** *(kahm-bee-'ahr too oh-'rah-ree·oh deh'klah-sehs)*

You shouldn't...	No debes... *(noh'deh-behs...)*
antagonize	**antagonizar** *(ahn-tah-goh-nee-'sahr)*
argue	**discutir** *(dees-koo-'teer)*
bother	**molestar** *(moh-leh-'stahr)*
curse	**maldecir** *(mahl-deh-'seer)*

gossip	**chismear** *(chees-meh-'ahr)*
humiliate	**humillar** *(oo-mee-'yahr)*
joke	**bromear** *(broh-meh-'ahr)*
lie	**mentir** *(mehn-'teer)*
tease	**burlarte** *(boor-'lahr-teh)*

Keep mentioning solutions or suggestions:

We offer (the)...	**Ofrecemos...** *(oh-freh-'seh-mohs...)*
different classes	**diferentes clases** *(dee-feh-'rehn-tehs 'klah-sehs)*
individualized plans	**planes individualizados** *('plah-nehs een-dee-vee-doo-ah-lee-'sah-dohs)*
intensive therapy	**terapia intensiva** *(teh-'rah-pee·ah een-tehn-'see-vah)*
personal contracts	**contratos personales** *(kohn-'trah-tohs pehr-soh-'nah-lehs)*
personality tests	**pruebas de personalidad** *(proo-'eh-bahs deh pehr-soh-nah-lee-'dahd)*
recovery groups	**grupos de recuperación** *('groo-pohs deh reh-koo-peh-rah-see-'ohn)*
rehabilitation	**rehabilitación** *(reh-ah-bee-lee-tah-see-'ohn)*
sign language	**lenguaje de sordomudos** *(lehn-'gwah-heh deh sohr-doh-'moo-dohs)*
special programs	**programas especiales** *(proh-'grah-mahs eh-speh-see-'ah-lehs)*
tutoring	**tutores** *(too-'toh-rehs)*
The program is...	**El programa es...** *(ehl proh-'grah-mah ehs...)*
adaptive	**adaptivo** *(ah-dahp-'tee-voh)*
educational	**educativo** *(eh-doo-kah-'tee-voh)*
for home study	**para estudiar en casa** *('pah-rah eh-stoo-dee-'ahr ehn 'kah-sah)*
private	**privado** *(pree-'vah-doh)*
vocational	**vocacional** *(voh-kah-see·oh-'nahl)*

➤ Get help from these professionals:

Talk to (the)...   **Habla con...** *('ah-blah kohn...)*

allergist   **el alergista** *(ehl ah-lehr-'hee-stah)*
chiropractor   **el quiropráctico** *(ehl kee-roh-'prahk-tee-koh)*
dentist   **el dentista** *(ehl dehn-'tee-stah)*
gynecologist   **el ginecólogo** *(ehl hee-neh-'koh-loh-goh)*
ophthalmologist   **el oftalmólogo** *(ehl ohf-tahl-'moh-loh-goh)*
optometrist   **el optometrista** *(ehl ohp-toh-meh-'tree-stah)*
orthodontist   **el ortodontista** *(ehl ohr-toh-dohn-'tee-stah)*
pediatrician   **el pediatra** *(ehl peh-dee-'ah-trah)*
physician   **el médico** *(ehl 'meh-dee-koh)*

Translate, and then connect the related vocabulary:

la vista *(lah 'vee-stah)*   **la silla de ruedas** *(lah 'see-yah deh roo-'eh-dahs)*
el oído *(ehl oh-'ee-doh)*   **los lentes** *(lohs 'lehn-tehs)*
el equilibrio *(ehl eh-*   **los audífonos** *(lohs ow-'dee-foh-nohs)*
   kee-'lee-bree·oh)

Name in Spanish three internal organs:

_____   _____   _____

Name in Spanish three traumatic events that often result in emotional problems:

_____   _____   _____

Complete each sentence with words you've just learned:

terapia, calmarse, bastón, polio, dolorido *(teh-'rah-pee·ah, kahl-'mahr-seh, bah-'stohn,'poh-lee·oh, doh-loh-'ree-doh)*

Debes _____ *('deh-behs _____)*

Me siento _____ *(meh see-'ehn-toh _____)*

Es un caso de _____ *(ehs oon'kah-soh deh _____)*

Ofrecemos _____ *(oh-freh-'seh-mohs _____)*

Usa _____ *('oo-sah _____)*

WORDS OF ENCOURAGEMENT
Palabras de ánimo *(pah-'lah-brahs deh'ah-nee-moh)*

Personal problems can be helped once the comment focuses on the positive. The following list of questions ask the student to come up with a solution. Have an interpreter at your side.

I'd like to hear your ideas.
Quisiera escuchar tus ideas.
(kee-see-'eh-rah eh-skoo-'chahr toos ee-'deh-ahs)

What other possibilities do you see?
¿Cuáles son las otras posibilidades que ves?
('kwah-lehs sohn lahs'oh-trahs poh-see-bee-lee-'dah-dehs keh vehs)

What steps would you take to correct the problem?
¿Qué medidas tomarías para corregir el problema?
(keh meh-'dee-dahs toh-mah-'ree-ahs'pah-rah koh-rreh-'heer ehl proh-'bleh-mah)

Are you convinced that this is the best solution?
¿Estás seguro de que ésta es la mejor solución?
(eh-'stahs seh-'goo-roh deh keh'eh-stah ehs lah meh-'hohr soh-loo-see-'ohn)

How do you feel about it?
¿Cómo te sientes acerca de eso?
('koh-moh teh see-'ehn-tehs ah-'sehr-kah deh'eh-soh)

Let's analyze and resolve the problem.
Vamos a analizar y resolver el problema.
(vah-mohs ah ah-nah-lee-'sahr ee reh-sohl-'vehr ehl proh-'bleh-mah)

I'd like to hear your...   **Quisiera escuchar tu...**
                             (kee-see-'eh-rah eh-skoo-'chahr too...)

comment	**comentario** *(koh-mehn-'tah-ree·oh)*
idea	**idea** *(ee-'deh-ah)*
interpretation	**interpretación** *(een-tehr-preh-tah-see-'ohn)*
opinion	**opinión** *(oh-pee-nee-'ohn)*
response	**respuesta** *(reh-'spweh-stah)*

This time, add a smile as you motivate others around you:

You have...	**Tú tienes...** *(too tee-'eh-nehs...)*
I see...	**Yo veo...** *(yoh 'veh-oh...)*
These is/are...	**Hay...** *('ah·ee...)*

excellent achievements
logros excelentes
('loh-grohs eks-seh-'lehn-tehs)

fast development
desarrollo rápido
(dehs-ah-'rroh-yoh 'rah-pee-doh)

good effort
buen esfuerzo
(bwehn ehs-'fwehr-soh)

great potential
gran potencial
(grahn poh-tehn-see-'ahl)

lots of desire
mucho deseo
('moo-choh deh-'seh-oh)

more success
más éxito
(mahs'ehk-see-toh)

obvious progress
progreso obvio
(proh-'greh-soh'ohb-vee·oh)

outstanding conduct
conducta destacada
(kohn-'dook-tah deh-stah-'kah-dah)

self-motivation
motivación personal
(moh-tee-vah-see-'ohn pehr-soh-'nahl)

sense of accomplishment
sentido de logro
(sehn-'tee-doh deh'loh-groh)

tremendous growth
crecimiento tremendo
(kreh-see-mee-'ehn-toh treh-'mehn-doh)

Now, say something to the students that will motivate them:

You are...	**Tú eres...** *(too'eh-rehs...)*
attentive	**atento** *(ah-'tehn-toh)*
bright	**brillante** *(bree-'yahn-teh)*
capable	**capaz** *(kah-'pahs)*
clever	**listo** *('lee-stoh)*
compassionate	**compasivo** *(kohm-pah-'see-voh)*
confident	**seguro** *(seh-'goo-roh)*
cooperative	**dispuesto** *(dee-'spweh-stoh)*
courageous	**valiente** *(vah-lee-'ehn-teh)*
decent	**decente** *(deh-'sehn-teh)*
ethical	**ético** *('eh-tee-koh)*
fair	**justo** *('hoo-stoh)*
friendly	**amistoso** *(ah-mee-'stoh-soh)*
healthy	**sano** *('sah-noh)*

helpful	**servicial** *(sehr-vee-see-'ahl)*
honest	**honesto** *(oh-'neh-stoh)*
intelligent	**inteligente** *(een-teh-lee-'hehn-teh)*
kind	**amable** *(ah-'mah-bleh)*
loved	**querido** *(keh-'ree-doh)*
nice	**simpático** *(seem-'pah-tee-koh)*
patient	**paciente** *(pah-see-'ehn-teh)*
polite	**cortés** *(kohr-'tehs)*
respectful	**respetuoso** *(reh-speh-too-'oh-soh)*
responsible	**responsable** *(reh-spohn-'sah-bleh)*
thoughtful	**considerado** *(kohn-see-deh-'rah-doh)*

MÁS INFORMACIÓN

➤ Let the family know how you feel about their child:

He has...	**Tiene...** *(tee-'eh-neh...)*

self-respect	**amor propio** *(ah-'mohr'proh-pee·oh)*
self-control	**control de sí mismo** *(kohn-'trohl deh see'mees-moh)*
nice manners	**buenos modales** *('bweh-nohs moh-'dah-lehs)*
strong values	**valores fuertes** *(vah-'loh-rehs'fwehr-tehs)*
personal convictions	**convicciones personales** *(kohn-veek-see-'oh-nehs pehr-soh-'nah-lehs)*

CAN YOU GIVE A DESCRIPTION?
¿Puedes dar una descripción? *('pweh-dehs dahr'oo-nah deh-skreep-see-'ohn)*

How well do you know your students? While practicing the next series of words, picture a person who fits the descriptive word. As usual, some of these need to be changed when you refer to a female:

The student is...	**El estudiante es...** *(ehl eh-stoo-dee-'ahn-teh ehs...)*

beautiful	**bella** *('beh-yah)*
blonde	**rubio** *('roo-bee·oh)*

brunette	**moreno** *(moh-'reh-noh)*
fat	**gordo** *('gohr-doh)*
funny	**chistoso** *(chee-'stoh-soh)*
handsome	**guapo** *('gwah-poh)*
immature	**inmaduro** *(een-mah-'doo-roh)*
left-handed	**zurdo** *('soor-doh)*
loud	**ruidoso** *(roo-ee-'doh-soh)*
mature	**maduro** *(mah-'doo-roh)*
older	**mayor** *(mah-'yohr)*
poor	**pobre** *('poh-breh)*
quiet	**quieto** *(kee-'eh-toh)*
red-headed	**pelirrojo** *(peh-lee-'rroh-hoh)*
rich	**rico** *('ree-koh)*
right-handed	**diestro** *(dee-'eh-stroh)*
short	**bajo** *('bah-hoh)*
shy	**tímido** *('tee-mee-doh)*
sloppy	**descuidado** *(dehs-kwee-'dah-doh)*
strong	**fuerte** *('fwehr-teh)*
tall	**alto** *('ahl-toh)*
thin	**delgado** *(dehl-'gah-doh)*
weak	**débil** *('deh-beel)*
young	**joven** *('hoh-vehn)*
younger	**menor** *(meh-'nohr)*

MÁS INFORMACIÓN

➤ Look a little closer at your student. Did you mention everything?

I see (the)...	**Veo...** *('veh-oh...)*

goatee	**la perita** *(lah peh-'ree-tah)*
ponytail	**la coleta** *(lah koh-'leh-tah)*
sideburns	**las patillas** *(lahs pah-'tee-yahs)*

THE FAMILY CONFERENCE
La reunión con la familia *(lah reh-oo-nee-'ohn kohn lah fah-'mee-lee·ah)*

Working on issues with students is one thing, but sharing that information with their families is something else. Why not start at the beginning. Either by phone or in person, let the family know why you need to meet.

Could you come to the office?
¿Puede venir a la oficina? *('pweh-deh veh-'neer ah lah oh-fee-'see-nah)*

I would like to talk to you.
Quisiera hablar con usted. *(kee-see-'eh-rah ah-'blahr kohn oo-'stehd)*

It's about _____ .
Tiene que ver con _____ . *(tee-'eh-neh keh vehr kohn _____)*

It's important that you come.
Es importante que venga usted. *(ehs eem-pohr-'tahn-teh keh'vehn-gah oo-'stehd)*

Be here at _____ .
Venga a _____ . *('vehn-gah ah _____)*

It's a...   **Es...** *(ehs...)*

serious   **serio** *('seh-ree·oh)*
urgent   **urgente** *(oor-'hehn-teh)*
necessary   **necesario** *(neh-seh-'sah-ree·oh)*

Invite the appropriate person. Use this pattern to clarify who everyone is.

Are you the...?   **¿Es usted...?** *(ehs oo-'stehd...)*

aunt   **la tía** *(lah 'tee-ah)*
brother   **el hermano** *(ehl ehr-'mah-noh)*

cousin	**el primo** *(ehl'pree-moh)*
daughter	**la hija** *(lah'ee-hah)*
father	**el padre** *(ehl'pah-dreh)*
granddaughter	**la nieta** *(lah nee-'eh-tah)*
grandfather	**el abuelo** *(ehl ah-'bweh-loh)*
grandmother	**la abuela** *(lah ah-'bweh-lah)*
grandson	**el nieto** *(ehl nee-'eh-toh)*
husband	**el esposo** *(ehl eh-spoh-soh)*
mother	**la madre** *(lah'mah-dreh)*
nephew	**el sobrino** *(ehl soh-'bree-noh)*
niece	**la sobrina** *(lah soh-'bree-nah)*
sister	**la hermana** *(lah ehr-'mah-nah)*
son	**el hijo** *(ehl'ee-hoh)*
uncle	**el tío** *(ehl'tee-oh)*
wife	**la esposa** *(lah eh-'spoh-sah)*

 CONFLICTOS CULTURALES

Because the traditional Hispanic family includes more than just its immediate members, you may want to consider learning the names for relatives outside the immediate family:

acquaintance	**el compañero** *(ehl kohm-pah-'nyeh-roh)*
boyfriend	**el novio** *(ehl'noh-vee·oh)*
brother-in-law	**el cuñado** *(ehl koo-'nyah-doh)*
close friend	**el amigo** *(ehl ah-'mee-goh)*
daughter-in-law	**la nuera** *(lah noo-'eh-rah)*
father-in-law	**el suegro** *(ehl'sweh-groh)*
foster family	**los padres sustitutos** *(lohs'pah-drehs soo-stee-'too-tohs)*
goddaughter	**la ahijada** *(lah ah-ee-'hah-dah)*
godson	**el ahijado** *(ehl ah-ee-'hah-doh)*
godfather	**el compadre** *(ehl kohm-'pah-dreh)*
godmother	**la comadre** *(lah koh-'mah-dreh)*
godparents	**los padrinos** *(lohs pah-'dree-nohs)*
girlfriend	**la novia** *(lah'noh-vee·ah)*
legal guardian	**el tutor legal** *(ehl too-'tohr leh-'gahl)*
mother-in-law	**la suegra** *(lah'sweh-grah)*

relative	**el pariente** *(ehl pah-ree-'ehn-teh)*
sister-in-law	**la cuñada** *(lah koo-'nyah-dah)*
son-in-law	**el yerno** *(ehl'yehr-noh)*
stepfather	**el padrastro** *(ehl pah-'drah-stroh)*
stepmother	**la madrastra** *(lah mah-'drah-strah)*

HOW ARE THEY DOING IN SCHOOL?
¿Cómo van en la escuela? *('koh-moh vahn ehn lah eh-'skweh-lah)*

In most cases, educators invite relatives and friends to visit in order to discuss student progress. Let's begin with the positive.

The student is very...	**El estudiante es muy...** *(ehl eh-stoo-dee-'ahn-teh ehs 'moo·ee...)*

artistic	**artístico** *(ahr-'tee-stee-koh)*
athletic	**atlético** *(aht-'leh-tee-koh)*
industrious	**aplicado** *(ah-plee-'kah-doh)*
neat	**limpio** *('leem-pee·oh)*
obedient	**obediente** *(oh-beh-dee-'ehn-teh)*
organized	**organizado** *(ohr-gah-nee-'sah-doh)*
punctual	**puntual** *(poon-too-'ahl)*
respectful	**respetuoso** *(reh-speh-too-'oh-soh)*
studious	**aplicado** *(ah-plee-'kah-doh)*

He/She...	El/Ella... *(ehl/'eh-yah)*
retains information	**retiene la información** *(reh-tee-'eh-neh lah een-fohr-mah-see-'ohn)*
is good at it	**tiene facilidad para eso** *(tee-'eh-neh fah-see-lee-'dahd 'pah-rah 'eh-soh)*
takes the time	**toma su tiempo** *('toh-mah soo tee-'ehm-poh)*
behaves well	**se porta bien** *(seh 'pohr-tah 'bee·ehn)*
follows directions	**sigue instrucciones** *('see-geh een-strook-see-'oh-nehs)*
obeys the rules	**obedece las reglas** *(oh-beh-'deh-seh lahs 'reh-glahs)*
does the homework	**hace la tarea** *('ah-seh lah tah-'reh-ah)*
pays attention	**presta atención** *('preh-stah ah-tehn-see-'ohn)*
is very advanced	**es muy adelantado(a)** *(ehs 'moo·ee ah-deh-lahn-'tah-doh[ah])*

You're welcome to add phrases to the lists above. Also remember that in order to create a negative statement in Spanish, all you need to do is add **no** in front of the verb:

She doesn't behave well.	**Ella no se porta bien.** *('eh-yah noh seh 'pohr-tah 'bee·ehn)*

Speaking of negative statements, here are a few more words you might want to know:

He is...	Es... *(ehs...)*
cruel	**cruel** *(kroo-'ehl)*
forgetful	**olvidadizo** *(ohl-vee-dah-'dee-soh)*
lazy	**perezoso** *(peh-reh-'soh-soh)*
restless	**inquieto** *(een-kee-'eh-toh)*
rude	**grosero** *(groh-'seh-roh)*
sassy	**fresco** *('freh-skoh)*
selfish	**egoísta** *(eh-goh-'ee-stah)*

Close out the conference by asking a few questions or sharing your opinion. If you studied hard and feel brave, make any recommendations that you feel may be necessary:

Why do you think he...?
¿Por qué piensa usted que...? *(pohr keh pee-'ehn-sah oo-'stehd keh...)*

isn't interested   **no está interesado** *(noh eh-'stah een-teh-reh-'sah-doh)*

doesn't study   **no estudia** *(noh eh-'stoo-dee·ah)*

stays quiet   **se queda quieto** *(seh'keh-dah kee-'eh-toh)*

always arrives late   **siempre llega tarde** *(see-'ehm-preh'yeh-gah'tahr-deh)*

misses school   **falta a la escuela** *('fahl-tah ah lah eh-'skweh-lah)*

likes to fight   **le gusta pelear** *(leh'goo-stah peh-leh-'ahr)*

is failing classes   **está fallando en sus clases** *(eh-'stah fah-'yahn-doh ehn soos'klah-sehs)*

Ask your son what he learned.
Pregúnte a su hijo qué aprendió. *(preh-'goon-teh ah soo'ee-hoh keh ah-prehn-dee-'oh)*

Come to the parent meetings.
Venga a las reuniones de los padres. *('vehn-gah ah lahs reh-oo-nee-'oh-nehs deh lohs'pah-drehs)*

Call us if there is a problem.
Llámenos si hay un problema. *('yah-meh-nohs see'ah·ee oon proh-'bleh-mah)*

Students need...   **Los estudiantes necesitan...** *(lohs eh-stoo-dee-'ahn-tehs neh-seh-'see-tahn...)*

counseling   **consejos** *(kohn-'seh-hohs)*

discipline   **disciplina** *(dee-see-'plee-nah)*

independence   **independencia** *(een-deh-pehn-'dehn-see·ah)*

praise   **alabanzas** *(ah-lah-'bahn-sahs)*

support   **apoyo** *(ah-'poh-yoh)*

➤ Continue questioning the family members:

Do you help him?   **¿Le ayuda?** *(leh ah-'yoo-dah)*

Do you praise him?   **¿Le alaba?** *(leh ah-'lah-bah)*

Do you punish him?   **¿Le castiga?** *(leh kah-'stee-gah)*

> Sometimes meetings with counselors don't go exactly as planned:

It's cancelled. **Está cancelado.** *(eh-'stah kahn-seh-'lah-doh)*

I'm going to postpone it. **Voy a posponerlo.** *('voh·ee ah pohs-poh-'nehr-loh)*

They changed it. **Lo han cambiado.** *(loh ahn kahm-bee-'ah-doh)*

I have to go to a meeting. **Tengo que ir a una reunión.** *('tehn-goh keh eer ah 'oo-nah reh-oo-nee-'ohn)*

I'm with another student. **Estoy con otro estudiante.** *(eh-'stoh·ee kohn 'oh-troh eh-stoo-dee-'ahn-teh)*

Talk to me after school. **Hábleme después de horas de escuela.** *('ah-bleh-meh deh-'spwehs deh 'oh-rahs deh eh-'skweh-lah)*

Please come back later. **Regrese más tarde, por favor.** *(reh-'greh-seh mahs 'tahr-deh, pohr fah-'vohr)*

I can't meet right now. **No puedo tener reunión ahora.** *(noh 'pweh-doh teh-'nehr reh-oo-nee-'ohn ah-'oh-rah)*

¿LISTOS PARA PRACTICAR?

Make five positive comments about your favorite student:

_____ _____ _____ _____ _____

Match these opposites:

rubio *('roo-bee·oh)*   **delgado** *(dehl-'gah-doh)*
gordo *('gohr-doh)*   **alto** *('ahl-toh)*
fuerte *('fwehr-teh)*   **rico** *('ree-koh)*
bajo *('bah-hoh)*   **moreno** *(moh-'reh-noh)*
pobre *('poh-breh)*   **débil** *('deh-beel)*

Translate into English:

Ella no se porta bien. *('eh-yah noh seh 'pohr-tah 'bee·ehn)*
Ella falta a la escuela. *('eh-yah 'fahl-tah ah lah eh-'skweh-lah)*
Ella es fresca y ruda. *('eh-yah ehs 'freh-skah ee 'roo-dah)*

Complete these sets: **tío:tía** *('tee-oh, 'tee-ah)*
                                         sobrino:sobrina *(soh-'bree-noh, soh-'bree-nah)*

yerno: _____ *('yehr-noh)*

nieto: _____ *(nee-'eh-toh)*

padrino: _____ *(pah-'dree-noh)*

novia: _____ *('noh-vee·ah)*

madrastra: _____ *(mah-'drah-strah)*

PLANNING FOR THE FUTURE
La planificación para el futuro
(lah plah-nee-fee-kah-see-'ohn 'pah-rah ehl foo-'too-roh)

Guidance and career counselors take on special duties as they deal with older students. These sample phrases should help:

There are...	**Hay...** *('ah·ee...)*
job opportunities	**oportunidades para trabajar** *(oh-pohr-too-nee-'dah-dehs 'pah-rah trah-bah-'hahr)*
job placement	**asignación de trabajo** *(ah-seeg-nah-see-'ohn deh trah-'bah-hoh)*
job requirements	**requisitos para el trabajo** *(reh-kee-'see-tohs 'pah-rah ehl trah-'bah-hoh)*
It's (the)...	**Es...** *(ehs...)*
career planning	**la planificación de carreras** *(lah plah-nee-fee-kah-see-'ohn deh kah-'rreh-rahs)*
summer school	**la escuela del verano** *(lah eh-'skweh-lah deh veh-'rah-noh)*
technical training	**el entrenamiento técnico** *(ehl ehn-treh-nah-mee-'ehn-toh 'tehk-nee-koh)*
volunteer program	**el programa voluntario** *(ehl proh-'grah-mah voh-loon-'tah-ree·oh)*
work experience	**la experiencia en el trabajo** *(lah ehk-speh-ree-'ehn-see·ah ehn ehl trah-'bah-hoh)*

Here's information about (the)...
Aquí tiene información acerca de... *(ah-'kee tee-'eh-neh een-fohr-mah-see-'ohn ah-'sehr-kah deh...)*

application	**la solicitud** *(lah soh-lee-see-'tood)*
armed forces	**las fuerzas armadas** *(lahs 'fwehr-sahs ahr-'mah-dahs)*
degree	**la licenciatura** *(lah lee-sehn-see·ah-'too-rah)*
electives	**la materia optativa** *(lah mah-'teh-ree·ah ohp-tah-'tee-vah)*
entrance exams	**los exámenes de entrada** *(lohs ehk-'sah-meh-nehs deh ehn-'trah-dah)*
financial aid	**la ayuda financiera** *(lah ah-'yoo-dah fee-nahn-see-'eh-rah)*
funding	**la obtención de fondos** *(lah ohb-tehn-see-'ohn deh 'fohn-dohs)*
letters of recommendation	**las cartas de recomendación** *(lahs 'kahr-tahs deh reh-koh-mehn-dah-see-'ohn)*
loan	**el préstamo** *(ehl 'preh-stah-moh)*
prerequisites	**los prerrequisitos** *(lohs preh-rreh-kee-'see-tohs)*
registration	**la inscripción** *(lah een-skreep-see-'ohn)*
scholarship	**la beca** *(lah 'beh-kah)*
testing	**los exámenes** *(lohs ehk-'sah-meh-nehs)*
transcripts	**la copia de los certificados de estudio** *(lah 'koh-pee·ah deh lohs sehr-tee-fee-'kah-dohs deh eh-'stoo-dee·oh)*

MÁS INFORMACIÓN

➤ How about summer employment:

There's work at (the)...   **Hay trabajo en...** *('ah·ee trah-'bah-hoh ehn...)*

camp	**el campamento** *(ehl kahm-pah-'mehn-toh)*
club	**el club** *(ehl kloob)*
hotel	**el hotel** *(ehl oh-'tehl)*
lodge	**la logia** *(lah 'loh-hee·ah)*

ranch	**el rancho** *(ehl'rahn-choh)*
resort	**el lugar de vacaciones** *(ehl loo-'gahr deh vah-kah-see-'oh-nehs)*

➤ These terms should be familiar to most educators:

Bachelor of Arts	**la licenciatura de letras** *(lah lee-sehn-see·ah-'too-rah deh'leh-trahs)*
Bachelor of Science	**la licenciatura de ciencias** *(lah lee-sehn-see·ah-'too-rah deh see-'ehn-see·ahs)*
Doctorate degree	**el doctorado** *(ehl dohk-toh-'rah-doh)*
Master of Arts	**la maestría en letras** *(lah mah-eh-'stree-ah ehn 'leh-trahs)*
Master of Science	**la maestría en ciencias** *(lah mah-eh-'stree-ah ehn see-'ehn-see·ahs)*
Ph.D.	**el doctorado en el campo de las humanidades** *(ehl dohk-toh-'rah-doh ehn ehl'kahm-poh deh lahs oo-mah-nee-'dah-dehs)*

CONFLICTOS CULTURALES

Many of the words here can be used to assist educators at schools of higher learning. The only difference might be in the way you talk to students. Instead of using the "**tú**" form, try sending messages formally with "**usted**."

¡ACCIÓN!

Here's still another way to talk about past actions. The past progressive tense has two parts, so pay attention:

First, give your **-ar** verbs the **-ando** endings and the **-er** or **-ir** verbs the **-iendo** endings. You've done this before:

hablar *(ah-'blahr)*	**hablando** *(ah-'blahn-doh)*
comer *(koh-'mehr)*	**comiendo** *(koh-mee-'ehn-doh)*
escribir *(eh-skree-'beer)*	**escribiendo** *(eh-skree-bee-'ehn-doh)*

Second, change the verb **estar** *(eh-'stahr)* to the following past tense form:

I was	**estaba** *(eh-'stah-bah)*
You were (informal)	**estabas** *(eh-'stah-bahs)*
You (formal) were; He, She was	**estaba** *(eh-'stah-bah)*
You (pl.), They were	**estaban** *(eh-'stah-bahn)*
We were	**estábamos** *(eh-'stah-bah-mohs)*

Now, put them together. This past progressive is like the present progressive because it gets easier the more you practice:

I was studying.	**Estaba estudiando.** *(eh-'stah-bah eh-stoo-dee-'ahn-doh)*
She was reading.	**Estaba leyendo.** *(eh-'stah-bah leh-'yehn-doh)*
They were leaving.	**Estaban saliendo.** *(eh-'stah-bah sah-lee-'ehn-doh)*
We were calling.	**Estábamos llamando.** *(eh-'stah-bah-mohs yah-'mahn-doh)*

 ¡ÓRDENES!

Generally speaking, the words **lo** *(loh)* or **la** *(lah)* refer to "it" in Spanish (**lo** for masculine, **la** for feminine). They can be very useful when they are added to your formal or informal commands:

Bring	**Traiga** *('trah·ee-gah)*
Bring it.	**Tráigala.** *('trah·ee-gah-lah)*
Do	**Haz** *(ahs)*
Do it.	**Hazlo.** *('ahs-loh)*

All set to put a few together? Try talking to several students at once:

Everyone, pick it up and put it in the trash!
¡Todos, recójanlo y métanlo en la basura!
('toh-dohs, reh-'koh-hahn-loh ee 'meh-tahn-loh ehn lah bah-'soo-rah)

228

➤ Check the pattern in these negative commands:

Don't do it!	**¡No lo hagas!** *(noh loh'ah-gahs)*
Don't throw it!	**¡No la tires!** *(noh lah'tee-rehs)*
Don't move it!	**¡No lo muevas!** *(noh loh'mweh-vahs)*

➤ Obviously, when you refer to more than one object in a command phrase, the pronouns are in the plural:

Don't throw them!	**¡No las tires!** *(noh lahs'tee-rehs)*
Don't move them!	**¡No los muevas!** *(noh lohs'mweh-vahs)*

➤ And just like the other pronouns, these little words go before your actions in a standard sentence:

I'm writing it.	**Lo estoy escribiendo.** *(loh eh-'stoh·ee eh-skree-bee-'ehn-doh)*
She studies them.	**Los estudia.** *(lohs eh-'stoo-dee·ah)*
We have it.	**La tenemos.** *(lah teh-'neh-mohs)*

¿LISTOS PARA PRACTICAR?

Practice this dialog with a Spanish speaker:

—**Necesito información acerca de la universidad.** *(neh-seh-'see-toh een-fohr-mah-see-'ohn ah-'sehr-kah deh lah oo-nee-vehr-see-'dahd)*

  —**¡Muy bien! ¿Cómo puedo ayudarle?** *('moo·ee bee·'ehn. 'koh-moh 'pweh-doh ah-yoo-'dahr-leh)*

—**¿Hay becas?** *('ah·ee 'beh-kahs)*

  —**Sí, y hay préstamos, también.** *(see, ee 'ah·ee 'preh-stah-mohs, tahm-bee-'ehn)*

Follow the examples and fill in the blanks:

I'm studying.   I was studying.
Estoy estudiando.   *(eh-'stoh·ee eh-stoo-dee-'ahn-doh)*
Estaba estudiando.   *(eh-'stah-bah eh-stoo-dee-'ahn-doh)*

Estoy leyendo.   _____
(eh-'stoh·ee leh-'yehn
   -doh)
Estoy escribiendo.   _____
(eh-'stoh·ee eh-skree-bee-
   'ehn-doh)
Estoy comiendo.   _____
(eh-'stoh·ee koh-mee-
   'ehn-doh)

Watch out for **le** and **lo**. Translate!

Don't talk to <u>him</u>.   _____

Don't throw <u>it</u>.   _____

Don't hit <u>her</u>.   _____

230

CHAPTER SEVEN
Capítulo Siete
(kah-'pee-too-loh see-'eh-teh)

THE ADMINISTRATORS
Los administradores
(lohs ahd-mee-nee-strah-'doh-rehs)

ADMINISTRATION

La administración *(lah ahd-mee-nees-trah-see-'on)*

Some professionals are the administrators. Perhaps as you introduce yourself to a Spanish speaker, you will remember to say one of these:

I'm (the)...	**Soy...** *('soh·ee)*
assistant principal	**el subdirector** *(ehl soob-dee-rehk-'tohr)*
assistant superintendent	**el subsuperintendente** *(ehl soob-soo-pehr-een-tehn-'dehn-teh)*
principal	**el director** *(ehl dee-rehk-'tohr)*
superintendent	**el superintendente** *(ehl soo-pehr-een-tehn-'dehn-teh)*

Fill in the blanks with English, and see if you can translate them.

I'm (the)...	**Soy...** *('soh·ee...)*
_____ administrator	**el administrador** _____ *(ehl ahd-mee-nee-strah-'dohr ____)*
_____ coordinator	**el coordinador de** _____ *(ehl koh-ohr-dee-nah-'dohr deh ____)*
_____ dean	**el decano de** _____ *(ehl deh-'kah-noh deh ____)*
_____ director	**el director de** _____ *(ehl dee-rehk-'tohr deh ____)*
_____ manager	**el gerente de** _____ *(ehl heh-'rehn-teh deh ____)*
_____ specialist	**el especialista de** _____ *(ehl eh-speh-see·ah-'lee-stah deh)*
_____ supervisor	**el supervisor de** _____ *(ehl soo-pehr-vee-'sohr deh ____)*
_____ trainer	**el entrenador de** _____ *(ehl ehn-treh-nah-'dohr deh ____)*

➤ The word *board* is used all the time in education:

Board of Education	**la junta de educadores** *(lah 'hoon-tah deh eh-doo-kah-'doh-rehs)*
Board of Supervisors	**la junta de supervisores** *(lah 'hoon-tah deh soo-pehr-vee-'soh-rehs)*
Board of Trustees	**la junta de fideicomisarios** *(lah 'hoon-tah deh fee-deh-ee-koh-mee-'sah-ree·ohs)*

➤ Schools vary, so fill in the blanks with words of your choice:

It's the director of _____ **Es el director de** _____ *(ehs ehl dee-rehk-'tohr deh ___)*

finance	**las finanzas** *(lahs fee-'nahn-sahs)*
personnel	**el personal** *(ehl pehr-soh-'nahl)*
special services	**los servicios especiales** *(lohs sehr-'vee-see·ohs eh-speh-see-'ah-lehs)*

➤ As you are aware, many words in Spanish are very close to their English equivalents. Do you see any patterns?

aide	**el ayudante** *(ehl ah-yoo-'dahn-teh)*
assistant	**el asistente** *(ehl ah-see-'stehn-teh)*
associate	**el asociado** *(ehl ah-soh-see-'ah-doh)*
clerk	**el dependiente** *(ehl deh-pehn-dee-'ehn-teh)*
consultant	**el consultor** *(ehl kohn-sool-'tohr)*
facilitator	**el facilitador** *(ehl fah-see-lee-tah-'dohr)*
leader	**el líder** *(ehl 'lee-dehr)*
official	**el funcionario** *(ehl foon-see·oh-'nah-ree·oh)*
operator	**el operador** *(ehl oh-peh-rah-'dohr)*
programmer	**el programador** *(ehl proh-grah-mah-'dohr)*
secretary	**el secretario** *(ehl seh-kreh-'tah-ree·oh)*
technician	**el técnico** *(ehl 'tehk-nee-koh)*

LOTS OF RESPONSIBILITY
Mucha responsabilidad *('moo-chah reh-spohn-sah-bee-lee-'dahd)*

Can you name some of the common duties of a school or district administrator? This is only a sample, so feel free to add to the list:

I'm in charge of (the)... **Estoy encargado de...** *(eh-'stoh·ee ehn-kahr-'gah-doh deh...)*

announcements	**los anuncios** *(lohs ah-'noon-see·ohs)*
attendance	**la asistencia** *(lah ah-see-'stehn-see·ah)*
budget	**el presupuesto** *(ehl preh-soo-'pweh-stoh)*
contracts	**los contratos** *(lohs kohn-'trah-tohs)*

curriculum	**el plan de estudios** *(ehl plahn deh eh-'stoo-dee·ohs)*
discipline	**la disciplina** *(lah dee-see-'plee-nah)*
food service	**la alimentación** *(lah ah-lee-mehn-tah-see-'ohn)*
grades	**las notas** *(lahs'noh-tahs)*
graduation	**la graduación** *(lah grah-doo-ah-see-'ohn)*
health care	**el cuidado de la salud** *(ehl kwee-'dah-doh deh lah sah-'lood)*
maintenance	**el mantenimiento** *(ehl mahn-teh-nee-mee-'ehn-toh)*
orientation	**la orientación** *(lah oh-ree-ehn-tah-see-'ohn)*
promotion	**la promoción** *(lah proh-moh-see-'ohn)*
public relations	**las relaciones públicas** *(lahs reh-lah-see-'oh-nehs 'poo-blee-kahs)*
registration	**la inscripción** *(lah een-skreep-see-'ohn)*
security	**la seguridad** *(lah seh-goo-ree-'dahd)*
supplies	**los materiales** *(lohs mah-teh-ree-'ah-lehs)*
training	**el entrenamiento** *(ehl ehn-treh-nah-mee-'ehn-toh)*
I work in (the)...	**Trabajo en...** *(trah-'bah-hoh ehn...)*
city	**la ciudad** *(lah see-oo-'dahd)*
county	**el condado** *(ehl kohn-'dah-doh)*
department	**el departamento** *(ehl deh-pahr-tah-'mehn-toh)*
district	**el distrito** *(ehl dee-'stree-toh)*
main office	**la sede** *(lah'seh-deh)*
region	**la región** *(lah reh-hee-'ohn)*
I teach at (the)...	**Enseño en...** *(ehn-'seh-nyoh ehn...)*
conference	**la conferencia** *(lah kohn-feh-'rehn-see·ah)*
convention	**la convención** *(lah kohn-vehn-see-'ohn)*
inservice	**la práctica** *(lah'prahk-tee-kah)*
seminar	**el seminario** *(ehl seh-mee-'nah-ree·oh)*
workshop	**el entrenamiento** *(ehl ehn-treh-nah-mee-'ehn-toh)*
I speak with my...	**Hablo con mi/mis...** *('ah-bloh kohn mee / mees...)*
employees	**empleados** *(ehm-pleh-'ah-dohs)*
faculty	**facultad** *(fah-kool-'tahd)*
staff	**personal** *(pehr-soh-'nahl)*

➤ Learn everyone's title as introductions are made:

He's (the)...   **Es...** *(ehs...)*

advisor   **el aconsejador** *(ehl ah-kohn-seh-hah-'dohr)*
mentor   **el mentor** *(ehl mehn-'tohr)*
neighbor   **el vecino** *(ehl veh-'see-noh)*
partner   **el socio** *(ehl'soh-see·oh)*
sponsor   **el patrocinador** *(ehl pah-troh-see-nah-'dohr)*

➤ You might be asked to discuss your affiliation:

I'm a member of (the)... **Soy miembro de...** *('soh·ee mee-'ehm-broh deh...)*

association   **la asociación** *(lah ah-soh-see-ah-see-'ohn)*
coalition   **la coalición** *(lah koh-ah-lee-see-'ohn)*
commission   **la comisión** *(lah koh-mee-see-'ohn)*
council   **el consejo** *(ehl kohn-'seh-hoh)*
organization   **la organización** *(lah ohr-gah-nee-sah-see-'ohn)*

¿LISTOS PARA PRACTICAR?

What do these words mean? Write it down!

La escuela necesita más materiales y el dinero no está en el presupuesto.
(lah eh-'skweh-lah neh-seh-'see-tah mahs mah-teh-ree-'ah-lehs ee ehl dee-'neh-roh noh eh-'stah ehn ehl preh-soo-'pweh-stoh)

_____

Tenemos problemas con la asistencia y disciplina de los estudiantes.
(teh-'neh-mohs proh-'bleh-mahs kohn lah ah-see-'stehn-see·ah ee dee-see-'plee-nah deh lohs eh-stoo-dee-'ahn-tehs)

_____

Me gusta mucho nuestro plan de estudio para el próximo año.
(meh'goo-stah'moo-choh'nweh-stroh plahn deh eh-'stoo-dee·oh'pah-rah ehl'prohk-see-moh'ah-nyoh)

_____

LET'S EVALUATE!

¡**Vamos a evaluar!** *('vah-mohs ah eh-vah-loo-'ahr)*

One of the primary jobs of the school administrator is to help assess student success. Numerous tools are used for testing, so the Spanish that you'll need may vary. The sample sentences that follow should be useful to anyone who evaluates student progress in school:

We are using (the)...	**Estamos usando...** *(eh-'stah-mohs oo-'sahn-doh...)*
analysis	**el análisis** *(ehl ah-'nah-lee-sees)*
check-up	**la comprobación** *(lah kohm-proh-bah-see-'ohn)*
diagnosis	**el diagnóstico** *(ehl dee-ahg-'noh-stee-koh)*
evaluation	**la evaluación** *(lah eh-vah-loo-ah-see-'ohn)*
exam	**el examen** *(ehl ehk-'sah-mehn)*
follow-up	**la continuación** *(lah kohn-tee-noo-ah-see-'ohn)*
instrument	**el instrumento** *(ehl een-stroo-'mehn-toh)*
test	**la prueba** *(lah proo-'eh-bah)*
It's from the...	**Es de...** *(ehs deh...)*
college	**la universidad** *(lah oo-nee-vehr-see-'dahd)*
company	**la compañía** *(lah kohm-pah-'nyee-ah)*
county	**el condado** *(ehl kohn-'dah-doh)*
district	**el distrito** *(ehl dee-'stree-toh)*
government	**el gobierno** *(ehl goh-bee-'ehr-noh)*
school	**la escuela** *(lah eh-'skweh-lah)*
state	**el estado** *(ehl eh-'stah-doh)*
The level is...	**El nivel es...** *(ehl nee-'vehl ehs...)*
advanced	**avanzado** *(ah-vahn-'sah-doh)*
average	**promedio** *(proh-'meh-dee·oh)*
beginning	**inicial** *(ee-nee-see-'ahl)*
high	**alto** *('ahl-toh)*
intermediate	**intermedio** *(een-tehr-'meh-dee·oh)*
low	**bajo** *('bah-hoh)*

Stay on a roll. All of these words are important:

The purpose is to evaluate...
El propósito es evaluar...
(ehl proh-'poh-see-toh ehs eh-vah-loo-'ahr)

intelligence	**la inteligencia** *(lah een-teh-lee-'hehn-see·ah)*
knowledge	**el conocimiento** *(ehl koh-noh-see-mee-'ehn-toh)*
language	**el lenguaje** *(ehl lehn-'gwah-heh)*
performance	**el rendimiento** *(ehl rehn-dee-mee-'ehn-toh)*
personality	**la personalidad** *(lah pehr-soh-nah-lee-'dahd)*
potential	**el potencial** *(ehl poh-tehn-see-'ahl)*
skill	**la habilidad** *(lah ah-bee-lee-'dahd)*
strengths	**los puntos fuertes** *(lohs 'poon-tohs 'fwehr-tehs)*
talent	**el talento** *(ehl tah-'lehn-toh)*
weaknesses	**las debilidades** *(lahs deh-bee-lee-'dah-dehs)*

We count (the)...	**Contamos...** *(kohn-'tah-mohs...)*
credits	**los créditos** *(lohs 'kreh-dee-tohs)*
grades	**las notas** *(lahs 'noh-tahs)* ,
hours	**las horas** *(lahs 'oh-rahs)*
points	**los puntos** *(lohs 'poon-tohs)*
units	**las unidades** *(lahs oo-nee-'dah-dehs)*

I have (the)...	**Tengo...** *('tehn-goh...)*
answers	**las respuestas** *(lahs reh-'spweh-stahs)*
data	**los datos** *(lohs 'dah-tohs)*
information	**la información** *(lah een-fohr-mah-see-'ohn)*
report card	**el boletín de evaluación** *(ehl boh-leh-'teen deh eh-vah-loo-ah-see-'ohn)*
results	**los resultados** *(lohs reh-sool-'tah-dohs)*
scores	**las calificaciones** *(lahs kah-lee-fee-kah-see-'oh-nehs)*
summary	**el resumen** *(ehl reh-'soo-mehn)*

Now use these one-liners as you explain the evaluation process to the students and their families:

These are the times and dates.
Estas son las horas y fechas.
('eh-stahs sohn lahs'on-rahs ee'feh-chahs)

You have time to prepare.
Tienes tiempo para prepararte.
(tee-'eh-nehs tee-'ehm-poh'pah-rah preh-pah-'rahr-teh)

The evaluation will last...
La evaluación durará...
(lah eh-vah-loo-ah-see-'ohn doo-rah-'rah...)

Let me explain the procedure.
Déjame explicar el procedimiento.
('deh-hah-meh ehks-plee-'kahr ehl proh-seh-dee-mee-'ehn-toh)

It will help the school.
Ayudará a la escuela.
(ah-yoo-dah-'rah ah lah ehs-'kweh-lah)

MÁS INFORMACIÓN

➤ If you're asked to describe the evaluation, these words will get the message across:

It is...   **Es...** *(ehs...)*

acceptable   **aceptable** *(ah-sehp-'tah-bleh)*
cognitive   **cognitivo** *(kohg-nee-'tee-voh)*
constructive   **constructivo** *(kohn-strook-'tee-voh)*
convenient   **conveniente** *(kohn-veh-nee-'ehn-teh)*
critical   **crítico** *('kree-tee-koh)*
customized   **personalizado** *(pehr-soh-nah-lee-'sah-doh)*
diagnostic   **diagnóstico** *(dee-ahg-'noh-stee-koh)*

238

effective	**eficaz** *(eh-fee-'kahs)*
fair	**justo** *('hoo-stoh)*
functional	**funcional** *(foon-see·oh-'nahl)*
generalized	**generalizado** *(heh-neh-rah-lee-'sah-doh)*
objective	**objetivo** *(ohb-heh-'tee-voh)*
optional	**opcional** *(ohp-see·oh-'nahl)*
positive	**positivo** *(poh-see-'tee-voh)*
significant	**significativo** *(seeg-nee-fee-kah-'tee-voh)*
subjective	**subjetivo** *(soob-heh-'tee-voh)*
transitional	**transicional** *(trahn-see-see·ohn-'nahl)*

➤ Do you have students who always seem to excel?

They are...	**Son...** *(sohn...)*

accelerated	**avanzados** *(ah-vahn-'sah-dohs)*
gifted	**talentosos** *(tah-lehn-'toh-sohs)*
high-achievers	**acelerados** *(ah-seh-leh-'rah-dohs)*

THE TEST
El examen *(ehl ehk-'sah-mehn)*

If some form of testing is part of the evaluation, guide the students carefully through each phase. Try these lines:

Come on this date.	**Venga en esta fecha.** *('vehn-gah ehn'eh-stah'feh-chah)*
Don't be nervous.	**No se ponga nervioso.** *(noh seh'pohn-gah nehr-vee-'oh-soh)*
Don't take too long.	**No se demore mucho.** *(noh seh deh-'moh-reh'moo-choh)*
This is the evaluation.	**Esta es la evaluación.** *('eh-stah ehs lah eh-vah-loo-ah-see-'ohn)*

Just do the best you can. **Háganlo lo mejor que puedan.**
(*'ah-gahn-loh loh meh-'hohr keh'pweh-dahn*)

You'll receive the results soon. **Recibirán los resultados pronto.**
(*reh-see-bee-'rahn lohs reh-sool-'tah-dohs'prohn-toh*)

Now, be helpful, using this vocabulary from previous lessons:

Use (the)...	**Usen...** (*'oo-sehn...*)
approach	**el enfoque** (*ehl ehn-'foh-keh*)
method	**el método** (*ehl'meh-toh-doh*)
model	**el modelo** (*ehl moh-'deh-loh*)
principle	**el principio** (*ehl preen-'see-pee·oh*)
strategy	**la estrategia** (*lah eh-strah-'teh-hee·ah*)
technique	**la técnica** (*lah'tehk-nee-kah*)
Look at (the)...	**Miren...** (*'mee-rehn...*)
examples	**los ejemplos** (*lohs eh-'hehm-plohs*)
instructions	**las instrucciones** (*lahs een-strook-see-'oh-nehs*)
questions	**las preguntas** (*lahs preh-'goon-tahs*)

Continue to explain, but this time get some feedback from everyone about the evaluation. Keep it simple with the patterns shown:

Are you...?	**¿Está...?** (*eh-'stah...*)
capable	**capacitado** (*kah-pah-see-'tah-doh*)
interested	**interesado** (*een-teh-reh-'sah-doh*)

motivated	**motivado** *(moh-tee-'vah-doh)*
optimistic	**optimista** *(ohp-tee-'mee-stah)*
prepared	**preparado** *(preh-pah-'rah-doh)*
satisfied	**satisfecho** *(sah-tees-'feh-choh)*

MÁS INFORMACIÓN

➤ Very technical words will be required, so keep a few nearby:

data collection	**el banco de datos** *(ehl'bahn-koh deh'dah-tohs)*
learning curve	**la curva de aprendizaje** *(lah'koor-vah deh ah-prehn-dee-'sah-heh)*
pre-test	**el pre-examen** *(ehl preh-ehk-'sah-mehn)*
post-test	**el post-examen** *(ehl pohst-ehk-'sah-mehn)*
time frame	**el lapso de tiempo** *(ehl'lahp-soh deh tee-'ehm-poh)*
top priority	**la prioridad máxima** *(lah pree-oh-ree-'dahd'makh-see-mah)*
track record	**el récord de trabajo** *(ehl'reh-kohrd deh trah-'bah-hoh)*
workload	**la cantidad de trabajo** *(lah kahn-tee-'dahd deh trah-'bah-hoh)*

➤ Watch for word patterns.

cooperation	**la cooperación** *(lah koh-oh-peh-rah-see-'ohn)*
correction	**la corrección** *(lah koh-rrehk-see-'ohn)*
implementation	**la implementación** *(lah eem-pleh-mehn-tah-see-'ohn)*
initiation	**la iniciación** *(lah ee-nee-see-ah-see-'ohn)*
limitation	**la limitación** *(lah lee-mee-tah-see-'ohn)*
observation	**la observación** *(lah ohb-sehr-vah-see-'ohn)*

preparation	**la preparación**
	(lah preh-pah-rah-see-'ohn)
satisfaction	**la satisfacción**
	(lah sah-tees-fahk-see-'ohn)
specification	**la especificación**
	(lah eh-speh-see-fee-kah-see-'ohn)

➤ But stay alert—not every word follows the rule

competition	**la competencia** *(lah kohm-peh-'tehn-see-ah)*
examination	**el examen** *(ehl ehk-'sah-mehn)*
expectation	**la esperanza** *(lah eh-speh-'rahn-sah)*

TELL US THE RESULTS!
¡Díganos los resultados! *('dee-gah-nohs lohs reh-sool-'tah-dohs)*

In many cases, the administrator must share the evaluation with students and their families. When you speak Spanish, sometimes only a few brief comments are all that's required to get your messages across. Here are the patterns.

Begin with a group of positive action words. Notice how the word **le** *(leh)* can refer to "you":

I would like to _____ you.	**Quisiera ____.** *(kee-see-'eh-rah)*
assure	**asegurarle** *(ah-seh-goo-'rahr-leh)*
commend	**alabarle** *(ah-lah-'bahr-leh)*
compliment	**felicitarle** *(feh-lee-see-'tahr-leh)*
encourage	**animarle** *(ah-nee-'mahr-leh)*
motivate	**motivarle** *(moh-tee-'vahr-leh)*
persuade	**persuadirle** *(pehr-swah-'deer-leh)*
reward	**recompensarle** *(reh-kohm-pehn-'sahr-leh)*
support	**apoyarle** *(ah-poh-'yahr-leh)*
thank	**agradecerle** *(ah-grah-deh-'sehr-leh)*

Your post-evaluation meeting could last awhile, so don't run out of things to say:

I'm going to...   **Voy a...** *('voh·ee ah)*

clarify	**clarificar** *(klah-ree-fee-'kahr)*
confirm	**confirmar** *(kohn-feer-'mahr)*
explain	**explicar** *(ehk-splee-'kahr)*
identify	**identificar** *(ee-dehn-tee-fee-'kahr)*
suggest	**sugerir** *(soo-heh-'reer)*

If you need to reveal specific test results, try out the following key terms:

It's acceptable	**Es aceptable** *(ehs ah-sehp-'tah-bleh)*
It's adequate	**Es adecuado** *(ehs ah-deh-'kwah-doh)*
It's appropriate	**Es apropiado** *(ehs ah-proh-pee-'ah-doh)*
It's approved	**Está aprobado** *(eh-'stah ah-proh-'bah-doh)*
It's better	**Está mejor** *(eh-'stah meh-'hohr)*
It's correct	**Está correcto** *(eh-'stah koh-'rrehk-toh)*
It's excellent	**Es excelente** *(ehs ehk-seh-'lehn-teh)*
It's good	**Es bueno** *(ehs 'bweh-noh)*
It's high	**Es alto** *(ehs 'ahl-toh)*
It's more	**Es más** *(ehs mahs)*
It's outstanding	**Es fantástico** *(ehs fahn-'tah-stee-koh)*
It's satisfactory	**Está satisfactorio** *(eh-'stah sah-tees-fahk-'toh-ree·oh)*

It's (the)...   **Es...** *(ehs...)*

average	**el promedio** *(ehl proh-'meh-dee-oh)*
maximum	**el máximo** *(ehl 'mahk-see-moh)*
minimum	**el mínimo** *(ehl 'mee-nee-moh)*

Unfortunately, the results aren't always positive:

It's less than expected.	**Es menos de lo esperado.** *(ehs 'meh-nohs deh loh eh-speh-'rah-doh)*
It's a low result.	**Es un resultado bajo.** *(ehs oon reh-sool-'tah-doh 'bah-hoh)*

It's unacceptable.	**Es inaceptable.**
	(ehs een-ah-sehp-'tah-bleh)
It's incorrect.	**Está incorrecto.**
	(eh-'stah een-koh-'rrehk-toh)
poor	**Está mal.**
	(eh-'stah mahl)
worse	**Está peor.**
	(eh-'stah peh-'ohr)

MÁS INFORMACIÓN

➤ The verb, "to make a mistake" is **equivocarse** *(eh-kee-voh-'kahr-seh)*:

You make mistakes sometimes.
A veces usted se equivoca.
(ah'veh-sehs oo-'stehd seh eh-kee-'voh-kah)

➤ Here are more words and phrases that deal with assessments:

I agree.	**Estoy de acuerdo.**
	(eh-'stoh·ee deh ah-'kwehr-doh)
I disagree.	**No estoy de acuerdo.** *(noh eh-'stoh·ee deh ah-'kwehr-doh)*
It needs improvement.	**Necesita mejorar.**
	(neh-seh-'see-tah meh-hoh-'rahr)
There were a lot of mistakes.	**Había muchos errores.**
	(ah-'bee-ah'moo-chohs eh-'rroh-rehs)

¿LISTOS PARA PRACTICAR?

Connect the words that are similar in meaning:

el examen *(ehl ehk-'sah-mehn)*   **la universidad**   *(lah oo-nee-vehr-see-'dahd)*

la habilidad *(lah ah-bee-lee-'dahd)*   **el técnico** *(ehl'tehk-nee-koh)*

el método *(ehl'meh-toh-doh)*   **la respuesta** *(lah reh-'spweh-stah)*

el crédito *(ehl'kreh-dee-toh)* **la unidad** *(lah oo-nee-'dahd)*
la escuela *(lah eh-'skweh-lah)* **la prueba** *(lah proo-'eh-bah)*
el resultado *(ehl reh-sool-'tah-doh)* **el talento** *(ehl tah-'lehn-toh)*

You know what to do here. Simply follow the example:

encourage	**<u>Quisiera animarle.</u>** *(kee-see-'eh-rah ah-nee-'mahr-leh)*
thank	_____
commend	_____
tell	_____

TO BE ON DUTY
Estar de servicio *(eh-'stahr deh sehr-'vee-see·oh)*

Many administrators also are responsible for campus control. Let's break our new Spanish phrases into areas where students generally tend to congregate. See if you can find any familiar patterns that can be used just about anywhere. Walk around as you practice talking to groups of children:

In the Halls—En los corredores *(ehn lohs koh-rreh-'doh-rehs)*

Stay in line.	**Quédense en fila.** *('keh-dehn-seh ehn'fee-lah)*
Keep to the right.	**Quédense a la derecha.** *('keh-dehn-seh ah lah deh-'reh-chah)*
Remain quiet.	**Quédense quietos.** *('keh-dehn-seh kee-'eh-tohs)*
Don't push.	**No empujen.** *(noh ehm-'poo-hehn)*
Don't run.	**No corran.** *(noh'koh-rrahn)*
Don't yell.	**No griten.** *(noh'gree-tehn)*
Please put those away.	**Favor de guardar las cosas.** *(fah-'vohr deh gwahr-'dahr lahs'koh-sahs)*
Please don't touch the doors.	**Favor de no tocar los puertas.** *(fah-'vohr deh noh toh-'kahr lahs'pwehr-tahs)*
Please hurry up.	**Favor de apurarse.** *(fah-'vohr deh ah-poo-'rahr-seh)*

Where are you going?	**¿Adónde van?** *(ah-'dohn-deh vahn)*
Where is your teacher?	**¿Dónde está su maestro?** *('dohn-deh eh-'stah soo mah-'eh-stroh)*
Where are you coming from?	**¿De dónde vienen?** *(deh'dohn-deh vee-'eh-nehn)*

In the Restrooms—En los cuartos de baño *(ehn lohs 'kwahr-tohs deh 'bah-nyoh)*

Go before class.	**Vayan antes de la clase.** *('vah-yahn'ahn-tehs deh lah'klah-seh)*
Go to your classes.	**Vayan a sus clases.** *('vah-yahn ah soos'klah-sehs)*
Go quickly.	**Vayan rápido.** *('vah-yahn'rah-pee-doh)*
Put the paper in the toilet.	**Pongan el papel en el excusado.** *('pohn-gahn ehl pah-'pehl ehn ehl ehk-skoo-'sah-doh)*
Put the soap on the sink.	**Pongan el jabón en el lavabo.** *('pohn-gahn ehl hah-'bohn ehn ehl lah-'vah-boh)*
Put the trash in the can.	**Pongan la basura en el bote.** *('pohn-gahn lah bah-'soo-rah ehn ehl'boh-teh)*
Flush the toilet, please.	**Descarguen el agua, por favor.** *(dehs-'kahr-gehn ehl'ah-gwah, pohr fah-'vohr)*
Turn off the water, please.	**Cierren el agua, por favor.** *(see-'eh-rrehn ehl'ah-gwah pohr fah-'vohr)*
Close the door, please.	**Cierren la puerta, por favor.** *(see-'eh-rehn lah 'pwehr-tah, pohr fah-'vohr)*
Who is inside?	**¿Quién está adentro?** *(kee-'ehn eh-'stah ah-'dehn-troh)*
Who did this?	**¿Quién hizo esto?** *(kee-'ehn'ee-soh'eh-stoh)*
Who turned off the light?	**¿Quién apagó la luz?** *(kee-'ehn ah-pah-'goh lah loos)*

In the Lunch Area—En el comedor *(ehn ehl koh-meh-'dohr)*

You need to line up.	**Necesitan hacer fila.** *(neh-seh-'see-tahn ah-'sehr 'fee-lah)*

You need to have tickets.	**Necesitan tener boletos.** *(neh-seh-'see-tahn teh-'nehr boh-'leh-tohs)*
You need to pay.	**Necesitan pagar.** *(neh-seh-'see-tahn pah-'gahr)*
Wait for your turn.	**Esperen su turno.** *(eh-'speh-rehn soo'toor-noh)*
Wait for the bell.	**Esperen hasta que suene el timbre.** *(eh-'speh-rehn'ah-stah keh'sweh-neh ehl'teem-breh)*
Wait for your class.	**Esperen su clase.** *(eh-'speh-rehn soo'klah-seh)*
You are dismissed.	**Pueden irse.** *('pweh-dehn'eer-seh)*
You can clear the table.	**Pueden limpiar la mesa.** *('pweh-dehn leem-pee-'ahr lah'meh-sah)*
You can bring your lunch.	**Pueden traer su almuerzo.** *('pweh-dehn trah-'ehr soo ahl-moo-'ehr-soh)*
Pick up the food.	**Recojan la comida.** *(reh-'koh-hahn lah koh-'mee-dah)*
Pick up the trash.	**Recojan la basura.** *(reh-'koh-hahn lah bah-'soo-rah)*
Pick up the drinks.	**Recojan las bebidas.** *(reh-'koh-hahn lahs beh-'bee-dahs)*
There is a lunch pass.	**Hay un pase para almorzar afuera.** *(ah·ee oon'pah-seh'pah-rah ahl-mohr-'sahr ah-'fweh-rah)*
There is a free lunch.	**Hay un almuerzo gratis.** *(ah·ee oon ahl-moo-'ehr-soh'grah-tees)*
There is a sack lunch.	**Hay un almuerzo en bolsa.** *(ah·ee oon ahl-moo-'ehr-soh ehn'bohl-sah)*

On the Playground—En el campo de recreo *(ehn ehl 'kahm-poh deh reh-'kreh-oh)*

Talk to the team captain.	**Hablen con el capitán del equipo.** *('ah-blehn kohn ehl kah-pee-'tahn dehl eh-'kee-poh)*
Talk to the teacher.	**Hablen con el maestro.** *('ah-blehn kohn ehl mah-'eh-stroh)*
Talk to the coach.	**Hablen con el entrenador.** *('ah-blehn kohn ehl ehn-treh-nah-'dohr)*

Why aren't you playing?	**¿Por qué no están jugando?** *(pohr keh noh eh-'stahn hoo-'gahn-doh)*
Why are you fighting?	**¿Por qué están peleando?** *(pohr keh eh-'stahn peh-leh-'ahn-doh)*
Why are you crying?	**¿Por qué están llorando?** *(pohr keh eh-'stahn yoh-'rahn-doh)*

They're going to choose teams.
Van a escoger miembros del equipo. *(vahn ah ehs-koh-'hehr mee-'ehm-brohs dehl eh-'kee-poh)*

They're going to win.
Van a ganar. *(vahn ah gah-'nahr)*

They're going to play there.
Van a jugar ahí. *(vahn ah hoo-'gahr ah-'ee)*

You should go to the office.	**Deben ir a la oficina.** *('deh-behn eer ah lah oh-fee-'see-nah)*
You should go to the nurse.	**Deben ir a la enfermera.** *('deh-behn eer ah lah ehn-fehr-'meh-rah)*
You should go to the class.	**Deben ir a la clase.** *('deh-behn eer ah lah 'klah-seh)*

MÁS INFORMACIÓN

➤ Use brief phrases to give commands:

Stop it!	**¡No hagas eso!** *(noh 'ah-gahs 'eh-soh)*
Don't be late!	**¡No llegue tarde!** *(noh 'yeh-geh 'tahr-deh)*
Come here!	**¡Ven aquí!** *(vehn ah-'kee)*

Note that here and throughout the book we constantly switch between the polite **usted** *(oo-'stehd)* and the familiar **tú** *(too)*. In the first two commands above, for example, **hagas** *('ah-gahs)* implies **tú, (Tú no hagas eso),** *(too noh 'ah-gahs 'eh-soh)* whereas **llegue** *('yeh-'geh)* corresponds to **usted, (Usted, no llegue tarde)** *(oo-'stehd, noh 'yeh-geh 'tahr-deh)*.

➤ Notice this pattern:

Keep moving. **Sigan caminando.** *('see-gahn kah-mee-'nahn-doh)*
Keep studying. **Sigan estudiando.** *('see-gahn eh-stoo-dee-'ahn-doh)*
Keep working. **Sigan trabajando.** *('see-gahn trah-bah-'hahn-doh)*

➤ Do you know what to say when suspicious characters wander onto school property?

Are you visiting? **¿Estás visitando?** *(eh-'stahs vee-see-'tahn-doh)*

Do you have an appointment? **¿Tienes una cita?** *(tee-'eh-nehs 'oo-nah 'see-tah)*

Who are you waiting for? **¿Por quién estás esperando?** *(pohr kee-'ehn eh-'stahs eh-speh-'rahn-doh)*

You cannot stay on school property.
No puedes quedarte en el terreno de la escuela. *(noh 'pweh-dehs keh-'dahr-teh ehn ehl teh-'rreh-noh deh lah eh-'skweh-lah)*

You have to leave now.
Tienes que irte ahora. *(tee-'eh-nehs keh 'eer-teh ah-'oh-rah)*

You need to show me identification.
Necesitas mostrarme identificación. *(neh-seh-'see-tahs mohs-'trahr-meh ee-dehn-tee-fee-kah-see-'ohn)*

 ¿LISTOS PARA PRACTICAR?

Try out your new Spanish skills all around the campus!

Give three commands to children who are moving through a school hallway:

_____ _____ _____

Give three commands to children who are crowded in a school bathroom:

_____ _____ _____

Give three commands to children who are having lunch in a school cafeteria:

_____ _____ _____

SERIOUS PROBLEMS
Los problemas serios *(lohs proh-'bleh-mahs 'seh-ree·ohs)*

Perhaps the toughest job for school officials is dealing with on-site emergencies and disasters. Not only a lot of preparation is required, but there's no guarantee that everything will run smoothly. Here's a list of events that demands an immediate response:

We had a/an...	**Tuvimos un/una...** *(too-'vee-mohs oon / 'oo-nah...)*
blackout	**apagón** *(ah-pah-'gohn)*
bomb	**bomba** *('bohm-bah)*
car accident	**accidente de carro** *(ahk-see-'dehn-teh deh 'kah-rroh)*
chemical spill	**derrame de sustancia química** *(deh-'rrah-meh deh soo-'stahn-see·ah 'kee-mee-kah)*
explosion	**explosión** *(ehk-sploh-see-'ohn)*
fire	**incendio** *(een-'sehn-dee·oh)*
overdose	**sobredosis** *(soh-breh-'doh-sees)*
raid	**incursión** *(een-koor-see-'ohn)*
rape	**violación** *(vee-oh-lah-see-'ohn)*
riot	**disturbio** *(dee-'stoor-bee·oh)*
robbery	**robo** *('roh-boh)*
shooting	**disparo** *(dee-'spah-roh)*
smog alert	**alerta de smog** *(ah-'lehr-tah deh eh-'smohg)*
stabbing	**puñalada** *(poo-nyah-'lah-dah)*
strike	**huelga** *('wehl-gah)*
suicide	**suicidio** *(soo-ee-'see-dee·oh)*
There is/are...	**Hay...** *('ah·ee...)*
flames	**llamas** *('yah-mahs)*
fumes	**vapores** *(vah-'poh-rehs)*
gas	**gas** *(gahs)*

poison	**veneno** *(veh-'neh-noh)*
smoke	**humo** *('oo-moh)*
toxic materials	**materiales tóxicos** *(mah-teh-ree-'ah-lehs 'tohk-see-kohs)*

Is everything secured? For safety purposes, these things should be memorized also:

Always use (the)...	**Siempre usa...** *(see-'ehm-preh 'oo-sah)*
alarm	**la alarma** *(lah ah-'lahr-mah)*
chain	**la cadena** *(lah kah-'deh-nah)*
deadbolt	**el pestillo** *(ehl peh-'stee-yoh)*
key	**la llave** *(lah 'yah-veh)*
latch	**el cerrojo** *(ehl seh-'rroh-hoh)*
lock	**la cerradura** *(lah seh-rrah-'doo-rah)*
padlock	**el candado** *(ehl kahn-'dah-doh)*
safe	**la caja fuerte** *(lah 'kah-hah 'fwehr-teh)*
shelter	**el refugio** *(ehl reh-'foo-hee·oh)*

Now post labels in both languages on each piece of emergency equipment in your building. Check out the examples:

Use (the)...	**Usa...** *('oo-sah...)*
binoculars	**los binoculares** *(lohs bee-noh-koo-'lah-rehs)*
candle	**la vela** *(lah 'veh-lah)*
cone	**el cono** *(ehl 'koh-noh)*
fire extinguisher	**el extintor** *(ehl ehks-teen-'tohr)*
first aid kit	**el botiquín de primeros auxilios** *(ehl boh-tee-'keen deh pree-'meh-rohs owk-'see-lee·ohs)*
flare	**la luz de bengala** *(lah loos deh behn-'gah-lah)*
flashlight	**la linterna** *(lah leen-'tehr-nah)*
hydrant	**la llave de agua** *(lah 'yah-veh deh 'ah-gwah)*
matches	**los fósforos** *(lohs 'fohs-foh-rohs)*

Let's talk about (the)...	**Vamos a hablar de...** *('vah-mohs ah ah-'blahr deh...)*
exercise	**el ejercicio** *(ehl eh-hehr-'see-see·oh)*
instructions	**las instrucciones** *(lahs een-strook-see-'oh-nehs)*
phases	**las etapas** *(lahs eh-'tah-pahs)*
plan	**el plan** *(ehl plahn)*
procedures	**los procedimientos** *(lohs proh-seh-dee-mee-'ehn-tohs)*
steps	**los pasos** *(lohs 'pah-sohs)*
system	**el sistema** *(ehl see-'steh-mah)*

Listen to (the)...	**Escucha a...** *(eh-'skoo-chah ah...)*
alarm	**la alarma** *(lah ah-'lahr-mah)*
bell	**la campana** *(lah kahm-'pah-nah)*
bulletin	**el anuncio** *(ehl ah-'noon-see·oh)*
buzzer	**el timbre** *(ehl 'teem-breh)*
code	**el código** *(ehl 'koh-dee-goh)*
drill	**el simulacro** *(ehl see-moo-'lah-kroh)*
horn	**la bocina** *(lah boh-'see-nah)*
report	**el reporte** *(ehl reh-'pohr-teh)*
signal	**la señal** *(lah seh-'nyahl)*
siren	**la sirena** *(lah see-'reh-nah)*
warning	**la advertencia** *(lah ahd-vehr-'tehn-see·ah)*
whistle	**el silbato** *(ehl seel-'bah-toh)*

MÁS INFORMACIÓN

➤ Emergency vocabulary could be used to save lives, so don't treat this list lightly:

capacity	**la capacidad** *(lah kah-pah-see-'dahd)*
caution	**la advertencia** *(lah ahd-vehr-'tehn-see·ah)*
danger	**el peligro** *(ehl peh-'lee-groh)*
emergency	**la emergencia** *(lah eh-mehr-'hehn-see·ah)*
rescue	**el rescate** *(ehl reh-'skah-teh)*

| safety | **la seguridad** *(lah seh-goo-ree-'dahd)* |
| threat | **la amenaza** *(lah ah-meh-'nah-sah)* |

➤ Stick with an easy pattern:

evacuation	**la evacuación** *(lah eh-vah-koo-ah-see-'ohn)*
precaution	**la precaución** *(lah preh-kow-see-'ohn)*
preparation	**la preparación** *(lah preh-pah-rah-see-'ohn)*
prevention	**la prevención** *(lah preh-vehn-see-'ohn)*
protection	**la protección** *(lah proh-tehk-see-'ohn)*

➤ Try to put your new words together. All of these expressions will be useful:

emergency exit	**la salida de emergencia** *(lah sah-'lee-dah deh eh-mehr-'hehn-see·ah)*
evacuation procedure	**el plan de evacuación** *(ehl plahn deh eh-vah-koo-ah-see-'ohn)*
rescue team	**el equipo de rescate** *(ehl eh-'kee-poh deh reh-'skah-teh)*
room capacity	**la capacidad del salón** *(lah kah-pah-see-'dahd dehl sah-'lohn)*
safety manual	**el manual de seguridad** *(ehl mah-noo-'ahl deh seh-goo-ree-'dahd)*

CONFLICTOS CULTURALES

Did your student just move to this country? Is he or she confused about our language and culture? When you find the time, share a few insights on U.S. customs toward campus life, dress, dining, holidays, and social skills. Make them feel welcome by respecting their perspective and watch your relationship grow!

NATURAL DISASTERS
Los desastres naturales *(lohs deh-'sah-strehs nah-too-'rah-lehs)*

Instruction is often disrupted by Mother Nature. When you have to battle the elements, talk about the situation **en español** *(ehn eh-spah-'nyohl)*:

It was (the)...	**Fue...** *(fweh...)*
earthquake	**el terremoto** *(ehl teh-rreh-'moh-toh)*
flood	**la inundación** *(lah een-oon-dah-see-'ohn)*
frost	**la escarcha** *(lah eh-'skahr-chah)*
hail	**el granizo** *(ehl grah-'nee-soh)*
hurricane	**el huracán** *(ehl oo-rah-'kahn)*
ice	**el hielo** *(ehl 'yeh-loh)*
landslide	**el desprendimiento de tierra** *(ehl dehs-prehn-dee-mee-'ehn-toh deh tee-'eh-rrah)*
rain	**la lluvia** *(lah 'yoo-vee·ah)*
sleet	**el aguanieve** *(ehl ah-gwah-nee-'eh-veh)*
snow	**la nieve** *(lah nee-'eh-veh)*
storm	**la tormenta** *(lah tohr-'mehn-tah)*
tornado	**el tornado** *(ehl tohr-'nah-doh)*
wind	**el viento** *(ehl vee-'ehn-toh)*

When foul weather strikes, you may have to mention a few medical concerns:

It's...	**Es...** *(ehs...)*
a heart attack	**un ataque cardíaco** *(oon ah-'tah-keh kahr-'dee-ah-koh)*
dehydration	**deshidratación** *(lah dehs-ee-drah-tah-see-'ohn)*
frostbite	**congelamiento** *(kohn-heh-lah-mee-'ehn-toh)*
heatstroke	**postración** *(poh-strah-see-'ohn)*
sunstroke	**insolación** *(een-soh-lah-see-'ohn)*

HELP ME!

¡Ayúdeme! *(ah-'yoo-deh-meh)*

If the emergency situation persists, chances are someone is going to get hurt. Do you know enough Spanish to lend a hand?

He/She is...	**Está...** *(eh-'stah...)*
bleeding	**sangrando** *(sahn-'grahn-doh)*
choking	**asfixiándose** *(ahs-feek-see-'ahn-doh-seh)*
drowning	**ahogándose** *(ah-oh-'gahn-doh-seh)*
dying	**muriéndose** *(moo-ree-'ehn-doh-seh)*
unconscious	**inconsciente** *(een-kohn-see-'ehn-teh)*

Call (the)...	**Llame a...** *('ya-meh ah)*
911	**el nueve-uno-uno** *(ehl noo-'eh-veh'oo-noh'oo-noh)*
ambulance	**la ambulancia** *(lah ahm-boo-'lahn-see·ah)*
clinic	**la clínica** *(lah'klee-nee-kah)*
dentist	**el dentista** *(ehl dehn-'tee-stah)*
doctor	**el doctor** *(ehl dohk-'tohr)*
fire department	**el departamento de bomberos** *(ehl deh-pahr-tah-'mehn-toh deh bohm-'beh-rohs)*
home	**la casa** *(lah'kah-sah)*
hospital	**el hospital** *(ehl oh-spee-'tahl)*
neighbor	**el vecino** *(ehl veh-'see-noh)*
office	**la oficina** *(lah oh-fee-'see-nah)*
operator	**la operadora** *(lah oh-'peh-rah-'doh-rah)*
paramedic	**el paramédico** *(ehl pah-rah-'meh-dee-koh)*
pharmacy	**la farmacia** *(lah fahr-'mah-see·ah)*
police	**la policía** *(lah poh-lee-'see-ah)*
relative	**el pariente** *(ehl pah-ree-'ehn-teh)*
tow truck	**la grúa** *(lah'groo-ah)*

➤ In extreme circumstances, use these command phrases:

Cover yourselves!	**¡Cúbranse!** *('koo-brahn-seh)*
Danger!	**¡Peligro!** *(peh-'lee-groh)*
Fire!	**¡Fuego!** *('fweh-goh)*
Get under the table!	**¡Pónganse debajo de la mesa!** *('pohn-gahn-seh deh-'bah-hoh deh lah'meh-sah)*
Help!	**¡Socorro!** *(soh-'koh-rroh)*
Run outside!	**¡Corran hacia afuera!** *('koh-rrahn'ah-see-ah ah-'fweh-rah)*
Stay away from the windows!	**¡Quédense lejos de las ventanas!** *('keh-dehn-seh 'leh-hohs deh lahs vehn-'tah-nahs)*
Watch out!	**¡Ojo!** *('oh-hoh)*

➤ Local rescue organizations may need to be contacted. Tell the community who's coming to help:

Civil Defense	**la Milicia Civil** *(lah mee-'lee-see·ah see-'veel)*
National Guard	**la Guardia Nacional** *(lah'gwahr-dee·ah nah-see·oh-'nahl)*
Red Cross	**la Cruz Roja** *(lah kroos'roh-hah)*

¿LISTOS PARA PRACTICAR?

Choose the *best* word to complete each sentence below:

plan, paramédico, lluvia, campana, cadena, humo *(plahn, pah-rah-'meh-dee-koh,'yoo-vee·ah, kahm-'pah-nah, kah-'deh-nah,'oo-moh)*

El incendio tiene _____. *(ehl een-'sehn-dee·oh tee-'eh-neh _____)*

El candado tiene _____. *(ehl kahn-'dah-doh tee-'eh-neh _____)*

El ejercicio tiene _____. *(ehl eh-hehr-'see-see·oh tee-'eh-neh _____)*

La tormenta tiene _____. *(lah tohr-'mehn-tah tee-'eh-neh _____)*

La ambulancia tiene _____. *(lah ahm-boo-'lahn-see·ah tee-'eh-neh _____)*

La clase tiene _____. *(lah'klah-seh tee-'eh-neh _____)*

What would you shout in Spanish if there were a fire?

¡_____!

IT'S A CRIME!

¡Es un crimen! *(ehs oon'kree-mehn)*

At some schools, administrators are in a battle with campus crime. For the protection of all students and their families, let the Spanish-speaking public know exactly what the situation is:

He was arrested for...	**Fue arrestado por...**
	(fweh ah-rreh-'stah-doh pohr)
arson	**el incendio premeditado**
	(ehl een-'sehn-dee·oh preh-meh-dee-'tah-doh)
battery	**la agresión** *(lah ah-greh-see-'ohn)*
counterfeiting	**la falsificación**
	(lah fahl-see-fee-kah-see-'ohn)
embezzling	**el desfalco** *(ehl dehs-'fahl-koh)*
extortion	**la extorsión** *(lah ehks-tohr-see-'ohn)*
fraud	**el fraude** *(ehl'frow-deh)*
gambling	**los juegos de apuestas**
	(ehl'hweh-gohs deh ah-'pweh-stahs)
hijacking	**el robo en tránsito**
	(lohs'roh-boh ehn'trahn-see-toh)
kidnapping	**el secuestro** *(ehl seh-'kweh-stroh)*
larceny	**el hurto** *(ehl'oor-toh)*
manslaughter	**el homicidio involuntario**
	(ehl oh-mee-'see-dee·oh een-voh-loon-'tah-ree·oh)
vandalism	**el vandalismo** *(ehl vahn-dah-'lees-moh)*

These crimes are related to sex:

It was...	**Fue...** *(fweh...)*
incest	**el incesto** *(ehl een-'seh-stoh)*
lewd behavior	**el comportamiento indecente** *(ehl kohm-pohr-tah-mee-'ehn-toh een-deh-'sehn-teh)*
molestation	**el abuso sexual** *(ehl ah-'boo-soh sehk-soo-'ahl)*
obscene phone call	**la llamada obscena** *(lah yah-'mah-dah ohb-'seh-nah)*
pornography	**la pornografía** *(lah pohr-noh-grah-'fee-ah)*
prostitution	**la prostitución** *(lah proh-stee-too-see-'ohn)*
rape	**la violación** *(lah vee·oh-lah-see-'ohn)*
solicitation	**la incitación** *(lah een-see-tah-see-'ohn)*

If you have the legal authority, you should now have enough language to make the arrest:

I am going to...	**Voy a...** *('voh·ee ah...)*
arrest you	**arrestarlo** *(ah-rreh-'stahr-loh)*
frisk you	**registrarlo** *(reh-hee-'strahr-loh)*
handcuff you	**esposarlo** *(eh-spoh-'sahr-loh)*
use a police dog	**usar un perro policía** *(oo-'sahr oon 'peh-rroh poh-lee-'see-ah)*

When a child's behavior is headed in the wrong direction, some of these words and phrases surface in conversation. Take the ones you need:

We talked about (the)...	**Hablamos de...** *(ah-'blah-mohs deh...)*
community service	**el servicio para la comunidad** *(ehl sehr-'vee-see·oh 'pah-rah lah koh-moo-nee-'dahd)*

continuation school	**la escuela secundaria especial**
	(lah eh-'skweh-lah seh-koon-'dah-ree-ah eh-speh-see-'ahl)
county jail	**la cárcel del condado**
	(lah 'kahr-sehl dehl kohn-'dah-doh)
federal prison	**la prisión federal**
	(lah pree-see-'ohn feh-deh-'rahl)
felony	**el delito mayor**
	(ehl deh-'lee-toh mah-'yohr)
juvenile court	**la corte de menores**
	(lah 'kohr-teh deh meh-'noh-rehs)
lawsuit	**el pleito**
	(ehl 'pleh·ee-toh)
legal aid	**la ayuda legal**
	(lah ah-'yoo-dah leh-'gahl)
misdemeanor	**el delito menor** *(ehl deh-'lee-toh meh-'nohr)*
parole	**la libertad bajo palabra**
	(lah lee-behr-'tahd 'bah-hoh pah-'lah-brah)
penitentiary	**la penitenciaría**
	(lah peh-nee-tehn-see-ah-'ree-ah)
probation officer	**el agente encargado de la libertad provisional**
	(ehl ah-'hehn-teh ehn-kahr-'gah-doh deh lah lee-behr-'tahd proh-vee-see·oh-'nahl)
reformatory	**el reformatorio**
	(ehl reh-fohr-mah-'toh-ree-oh)
rehabilitation	**la rehabilitación**
	(lah reh-ah-bee-lee-tah-see-'ohn)
state prison	**la prisión del estado**
	(lah pree-see-'ohn dehl eh-'stah-doh)

MÁS INFORMACIÓN

➤ Kids may be drinking these at parties:

beer	**la cerveza** *(lah sehr-'veh-sah)*
liquor	**el licor** *(ehl lee-'kohr)*
wine	**el vino** *(ehl 'vee-noh)*

DRUG ABUSE

El abuso de las drogas *(ehl ah-'boo-soh deh lahs'droh-gahs)*

Does the crime involve drugs? Here are a few that you may hear about. Most look a lot like English:

He/She had (the)	**Tenía...** *(teh-'nee-ah...)*
acid	**el ácido** *(ehl'ah-see-doh)*
amphetamine	**la anfetamina** *(lah ahn-feh-tah-'mee-nah)*
barbiturate	**el barbitúrico** *(ehl bahr-bee-'too-ree-koh)*
benzedrine	**la bencedrina** *(lah behn-seh-'dree-nah)*
cocaine	**la cocaína** *(lah koh-kah-'ee-nah)*
crack	**el crack** *(ehl krahk)*
crank	**el crank** *(ehl'krahnk)*
hashish	**el hashish** *(ehl ah-'sheesh)*
heroin	**la heroína** *(lah eh-roh-'ee-nah)*
marijuana	**la marijuana** *(lah mah-ree-'wah-nah)*
mescaline	**la mescalina** *(lah meh-skah-'lee-nah)*
seconal	**el seconal** *(ehl seh-koh-'nahl)*

Don't forget to mention the inhalants:

We found...	**Encontramos...** *(ehn-kohn-'trah-mohs)*
cleaning fluid	**el líquido para limpiar** *(ehl'lee-kee-doh'pah-rah leem-pee-'ahr)*
ether	**el éter** *(ehl'eh-tehr)*
freon	**el freón** *(ehl freh-'ohn)*
gasoline	**la gasolina** *(lah gah-soh-'lee-nah)*
hydrocarbons	**los hidrocarbonos** *(lohs ee-droh-kahr-'boh-nohs)*
lighter fluid	**el líquido de encendedor** *(ehl'lee-kee-doh deh ehn-sehn-deh-'dohr)*
model glue	**el pegamento de modelos** *(ehl peh-gah-'mehn-toh deh moh-'deh-lohs)*

Drug conversations could also require this important terminology:

dealer	**el droguero** *(ehl droh-'geh-roh)*
drug addict	**el drogadicto** *(ehl drohg-ah-'deek-toh)*
habit	**el hábito** *(ehl 'ah-bee-toh)*
illegal possession	**la posesión ilegal** *(lah poh-seh-see-'ohn ee-leh-'gahl)*
overdose	**la sobredosis** *(lah soh-breh-'doh-sees)*

Formulate more quesions using the language you know:

Where did you get that?	**¿Dónde conseguiste eso?** *('dohn-deh kohn-seh-'gee-steh 'eh-soh)*
Do you have a prescription?	**¿Tiene una receta?** *(tee-'eh-neh 'oo-nah reh-'seh-tah)*
Have you been arrested before?	**¿Has estado arrestado antes?** *(ahs eh-'stah-doh ah-rreh-'stah-doh 'ahn-tehs)*
How long have you been using...?	**¿Por cuánto tiempo has estado usando?** *(pohr 'kwahn-toh tee-'ehm-poh ahs eh-'stah-doh oo-'sahn-doh...)*
Do you have any scars or tattoos?	**¿Tienes cicatrices o tatuajes?** *(tee-'eh-nehs see-kah-'tree-sehs oh tah-too-'ah-hehs)*
What's the name of your contact?	**¿Cuál es el nombre de tu conexión?** *(kwahl ehs ehl 'nohm-breh deh too koh-nehk-see-'ohn)*
What is the beeper for?	**¿Para qué es el beeper?** *('pah-rah keh ehs ehl 'bee-pehr)*
When did you buy it?	**¿Cuándo lo compraste?** *('kwahn-doh loh kohm-'prah-steh)*
Where did you buy it?	**¿Dónde lo compraste?** *('dohn-deh loh kohm-'prah-steh)*
When did you start using drugs?	**¿Cuándo comenzaste a tomar drogas?** *('kwahn-doh koh-mehn-'sah-steh ah toh-'mahr 'droh-gahs)*
What kind have you taken?	**¿Qué clase has tomado?** *(keh 'klah-seh ahs toh-'mah-doh)*

If the crime is robbery:

They stole (the)...	**Robaron...** *(roh-'bah-rohn...)*
backpack	**la mochila** *(lah moh-'chee-lah)*
bicycle	**la bicicleta** *(lah bee-see-'kleh-tah)*
clothing	**la ropa** *(lah 'roh-pah)*
equipment	**el equipo** *(ehl eh-'kee-poh)*
jewelry	**las joyas** *(lahs 'hoh-yahs)*
machine	**la máquina** *(lah 'mah-kee-nah)*
money	**el dinero** *(ehl dee-'neh-roh)*

➤ Assure the families that things are back to normal:

The students are safe.	**Los estudiantes están seguros.** *(lohs eh-stoo-dee-'ahn-tehs eh-'stahn seh-'goo-rohs)*
Everything is under control.	**Todo está bajo nuestro control.** *('toh-doh eh-'stah 'bah-hoh 'nweh-stroh kohn-'trohl)*
We have called the police.	**Hemos llamado a la policía.** *('eh-mohs yah-'mah-doh ah lah poh-lee-'see-ah)*
There is proof.	**Hay evidencia.** *('ah·ee eh-vee-'dehn-see·ah)*
There will be an investigation.	**Habrá una investigación.** *(ah-'brah 'oo-nah een-veh-stee-gah-see-'ohn)*

We know (the)...	**Conocemos a...** *(koh-noh-'seh-mohs ah...)*
suspect	**el sospechoso** *(ehl soh-speh-'choh-soh)*
victim	**la víctima** *(lah 'veek-tee-mah)*
witness	**el testigo** *(ehl teh-'stee-goh)*

➤ Stay alert as you confront the suspects with the following command words:

Come here!	**¡Vengan aquí !**
	('vehn-gahn ah-'kee)
Raise your hands!	**¡Levanten las manos!**
	(leh-'vahn-tehn lahs'mah-nohs)
Sit down!	**¡Siéntense!**
	(see-'ehn-tehn-seh)
Turn around!	**¡Dénse vuelta!**
	('dehn-seh'vwehl-tah)
Empty your pockets!	**¡Vacíen los bolsillos!**
	(vah-'see-ehn lohs bohl-'see-yohs)
Give it to me!	**¡Dénmelo!**
	('dehn-meh-loh)
Show me your hands!	**¡Muéstrenme las manos!**
	('mweh-strehn-meh lahs'mah-nohs)

 CONFLICTOS CULTURALES

One of the most difficult things to discuss in a foreign language concerns social ethics and values. Your personal feelings, attitudes, and beliefs cannot be communicated in a few short sentences. Therefore, the best way to express any serious matter such as criminal behavior is either through an interpreter or by preparing a written note. Be sure that your students know exactly what is right and what is wrong in your institution.

TELL THEM, PLEASE
Dígales, por favor *('dee-gah-lehs, pohr fah-'vohr)*

Don't try to handle every situation all by yourself. Ask the nearest Spanish speaker to assist you when valuable information needs to be shared. This pattern works well with the words and phrases below:

Tell them that...	**Dígales que...** *('dee-gah-lehs keh...)*
they have to calm down	**tienen que calmarse** *(tee-'eh-nehn keh kahl-'mahr-seh)*
they should obey the rules	**deben obedecer las reglas** *('deh-behn oh-beh-deh-'sehr lahs 'reh-glahs)*
they need to be careful	**necesitan tener cuidado** *(neh-seh-'see-tahn teh-'nehr kwee-'dah-doh)*
they cannot do that	**no pueden hacer eso** *(noh 'pweh-dehn ah-'sehr 'eh-soh)*
it is an emergency	**es una emergencia** *(ehs 'oo-nah eh-mehr-'hehn-see·ah)*
I need to call their parents	**necesito hablar con sus padres** *(neh-seh-'see-toh ah-'blahr kohn soos 'pah-drehs)*

Now, tell one student to advise another. Use this pattern to make an administrative decision:

Tell him/her that...	**Dígale que...** *('dee-gah-leh keh...)*
this is a warning	**ésta es una advertencia** *('eh-stah ehs 'oo-nah ahd-vehr-'tehn-see-ah)*
this is going in his file	**ésto va en su archivo personal** *('eh-stoh vah ehn soo ahr-'chee-voh pehr-soh-'nahl)*
we are going to make some changes	**vamos a hacer algunos cambios** *('vah-mohs ah ah-'sehr ahl-'goo-nohs 'kahm-bee·ohs)*
this is the last time	**ésta es la última vez** *('eh-stah ehs lah 'ool-tee-mah vehs)*
I'm calling security	**estoy llamando a los guardias** *(eh-'stoh·ee yah-'mahn-doh ah lohs 'gwahr-dee-ahs)*

MÁS INFORMACIÓN

➤ Continue to discuss the situation in detail:

If it happens again...	**Si pasa de nuevo...** *(see 'pah-sah deh noo-'eh-voh)*

you will be expelled	**serás expulsado**
	(seh-'rahs eks-pool-'sah-doh)
you will be transferred	**serás transferido**
	(seh-'rahs trahns-feh-'ree-doh)
you will be suspended	**serás suspendido**
	(seh-'rahs soo-spehn-'dee-doh)

➤ Copy these down. They make good opening phrases:

I told you that...
Le dije que... *(leh 'dee-heh keh)*

Remember that...
Recuerde que... *(reh-'kwehr-deh keh)*

It's important that...
Es importante que... *(ehs eem-pohr-'tahn-teh keh)*

When you finish...
Cuando termine... *('kwahn-doh tehr-'mee-neh)*

If it's possible...
Si es posible... *(see ehs poh-'see-bleh)*

Before you go...
Antes de irse... *('ahn-tehs deh 'eer-seh)*

Translate:
Cuando termines, apaga la luz.
('kwahn-doh tehr-'mee-nehs, ah-'pah-gah lah loos)

_____

Si es posible, ven temprano.
(see ehs poh-'see-bleh, 'vehn tehm-'prah-noh)

_____

Antes de irse, cierre la puerta.
('ahn-tehs deh 'eer-seh, see-'eh-reh lah 'pwehr-tah)

_____

265

➤ And here's a pattern that requires more verb infinitives:

Make sure that you guys...   **Asegúrense de...** *(ah-seh-'goo-rehn-seh deh...)*

ask me   **preguntarme** *(preh-goon-'tahr-meh)*
call them   **llamarles** *(yah-'mahr-lehs)*
read it   **leerlo** *(leh-'ehr-loh)*

¿LISTOS PARA PRACTICAR?

In Spanish, name three serious crimes:

_____   _____   _____

Connect the related terms:

la cárcel *(lah'kahr-sehl)*   **la cicatriz** *(lah see-kah-'trees)*
la droga *(lah'droh-gah)*   **la prisión** *(lah pree-see-'ohn)*
el tatuaje *(ehl tah-too-'ah-heh)*   **la medicina** *(lah meh-dee-'see-nah)*

Follow these commands:

¡Dése vuelta y levante las manos! *('deh-seh'vwehl-tah ee leh-'vahn-teh las 'mah-nohs)*

Translate into Spanish:

Remember that it is an emergency. _____

If it happens again, you will be expelled. _____

Tell them that they can't do that. _____

TO TALK TO THE PUBLIC!

¡Hablar con el público! *(ah-'blahr kohn ehl 'poo-blee-koh)*

Educators in administrative positions are often overloaded with duties and responsibilities on campus, as well as public gatherings. Maybe they're headed to one of these:

He/She went to (the)...   **Fue a...** *(fweh ah...)*

assembly	**la asamblea** *(lah ah-sahm-'bleh-ah)*
committee	**el comité** *(ehl koh-mee-'teh)*
conference	**la conferencia** *(lah kohn-feh-'rehn-see·ah)*
council	**la junta** *(lah 'hoon-tah)*
meeting	**la reunión** *(lah reh-oo-nee-'ohn)*
seminar	**el seminario** *(ehl seh-mee-'nah-ree·oh)*

He/She is...   **Está...** *(eh-'stah...)*

discussing	**conversando** *(kohn-vehr-'sahn-doh)*
hiring	**contratando** *(kohn-trah-'tahn-doh)*
organizing	**organizando** *(ohr-gah-nee-'sahn-doh)*
planning	**planeando** *(plah-neh-'ahn-doh)*
presenting	**presentando** *(preh-sehn-'tahn-doh)*
speaking	**hablando** *(ah-'blahn-doh)*
teaching	**enseñando** *(ehn-seh-'nyahn-doh)*
training	**entrenando** *(ehn-treh-'nahn-doh)*
traveling	**viajando** *(vee-ah-'hahn-doh)*
visiting	**visitando** *(vee-see-'tahn-doh)*

EL COMITE ESTÁ PRESENTANDO, ORGANIZANDO Y PLANEANDO.

And, what's the topic for discussion? At your next public gathering, step up to the microphone and refer to any important issue:

I'd like to talk about (the)...   **Quisiera discutir...** *(kee-see-'eh-rah dee-skoo-'teer...)*

graduation requirements   **los requisitos para la graduación** *(lohs reh-kee-'see-tohs 'pah-rah lah grah-doo-ah-see-'ohn)*

proficiency testing   **los exámenes de competencia** *(lohs ehk-'sah-meh-nehs deh kohm-peh-'tehn-see·ah)*

course of study   **el curso de estudio** *(ehl 'koor-soh deh eh-'stoo-dee·oh)*

school budget   **el presupuesto de la escuela** *(ehl preh-soo-'pweh-stoh deh lah eh-'skweh-lah)*

substitute teachers   **los profesores suplentes** *(lohs proh-feh-'soh-rehs soo-'plehn-tehs)*

drop out rate   **la proporción de estudiantes que dejan sus estudios** *(lah proh-pohr-see-'ohn deh eh-stoo-dee-'ahn-tehs keh 'deh-hahn soos eh-'stoo-dee·ohs)*

remedial programs   **los programas de refuerzo** *(lohs proh-'grah-mahs deh reh-'fwehr-soh)*

district boundaries   **las fronteras del distrito** *(lahs frohn-'teh-rahs dehl dee-'stree-toh)*

PTA   **la asociación de los padres de alumnos** *(lah ah-soh-see-ah-see-'ohn deh lohs 'pah-drehs deh ah-'loom-nohs)*

community support   **el apoyo de la comunidad** *(ehl ah-'poh-yoh deh lah koh-moo-nee-'dahd)*

sanitary conditions   **las condiciones sanitarias** *(lahs kohn-dee-see-'oh-nehs sah-nee-'tah-ree·ahs)*

special services   **los servicios especiales** *(lohs sehr-'vee-see·ohs eh-speh-see-'ah-lehs)*

new construction   **la nueva construcción** *(lah noo-'eh-vah kohn-strook-see-'ohn)*

268

Insert a key word once in a while. Make sure your pronunciation is clear:

We have (the)...	**Tenemos...** *(teh-'neh-mohs...)*
alternatives	**las alternativas** *(lahs ahl-tehr-nah-'tee-vahs)*
goals	**las metas** *(lahs 'meh-tahs)*
instructions	**las instrucciones** *(lahs een-strook-see-'oh-nehs)*
needs	**los requisitos** *(lohs reh-kee-'see-tohs)*
objectives	**los objetivos** *(lohs ohb-heh-'tee-vohs)*
recommendations	**las recomendaciones** *(lahs reh-koh-mehn-dah-see-'oh-nehs)*
solutions	**las soluciones** *(lahs soh-loo-see-'oh-nehs)*
studies	**las investigaciones** *(las een-veh-stee-gah-see-'ohn-ehs)*
suggestions	**las sugerencias** *(lahs soo-heh-'rehn-see·ahs)*

Stress each point using descriptive words. Do any of the following look like English?

It's...	**Es/Está...** *(ehs/eh-'stah...)*
flexible	**(Es) flexible** *(ehs flehk-'see-bleh)*
formal	**(Es) formal** *(ehs fohr-'mahl)*
individualized	**(Está) individualizado** *(eh-'stah een-dee-vee-doo-ah-lee-'sah-doh)*
modified	**(Está) modificado** *(eh'stah moh-dee-fee-'kah-doh)*
modular	**(Es) modular** *(ehs moh-doo-'lahr)*
programmed	**(Está) programado** *(eh-'stah proh-grah-'mah-doh)*
recorded	**(Está) documentado** *(eh-'stah doh-koo-mehn-'tah-doh)*
supplementary	**(Es) suplementario** *(ehs soo-pleh-mehn-'tah-ree·oh)*
tracked	**(Está) seguido** *(eh-'stah seh-'gee-doh)*

Let the audience know that you are there to help. Eagerly mention what you are willing to do:

We offer (the)...	**Ofrecemos...** *(oh-freh-'seh-mohs)*
day care center	**la guardería infantil** *(lah gwahr-deh-'ree-ah een-fahn-'teel)*

donation	**la donación** *(lah doh-nah-see-'ohn)*
food stamps	**los cupones de alimentos** *(lohs koo-'poh-nehs deh ah-lee-'mehn-tohs)*
housing	**la vivienda** *(lah vee-vee-'ehn-dah)*
insurance	**el seguro** *(ehl seh-'goo-roh)*
legal service	**el servicio legal** *(ehl sehr-'vee-see·oh leh-'gahl)*
medical care	**el cuidado médico** *(ehl kwee-'dah-doh 'meh-dee-koh)*
vaccination	**la vacunación** *(lah vah-koo-nah-see-'ohn)*
welfare	**el bienestar social** *(ehl bee-ehn-eh-'stahr soh-see-'ahl)*

MÁS INFORMACIÓN

➤ Keep student family needs on target:

assistance	**la ayuda** *(lah ah-'yoo-dah)*
resource	**el recurso** *(ehl reh-'koor-soh)*
shelter	**el amparo** *(ehl ahm-'pah-roh)*
support	**el apoyo** *(ehl ah-'poh-yoh)*
therapy	**la terapia** *(lah teh-'rah-pee·ah)*

➤ Nobody can survive without the following expressions:

Above all...	**Sobre todo...** *('soh-breh 'toh-doh...)*
At first...	**Al principio...** *(ahl preen-'see-pee·oh...)*
At last...	**Por fin...** *(pohr feen...)*
At least...	**Por lo menos...** *(pohr loh 'meh-nohs...)*
By the way...	**A propósito...** *(ah proh-'poh-see-toh...)*
For example...	**Por ejemplo...** *(pohr eh-'hehm-ploh)*
In general...	**En general...** *(ehn heh-neh-'rahl...)*
In other words...	**Es decir...** *(ehs deh-'seer...)*
On the other hand...	**En cambio...** *(ehn 'kahm-bee·oh...)*

Try some:

En general, estoy bien.
(ehn heh-neh-'rahl, eh-'stoh·ee bee·ehn)

A propósito, mañana no hay escuela.
(a proh-'poh-see-toh, mah-'nyah-nah noh'ah-ee eh-'skweh-lah)

Al principio, vengan a la clase.
(ahl preen-'see-pee·oh'vehn-gahn ah lah'klah-seh)

 CONFLICTOS CULTURALES

Spanish-speaking people are identical to us in that they use slang or idiomatic expressions to talk about routine activities. Many also use Spanglish, that is, English words adapted for Spanish use (**la troca** *[lah'troh-kah]* for "the truck" and **el rufo** *[ehl'roo-foh]* for "the roof.)" If you're having trouble understanding certain words or expressions, use the phrase **¿Qué significa eso?** *[keh seeg-nee-'fee-kah'eh-soh]*, which translates, "What does that mean?" Chances are they'll come up with the Spanish words that are more familiar to you. Just be patient and take note of what they're saying for future reference.

POLITICS
La política *(lah poh-'lee-tee-kah)*

Make references to what's going on in the political arena. Decisions at the top affect educational policies:

It has to do with...	**Tiene que ver con...** *(tee-'eh-neh keh'vehr kohn...)*
affirmative action	**la acción afirmativa** *(lah ahk-see-'ohn ah-feer-mah-'tee-vah)*
bilingual education	**la educación bilingüe** *(lah eh-doo-kah-see·'ohn bee-'leen-gweh)*
civil rights	**los derechos civiles** *(lohs deh-'reh-chohs see-'vee-'lehs)*
election	**la elección** *(lah eh-lehk-see-'ohn)*
government	**el gobierno** *(ehl goh-bee-'ehr-noh)*
law	**la ley** *(lah'leh·ee)*

media	**los medios de comunicación** *(lohs'meh-dee·ohs deh koh-moo-nee-kah-see-'ohn)*
population	**la población** *(lah poh-blah-see-'ohn)*

Negative themes are bound to surface, so prepare yourself for trouble:

There is/are...	**Hay...** *('ah·ee...)*
alcoholism	**el alcoholismo** *(ehl ahl-koh-oh-'lees-moh)*
crime rate	**el índice de crimen** *(ehl'een-dee-seh deh'kree-mehn)*
disease	**las enfermedades** *(lahs ehn-fehr-meh-'dah-dehs)*
domestic violence	**la violencia doméstica** *(lah vee-oh-'lehn-see·ah doh-'meh-stee-kah)*
drug abuse	**el abuso de drogas** *(ehl ah-'boo-soh deh'droh-gahs)*
drug addiction	**la drogadicción** *(lah drohg-ah-deek-see-'ohn)*
drug traffic	**el narcotráfico** *(ehl nahr-koh-'trah-fee-koh)*
gangs	**las pandillas** *(lahs pahn-'dee-yahs)*
homelessness	**la gente desamparada** *(lah'hehn-teh dehs-ahm-pah-'rah-dah)*
hunger	**el hambre** *(ehl'ahm-breh)*
juvenile delinquency	**la delincuencia juvenil** *(lah deh-leen-'kwehn-see·ah hoo-veh-'neel)*
poverty	**la pobreza** *(lah poh-'breh-sah)*
racism	**el racismo** *(ehl rah-'sees-moh)*
runaway children	**los niños fugitivos** *(lohs'nee-nyohs foo-hee-'tee-vohs)*
segregation	**la segregación** *(lah seh-greh-gah-see-'ohn)*
teen suicide	**el suicidio de adolescentes** *(ehl soo-ee-'see-dee·oh deh ah-doh-leh-'sehn-tehs)*
unemployment	**el desempleo** *(ehl dehs-ehm-'pleh-oh)*
violence	**la violencia** *(lah vee-oh-'lehn-see·ah)*

➤ Group all your vocabulary according to patterns:

It's...	**Es...** *(ehs...)*
bi-cultural	**bicultural** *(bee-kool-too-'rahl)*
cross-cultural	**intercultural** *(een-tehr-kool-too-'rahl)*
multi-cultural	**multicultural** *(mool-tee-kool-too-'rahl)*

Take (the)...	**Toma...** *('toh-mah...)*
brochure	**el folleto** *(ehl foh-'yeh-toh)*
flyer	**la hoja informativa** *(lah 'oh-hah een-fohr-mah-'tee-vah)*
syllabus	**el programa de estudio** *(ehl proh-'grah-mah deh eh-'stoo-dee·oh)*

We have (the)...	**Tenemos...** *(teh-'neh-mohs...)*
home school	**la escuela en casa** *(lah eh-'skweh-lah ehn 'kah-sah)*
night school	**la escuela de noche** *(lah eh-'skweh-lah deh 'noh-cheh)*
summer school	**la escuela de verano** *(lah eh-'skweh-lah deh veh-'rah-noh)*

There's...	**Hay...** *('ah·ee...)*
teacher shortage	**falta de maestros** *('fahl-tah deh mah-'eh-strohs)*
teacher recruitment	**contratación de maestros** *(kohn-trah-tah-see-'ohn deh mah-'eh-strohs)*
teacher certification	**certificación de maestros** *(sehr-tee-fee-kah-see-'ohn deh mah-'eh-strohs)*

It isn't...	**No es...** *(noh ehs...)*
co-ed	**colegio mixto** *(koh-'leh-hee·oh'meek-stoh)*
non-profit	**sin fines de lucro** *(seen'fee-nehs deh'loo-kroh)*
year-round	**para todo el año** *('pah-rah'toh-doh ehl'ah-nyoh)*

➤ End your presentation with a kind word or two.

Thank you very much for coming.
Muchas gracias por venir. *('moo-chahs'grah-see·ahs pohr veh-'neer)*

The students will receive...	**Los estudiantes van a recibir...** *(lohs eh-stoo-dee-'ahn-tehs vahn ah reh-see-'beer...)*
awards	**galardones** *(gah-lahr-'doh-nehs)*
certificates	**certificados** *(sehr-tee-fee-'kah-dohs)*
gifts	**regalos** *(reh-'gah-lohs)*
medals	**medallas** *(meh-'dah-yahs)*
prizes	**premios** *('preh-mee·ohs)*
rewards	**recompensas** *(reh-kohm-'pehn-sahs)*
ribbons	**cintas meritorias** *('seen-tahs meh-ree-'toh-ree-ahs)*
trophies	**trofeos** *(troh-'feh-ohs)*

TO CONVERSE WITH EMPLOYEES

Conversar con los empleados *(kohn-vehr-'sahr kohn lohs ehm-pleh-'ah-dohs)*

Besides using Spanish with students, families, and the community, there's also an occasional opportunity to chat with fellow employees. If a Spanish speaker works for you, you may have to discuss the following topics:

Let's talk about (the)....	**Hablamos de...** *(ah-'blah-mohs deh)*
benefits	**los beneficios** *(lohs beh-neh-'fee-see·ohs)*
contracts	**los contratos** *(lohs kohn-'trah-tohs)*
credit union	**el banco cooperativo** *(ehl'bahn-koh koh-oh-peh-rah-'tee-voh)*

employee party	**la fiesta para los empleados** *(lah fee-'eh-stah 'pah-rah lohs ehm-pleh-'ah-dohs)*
holidays	**los días feriados** *(lohs 'dee-ahs feh-ree-'ah-dohs)*
insurance	**el seguro** *(ehl seh-'goo-roh)*
interviews	**las entrevistas** *(lahs ehn-treh-'vee-stahs)*
job description	**la descripción del trabajo** *(lah deh-skreep-see-'ohn dehl trah-'bah-hoh)*
overtime	**el sobretiempo** *(ehl soh-breh-tee-'ehm-poh)*
raise	**el aumento de sueldo** *(ehl ow-'mehn-toh deh 'swehl-doh)*
retirement	**la jubilación** *(lah hoo-bee-lah-see-'ohn)*
staff development	**el entrenamiento del personal** *(ehl ehn-treh-nah-mee-'ehn-toh dehl pehr-soh-'nahl)*
trade union	**el sindicato** *(ehl seen-dee-'kah-toh)*
vacations	**las vacaciones** *(lahs vah-kah-see-'oh-nehs)*
wages	**el sueldo** *(ehl 'swehl-doh)*

This time give a schedule to anyone who asks:

Be here at _____. **Esté aquí a _____ .**

(eh-'steh ah-'kee-ah _____)

You may leave at _____. **Se puede ir a _____ .**

(seh 'pweh-deh eer ah _____)

Take a break at _____. **Tome un descanso a _____ .**

('toh-meh oon deh-'skahn-soh ah _____)

Return at _____. **Regrese a _____ .**

(reh-'greh-seh ah _____)

You will work on _____. **Va a trabajar en _____ .**

(vah ah trah-bah-'hahr ehn _____)

And do the Spanish-speaking employees know all the regulations around the worksite?

Use (the)... **Use...** *('oo-seh)*

authorized area **la zona autorizada**

(lah 'soh-nah ow-toh-ree-'sah-dah)

personal identification	**la identificación personal** *(lah ee-dehn-tee-fee-kah-see-'ohn pehr-soh-'nahl)*
security code	**el código de seguridad** *(ehl'koh-dee-goh deh seh-goo-ree-'dahd)*
sign-in sheet	**la lista de registro** *(lah'lee-stah deh reh-'hee-stroh)*
time card	**la tarjeta de trabajo** *(lah tahr-'heh-tah deh trah-'bah-hoh)*
time clock	**el reloj de trabajo** *(ehl reh-'loh deh trah-'bah-hoh)*

Use the employee _____ .	**Use _____ para los empleados.** *('oo-seh _____ 'pah-rah lohs ehm-pleh-'ah-dohs)*

cafeteria	**la cafetería** *(lah kah-feh-teh-'ree-ah)*
entrance	**la entrada** *(lah ehn-'trah-dah)*
lounge	**el salón de espera** *(ehl sah-'lohn deh eh-'speh-rah)*
parking area	**la zona de estacionamiento** *(lah'soh-nah deh eh-stah-see·oh-nah-mee-'ehn-toh)*
restroom	**el baño** *(ehl'bah-nyoh)*
telephone	**el teléfono** *(ehl teh-'leh-foh-noh)*

MÁS INFORMACIÓN

➤ These words are used for special occasions:

Let's...	**Vamos a...** *('vah-mohs ah...)*

contribute	**contribuir** *(kohn-tree-boo-'eer)*
donate	**donar** *(doh-'nahr)*
volunteer	**ser voluntarios** *(sehr voh-loon-'tah-ree·ohs)*

Once Hispanics establish friendly relationships, they often use nicknames when referring to each other. It is meant to show intimacy, and not disrespect. Besides, it might be fun to look up the translations for any terms of endearment that you hear.

¿LISTOS PARA PRACTICAR?

Pick the *best* word to fill in the blank:

los premios, la junta, el presupuesto *(lohs 'preh-mee·ohs, lah 'hoon-tah, ehl preh-soo-'pweh-stoh)*

El director fue a _____ . *(ehl dee-rehk-'tohr fweh ah _____)*

Los niños reciben _____ . *(lohs 'nee-nyohs reh-'see-behn _____)*

Quiero discutir _____ . *(kee-'eh-roh dees-koo-'teer _____)*

Connect the terms that seem to relate best:

la ley *(lah 'leh·ee)*   **la conferencia** *(lah kohn-feh-'rehn-see·ah)*

las metas *(lahs 'meh-tahs)*   **la pobreza** *(lah poh-'breh-sah)*

el sobretiempo *(ehl soh-breh-tee-'ehm-poh)*   **los objetivos** *(lohs ohb-heh-'tee-vohs)*

el hambre *(ehl 'ahm-breh)*   **el sueldo** *(ehl 'swehl-doh)*

la reunión *(lah reh-oo-nee-'ohn)*   **el gobierno** *(ehl goh-bee-'ehr-noh)*

Review the verb forms we've studied so far in this guidebook. Note the spelling and pronunciation changes that take place when you shift from one time reference to the next:

I'm working now.	**Estoy trabajando ahora.** *(eh-'stoh·ee trah-bah-'hahn-doh ah-oh-rah)*
I work every day.	**Trabajo todos los días.** *(trah-'bah-hoh 'toh-dohs lohs 'dee-ahs)*
I will work tomorrow.	**Trabajaré mañana.** *(trah-bah-hah-'reh mah-'nyah-nah)*
I worked yesterday.	**Trabajé ayer.** *(trah-bah-'heh ah-'yehr)*

Now, study the following two-part verb pattern. It's extremely important in school-related conversations because it refers to actions that have already taken place. It's a past action pattern that is used frequently in everyday communication, so pay close attention to each example. Here's how the words go together.

The first part consists of forms of the verb "to have" **haber** *(ah-'behr)*.

The second part consists of the past participle of the action word. Both parts must be used together.

I've	**He**	left	**salido** *(sah-'lee-doh)*
		eaten	**comido** *(koh-'mee-doh)*
You've (informal)	**Has**	studied	**estudiado** *(ehs-too-dee-'ah-doh)*
		written	**escrito** *(ehs-'kree-toh)*

278

You've (formal), She's, He's	**Ha**	closed	**cerrado** *(seh-'rrah-doh)*
		cleaned	**limpiado** *(leem-pee-'ah-doh)*
You've (pl.), They've	**Han**	worked	**trabajado** *(trah-bah-'hah-doh)*
		arrived	**llegado** *(yeh-'gah-doh)*
We've	**Hemos**	learned	**aprendido** *(ah-prehn-'dee-doh)*

To learn more about these past participle verb forms, consider taking a beginning Spanish class. It's worth the effort, because in education this two-part verb tense can be very useful. Watch:

I've arrived late many times.
He llegado tarde muchas veces.
(eh yeh-'gah-doh 'tahr-deh 'moo-chahs 'veh-sehs)

She's passed the test.
Ella ha pasado el examen.
('eh-yah ah pah-'sah-doh ehl ek-'sah-mehn)

We've cleaned the desks.
Hemos limpiado los escritorios.
('eh-mohs leem-pee-'ah-doh lohs eh-skree-'toh-ree-ohs)

MÁS INFORMACIÓN

➤ Some past participles can be used as descriptive words:

They are parked cars.	**Son carros <u>estacionados</u>.** *(sohn 'kah-rrohs eh-stah-see·oh-'nah-dohs)*
They are painted doors.	**Son puertas <u>pintadas</u>.** *(sohn 'pwehr-tahs peen-'tah-dahs)*
They are washed floors.	**Son pisos <u>lavados</u>.** *(sohn 'pee-sohs lah-'vah-dohs)*

➤ A handful of past participles are considered irregular. Memorize these examples:

I've broken the pencil.	**He <u>roto</u> el lápiz.** *(eh'roh-toh ehl'lah-pees)*
We've written the report.	**Hemos <u>escrito</u> el reporte.** *('eh-mohs eh-'skree-toh ehl reh-'pohr-teh)*
He's seen the program.	**Ha <u>visto</u> el programa.** *(ah'vee-stoh ehl proh-'grah-mah)*

¡ÓRDENES!

Now that we can add pronouns to our command words, let's attempt to create a few one-word expressions for everyday use.

Tell it to me	**Dímelo** *('dee-meh-loh)*
Show it to me	**Enséñamela** *(ehn-'seh-nyah-meh-lah)*
Give it to me	**Dámelo** *('dah-meh-loh)*
Turn it in to me	**Entrégamela** *(ehn-'treh-gah-meh-lah)*
Bring it to me	**Tráemelo** *('trah-eh-meh-loh)*
Throw it to me	**Tíramela** *('tee-rah-meh-lah)*

Watch what happens when the same commands are in the formal mode:

Tell it to me	**Dígamelo** *('dee-gah-meh-loh)*
Show it to me	**Enséñemela** *(ehn-'seh-nyeh-meh-lah)*
Give it to me	**Démelo** *('deh-meh-loh)*
Turn it in to me	**Entréguemela** *(ehn-'treh-geh-meh-lah)*
Bring it to me	**Tráigamelo** *('trah·ee-gah-meh-loh)*
Throw it to me	**Tíremela** *('tee-reh-meh-lah)*

¿LISTOS PARA PRACTICAR?

Study the examples, and then write in the missing verb forms:

enseñar *(ehn-seh-'nyahr)* **trabajar** *(trah-bah-'hahr)* **hablar** *(ah-'blahr)*

Estoy enseñando. *(eh-'stoh·ee ehn-seh-'nyahn-doh)*
Enseño. *(ehn-'seh-'nyoh)*
Enseñaré. *(ehn-seh-nyah-'reh)*
Enseñé. *(ehn-seh-'nyeh)*
Estaba enseñando. *(eh-'stah-bah ehn-seh-'nyahn-doh)*
He enseñado. *(eh ehn-seh-'nyah-doh)*

aprender *(ah-prehn-'dehr)* **comer** *(koh-'mehr)* **escribir** *(eh-skree-'beer)*

Estoy aprendiendo.
(eh-'stoh·ee ah-prehn-dee-'ehn-doh)
Aprendo. *(ah-'prehn-doh)*
Aprenderé.
(ah-prehn-deh-'reh)
Aprendí. *(ah-prehn-'dee)*
Estaba aprendiendo.
(eh-'stah-bah ah-prehn-dee-'ehn-doh)
He aprendido.
(eh ah-prehn-'dee-doh)

CHAPTER EIGHT
Capítulo Ocho
(kah-'pee-too-loh 'oh-choh)

SUPPORT STAFF
El personal auxiliar
(ehl pehr-soh-'nahl owk-see-lee-'ahr)

OFFICE ASSISTANCE
Ayuda en la oficina *(ah-'yoo-dah ehn lah oh-fee-'see-nah)*

At educational facilities everywhere, nothing gets done without the help of skilled office professionals. Spend time with this series of words and phrases designed specifically for clerical staff who need to use Spanish:

May I help you?
¿Puedo ayudarle? *('pweh-doh ah-yoo-'dahr-leh)*

You need to talk to _____ .
Necesita hablar con _____ .*(neh-seh-'see-tah ah-'blahr kohn _____)*

Do you know where it is?
¿Sabe dónde está? *('sah-beh 'dohn-deh eh-'stah)*

Someone will help you in a few minutes.
Alguien le atenderá en algunos minutos. *('ahl-gee·ehn·leh ah-tehn-deh-'rah ehn ahl-'goo-nohs mee-'noo-tohs)*

Please have a seat.
Por favor, tome asiento. *(pohr fah-'vohr, 'toh-meh ah-see-'ehn-toh)*

These are the office hours.
Estas son las horas de oficina. *('eh-stahs sohn lahs 'oh-rahs deh oh-fee-'see-nah)*

I NEED INFORMATION, PLEASE
Necesito información, por favor
(neh-seh-'see-toh een-fohr-mah-see-'ohn, pohr fah-'vohr)

For those situations involving orientation, registration, or minor emergencies, utilize the one-liners below. Start off by talking to the student:

Where do you go to school?
¿Adónde vas a la escuela? *(ah-'dohn-deh vahs ah lah eh-'skweh-lah)*

You need to go back to class.
Necesitas regresar a tu clase. *(neh-seh-'see-tahs reh-greh-'sahr ah too 'klah-seh)*

What grade are you in?
¿En qué grado estás? *(ehn keh 'grah-doh eh-'stahs)*

Are your parents at home?
¿Están tus padres en casa? *(eh-'stahn toos 'pah-drehs ehn 'kah-sah)*

Do any of your brothers or sisters attend this school?
¿Asiste algún hermano o hermana a esta escuela? *(ah-'see-steh ahl-'goon ehr-'mah-noh oh ehr-'mah-nah ah 'eh-stah eh-'skweh-lah)*

Who would you like to talk to?
¿Con quién te gustaría hablar? *(kohn kee-'ehn teh goo-stah-'ree-ah ah-'blahr)*

What is your student ID number?
¿Cuál es tu número de estudiante? *(kwahl ehs too 'noo-meh-roh deh eh-stoo-dee-'ahn-teh)*

Who sent you here?
¿Quién te mandó aquí? *(kee-'ehn teh mahn-'doh ah-'kee)*

Now, say a few things to the parents, families, and friends:

Read all of the information.
Lea toda la información. *('leh-ah 'toh-dah lah een-fohr-mah-see-'ohn)*

Do you have all the forms?
¿Tiene todos los formularios? *(tee-'eh-neh 'toh-dohs lohs fohr-moo-'lah-ree·ohs)*

Who is the legal parent or guardian?
¿Quién es el padre o guardián legal? *(kee-'ehn ehs ehl 'pah-dreh oh gwahr-dee-'ahn leh-'gahl)*

These are the instructions.
Estas son las instrucciones. *('eh-stahs sohn lahs een-strook-see-'oh-nehs)*

Is there someone in the home who speaks English?
¿Hay alguien en la casa que hable inglés? *('ah·ee 'ahl-gee·ehn ehn lah 'kah-sah keh 'ah-bleh een-'glehs)*

Please fill out everything and sign here.
Llene todo y firme aquí, por favor. *('yeh-neh 'toh-doh ee 'feer-meh ah-'kee, pohr fah-'vohr)*

Who can we call in case of emergency?
¿A quién podemos llamar en caso de emergencia? *(ah kee-'ehn poh-'deh-mohs yah-'mahr ehn 'kah-soh deh eh-mehr-'hehn-see·ah)*

MÁS INFORMACIÓN

➤ At the front counter, employees discuss various costs, fees, and charges with students and their families, and these phrases are used all the time:

How much does it cost?	**¿Cuánto cuesta?** *('kwahn-toh 'kweh-stah)*
When do I have to pay?	**¿Cuándo tengo que pagar?** *('kwahn-doh 'tehn-goh keh pah-'gahr)*
Who do I give the money to?	**¿A quién doy el dinero?** *(ah kee-'ehn 'doh·ee ehl dee-'neh-roh)*
Please give me (the)...	**Por favor, deme...** *(pohr fah-'vohr, 'deh-meh...)*
bill	**la cuenta** *(lah 'kwehn-tah)*
bills	**los billetes** *(lohs bee-'yeh-tehs)*
change	**el cambio** *(ehl 'kahm-bee·oh)*
check	**el cheque** *(ehl 'cheh-keh)*
coins	**las monedas** *(lahs moh-'neh-dahs)*
credit card	**la tarjeta de crédito** *(lah tahr-'heh-tah deh 'kreh-dee-toh)*
invoice	**la factura** *(lah fahk-'too-rah)*
money	**el dinero** *(ehl dee-'neh-roh)*
order	**la orden** *(lah 'ohr-dehn)*
payment	**el pago** *(ehl 'pah-goh)*
receipt	**el recibo** *(ehl reh-'see-boh)*
dollar	**el dólar** *(ehl 'doh-lahr)*
cent	**el centavo** *(ehl sehn-'tah-voh)*

Many front office employees work with new immigrant families who are unfamiliar with local, state, or federal laws and regulations. If you plan to establish a long-term relationship, you can prevent potential problems by giving them as much legal information as possible. By contacting a variety of service agencies, one can pick up literature in Spanish concerning citizenship, taxes, health care, housing, employment, transportation, and residence, as well as personal rights and privileges.

THE SCHOOL NURSE

La enfermera en la escuela *(lah ehn-fehr-'meh-rah ehn lah eh-'skweh-lah)*

Right up the hallway from the main office, a school nurse prepares for the day's activities. These questions only require a **sí** or **no** for an answer. Start with those words that you already know:

Do you have...?	**¿Tienes...?** *(tee-'eh-nehs)*
acne	**el acné** *(ehl ahk-'neh)*
backaches	**los dolores de espalda** *(lohs doh-'loh rehs deh eh-'spahl-dah)*
blister	**la ampolla** *(lah ahm-'poh-yah)*
bruise	**la contusión** *(lah kohn-too-see-'ohn)*
chills	**los escalofríos** *(lohs eh-skah-loh-'free-ohs)*
cold	**el resfriado** *(ehl rehs-free-'ah-doh)*
constipation	**el estreñimiento** *(ehl eh-streh-nyee-mee-'ehn-toh)*
convulsions	**las convulsiones** *(lahs kohn-vool-see-'oh-nehs)*
cramps	**los calambres** *(lohs kah-'lahm-brehs)*
cut	**la cortadura** *(lah kohr-tah-'doo-rah)*
diarrhea	**la diarrea** *(lah dee-ah-'rreh-ah)*
dizziness	**los mareos** *(lohs mah-'reh-ohs)*
fever	**la fiebre** *(lah fee-'eh-breh)*
gas	**el gas** *(ehl gahs)*
headaches	**los dolores de cabeza** *(lohs doh-'loh-rehs deh kah-'beh-sah)*

insomnia	**el insomnio** *(ehl een-'sohm-nee·oh)*
itching	**la picazón** *(lahl pee-kah-'sohn)*
menstruation	**la menstruación** *(lah mehn-stroo-ah-see-'ohn)*
nausea	**la náusea** *(lah 'now-seh-ah)*
numbness	**el adormecimiento** *(ehl ah-dohr-meh-see-mee-'ehn-toh)*
phlegm	**la flema** *(lah 'fleh-mah)*
scratch	**el rasguño** *(ehl rahs-'goo-nyoh)*
seizures	**los ataques** *(lohs ah-'tah-kehs)*
stomachaches	**los dolores de estómago** *(lohs doh-'loh-rehs deh eh-'stoh-mah-goh)*
swelling	**la hinchazón** *(lah een-chah-'sohn)*
toothache	**el dolor de muelas** *(ehl doh-'lohr deh 'mweh-lahs)*

Keep mentioning your concerns about their health:

It could be (the)...	**Podría ser...** *(poh-'dree-ah sehr...)*
allergies	**las alergias** *(ah-'lehr-hee·ahs)*
contagious disease	**la enfermedad contagiosa** *(lah ehn-fehr-meh-'dahd kohn-tah-hee-'oh-sah)*
dog bite	**la mordedura de perro** *(lah mohr-deh-'doo-rah deh 'peh-rroh)*
high blood pressure	**la presión alta** *(lah preh-see-'ohn 'ahl-tah)*
illness	**la enfermedad** *(lah ehn-fehr-meh-'dahd)*
infection	**la infección** *(lah een-fehk-see-'ohn)*
injury	**la herida** *(lah eh-'ree-dah)*

insect bite	**la picadura de insecto** *(lah pee-kah-'doo-rah deh een-'sehk-toh)*
poisoning	**el envenenamiento** *(ehl ehn-veh-neh-nah-mee-'ehn-toh)*
shock	**la prostración nerviosa** *(lah proh-strah-see-'ohn nehr-vee-'oh-sah)*

MÁS INFORMACIÓN

➤ Isolate the problem:

There are...	**Hay...** *('ah·ee...)*
physical problems	**problemas físicos** *(proh-'bleh-mahs 'fee-see-kohs)*
respiratory problems	**problemas respiratorios** *(proh-'bleh-mahs reh-spee-rah-'toh-ree·ohs)*
visual problems	**problemas de visión** *(proh-'bleh-mahs deh vee-see-'ohn)*

➤ There should be something on file about the child's health history. This can work as a checklist:

chicken pox	**varicela** *(vah-ree-'seh-lah)*
diabetes	**diabetes** *(dee-ah-'beh-tehs)*
measles	**sarampión** *(sah-rahm-pee-'ohn)*
mumps	**paperas** *(pah-'peh-rahs)*
scarlet fever	**escarlatina** *(eh-skahr-lah-'tee-nah)*

➤ All set to make a suggestion?

You need a _____ test.	**Necesitas un examen de _____ .** *(neh-seh-'see-tahs oon ehk-'sah-mehn deh _____)*
blood	**sangre** *('sahn-greh)*
urine	**orina** *(oh-'ree-nah)*
Pap smear	**Papinicolaou** *(pah-pee-nee-koh-'lah·oh-oo)*

288

➤ Can you figure out what these words mean?

difteria	**cáncer**	**leucemia**
(deef-'teh-ree·ah)	*('kahn-sehr)*	*(leh·oo-'seh-mee·ah)*
tétano	**tuberculosis**	
('teh-tah-noh)	*(too-behr-koo-'loh-sees)*	

TREATMENT
El tratamiento *(ehl trah-tah-mee-'ehn-toh)*

Anyone responsible for student health care should learn the medical terms below. Do you recall these terms from an earlier lesson?

We have (the)...   **Tenemos...** *(teh-'neh-mohs...)*

aspirin	**la aspirina** *(lah ah-spee-'ree-nah)*
bandage	**el vendaje** *(ehl vehn-'dah-heh)*
cream	**la crema** *(lah 'kreh-mah)*
lotion	**la loción** *(lah loh-see-'ohn)*
medicine	**la medicina** *(lah meh-deh-'see-nah)*
powder	**el talco** *(ehl 'tahl-koh)*

Now, use this pattern to explain the situation in greater detail:

He/She needs (the)...   **Necesita...** *(neh-seh-'see-tah...)*

antibiotic	**el antibiótico** *(ehl ahn-tee-bee-'oh-tee-koh)*
alcohol	**el alcohol** *(ehl ahl-koh-'ohl)*
Band-Aid®	**la curita** *(lah koo-'ree-tah)*
calamine lotion	**la loción de calamina** *(lah loh-see-'ohn deh kah-lah-'mee-nah)*
capsules	**las cápsulas** *(lahs 'kahp-soo-lahs)*
cast	**la armadura de yeso** *(lah ahr-mah-'doo-rah deh 'yeh-soh)*
cough syrup	**el jarabe para la tos** *(ehl hah-'rah-beh 'pah-rah lah tohs)*

CPR	**la respiración artificial**
	(lah reh-spee-rah-see-'ohn ahr-tee-fee-see-'ahl)
disinfectant	**el desinfectante** *(ehl dehs-een-fehk-'tahn-teh)*
drops	**las gotas** *(lahs 'goh-tahs)*
iodine	**el yodo** *(ehl 'yoh-doh)*
liniment	**el linimento** *(ehl lee-nee-'mehn-toh)*
lozenges	**las pastillas** *(lahs pah-'stee-yahs)*
pills	**las píldoras** *(lahs 'peel-doh-rahs)*
prescription	**la receta** *(lah reh-'seh-tah)*
shot	**la inyección** *(lah een-yehk-see-'ohn)*
stitches	**las puntadas** *(lahs poon-'tah-dahs)*
tablets	**las tabletas** *(lahs tah-'bleh-tahs)*
thermometer	**el termómetro** *(ehl tehr-'moh-meh-troh)*
vaseline	**la vaselina** *(lah vah-seh-'lee-nah)*
vitamins	**las vitaminas** *(lahs vee-tah-'mee-nahs)*
X rays	**los rayos equis** *(lohs 'rah-yohs 'eh-kees)*

MÁS INFORMACIÓN

➤ While treating the child, keep an eye out for these little critters:

fleas	**las pulgas** *(lahs 'pool-gahs)*
lice	**los piojos** *(lohs pee-'oh-hohs)*
ticks	**las garrapatas** *(lahs gah-rrah-'pah-tahs)*
worms	**los gusanos** *(lohs goo-'sah-nohs)*

SCHOOL MAINTENANCE
El mantenimiento de la escuela
(ehl mah-teh-nee-mee-'ehn-toh deh lah eh-'skweh-lah)

Look at all the employees around the campus. Perhaps one of the most noticeable staff members is the janitor or maintenance professional. When they use Spanish, here's their favorite set of vocabulary words:

I need (the)...	**Necesito...** *(neh-seh-'see-toh...)*
Give me (the)...	**Dame...** *('dah-meh...)*

Where's (the) ...	¿Dónde está ...? *('dohn-deh eh-'stah...)*
ammonia	**el amoníaco** *(ehl ah-moh-'nee-ah-koh)*
bleach	**el blanqueador** *(ehl blahn-keh-ah-'dohr)*
cleaner	**el limpiador** *(ehl leem-pee ah-'dohr)*
polish	**el lustrador** *(ehl loo-strah-'dohr)*
powder	**el polvo** *(ehl 'pohl-voh)*
soap	**el jabón** *(ehl hah-'bohn)*
spray gun	**el rociador** *(ehl roh-see ah-'dohr)*
wax	**la cera** *(lah 'seh-rah)*

Can you guess what these words mean?

el detergente *(ehl deh-tehr-'hehn-teh)*

_____

el desinfectante *(ehl dehs-een-fehk-'tahn-teh)*

_____

la solución *(lah soh-loo-see-'ohn)*

_____

When there's cleaning to do, be sure that the mess is clearly defined:

There is/are...	Hay... *('ah ee)*
crumbs	**las migas** *(lahs 'mee-gahs)*
dirt	**la tierra** *(lah tee-'eh-rrah)*
dust	**el polvo** *(ehl 'pohl-voh)*
fungi	**los hongos** *(lohs 'ohn-gohs)*
grime	**la mugre** *(lah 'moo-greh)*
mold	**el moho** *(ehl 'moh-oh)*
mud	**el lodo** *(ehl 'loh-doh)*
rust	**la herrumbre** *(lah eh-'rroom-breh)*
sewage	**el desagüe** *(ehl dehs-'ah-gweh)*
trash	**la basura** *(lah bah-'soo-rah)*
waste	**los desperdicios** *(lohs dehs-pehr-'dee-see-ohs)*

And be aware of any tools that are being used on campus:

Bring (the)...   **Trae...** *('trah-eh)*

broom   **la escoba** *(lah eh-'skoh-bah)*
brush   **el cepillo** *(ehl seh-'pee-yoh)*
bucket   **el balde** *(ehl 'bahl-deh)*
feather duster   **el plumero** *(ehl ploo-'meh-roh)*
hose   **la manguera** *(lah mahn-'geh-rah)*
mask   **la máscara** *(lah 'mah-skah-rah)*
mop   **el trapeador** *(ehl trah-peh-ah-'dohr)*
rag   **el trapo** *(ehl 'trah-poh)*
scraper   **el raspador** *(ehl rah-spah-'dohr)*
sponge   **la esponja** *(lah eh-'spohn-hah)*
stepladder   **la escalera** *(lah eh-skah-'leh-rah)*
towel   **la toalla** *(lah toh-'ah-yah)*
trashbag   **la bolsa para basura**
                         (lah 'bohl-sah 'pah-rah bah-'soo-rah)
vacuum cleaner   **la aspiradora** *(lah ah-spee-rah-'doh-rah)*

If students gather around, keep them away from dangerous items. Follow the patterns:

Don't touch (the) ...   **No toques ...** *(noh 'toh-kehs...)*

cart   **la carreta** *(lah kah-'rreh-tah)*
equipment   **el equipo** *(ehl eh-'kee-poh)*
extension cord   **el cable de extensión** *(ehl 'kah-bleh deh ehk-stehn-*
                         see-'ohn)
glass   **el vidrio** *(ehl 'vee-dree oh)*
machinery   **la maquinaria** *(lah mah-kee-'nah-ree ah)*
pipe   **la tubería** *(lah too-beh-'ree-ah)*
rope   **la soga** *(lah 'soh-gah)*
switch   **el interruptor** *(ehl een-teh-rroop-'tohr)*
tool   **la herramienta** *(lah eh-rrah-mee-'ehn-tah)*
wire   **el alambre** *(ehl ah-'lahm-breh)*

Continue making phrases, but this time, only mention the tools:

drill	**el taladro** *(ehl tah-'lah-droh)*
file	**la lima** *(lah 'lee-mah)*
hammer	**el martillo** *(ehl mahr-'tee-yoh)*
paintbrush	**la brocha** *(lah 'broh-chah)*
pliers	**el alicate** *(ehl ah-lee-'kah-teh)*
saw	**el serrucho** *(ehl seh-'rroo-choh)*
screwdriver	**el atornillador** *(ehl ah-tohr-nee-yah-'dohr)*
tape measure	**la cinta para medir** *(lah 'seen-tah 'pah-rah meh-'deer)*
wrench	**la llave inglesa** *(lah 'yah-veh een-'gleh-sah)*

 MÁS INFORMACIÓN

When children are near, these one-liners should help:

Don't press (the)...	**No oprimas...** *(noh oh-'pree-mahs...)*
button	**el botón** *(ehl boh-'tohn)*
dial	**el marcador** *(ehl mahr-kah-'dohr)*
key	**la tecla** *(lah 'teh-klah)*
knob	**el tirador** *(ehl tee-rah-'dohr)*
timer	**el reloj** *(ehl reh-'loh)*
Don't touch (the)...	**No toques...** *(noh 'toh-kehs...)*
fuse box	**la caja de fusibles** *(lah 'kah-hah deh foo-'see-blehs)*
gas meter	**el medidor de gas** *(ehl meh-dee-'dohr deh gahs)*
smoke alarm	**el detector de humo** *(ehl deh-tehk-'tohr deh 'oo-moh)*
thermostat	**el termostato** *(ehl tehr-moh-'stah-toh)*
water valve	**la válvula de agua** *(lah 'vahl-voo-lah deh 'ah-gwah)*

Name three common physical ailments in Spanish:

_____   _____   _____

Name three things in Spanish that belong in a first-aid kit:

_____   _____   _____

Put in the word that best completes each series:

el dinero, la cápsula, la basura, el detergente, el equipo *(ehl dee-'neh-roh, lah 'kahp-soo-lah, lah bah-'soo-rah, ehl deh-tehr-'hehn-teh, ehl eh-'kee-poh)*

el jabón, el limpiador, _____ *(ehl hah-'bohn, ehl leem-pee ah-'dohr)*

la tableta, la píldora, _____ *(lah tah-'bleh-tah, lah 'peel-doh-rah)*

el billete, la moneda, _____ *(ehl bee-'yeh-teh, lah moh-'neh-dah)*

la herramienta, la maquinaria, _____ *(lah eh-rrah-'mee-'ehn-tah, lah mah-kee-'nah-ree ah)*

la tierra, el desagüe, _____ *(lah tee-'eh-rrah, ehl dehs-'ah-gweh)*

Name three tools in Spanish that are used by a school janitor:

_____   _____   _____

THE GARDENER
El jardinero *(ehl hahr-dee-'neh-roh)*

The landscapers also need language skills if they consistently meet people who speak Spanish. Don't hesitate to practice saying the following terms:

We're working with the...	**Estamos trabajando con...**
	(eh-'stah-mohs trah-bah-'hahn-doh kohn)

branches	**las ramas** *(lahs 'rah-mahs)*
bushes	**los arbustos** *(lohs ahr-'boo-stohs)*
flowers	**las flores** *(lahs 'floh-rehs)*
foliage	**el follaje** *(ehl foh-'yah-heh)*
grass	**el pasto** *(ehl 'pah-stoh)*
gravel	**la grava** *(lah 'grah-vah)*
land	**el terreno** *(ehl teh-'rreh-noh)*
lawn	**el césped** *(ehl sehs-'pehd)*
leaves	**las hojas** *(lahs 'oh-hahs)*
plants	**las plantas** *(lahs 'plahn-tahs)*
rocks	**las piedras** *(lahs pee-'eh-drahs)*
roots	**las raíces** *(lah rah-'ee-sehs)*
sand	**la arena** *(lah ah-'reh-nah)*
seeds	**las semillas** *(lahs seh-'mee-yahs)*
tree	**el árbol** *(ehl 'ahr-bohl)*
weeds	**las malas hierbas** *(lahs 'mah-lahs 'yehr-bahs)*

Look at (the) ...	**Mira...** *('mee-rah)*

flower bed	**el arriate** *(ehl ah-rree-'ah-teh)*
greenhouse	**el invernadero**
	(ehl een-vehr-nah-'deh-roh)
grove	**la arboleda** *(lah arh-boh-'leh-dah)*
nursery	**el criadero** *(ehl kree ah-'deh-roh)*
orchard	**la huerta** *(lah 'wehr-tah)*

Tell the kids to stay away from hazardous areas:

Do not go near (the)...	**No acercarse a...** *(noh ah-sehr-'kahr-seh ah...)*

channel	**el canal** *(ehl kah-'nahl)*
ditch	**la zanja** *(lah 'sahn-hah)*
drainage	**el drenaje** *(ehl dreh-'nah-heh)*
hole	**el hoyo** *(ehl 'oh-yoh)*
irrigation	**la irrigación** *(lah ee-rree-gah-see-'ohn)*
slope	**el declive** *(ehl deh-'klee-veh)*
sprinklers	**las rociadoras**
	(lahs roh-see ah-'doh-rahs)

➤ Although you've learned a few tools and materials already, there are some that are generally used by employees who do most of their work outdoors:

Move (the)...	**Mueva...** *('mweh-vah)*
ax	**el hacha** *(ehl 'ah-chah)*
blower	**el soplador** *(ehl soh-plah-'dohr)*
chain saw	**la motosierra** *(lah 'moh-toh-see-'eh-rrah)*
fertilizer	**el abono** *(ehl ah-'boh-noh)*
hoe	**el azadón** *(ehl ah-sah-'dohn)*
insecticide	**el insecticida** *(ehl een-sehk-tee-'see-dah)*
lawn mower	**la cortadora de césped** *(lah kohr-tah-'doh-rah deh 'sehs-pehd)*
pick	**el pico** *(ehl 'pee-koh)*
pitchfork	**la horquilla** *(lah ohr-'kee-yah)*
rake	**el rastrillo** *(ehl rah-'stree-yoh)*
shovel	**la pala** *(lah 'pah-lah)*
tractor	**el tractor** *(ehl trahk-'tohr)*
wheelbarrow	**la carretilla** *(lah kah-rreh-'tee-yah)*

ALL AROUND TOWN
Por toda la ciudad *(pohr 'toh-dah lah see-oo-'dahd)*

Several staff members conduct their business off-site, and therefore communicate at different locations throughout the city. Check over the following list, which identifies parts of your local community. We learned some of these already:

I went to (the)...	**Fui a...** *(fwee ah...)*
airport	**el aeropuerto** *(ehl ah-eh-roh-'pwehr-toh)*
bank	**el banco** *(ehl 'bahn-koh)*
church	**la iglesia** *(lah ee-'gleh-see·ah)*
city hall	**el municipio** *(ehl moo-nee-'see-pee·oh)*

courthouse	**la corte** *(lah 'kohr-teh)*
warehouse	**el almacén** *(ehl ahl-mah-'sehn)*
factory	**la fábrica** *(lah 'fah-bree-kah)*
gas station	**la gasolinera** *(lah gah-soh-lee-'neh-rah)*
hospital	**el hospital** *(ehl oh-spee-'tahl)*
library	**la biblioteca** *(lah beeb-lee oh-'teh-kah)*
movie theater	**el cine** *(ehl 'see-neh)*
office	**la oficina** *(lah oh-fee-'see-nah)*
pharmacy	**la farmacia** *(lah fahr-'mah-see ah)*
police station	**la estación de policía** *(lah eh-stah-see-'ohn deh poh-lee-'see-ah)*
post office	**el correo** *(ehl koh-'rreh-oh)*
restaurant	**el restaurante** *(ehl reh-stah-oo-'rahn-teh)*
store	**la tienda** *(lah tee-'ehn-dah)*
supermarket	**el supermercado** *(ehl soo-pehr-mehr-'kah-doh)*

This new vocabulary will assist anyone who travels, delivers, or visits around town:

It's near (the)...	**Está cerca de...** *(eh-'stah 'sehr-kah deh...)*
alley	**el callejón** *(ehl kah-yeh-'hohn)*
apartment building	**el edificio de departamentos** *(ehl eh-dee-'fee-see oh deh deh-pahr-tah-'mehn-tohs)*
avenue	**la avenida** *(lah ah-veh-'nee-dah)*
billboard	**el letrero** *(ehl leh-'treh-roh)*
bridge	**el puente** *(ehl 'pwehn-teh)*
bus stop	**la parada de autobús** *(lah pah-'rah-dah deh ow-toh-'boos)*
car lot	**el lote de carros** *(ehl 'loh-teh deh 'kah-rrohs)*
corner	**la esquina** *(lah eh-'skee-nah)*
crosswalk	**el cruce de peatones** *(ehl 'kroo-seh deh peh-ah-'toh-nehs)*
downtown	**el centro** *(ehl 'sehn-troh)*
fountain	**la fuente** *(lah 'fwehn-teh)*
highway	**la carretera** *(lah kah-rreh-'teh-rah)*
neighborhood	**el barrio** *(ehl 'bah-rree·oh)*
outskirts	**las afueras** *(lahs ah-'fweh-rahs)*

railroad track	**la vía del ferrocarril** *(lah 'vee-ah dehl feh-rroh-kah-'rreel)*
road	**el camino** *(ehl kah-'mee-noh)*
sidewalk	**la acera** *(lah ah-'seh-rah)*
statue	**la estatua** *(lah eh-'stah-too-ah)*
stop sign	**el señal de parada** *(ehl seh-'nyahl deh pah-'rah-dah)*
street	**la calle** *(lah 'kah-yeh)*
telephone pole	**el poste de teléfono** *(ehl 'poh-steh deh teh-'leh-foh-noh)*
tower	**la torre** *(lah 'toh-rreh)*
traffic signal	**el semáforo** *(ehl seh-'mah-foh-roh)*
tunnel	**el túnel** *(ehl 'too-nehl)*

MÁS INFORMACIÓN

➤ The names for some businesses follow a similar pattern in the Spanish language. They end in the letters **-ería**. This is just a sample:

bakery	**la panadería** *(lah pah-nah-deh-'ree-ah)*
barber shop	**la peluquería** *(lah peh-loo-keh-'ree-ah)*
book store	**la librería** *(lah lee-breh-'ree-ah)*
butcher shop	**la carnicería** *(lah kahr-nee-seh-'ree-ah)*
laundromat	**la lavandería** *(lah lah-vahn-deh-'ree-ah)*
shoe store	**la zapatería** *(lah sah-pah-teh-'ree-ah)*

➤ Can you relate to any of these places of worship?

They go to (the) ...	**Van a ...** *(vahn ah...)*
cathedral	**la catedral** *(lah kah-teh-'drahl)*
chapel	**la capilla** *(lah kah-'pee-yah)*
church	**la iglesia** *(lah ee-'gleh-see·ah)*
mosque	**la mezquita** *(lah mehs-'kee-tah)*
synagogue	**la sinagoga** *(lah see-nah-'goh-gah)*
temple	**el templo** *(ehl 'tehm-ploh)*

Translate into English:

Tráigame la pala, el rastrillo y el azadón. *('trah ee-gah-meh lah 'pah-lah, ehl rah-'stree-yoh ee ehl ah-sah-'dohn)*

Cortaré el arbusto, el césped y el árbol. *(kohr-tah-'reh ehl ahr-'boo-stoh, ehl 'sehs-pehd ee ehl 'ahr-bohl)*

Fui a la tienda, el correo y el banco. *(fwee ah lah tee-'ehn-dah, ehl koh-'rreh-oh, ee ehl 'bahn-koh)*

Mire la fuente, el puente y la estatua. *('mee-reh lah 'fwehn-teh, ehl 'pwehn-teh ee lah eh-'stah-too-ah)*

He hablado con el jardinero, la enfermera y el bedel. *(eh ah-'blah-doh kohn ehl hahr-dee-'neh-roh, lah ehn-fehr-'meh-rah ee ehl beh-'dehl)*

READ THE SIGN!
¡Lee el letrero! *('leh-eh ehl leh-'treh-roh)*

Do all the students and their families know what these words mean?

Curve	**CURVA** *('koor-vah)*
Detour	**DESVIACION** *(dehs-vee-ah-see-'ohn)*
Do Not Cross	**NO CRUZAR** *(noh kroo-'sahr)*
Do Not Litter	**NO TIRE BASURA** *(noh 'tee-reh bah-'soo-rah)*
Emergency	**EMERGENCIA** *(eh-mehr-'hehn-see·ah)*
Entrance	**ENTRADA** *(ehn-'trah-dah)*
Exit	**SALIDA** *(sah-'lee-dah)*
Handicapped	**MINUSVALIDOS** *(mee-noos-'vah-lee-dohs)*
Narrow Road	**CAMINO ESTRECHO** *(kah-'mee-noh eh-'streh-choh)*
No Entrance	**PASO PROHIBIDO** *('pah-soh proh-ee-'bee-doh)*
No Passing	**NO PASAR** *(noh pah-'sahr)*
No U Turn	**PROHIBIDA LA VUELTA EN U** *(proh-ee-'bee-dah lah 'vwehl-tah ehn oo)*
One Way	**CIRCULACION** *(seer-koo-lah-see-'ohn)*

Parking	**ESTACIONAMIENTO**
	(eh-stah-see oh-nah-mee-'ehn-toh)
Pedestrian Crossing	**PASO DE PEATONES**
	('pah-soh deh peh-ah-'toh-nehs)
Railroad Crossing	**CRUCE DE VIAS** *('kroo-seh deh 'vee-ahs)*
Slow	**DESPACIO** *(deh-'spah-see·oh)*
Speed Limit	**LIMITE DE VELOCIDAD**
	('lee-mee-teh deh veh-loh-see-'dahd)
Stop	**ALTO** *('ahl-toh)*
Tow Away Zone	**SE USARA GRUA** *(seh oo-sah-'rah 'groo-ah)*
Traffic Circle	**GLORIETA** *(gloh-ree-'eh-tah)*
Wait	**ESPERE** *(eh-'speh-reh)*
Walk	**CAMINE** *(kah-'mee-neh)*
Wrong Way	**VIA EQUIVOCADA**
	('vee-ah eh-kee-voh-'kah-dah)
Yield	**CEDA EL PASO** *('seh-dah ehl 'pah-soh)*

Speaking of written signs, what about those around the school grounds? Post these words in two languages today!

Closed	**CERRADO** *(seh-'rrah-doh)*
Danger	**PELIGRO** *(peh-'lee-groh)*
For Rent	**SE ALQUILA** *(seh ahl-'kee-lah)*
For Sale	**SE VENDE** *(seh 'vehn-deh)*
No Smoking	**NO FUMAR** *(noh foo-'mahr)*
Open	**ABIERTO** *(ah-bee-'ehr-toh)*
Out of Order	**DESCOMPUESTO** *(dehs-kohm-'pweh-stoh)*
Pull	**JALE** *('hah-leh)*
Push	**EMPUJE** *(ehm-'poo-heh)*
Red Cross	**CRUZ ROJA** *(kroos 'roh-hah)*
Restrooms	**BAÑOS** *('bah-nyohs)*

Keep going:

Authorized Personnel Only	**SÓLO PARA PERSONAL AUTORIZADO**
	('soh-loh 'pah-rah pehr-soh-'nahl ow-toh-ree-
	'sah-doh)
Change Machine	**MÁQUINA DE CAMBIO**
	('mah-kee-nah deh 'kahm-bee·oh)
Do Not Block Entrance	**NO OBSTRUIR LA ENTRADA**
	(noh ohb-stroo-'eer lah ehn-'trah-dah)

Emergency Exit	**SALIDA DE EMERGENCIA**
	(sah-'lee-dah deh eh-mehr-'hehn-see-ah)
Employee Parking	**ESTACIONAMIENTO PARA EMPLEADOS**
	(eh-stah-see-oh-nah-mee-'ehn-toh 'pah-rah ehm-pleh-'ah-dohs)
Next Window Please	**PASAR A LA SIGUIENTE VENTANILLA**
	(pah-'sahr ah lah see-gee-'ehn-teh vehn-tah-'nee-yah)

CONFLICTOS CULTURALES

Do not translate names of businesses, brands, streets. All over the world, most formal titles in English remain the same.

KITCHEN EMPLOYEES

Los empleados de la cocina *(lohs ehm-pleh-'ah-dohs deh lah koh-'see-nah)*

When the bell rings, and everyone fills the cafeteria or lunch area, numerous conversations begin. Here are the names for a few condiments:

We need more of (the) ...	**Necesitamos más de ...** *(neh-seh-see-'tah-mohs mahs deh...)*
chocolate	**el chocolate** *(ehl choh-koh-'lah-teh)*
cinnamon	**la canela** *(lah kah-'neh-lah)*
garlic	**el ajo** *(ehl 'ah-hoh)*
honey	**la miel** *(lah mee-'ehl)*
hot pepper	**el chile** *(ehl 'chee-leh)*
marmalade	**la mermelada** *(lah mehr-meh-'lah-dah)*
mayonnaise	**la mayonesa** *(lah mah-yoh-'neh-sah)*
mustard	**la mostaza** *(lah moh-'stah-sah)*
nuts	**las nueces** *(lahs noo-'eh-sehs)*
oil	**el aceite** *(ehl ah-'seh ee-teh)*
olive	**la aceituna** *(lah ah-seh ee-'too-nah)*
peanut butter	**la crema de maní** *(lah 'kreh-mah deh mah-'nee)*

pepper	**la pimienta** *(lah pee-mee-'ehn-tah)*
pickle	**el encurtido** *(ehl ehn-koor-'tee-doh)*
salad dressing	**la salsa para la ensalada**
	(lah 'sahl-sah 'pah-rah lah ehn-sah-'lah-dah)
salt	**la sal** *(lah sahl)*
sauce	**la salsa** *(lah 'sahl-sah)*
sugar	**el azúcar** *(ehl ah-'soo-kahr)*
tomato sauce	**la salsa de tomate**
	(lah 'sahl-sah deh toh-'mah-teh)
vanilla	**la vainilla** *(lah vah·ee-'nee-yah)*
vinegar	**el vinagre** *(ehl vee-'nah-greh)*

Think about labeling some of these kitchen objects with removable stickers:

Bring (the)...	**Traiga...** *('trah ee-gah...)*
apron	**el delantal** *(ehl deh-lahn-'tahl)*
bowl	**el plato hondo** *(ehl 'plah-toh 'ohn-doh)*
butter dish	**la mantequillera** *(lah mahn-teh-kee-'yeh-rah)*
coffeepot	**la cafetera** *(lah kah-feh-'teh-rah)*
creamer	**la cremera** *(lah kreh-'meh-rah)*
cup	**la taza** *(lah 'tah-sah)*
fork	**el tenedor** *(ehl teh-neh-'dohr)*
glass	**el vaso** *(ehl 'vah-soh)*
grill	**la parrilla** *(lah pah-'rree-yah)*
knife	**el cuchillo** *(ehl koo-'chee-yoh)*
matches	**los fósforos** *(lohs 'fohs-foh-rohs)*
napkin	**la servilleta** *(lah sehr-vee-'yeh-tah)*
pan	**el sartén** *(ehl sahr-'tehn)*
pepper shaker	**el pimentero** *(ehl pee-mehn-'teh-roh)*
pitcher	**el cántaro** *(ehl 'kahn-tah-roh)*
plate	**el plato** *(ehl 'plah-toh)*
platter	**la fuente** *(lah 'fwehn-teh)*
pot	**la olla** *(lah 'oh-yah)*
rack	**el estilador** *(ehl eh-stee-lah-'dohr)*
salad bowl	**la ensaladera** *(lah ehn-sah-lah-'deh-rah)*
salt shaker	**el salero** *(ehl sah-'leh-roh)*
saucepan	**la cacerola** *(lah kah-seh-'roh-lah)*
saucer	**el platillo** *(ehl plah-'tee-yoh)*
spoon	**la cuchara** *(lah koo-'chah-rah)*

sugar bowl	**la azucarera** *(lah ah-soo-kah-'reh-rah)*
tablecloth	**el mantel** *(ehl mahn-'tehl)*
thermos	**el termo** *(ehl 'tehr-moh)*
towel	**la toalla** *(lah toh-'ah-yah)*
tray	**la bandeja** *(lah bahn-'deh-hah)*

Everyone has something to say about their meal. Listen to these comments in Spanish:

It's...	**Está...** *(eh-'stah)*

bitter	**amargo** *(ah-'mahr-goh)*
burned	**quemado** *(keh-'mah-doh)*
cooked	**cocido** *(koh-'see-doh)*
delicious	**delicioso** *(deh-lee-see-'oh-soh)*
dry	**seco** *('seh-koh)*
fresh	**fresco** *('frehs-koh)*
fried	**frito** *('free-toh)*
frozen	**congelado** *(kohn-heh-'lah-doh)*
hard	**duro** *('doo-roh)*
moist	**húmedo** *('oo-meh-doh)*
raw	**crudo** *('kroo-doh)*
rotten	**podrido** *(poh-'dree-doh)*
salty	**salado** *(sah-'lah-doh)*
soft	**suave** *('swah-veh)*
sour	**agrio** *('ah-gree·oh)*
spicy	**picante** *(pee-'kahn-teh)*
sweet	**dulce** *('dool-seh)*
tasty	**sabroso** *(sah-'broh-soh)*
warm	**tibio** *('tee-bee·oh)*

Keep it up, but with these words, talk to the students about good health:

It's...	**Es...** *(ehs)*

diet	**dietético** *(dee-eh-'teh-tee-koh)*
fat-free	**desgrasado** *(dehs-grah-'sah-doh)*
kosher	**preparado conforme a la ley judía**
	(preh-pah-'rah-doh kohn-'fohr-meh ah lah 'leh eehoo-'dee-ah)

natural	**natural** *(nah-too-'rahl)*
organic	**orgánico** *(ohr-'gah-nee-koh)*
sugar-free	**sin azúcar** *(seen ah-'soo-kahr)*
vegetarian	**vegetariano** *(veh-heh-tah-ree-'ah-noh)*

SECURITY PERSONNEL
El personal de seguridad *(ehl pehr-soh-'nahl deh seh-goo-ree-'dahd)*

Yet another key figure at school sites today is the campus security guard. When they address people in Spanish, their first question is to find out who everyone is:

Who is (the)...?	**¿Quién es...?** *(kee-'ehn ehs...)*
bystander	**el espectador** *(ehl eh-spehk-tah-'dohr)*
companion	**el compañero** *(ehl kohm-pah-'nyeh-roh)*
cyclist	**el ciclista** *(ehl see-'klee-stah)*
driver	**el chofer** *(ehl choh-'fehr)*
employee	**el empleado** *(ehl ehm-pleh-'ah-doh)*
friend	**el amigo** *(ehl ah-'mee-goh)*
minor	**el menor de edad** *(ehl meh-'nohr deh eh-'dahd)*
neighbor	**el vecino** *(ehl veh-'see-noh)*
passenger	**el pasajero** *(ehl pah-sah-'heh-roh)*
pedestrian	**el peatón** *(ehl peh-ah-'tohn)*
stranger	**el desconocido** *(ehl dehs-koh-noh-'see-doh)*
visitor	**el visitante** *(ehl vee-see-'tahn-teh)*

Now mention some of the folks who may create a problem. Do you recall any of these words from before?

I saw (the)...   **Yo ví...** *(yoh vee...)*

beggar   **el limosnero** *(ehl lee-mohs-'neh-roh)*
criminal   **el criminal** *(ehl kree-mee-'nahl)*
delinquent   **el delincuente** *(ehl deh-leen-'kwehn-teh)*
drug dealer   **el droguero** *(ehl droh-'geh-roh)*
drunkard   **el borracho** *(ehl boh-'rrah-choh)*
gang member   **el pandillero** *(ehl pahn-dee-'yeh-roh)*
loiterer   **el holgazán** *(ehl ohl-gah-'sahn)*
pickpocket   **el carterista** *(ehl kahr-teh-'ree-stah)*
prostitute   **la prostituta** *(lah proh-stee-'too-tah)*
thief   **el ladrón** *(ehl lah-'drohn)*
vagrant   **el vagabundo** *(ehl vah-gah-'boon-doh)*

When you confront and question all suspicious characters, combine your question words to collect the data you need. Write down a few of these phrases so that you won't forget. Fortunately, the answers to these questions are often brief and to the point:

Whose is it?   **¿De quién es?** *(deh kee-'ehn ehs)*
What's that?   **¿Qué es eso?** *(keh ehs 'eh-soh)*
Where are you from?   **¿De dónde es?** *(deh 'dohn-deh ehs)*
Where do you live?   **¿Dónde vive?** *('dohn-deh 'vee-veh)*
For what reason?   **¿Por qué razón?** *(pohr keh rah-'sohn)*
What kind?   **¿Qué clase?** *(keh 'klah-seh)*

This next Spanish action form is helpful in any conversation.

Have you been in jail?   **¿Ha estado en la cárcel?**
                                  (ah eh-'stah-doh ehn lah 'kahr-sehl)
Have you been drinking?   **¿Ha estado tomando alcohol?**
                                  (ah eh-'stah-doh toh-'mahn-doh ahl-koh-'ohl)
Have you been taking drugs?   **¿Ha estado tomando drogas?**
                                  (ah eh-'stah-doh toh-'mahn-doh 'droh-gahs)
Have you ever been arrested?   **¿Ha sido arrestado alguna vez?**
                                  *(ah 'see-doh ah-rreh-'stah-doh ahl-'goo-nah
                                    vehs)*

MÁS INFORMACIÓN

➤ To know the Spanish names of your uniform and equipment will be useful, and it will boost your self-confidence.

This is (the)...   **Esto es...** *('eh-stoh ehs...)*

badge	**el emblema** *(ehl ehm-'bleh-mah)*
bullhorn	**el altavoz** *(ehl ahl-tah-'vohs)*
equipment belt	**la correa de equipaje** *(lah koh-'rreh-ah deh eh-kee-'pah-heh)*
flashlight	**la linterna** *(lah leen-'tehr-nah)*
handcuff	**las esposas** *(lahs eh-'spoh-sahs)*
radio transmitter	**el radiotransmisor** *(ehl rah-dee oh-trahns-mee-sohr)*
uniform	**el uniforme** *(ehl oo-nee-'fohr-meh)*
whistle	**el silbato** *(ehl seel-'bah-toh)*

¿LISTOS PARA PRACTICAR?

Connect the opposites:

sal *(sahl)*   **suave** *('swah-veh)*
duro *('doo-roh)*   **tenedor** *(teh-neh-'dohr)*
cuchara *(koo-'chah-rah)* **pimienta** *(pee-mee-'ehn-tah)*

Select the word that should go next:

sartén, mostaza, delicuente, amigo, dulce *(sahr-'tehn, moh-'stah-sah, deh-leen-'kwehn-teh, ah-'mee-goh, 'dool-seh)*

agrio, picante, _____ *('ah-gree oh, pee-'kahn-teh)*

mayonesa, salsa de tomate, _____ *(mah-yoh-'neh-sah, 'sahl-sah deh toh-'mah-teh)*

cacerola, olla, _____ *(kah-seh-'roh-lah, 'oh-yah)*

compañero, vecino, _____ (kohm-pah-'nyeh-roh, veh-'see-noh)

ladrón, pandillero, _____ (lah-'drohn, pahn-dee-'yeh-roh)

Let's close out this guidebook with a quick review of the grammar material that was presented earlier. Instruction on verb usage can be found at the end of each chapter. Closely study this next example and then fill in the blanks below with the correct verb forms:

to buy   **comprar** (kohm-'prahr)

I'm buying   **Estoy comprando** (eh-'stoh·ee kohm-'prahn-doh)
I buy   **Compro** ('kohm-proh)
I will buy   **Compraré** (kohm-prahr-'reh)
I bought   **Compré** (kohm-'preh)
I have bought   **He comprado** (eh kohm-'prah-doh)

to walk   **caminar** (kah-mee-'nahr)

I'm walking   _____

I walk   _____

I will walk   _____

I walked   _____

I have walked   _____

to try   **tratar** (trah-'tahr)

I'm trying   _____

I try   _____

I will try   _____

I tried   _____

I have tried   _____

Again, one of the best methods for practicing verbs is to insert them into short, practical phrases. Here are some shortcuts that were presented earlier. Translate, and then choose one of the verb phrases below to complete a sentence:

No... *(noh)* _____

Puedo... *('pweh-doh)* _____

Me gusta... *(meh 'goo-stah)* _____

Voy a... *('voh·ee ah)* _____

Quiero... *(kee-'eh-roh)* _____

Quisiera... *(kee-see-'eh-rah)* _____

Favor de... *(fah-'vohr deh)* _____

Tienes que... *(tee-'eh-nehs keh)* _____

Necesitas... *(neh-seh-'see-tahs)* _____

Debes... *('deh-behs)* _____

> **estudiar la lección** *(eh-stoo-dee-'ahr lah lehk-see-'ohn)*
> **trabajar en el libro** *(trah-bah-'hahr ehn ehl 'lee-broh)*
> **leer el papel** *(leh-'ehr ehl pah-'pehl)*
> **escribir con el lápiz** *(eh-skree-'beer kohn ehl 'lah-pees)*
> **hablar inglés** *(ah-'blahr een-'glehs)*

 ¿LISTOS PARA PRACTICAR?

Create real-life scenarios every chance you get! Make up a situation, choose characters, and role-play the scene over and over again. Obviously, the more you practice, the easier it will become. The key is to select a dialog that you know will take place soon; practicing unreal or irrelevant scenarios will only slow down the process. And remember, if you worry too much about your grammar and pronunciation errors, you'll never get started at all!

MÁS INFORMACIÓN

➤ Take note of this new shortcut to using Spanish verbs. If you are struggling with the past tense, stick this one-liner in front of any infinitive:

I just finished...   **Acabo de...** *(ah-'kah-boh deh...)*

I just finished eating.   **Acabo de comer.** *(ah-'kah-boh deh koh-'mehr)*
I just finished reading.   **Acabo de leer.** *(ah-'kah-boh deh leh-'ehr)*
I just finished playing.   **Acabo de jugar.** *(ah-'kah-boh deh hoo-'gahr)*

¿LISTOS PARA PRACTICAR?

To practice the past tense, follow the pattern in the example. Don't forget to translate:

Acabo de hablar   <u>**Hablé**</u> *(ah-'bleh)*
(ah-'kah-boh deh ah-'blahr)
                                 _____
Acabo de aconsejar
(ah-'kah-boh deh ah-kohn-seh-'hahr)
                                 _____
Acabo de consultar
(ah-'kah-boh deh kohn-sool-'tahr)
                                 _____
Acabo de gritar
(ah-'kah-boh deh gree-'tahr)
                                 _____
Acabo de discutir
(ah-'kah-boh deh dee-skoo-'teer)
                                 _____
Acabo de dormir
(ah-'kah-boh deh dohr-'meer)
                                 _____
Acabo de escribir
(ah-'kah-boh deh eh-skree-'beer)
                                 _____

No educator who needs Spanish can last long without the command words. Let's review some of the key phrases. Translate as you read through these popular informal commands, and then create some expressions of your own:

Contesta *(kohn-'teh-stah)*
Contesta en inglés. *(kohn-'teh-stah ehn eeh-'glehs)*

Trae *('trah-eh)*
Trae el formulario. *('trah-eh ehl fohr-moo-'lah-ree·oh)*

Llama *('yah-mah)*
Llama a tus padres. *('yah-mah ah toos pah-'drehs)*

Escucha *(eh-'skoo-chah)*
Escucha la pregunta. *(eh-'skoo-chah lah preh-'goon-tah)*

Lee *('leh-eh)*
Lee el papel. *('leh-eh ehl pah-'pehl)*

Regresa *(reh-'greh-sah)*
Regresa mañana. *(reh-'greh-sah mah-'nyah-nah)*

Firma *('feer-mah)*
Firma aquí. *('feer-mah ah-'kee)*

Habla *('ah-blah)*
Habla más despacio. *('ah-blah mahs deh-'spah-see·oh)*

Toma *('toh-mah)*
Toma asiento. *('toh-mah ah-see-'ehn-toh)*

Keep it up; however, this time say things using the formal command form:

Try   **Trate** *('trah-teh)* _____

Study   **Estudie** *(eh-'stoo-dee-eh)* _____

Ask for   **Pida** *('pee-dah)* _____

Explain   **Explique** *(ehks-'plee-keh)* _____

Measure   **Mida** *('mee-dah)* _____

Check   **Verifique** *(veh-ree-'fee-keh)* _____

Let   **Deje** *('deh-heh)* _____

Touch   **Toque** *('toh-keh)* _____

Cut   **Corte** *('kohr-teh)* _____

Pass   **Pase** *('pah-seh)* _____

Learn   **Aprenda** *(ah-'prehn-dah)* _____

MÁS INFORMACIÓN

➤ Since we're talking about commands, do you recall the **le**, **lo** and **la** words? Follow the model as you review:

Bring it   **Tráigalo** *('trah ee-gah-loh)*

Choose it   _____

Deliver it   _____

Do it   _____

Change it   _____

Talk to him   **Háblele** *('ah-bleh-leh)*

Look for him   _____

311

Pay him	_____
Look at him	_____
Give it to him	_____

These phrases are a bit more complicated:

Send it to me	**Mándemelo** (*'mahn-deh-meh-loh*)
Lift it up	_____
Tell it to me	_____

CONFLICTOS CULTURALES

To get a true feel for communication in Spanish, find time to observe a group of Hispanics in public or at a social gathering. Facial expressions, touch, changes in tone, and hand signals are a few of the many non-verbal differences between the Latin American and U.S. cultures.

THAT'S IT, FELLOW EDUCATORS!
¡Eso es todo, colegas! (*'eh-soh ehs 'toh-doh, koh-'leh-gahs*)

Now that you have learned all the important vocabulary and phrases needed to converse in Spanish, are you ready to use them in public? No matter what you do in the field of education, the skills that are required to communicate have been presented somewhere in this guidebook. So, what's the delay? The Spanish-speaking world is waiting for you, so get out there and go for it! Trust me—once you get started, your life as an educator will never be the same!

Buena suerte, amigos, y Dios les bendiga, *('bweh-nah 'swehr-teh, ah-'mee-gohs, ee 'dee-ohs lehs behn-'dee-gah)*

Bill

Bill

ENGLISH-SPANISH VERBS

act, to	actuar	*ahk-too-'ahr*
add, to	sumar	*soo-'mahr*
advise, to	avisar	*ah-vee-'sahr*
allow, to	dejar	*deh-'hahr*
analyze, to	analizar	*ah-nah-lee-'sahr*
answer, to	contestar	*kohn-teh-'stahr*
apply, to	aplicar	*ah-plee-'kahr*
argue, to	discutir	*dee-skoo-'teer*
arrange, to	arreglar	*ah-rreh-'glahr*
arrest, to	arrestar	*ah-rreh-'stahr*
arrive, to	llegar	*yeh-'gahr*
ask for, to	pedir	*peh-'deer*
ask, to	preguntar	*preh-goon-'tahr*
assign, to	asignar	*ah-seeg-'nahr*
assure, to	asegurar	*ah-seh-goo-'rahr*
attend, to	asistir	*ah-see-'steer*
bathe, to	bañarse	*bah-'nyahr-seh*
be able, to	poder	*poh-'dehr*
be in charge, to	encargar	*ehn-kahr-'gahr*
be, to	estar, ser	*eh-'stahr, sehr*
beat up, to	golpear	*gohl-peh-'ahr*
begin, to	comenzar, empezar	*koh-mehn-'sahr, ehm-peh-'sahr*
behave, to	portarse	*pohr-'tahr-seh*
bite, to	morder	*mohr-'dehr*
bother, to	molestar	*moh-leh-'stahr*
bounce, to	rebotar	*reh-boh-'tahr*
break, to	quebrar, romper	*keh-'brahr, rohm-'pehr*
breathe, to	respirar	*reh-spee-'rahr*
bring, to	traer	*trah-'ehr*
build, to	construir	*kohn-stroo-'eer*
buy, to	comprar	*kohm-'prahr*
calculate, to	calcular	*kahl-koo-'lahr*
call, to	llamar	*yah-'mahr*
calm down, to	calmarse	*kahl-'mahr-seh*
cancel, to	cancelar	*kahn-seh-'lahr*
carry, to	llevar	*yeh-'vahr*
catch, to	agarrar	*ah-gah-'rrahr*
change, to	cambiar	*kahm-bee-'ahr*
chase, to	perseguir	*pehr-seh-'geer*
check, to	revisar	*reh-vee-'sahr*
chew, to	masticar	*mah-stee-'kahr*

choose, to	escoger	*eh-skoh-'hehr*
clarify, to	clarificar	*klah-ree-fee-'kahr*
clean, to	limpiar	*leem-pee-'ahr*
climb, to	subir	*soo-'beer*
close, to	cerrar	*seh-'rrahr*
comb one's hair, to	peinarse	*peh·ee-'nahr-seh*
come, to	venir	*veh-'neer*
commend, to	alabar	*ah-lah-'bahr*
communicate, to	comunicar	*koh-moo-nee-'kahr*
compare, to	comparar	*kohm-pah-'rahr*
compete, to	competir	*kohm-peh-'teer*
complain, to	quejarse	*keh-'hahr-seh*
complete, to	completar	*kohm-pleh-'tahr*
compliment, to	felicitar	*feh-lee-see-'tahr*
confirm, to	confirmar	*kohn-feer-'mahr*
confiscate, to	confiscar	*kohn-fee-'skahr*
consult, to	consultar	*kohn-sool-'tahr*
converse, to	conversar	*kohn-vehr-'sahr*
copy, to	copiar	*koh-pee-'ahr*
correct, to	corregir	*koh-rreh-'heer*
counsel, to	aconsejar	*ah-kohn-seh-'hahr*
count, to	contar	*kohn-'tahr*
cover, to	cubrir	*koo-'breer*
cry, to	llorar	*yoh-'rahr*
curse, to	decir groserías, maldecir	*deh-'seer groh-seh-'ree-ahs, mahl-deh-'seer*
cut, to	cortar	*kohr-'tahr*
dance, to	bailar	*'bah·ee-'lahr*
debate, to	debatir	*deh-bah-'teer*
defecate, to	defecar	*deh-feh-'kahr*
define, to	definir	*deh-fee-'neer*
deliver, to	entregar	*ehn-treh-'gahr*
deny, to	negarse	*neh-'gahr-seh*
deserve, to	merecer	*meh-reh-'sehr*
dial, to	marcar	*mahr-'kahr*
die, to	morir	*moh-'reer*
distract, to	distraer	*dee-strah-'ehr*
dive, to	zambullirse	*sahm-boo-'yeer-seh*
divide, to	dividir	*dee-vee-'deer*
do, to	hacer	*ah-'sehr*
draw, to	dibujar	*dee-boo-'hahr*
drink, to	beber	*beh-'behr*
drive, to	manejar	*mah-neh-'hahr*
eat, to	comer	*koh-'mehr*
empty, to	vaciar	*vah-see-'ahr*

encourage, to	animar	*ah-nee-'mahr*
end, to	terminar	*tehr-mee-'nahr*
enroll, to	inscribirse, matricularse	*een-skree-'beer-seh, mah-tree-koo-'lahr-seh*
enter, to	entrar	*ehn-'trahr*
erase, to	borrar	*boh-'rrahr*
evaluate, to	evaluar	*eh-vah-loo-'ahr*
examine, to	examinar	*ehk-sah-mee-'nahr*
expel, to	expulsar	*ehk-spool-'sahr*
explain, to	explicar	*ehk-splee-'kahr*
factor, to	factorar	*fahk-toh-'rahr*
fall, to	caerse	*kah-'ehr-seh*
feel, to	sentirse	*sehn-'teer-seh*
fight, to	pelear	*peh-leh-'ahr*
fill out, to	llenar	*yeh-'nahr*
find, to	encontrar	*ehn-kohn-'trahr*
fish, to	pescar	*peh-'skahr*
fold, to	doblar	*doh-'blahr*
follow, to	seguir	*seh-'geer*
forget, to	olvidar	*ohl-vee-'dahr*
get dressed, to	vestirse	*veh-'steer-seh*
get lost, to	perderse	*pehr-'dehr-seh*
get, to	conseguir	*kohn-seh-'geer*
give, to	dar	*dahr*
go, to	ir	*eer*
gossip, to	chismear	*chees-meh-'ahr*
grab, to	agarrar	*ah-gah-'rrahr*
graduate, to	graduarse	*grah-doo-'ahr-seh*
guess, to	adivinar	*ah-dee-vee-'nahr*
hang up, to	colgar	*kohl-'gahr*
hate, to	odiar	*oh-dee-'ahr*
have, to	tener	*teh-'nehr*
hear, to	oír	*oh-'eer*
help, to	ayudar	*ah-yoo-'dahr*
hide, to	esconder	*eh-skohn-'dehr*
hire, to	contratar	*kohn-trah-'tahr*
hit, to	pegar	*peh-'gahr*
hug, to	abrazar	*ah-brah-'sahr*
hurry, to	apurarse	*ah-poo-'rahr-seh*
hurt, to	herir	*eh-'reer*
identify, to	identificar	*ee-dehn-tee-fee-'kahr*
improve, to	mejorar	*meh-hoh-'rahr*
include, to	incluir	*een-kloo-'eer*
inform, to	informar	*een-fohr-'mahr*
invest, to	invertir	*een-vehr-'teer*

joke, to	bromear	*broh-meh-'ahr*
jump, to	saltar	*sahl-'tahr*
kick, to	patear	*pah-teh-'ahr*
know someone, to	conocer	*koh-noh-'sehr*
know something, to	saber	*sah-'behr*
learn, to	aprender	*ah-prehn-'dehr*
leave, to	irse, salir	*'eer-seh, sah-'leer*
lie down, to	acostarse	*ah-koh-'stahr-seh*
lie, to	mentir	*mehn-'teer*
listen, to	escuchar	*eh-skoo-'chahr*
loan, to	prestar	*preh-'stahr*
loiter, to	holgazanear	*ohl-gah-sah-neh-'ahr*
look for, to	buscar	*boo-'skahr*
look, to	mirar	*mee-'rahr*
lose, to	perder	*pehr-'dehr*
love, to	amar	*ah-'mahr*
make a mistake, to	equivocarse	*eh-kee-voh-'kahr-seh*
measure, to	medir	*meh-'deer*
miss, to	faltar	*fahl-'tahr*
motivate, to	motivar	*moh-tee-'vahr*
move, to	mover	*moh-'vehr*
multiply, to	multiplicar	*mool-tee-plee-'kahr*
obey, to	obedecer	*oh-beh-deh-'sehr*
observe, to	observar	*ohb-sehr-'vahr*
offer, to	ofrecer	*oh-freh-'sehr*
omit, to	eliminar	*eh-lee-mee-'nahr*
open, to	abrir	*ah-'breer*
organize, to	organizar	*ohr-gah-nee-'sahr*
owe, to	deber	*deh-'behr*
paint, to	pintar	*peen-'tahr*
park, to	estacionar	*eh-stah-see·oh-'nahr*
participate, to	participar	*pahr-tee-see-'pahr*
pass out, to	repartir	*reh-pahr-'teer*
pass, to	pasar	*pah-'sahr*
persuade, to	persuadir	*pehr-swah-'deer*
pitch, to	lanzar	*lahn-'sahr*
plan, to	planear	*plah-neh-'ahr*
play, to	jugar	*hoo-'gahr*
point, to	señalar	*seh-nyah-'lahr*
practice, to	practicar	*prahk-tee-'kahr*
present, to	presentar	*preh-sehn-'tahr*
press, to	oprimir	*oh-pree-'meer*
pronounce, to	pronunciar	*proh-noon-see-'ahr*
protect, to	proteger	*proh-teh-'hehr*
pull, to	jalar	*hah-'lahr*

push, to	empujar	*ehm-poo-'hahr*
put in, to	meter	*meh-'tehr*
put, to	poner	*poh-'nehr*
read, to	leer	*leh-'ehr*
reduce, to	reducir	*reh-doo-'seer*
relax, to	relajarse	*reh-lah-'hahr-seh*
remember, to	recordar	*reh-kohr-'dahr*
repeat, to	repetir	*reh-peh-'teer*
respect, to	respetar	*reh-speh-'tahr*
rest, to	descansar	*deh-skahn-'sahr*
retain, to	retener	*reh-teh-'nehr*
return, to	regresar	*reh-greh-'sahr*
reward, to	recompensar	*reh-kohm-pehn-'sahr*
ride, to	montar	*mohn-'tahr*
roll, to	rodar	*roh-'dahr*
run, to	correr	*koh-'rrehr*
sail, to	navegar	*nah-veh-'gahr*
say, to	decir	*deh-'seer*
search, to	registrar	*reh-hee-'strahr*
see, to	ver	*vehr*
seem, to	parecer	*pah-reh-'sehr*
sell, to	vender	*vehn-'dehr*
separate, to	separar	*seh-pah-'rahr*
serve, to	servir	*sehr-'veer*
sew, to	coser	*koh-'sehr*
shake, to	sacudir	*sah-koo-'deer*
shoot, to	disparar	*dee-spah-'rahr*
show, to	mostrar	*moh-'strahr*
sign, to	firmar	*feer-'mahr*
simplify, to	simplificar	*seem-plee-fee-'kahr*
sing, to	cantar	*kahn-'tahr*
skate, to	patinar	*pah-tee-'nahr*
ski, to	esquiar	*eh-skee-'ahr*
sleep, to	dormir	*dohr-'meer*
smoke, to	fumar	*foo-'mahr*
solve, to	resolver	*reh-sohl-'vehr*
speak, to	hablar	*ah-'blahr*
spell, to	deletrear	*deh-leh-treh-'ahr*
spit, to	escupir	*eh-skoo-'peer*
stack, to	amontonar	*ah-mohn-toh-'nahr*
steal, to	robar	*roh-'bahr*
stroll, to	pasear	*pah-seh-'ahr*
study, to	estudiar	*eh-stoo-dee-'ahr*
subtract, to	restar	*reh-'stahr*
suggest, to	sugerir	*soo-heh-'reer*

support, to	apoyar	*ah-poh-'yahr*
suspend, to	suspender	*soo-spehn-'dehr*
swallow, to	tragar	*trah-'gahr*
swim, to	nadar	*nah-'dahr*
take care of oneself, to	cuidarse	*kwee-'dahr-seh*
take out, to	sacar	*sah-'kahr*
take, to	tomar	*toh-'mahr*
teach, to	enseñar	*ehn-seh-'nyahr*
tease, to	burlarse	*boor-'lahr-seh*
tell, to	decir	*deh-'seer*
thank, to	agradecer	*ah-grah-deh-'sehr*
think, to	pensar	*pehn-'sahr*
threaten, to	amenazar	*ah-meh-nah-'sahr*
throw, to	tirar	*tee-'rahr*
tie, to	amarrar	*ah-mah-'rrahr*
touch, to	tocar	*toh-'kahr*
train, to	entrenar	*ehn-treh-'nahr*
travel, to	viajar	*vee-ah-'hahr*
trip, to	tropezar	*troh-peh-'sahr*
try, to	tratar	*trah-'tahr*
turn around, to	darse vuelta	*'dahr-seh 'vwehl-tah*
understand, to	entender	*ehn-tehn-'dehr*
urinate, to	orinar	*oh-ree-'nahr*
use, to	usar	*oo-'sahr*
verify, to	verificar	*veh-ree-fee-'kahr*
visit, to	visitar	*vee-see-'tahr*
vomit, to	vomitar	*voh-mee-'tahr*
wait, to	esperar	*eh-speh-'rahr*
want, to	querer	*keh-'rehr*
wash, to	lavar	*lah-'vahr*
win, to	ganar	*gah-'nahr*
work, to	trabajar	*trah-bah-'hahr*
worry, to	preocuparse	*preh-oh-koo-'pahr-seh*
wrestle, to	luchar	*loo-'chahr*
write, to	escribir	*eh-skree-'beer*
yell, to	gritar	*gree-'tahr*

SPANISH-ENGLISH VERBS

abrazar	hug, to	*ah-brah-'sahr*
abrir	open, to	*ah-'breer*
aconsejar	counsel, to	*ah-kohn-seh-'hahr*
acostarse	lie down, to	*ah-koh-'stahr-seh*
actuar	act, to	*ahk-too-'ahr*
adivinar	guess, to	*ah-dee-vee-'nahr*
agarrar	catch, to; to grab	*ah-gah-'rrahr*
agradecer	thank, to	*ah-grah-deh-'sehr*
alabar	commend, to	*ah-lah-'bahr*
amar	love, to	*ah-'mahr*
amarrar	tie, to	*ah-mah-'rrahr*
amenazar	threaten, to	*ah-meh-nah-'sahr*
amontonar	stack, to	*ah-mohn-toh-'nahr*
analizar	analyze, to	*ah-nah-lee-'sahr*
animar	encourage, to	*ah-nee-'mahr*
aplicar	apply, to	*ah-plee-'kahr*
apoyar	support, to	*ah-poh-'yahr*
aprender	learn, to	*ah-prehn-'dehr*
apurarse	hurry, to	*ah-poo-'rahr-seh*
arreglar	arrange, to	*ah-rreh-'glahr*
arrestar	arrest, to	*ah-rreh-'stahr*
asegurar	assure, to	*ah-seh-goo-'rahr*
asignar	assign, to	*ah-seeg-'nahr*
asistir	attend, to	*ah-see-'steer*
avisar	advise, to	*ah-vee-'sahr*
ayudar	help, to	*ah-yoo-'dahr*
bailar	dance, to	*'bah·ee-'lahr*
bañarse	bathe, to	*bah-'nyahr-seh*
beber	drink, to	*beh-'behr*
borrar	erase, to	*boh-'rrahr*
bromear	joke, to	*broh-meh-'ahr*
burlarse	tease, to	*boor-'lahr-seh*
buscar	look for, to	*boo-'skahr*
caerse	fall, to	*kah-'ehr-seh*
calcular	calculate, to	*kahl-koo-'lahr*
calmarse	calm down, to	*kahl-'mahr-seh*
cambiar	change, to	*kahm-bee-'ahr*
cancelar	cancel, to	*kahn-seh-'lahr*
cantar	sing, to	*kahn-'tahr*
cerrar	close, to	*seh-'rrahr*
chismear	gossip, to	*chees-meh-'ahr*
clarificar	clarify, to	*klah-ree-fee-'kahr*

colgar	hang up, to	*kohl-'gahr*
comenzar	begin, to	*koh-mehn-'sahr*
comer	eat, to	*koh-'mehr*
comparar	compare, to	*kohm-pah-'rahr*
competir	compete, to	*kohm-peh-'teer*
completar	complete, to	*kohm-pleh-'tahr*
comprar	buy, to	*kohm-'prahr*
comunicar	communicate, to	*koh-moo-nee-'kahr*
confirmar	confirm, to	*kohn-feer-'mahr*
confiscar	confiscate, to	*kohn-fee-'skahr*
conocer	know someone, to	*koh-noh-'sehr*
conseguir	get, to	*kohn-seh-'geer*
construir	build, to	*kohn-stroo-'eer*
consultar	consult, to	*kohn-sool-'tahr*
contar	count, to	*kohn-'tahr*
contestar	answer, to	*kohn-teh-'stahr*
contratar	hire, to	*kohn-trah-'tahr*
conversar	converse, to	*kohn-vehr-'sahr*
copiar	copy, to	*koh-pee-'ahr*
corregir	correct, to	*koh-rreh-'heer*
correr	run, to	*koh-'rrehr*
cortar	cut, to	*kohr-'tahr*
coser	sew, to	*koh-'sehr*
cubrir	cover, to	*koo-'breer*
cuidarse	take care of oneself, to	*kwee-'dahr-seh*
dar	give, to	*dahr*
darse vuelta	turn around, to	*'dahr-seh 'vwehl-tah*
debatir	debate, to	*deh-bah-'teer*
deber	owe, to	*deh-'behr*
decir	say, to; to tell	*deh-'seer*
decir groserías	curse, to	*deh-'seer groh-seh-'ree-ahs*
defecar	defecate, to	*deh-feh-'kahr*
definir	define, to	*deh-fee-'neer*
dejar	allow, to	*deh-'hahr*
deletrear	spell, to	*deh-leh-treh-'ahr*
descansar	rest, to	*deh-skahn-'sahr*
dibujar	draw, to	*dee-boo-'hahr*
discutir	argue, to	*dee-skoo-'teer*
disparar	shoot, to	*dee-spah-'rahr*
distraer	distract, to	*dee-strah-'ehr*
dividir	divide, to	*dee-vee-'deer*
doblar	fold, to	*doh-'blahr*
dormir	sleep, to	*dohr-'meer*
eliminar	omit, to	*eh-lee-mee-'nahr*
empezar	begin, to	*ehm-peh-'sahr*

empujar	push, to	*ehm-poo-'hahr*
encargar	be in charge, to	*ehn-kahr-'gahr*
encontrar	find, to	*ehn-kohn-'trahr*
enseñar	teach, to	*ehn-seh-'nyahr*
entender	understand, to	*ehn-tehn-'dehr*
entrar	enter, to	*ehn-'trahr*
entregar	deliver, to	*ehn-treh-'gahr*
entrenar	train, to	*ehn-treh-'nahr*
equivocarse	make a mistake, to	*eh-kee-voh-'kahr-seh*
escoger	choose, to	*eh-skoh-'hehr*
esconder	hide, to	*eh-skohn-'dehr*
escribir	write, to	*eh-skree-'beer*
escuchar	listen, to	*eh-skoo-'chahr*
escupir	spit, to	*eh-skoo-'peer*
esperar	wait, to	*eh-speh-'rahr*
esquiar	ski, to	*eh-skee-'ahr*
estacionar	park, to	*eh-stah-see·oh-'nahr*
estar	be, to	*eh-'stahr*
estudiar	study, to	*eh-stoo-dee-'ahr*
evaluar	evaluate, to	*eh-vah-loo-'ahr*
examinar	examine, to	*ehk-sah-mee-'nahr*
explicar	explain, to	*ehk-splee-'kahr*
expulsar	expel, to	*ehk-spool-'sahr*
factorar	factor, to	*fahk-toh-'rahr*
faltar	miss, to	*fahl-'tahr*
felicitar	compliment, to	*feh-lee-see-'tahr*
firmar	sign, to	*feer-'mahr*
fumar	smoke, to	*foo-'mahr*
ganar	win, to	*gah-'nahr*
golpear	beat up, to	*gohl-peh-'ahr*
graduarse	graduate, to	*grah-doo-'ahr-seh*
gritar	yell, to	*gree-'tahr*
hablar	speak, to	*ah-'blahr*
hacer	do, to	*ah-'sehr*
herir	hurt, to	*eh-'reer*
holgazanear	loiter, to	*ohl-gah-sah-neh-'ahr*
identificar	identify, to	*ee-dehn-tee-fee-'kahr*
incluir	include, to	*een-kloo-'eer*
informar	inform, to	*een-fohr-'mahr*
inscribirse	enroll, to	*een-skree-'beer-seh*
invertir	invest, to	*een-vehr-'teer*
ir	go, to	*eer*
irse	leave, to	*'eer-seh*
jalar	pull, to	*hah-'lahr*
jugar	play, to	*hoo-'gahr*

lanzar	pitch, to	*lahn-'sahr*
lavar	wash, to	*lah-'vahr*
leer	read, to	*leh-'ehr*
limpiar	clean, to	*leem-pee-'ahr*
llamar	call, to	*yah-'mahr*
llegar	arrive, to	*yeh-'gahr*
llenar	fill out, to	*yeh-'nahr*
llevar	carry, to	*yeh-'vahr*
llorar	cry, to	*yoh-'rahr*
luchar	wrestle, to	*loo-'chahr*
maldecir	curse, to	*mahl-deh-'seer*
manejar	drive, to	*mah-neh-'hahr*
marcar	dial, to	*mahr-'kahr*
masticar	chew, to	*mah-stee-'kahr*
matricularse	enroll, to	*mah-tree-koo-'lahr-seh*
medir	measure, to	*meh-'deer*
mejorar	improve, to	*meh-hoh-'rahr*
mentir	lie, to	*mehn-'teer*
merecer	deserve, to	*meh-reh-'sehr*
meter	put in, to	*meh-'tehr*
mirar	look, to	*mee-'rahr*
molestar	bother, to	*moh-leh-'stahr*
montar	ride, to	*mohn-'tahr*
morder	bite, to	*mohr-'dehr*
morir	die, to	*moh-'reer*
mostrar	show, to	*moh-'strahr*
motivar	motivate, to	*moh-tee-'vahr*
mover	move, to	*moh-'vehr*
multiplicar	multiply, to	*mool-tee-plee-'kahr*
nadar	swim, to	*nah-'dahr*
navegar	sail, to	*nah-veh-'gahr*
negarse	deny, to	*neh-'gahr-seh*
obedecer	obey, to	*oh-beh-deh-'sehr*
observar	observe, to	*ohb-sehr-'vahr*
odiar	hate, to	*oh-dee-'ahr*
ofrecer	offer, to	*oh-freh-'sehr*
oír	hear, to	*oh-'eer*
olvidar	forget, to	*ohl-vee-'dahr*
oprimir	press, to	*oh-pree-'meer*
organizar	organize, to	*ohr-gah-nee-'sahr*
orinar	urinate, to	*oh-ree-'nahr*
parecer	seem, to	*pah-reh-'sehr*
participar	participate, to	*pahr-tee-see-'pahr*
pasar	pass, to	*pah-'sahr*
pasear	stroll, to	*pah-seh-'ahr*

patear	kick, to	*pah-teh-'ahr*
patinar	skate, to	*pah-tee-'nahr*
pedir	ask for, to	*peh-'deer*
pegar	hit, to	*peh-'gahr*
peinarse	comb one's hair, to	*peh·ee-'nahr-seh*
pelear	fight, to	*peh-leh-'ahr-seh*
pensar	think, to	*pehn-'sahr*
perder	lose, to	*pehr-'dehr*
perderse	get lost, to	*pehr-'dehr-seh*
perseguir	chase, to	*pehr-seh-'geer*
persuadir	persuade, to	*pehr-swah-'deer*
pescar	fish, to	*peh-'skahr*
pintar	paint, to	*peen-'tahr*
planear	plan, to	*plah-neh-'ahr*
poder	be able, to	*poh-'dehr*
poner	put, to	*poh-'nehr*
portarse	behave, to	*pohr-'tahr-seh*
practicar	practice, to	*prahk-tee-'kahr*
preguntar	ask, to	*preh-goon-'tahr*
preocuparse	worry, to	*preh-oh-koo-'pahr-seh*
presentar	present, to	*preh-sehn-'tahr*
prestar	loan, to	*preh-'stahr*
pronunciar	pronounce, to	*proh-noon-see-'ahr*
proteger	protect, to	*proh-teh-'hehr*
quebrar	break, to	*keh-'brahr*
quejarse	complain, to	*keh-'hahr-seh*
querer	want, to	*keh-'rehr*
rebotar	bounce, to	*reh-boh-'tahr*
recompensar	reward, to	*reh-kohm-pehn-'sahr*
recordar	remember, to	*reh-kohr-'dahr*
reducir	reduce, to	*reh-doo-'seer*
registrar	search, to	*reh-hee-'strahr*
regresar	return, to	*reh-greh-'sahr*
relajarse	relax, to	*reh-lah-'hahr-seh*
repartir	pass out, to	*reh-pahr-'teer*
repetir	repeat, to	*reh-peh-'teer*
resolver	resolve, to; to solve	*reh-sohl-'vehr*
respetar	respect, to	*reh-speh-'tahr*
respirar	breathe, to	*reh-spee-'rahr*
restar	subtract, to	*reh-'stahr*
retener	retain, to	*reh-teh-'nehr*
revisar	check, to	*reh-vee-'sahr*
robar	steal, to	*roh-'bahr*
rodar	roll, to	*roh-'dahr*
romper	break, to	*rohm-'pehr*

saber	know something, to	*sah-'behr*
sacar	take out, to	*sah-'kahr*
sacudir	shake, to	*sah-koo-'deer*
salir	leave, to	*sah-'leer*
saltar	jump, to	*sahl-'tahr*
seguir	follow, to	*seh-'geer*
señalar	point, to	*seh-nyah-'lahr*
sentirse	feel, to	*sehn-'teer-seh*
separar	separate, to	*seh-pah-'rahr*
ser	be, to	*sehr*
servir	serve, to	*sehr-'veer*
simplificar	simplify, to	*seem-plee-fee-'kahr*
subir	climb, to	*soo-'beer*
sugerir	suggest, to	*soo-heh-'reer*
sumar	add, to	*soo-'mahr*
suspender	suspend, to	*soo-spehn-'dehr*
tener	have, to	*teh-'nehr*
terminar	end, to	*tehr-mee-'nahr*
tirar	throw, to	*tee-'rahr*
tocar	touch, to	*toh-'kahr*
tomar	take, to	*toh-'mahr*
trabajar	work, to	*trah-bah-'hahr*
traer	bring, to	*trah-'ehr*
tragar	swallow, to	*trah-'gahr*
tratar	try, to	*trah-'tahr*
tropezar	trip, to	*troh-peh-'sahr*
usar	use, to	*oo-'sahr*
vaciar	empty, to	*vah-see-'ahr*
vender	sell, to	*vehn-'dehr*
venir	come, to	*veh-'neer*
ver	see, to	*vehr*
verificar	verify, to	*veh-ree-fee-'kahr*
vestirse	get dressed, to	*veh-'steer-seh*
viajar	travel, to	*vee-ah-'hahr*
visitar	visit, to	*vee-see-'tahr*
vomitar	vomit, to	*voh-mee-'tahr*
zambullirse	dive, to	*sahm-boo-'yeer-seh*

ENGLISH-SPANISH DICTIONARY

➤ The gender of Spanish nouns is indicated by the article (**el** or **la**).
➤ When a noun can be either masculine or feminine, it is shown in the masculine form and then in the feminine form: **adulto, el (la adulta)**
➤ All adjectives are shown in the masculine form. An **(a)** is added to remind you of the feminine ending.

abortion	el aborto	*ehl ah-'bohr-toh*
above	encima	*ehn-'see-mah*
absences	ausencias, las	*lahs ow-'sehn-see·ah*
abuse	abuso, el	*ehl ah-'boo-soh*
academy	academia, la	*lah ah-kah-'deh-mee·ah*
accident	accidente, el	*ehl ahk-see-'dehn-teh*
acne	acné, el	*ehl ahk-'neh*
action	acción, la	*lah ahk-see-'ohn*
activity	actividad, la	*lah ahk-tee-vee-'dahd*
addiction	adicción, la	*lah ah-deek-see-'ohn*
address	dirección, la	*lah dee-rehk-see-'ohn*
administration	administración, la	*lah ahd-mee-nee-strah-see-'ohn*
administrator	administrador, el (la administradora)	*ehl ahd-mee-nee-strah-'dohr (lah ahd-mee-nee-strah-'doh-rah)*
admissions	admisiones, las	*lahs ahd-mee-see-'oh-nehs*
adult	adulto, el (la adulta)	*ehl ah-'dool-toh (lah ah-'dool-tah)*
advanced	avanzado(a)	*ah-vahn-'sah-doh(ah)*
advisor	consejero, el (la consejera)	*ehl kohn-seh-'heh-roh (lah kohn-seh-'heh-rah)*
afraid	asustado(a)	*ah-soo-'stah-doh(ah)*
afterward	después	*deh-'spwehs*
age	edad, la	*lah eh-'dahd*
agency	agencia, la	*lah ah-'hehn-see·ah*
ahead	adelante	*ah-deh-'lahn-teh*
aide	ayudante, el (la ayudanta)	*ehl ah-yoo-'dahn-teh, (lah ah-yoo-'dahn-tah)*
air conditioner	acondicionador de aire, el	*ehl ah-kohn-dee-see·oh-nah-'dohr deh 'ah·ee-reh*
airplane	avión, el	*ehl ah-vee-'ohn*
airport	aeropuerto, el	*ehl ah-eh-roh-'pwehr-toh*
aisle	pasillo, el	*ehl pah-'see-yoh*
alarm	alarma, la	*lah ah-'lahr-mah*
alcohol	alcohol, el	*ehl ahl-koh-'ohl*
algebra	álgebra, el	*ehl 'ahl-heh-'brah*

all	todo(a)(os)(as)	*'toh-doh (ah) (ohs) (ahs)*
allergies	alergias, las	*lahs ah-'lehr-hee-ahs*
alley	callejón, el	*ehl kah-yeh-'hohn*
alphabet	alfabeto, el	*ehl ahl-fah-'beh-toh*
already	ya	*yah*
alternative	alternativa, la	*lah ahl-tehr-nah-'tee-vah*
always	siempre	*see-'ehm-preh*
ambulance	ambulancia, la	*lah ahm-boo-'lahn-see·ah*
and	y	*ee*
angry	enojado(a)	*eh-noh-'hah-doh(ah)*
animal	animal, el	*ehl ah-nee-'mahl*
ankle	tobillo, el	*ehl toh-'bee-yoh*
announcement	anuncio, el	*ehl ah-'noon-see-oh*
answer	respuesta, la	*lah reh-'spweh-stah*
apartment	apartamento, el	*ehl ah-pahr-tah-'mehn-toh*
apple	manzana, la	*lah mahn-'sah-nah*
appliance	electrodoméstico, el	*ehl eh-lehk-troh-doh-'meh-stee-koh*
application	solicitud, la	*lah soh-lee-see-'tood*
appointment	cita, la	*lah 'see-tah*
approach	enfoque, el	*ehl ehn-'foh-keh*
April	abril	*ah-'breel*
apron	delantal, el	*ehl deh-lahn-'tahl*
aquarium	acuario, el	*ehl ah-'kwah-ree·oh*
architect	arquitecto, el *or* la	*ehl / lah ahr-kee-'tehk-toh*
area	área, el	*ehl 'ah-reh-ah*
arena	anfiteatro, el	*ehl ah-fee-teh-'ah-troh*
argument	argumento, el	*ehl ahr-goo-'mehn-toh*
arm	brazo, el	*ehl 'brah-soh*
armchair	sillón, el	*ehl see-'yohn*
armed forces	fuerzas armadas, las	*lahs 'fwehr-sahs ahr-'mah-dahs*
arrow	flecha, la	*lah 'fleh-chah*
art	arte, el	*ehl 'ahr-teh*
article	artículo, el	*ehl ahr-'tee-koo-loh*
aspirin	aspirina, la	*lah ah-spee-'ree-nah*
assembly	asamblea, la	*lah ah-sahm-'bleh-ah*
assessment	evaluación, la	*lah eh-vah-loo-ah-see-'ohn*
assignment	tarea, la	*lah tah-'reh-ah*
assistance	ayuda, la	*lah ah-'yoo-dah*
assistant	asistente, el (la asistenta)	*ehl ah-see-'stehn-teh (lah ah-see-'stehn-tah)*
associate	asociado, el (la asociada)	*ehl ah-soh-see-'ah-doh (lah ah-soh-see-'ah-dah)*
astronomy	astronomía, la	*lah ah-stroh-noh-'mee-ah*
at	en	*ehn*

atlas	atlas, el	*ehl 'aht-lahs*
attendance	asistencia, la	*lah ah-see-'stehn-see·ah*
attitude	actitud, la	*lah ahk-tee-'tood*
audience	audiencia, la	*lah ow-dee-'ehn-see·ah*
auditorium	auditorio, el	*ehl ow-dee-'toh-ree·oh*
August	agosto	*ah-'goh-stoh*
aunt	tía, la	*lah 'tee-ah*
author	autor, el (la autora)	*ehl ow-'tohr (lah ow-'toh-rah)*
available	disponible	*dee-spoh-'nee-bleh*
avenue	avenida, la	*lah ah-veh-'nee-dah*
average	promedio, el	*ehl proh-'meh-dee·oh*
award	galardón, el	*ehl gah-lahr-'dohn*
ax	hacha, el	*ehl 'ah-chah*
baby	bebé, el *or* la	*ehl / lah beh-'beh*
back	espalda, la	*lah eh-'spahl-dah*
backache	dolor de espalda, el	*ehl doh-'lohr deh eh-'spahl-dah*
backpack	mochila, la	*lah moh-'chee-yah*
backwards	revés, al	*ahl reh-'vehs*
bad	malo(a)	*'mah-loh(ah)*
badge	emblema, el	*ehl ehm-'bleh-mah*
badminton	bádminton, el	*ehl 'bahd-meen-tohn*
bag	bolsa, la	*lah 'bohl-sah*
balance	equilibrio, el	*ehl eh-kee-'lee-bree·oh*
balcony	balcón, el	*ehl bahl-'kohn*
bald	calvo(a)	*'kahl-voh(ah)*
ball	pelota, la	*lah peh-'loh-tah*
balloon	globo, el	*ehl 'gloh-boh*
banana	plátano, el	*ehl 'plah-tah-noh*
band	banda, la	*lah 'bahn-da*
bandage	vendaje, el	*ehl vehn-'dah-heh*
Band Aid®	curita, la	*lah koo-'ree-tah*
bank	banco, el	*ehl 'bahn-koh*
banquet	banquete, el	*ehl bahn-'keh-teh*
baseball	béisbol, el	*ehl 'beh·ees-bohl*
basket	canasta, la	*lah kah-'nah-stah*
basketball	básquetbol, el	*ehl 'bah-skeht-bohl*
bassinet	bacinete, el	*ehl bah-see-'neh-teh*
bat	bate, el	*ehl 'bah-teh*
bathing suit	trusa, la	*lah 'troo-sah*
bathrobe	bata de baño, la	*lah 'bah-tah deh 'bah-nyoh*
battle	batalla, la	*lah bah-'tah-yah*
beach	playa, la	*lah 'plah-yah*
beaker	tazón, el	*ehl tah-'sohn*
beans	frijoles, los	*lohs free-'hoh-lehs*

beautiful	bello(a)	'beh-yoh(ah)
bed	cama, la	lah 'kah-mah
beef	carne, la	lah 'kahr-neh
before	antes	'ahn-tehs
beggar	limosnero, el (la limosnera)	ehl lee-mohs-'neh-roh (lah lee-mohs-'neh-rah)
behavior	comportamiento, el	ehl kohm-pohr-tah-mee-'ehn-toh
behind	detrás	deh-'trahs
belief	creencia, la	lah kreh-'ehn-see·ah
bell	campana, la	lah kahm-'pah-nah
belt	cinturón, el	ehl seen-too-'rohn
benches	bancas, las	lahs 'bahn-kahs
benefits	beneficios, los	lohs beh-neh-'fee-see·ohs
better	mejor	meh-'hohr
bib	babero, el	ehl bah-'beh-roh
bicycle	bicicleta, la	lah bee-see-'kleh-tah
big	grande	'grahn-de
bilingual	bilingüe	bee-'leen-gweh
bill	cuenta, la	lah 'kwehn-tah
billboard	letrero, el	ehl leh-'treh-roh
bin	depósito, el	ehl deh-'poh-see-toh
binder	encuadernador, el	ehl ehn-kwah-dehr-nah-'dohr
biography	biografía, la	lah bee-oh-grah-'fee-ah
biology	biología, la	lah bee-oh-loh-'hee-ah
bird	pájaro, el	ehl 'pah-hah-roh
birth	nacimiento, el	ehl nah-see-mee-'ehn-toh
black	negro(a)	'neh-groh(ah)
blanket	cobija, la	lah koh-'bee-hah
blind	ciego(a)	see-'eh-goh(ah)
blister	ampolla, la	lah ahm-'poh-yah
block	cubito, el	ehl koo-'bee-toh
blond	rubio(a)	'roo-bee·oh(ah)
blood	sangre, la	lah 'sahn-greh
blouse	blusa, la	lah 'bloo-sa
blue	azul	ah-'sool
Board of Education	junta de educación	lah 'hoon-tah deh eh-doo-kah-see·'ohn
boat	barco, el	ehl 'bahr-koh
body	cuerpo, el	ehl 'kwehr-poh
bomb	bomba, la	lah 'bohm-bah
book	libro, el	ehl 'lee-broh
bookstore	librería, la	lah lee-breh-'ree-ah
boot	bota, la	lah 'boh-tah
bored	aburrido(a)	ah-boo-rree-doh(ah)

bowl	plato hondo, el	*ehl 'plah-toh 'ohn-doh*
box	caja, la	*lah 'kah-hah*
boxing	boxeo, el	*ehl bohk-'seh-oh*
boy	niño, el	*ehl 'nee-nyoh*
boyfriend	novio, el	*ehl 'noh-vee·oh*
bracelet	brazalete, el	*ehl brah-sah-'leh-teh*
brain	cerebro, el	*ehl seh-'reh-broh*
branch	rama, la	*lah 'rah-mah*
brassiere	sostén, el	*ehl soh-'stehn*
break	descanso, el	*ehl deh-'skahn-soh*
breakfast	desayuno, el	*ehl deh-sah-'yoo-noh*
breath	aliento, el	*ehl ah-lee-'ehn-toh*
bridge	puente, el	*ehl 'pwehn-teh*
brochure	folleto, el	*ehl foh-'yeh-toh*
broom	escoba, la	*lah eh-'skoh-bah*
brother	hermano, el	*ehl ehr-'mah-noh*
brown	café	*kah-'feh*
bruise	contusión, la	*lah kohn-too-see-'ohn*
brunette	moreno(a)	*moh-'reh-noh(ah)*
brush	brocha, la	*lah 'broh-chah*
bucket	balde, el	*ehl 'bahl-deh*
budget	presupuesto, el	*ehl preh-soo-'pweh-stoh*
building	edificio, el	*ehl eh-dee-'fee-see·oh*
bulletin	anuncio, el	*ehl ah-'noon-see·oh*
bulletin board	tablero de anuncios, el	*ehl tah-'bleh-roh deh ah-'noon-see·ohs*
bullhorn	altavoz, el	*ehl ahl-tah-'vohs*
burn	quemadura, la	*lah keh-mah-'doo-rah*
burp	eructo, el	*ehl eh-'rook-toh*
bus	autobús, el	*ehl ow-toh-'boos*
bus driver	chofer de autobús, el *or* la	*ehl / lah choh-'fehr deh ow-toh-'boos*
bus station	estación de autobús, la	*lah eh-stah-see-'ohn deh ow-toh-'boos*
bus stop	parada de autobús, la	*lah pah-'rah-dah deh ow-toh-'boos*
busy	ocupado(a)	*oh-koo-'pah-doh(ah)*
but	pero	*'peh-roh*
buzzer	timbre, el	*ehl 'teem-breh*
cabinet	gabinete, el	*ehl gah-bee-'neh-teh*
cable	cable, el	*ehl 'kah-bleh*
cafeteria	cafetería, la	*lah kah-feh-teh-'ree-ah*
cake	torta, la	*lah 'tohr-tah*
calculator	calculadora, la	*lah kahl-koo-lah-'doh-rah*
calculus	cálculo, el	*ehl 'kahl-koo-loh*

calendar	calendario, el	*ehl kah-lehn-'dah-ree·oh*
camp	campamento, el	*ehl kahm-pah-'mehn-toh*
campus	campo, el	*ehl 'kahm-poh*
candle	vela, la	*lah 'veh-lah*
candy	dulces, los	*lohs 'dool-sehs*
cap	gorra, la	*lah 'goh-rrah*
capacity	capacidad, la	*lah kah-pah-see-'dahd*
captain	capitán, el (la capitana)	*ehl kah-pee-'tahn (lah kah-pee-'tah-nah)*
car	carro, el	*ehl 'kah-rroh*
card	tarjeta, la	*lah tahr-'heh-tah*
cardboard	cartón, el	*ehl kahr-'tohn*
care	cuidado, el	*ehl kwee-'dah-doh*
careless	descuidado(a)	*dehs-kwee-'dah-doh(ah)*
carnival	carnaval, el	*ehl kahr-nah-'vahl*
carpenter	carpintero, el (la carpintera)	*ehl kahr-peen-'teh-roh (lah kahr-peen-'teh-rah)*
carrot	zanahoria, la	*lah sah-nah-'oh-ree·ah*
cart	carreta, la	*lah kah-'rreh-tah*
cartoons	dibujos animados, los	*lohs dee-'boo-hohs ah-nee-'mah-dohs*
cashier	cajero, el (la cajera)	*ehl kah-'heh-roh (lah kah-'heh-rah)*
cassette	casete, el	*ehl kah-'seh-teh*
cassette player	tocador de casetes, el	*ehl toh-kah-'dohr deh kah-'seh-tehs*
cat	gato, el (la gata)	*ehl 'gah-toh (lah 'gah-tah)*
cave	cueva, la	*lah 'kweh-vah*
CDs	discos compactos, los	*lohs 'dee-skohs kohm-'pahk-tohs*
cellular phone	teléfono celular, el	*ehl teh-'leh-foh-noh seh-loo-'lahr*
cemetery	cementerio, el	*ehl seh-mehn-'teh-ree·oh*
cent	centavo, el	*ehl sehn-'tah-voh*
center	centro, el	*ehl 'sehn-troh*
ceremony	ceremonia, la	*lah seh-reh-'moh-nee·ah*
certificate	certificado, el	*ehl sehr-tee-fee-'kah-doh*
chain	cadena, la	*lah kah-'deh-nah*
chair	silla, la	*lah 'see-yah*
chairperson	director del departamento, el (la directora)	*ehl dee-rehk-'tohr dehl deh-pahr-tah-'mehn-toh (lah dee-rehk-'toh-rah)*
chalk	tiza, la	*lah 'tee-sah*
chalkboard	pizarrón, el	*ehl pee-sah-'rrohn*

change	cambio, el	ehl 'kahm-bee·oh
chapter	capítulo, el	ehl kah-'pee-too-loh
chart	diagrama, el	ehl dee-ah-'grah-mah
cheap	barato(a)	bah-'rah-toh(ah)
cheating	fraude, el	ehl 'frow-deh
check	cheque, el	ehl 'cheh-keh
checkers	juego de damas, el	ehl 'hoo·ee-goh deh 'dah-mahs
cheek	mejilla, la	lah meh-'hee-yah
chemical	producto químico, el	ehl proh-'dook-toh 'kee-mee-koh
chemistry	química, la	lah 'kee-mee-kah
chess	ajedrez, el	ehl ah-heh-'drehs
chest (body)	pecho, el	ehl 'peh-choh
chest (trunk)	baúl, el	ehl bah-'ool
chicken	pollo, el	ehl 'poh-yoh
chin	barbilla, la	lah bahr-'bee-yah
chocolate	chocolate, el	ehl choh-koh-'lah-teh
choir	coro, el	ehl 'koh-roh
Christmas	Navidad, la	lah nah-vee-'dahd
church	iglesia, la	lah ee-'gleh-see·ah
cigarettes	cigarrillos, los	lohs see-gah-'rree-yohs
city	ciudad, la	lah see-oo-'dahd
city hall	municipio, el	ehl moo-nee-'see-pee·oh
civil rights	derechos civiles, los	lohs deh-'reh-chohs see-'vee-lehs
class	clase, la	lah 'klah-seh
classroom	sala de clase, la	lah 'sah-lah deh 'klah-seh
clean	limpio(a)	'leem-pee·oh(ah)
clerk	dependiente, el (la dependienta)	ehl deh-pehn-dee-'ehn-teh (lah deh-pehn-dee-'ehn-tah)
clever	listo(a)	'lee-stoh(ah)
climate	clima, el	ehl 'klee-mah
clinic	clínica, la	lah 'klee-nee-kah
clock	reloj, el	ehl reh-'hoh
cloth	tela, la	lah 'teh-lah
clothing	ropa, la	lah 'roh-pah
club	club, el	ehl kloob
coach	entrenador, el (la entrenadora)	ehl ehn-treh-nah-'dohr (lah ehn-treh-nah-'doh-rah)
coast	costa, la	lah 'koh-stah
code	código, el	ehl 'koh-dee-goh
coffee	café, el	ehl kah-'feh
cold	frío(a)	'free-oh(ah)
college	universidad, la	lah oo-nee-vehr-see-'dahd
color	color, el	ehl koh-'lohr

colors	colores, los	*lohs koh-'loh-rehs*
comb	peine, el	*ehl 'peh·ee-neh*
comfortable	cómodo(a)	*'koh-moh-doh(ah)*
comment	comentario, el	*ehl koh-mehn-'tah-ree·oh*
committee	comité, el	*ehl koh-mee-'teh*
communication	comunicación, la	*lah koh-moo-nee-kah-see-'ohn*
companion, acquaintance	compañero, el (la compañera)	*ehl kohm-pah-'nyeh-roh (lah kohm-pah-'nyeh-rah)*
competitive athletics	deportes competitivos, los	*lohs deh-'pohr-tehs kohm-peh-tee-'tee-vohs*
computer	computadora, la	*lah kohm-poo-tah-'doh-rah*
concept	concepto, el	*ehl kohn-'sehp-toh*
conduct	comportamiento, el	*ehl kohm-pohr-tah-'mee-'ehn toh*
cone	cono, el	*ehl 'koh-noh*
conference	conferencia, la	*lah kohn-feh-'rehn-see·ah*
conflict	conflicto, el	*ehl kohn-'fleek-toh*
confused	confundido(a)	*kohn-foon-'dee-doh(ah)*
congratulations	felicitaciones, las	*lahs feh-lee-see-tah-see-'oh-nehs*
consent	consentimiento, el	*ehl kohn-sehn-tee-mee-'ehn-toh*
consultant	consultor, el (la consultora)	*ehl kohn-sool-'tohr (lah kohn-sool-'toh-rah)*
content	contenido, el	*ehl kohn-teh-'nee-doh*
contest	concurso, el	*ehl kohn-'koor-soh*
contract	contrato, el	*ehl kohn-'trah-toh*
convention	convención, la	*lah kohn-vehn-see-'ohn*
cook	cocinero, el (la cocinera)	*ehl koh-see-'neh-roh (lah koh-see-'neh-rah)*
cookie	galleta, la	*lah gah-'yeh-tah*
cooperative	dispuesto	*dee-'spweh-stoh*
copier	copiadora, la	*lah koh-pee-ah-'doh-rah*
corn	maíz, el	*ehl mah-'ees*
corner	esquina, la	*lah eh-'skee-nah*
corporal punishment	castigo corporal, el	*ehl kah-'stee-goh kohr-poh-'rahl*
correct	correcto(a)	*koh-'rrehk-toh(ah)*
cost	costo, el	*ehl 'koh-stoh*
cotton	algodón, el	*ehl ahl-goh-'dohn*
cough	tos, la	*lah tohs*
council	junta, la	*lah 'hoon-tah*
counseling	consejo, el	*ehl koh-'seh-hoh*
counselor	consejero, el (la consejera)	*ehl kohn-seh-'heh-roh (lah kohn-seh-'heh-rah)*
country	país, el	*ehl pah-'ees*

county	condado, el	*ehl kohn-'dah-doh*
coupon	cupón, el	*ehl koo-'pohn*
course	curso, el	*ehl 'koor-soh*
court (law)	corte, la	*lah 'kohr-teh*
court (tennis)	cancha, la	*lah 'kahn-chah*
courthouse	corte, la	*lah 'kohr-teh*
courtyard	plaza, la	*lah 'plah-sah*
cousin	primo, el (la prima)	*ehl 'pree-moh (lah 'pree-mah)*
cow	vaca, la	*lah 'vah-kah*
cradle	cuna mecedora, la	*lah 'ko-onah meh-seh-'doh-rah*
crayon	gis, el	*ehl hees*
cream	crema, la	*lah 'kreh-mah*
creative	creativo(a)	*kreh-ah-'tee-voh(ah)*
credit	crédito, el	*ehl 'kreh-dee-toh*
crib	cuna, la	*lah 'koo-nah*
crime	crimen, el	*ehl 'kree-mehn*
criminal	criminal, el *or* la	*ehl / lah kree-mee-'nahl*
cross country	correr a campo traviesa, el	*ehl koh-'rrehr ah 'kahm-poh trah-vee-'eh-sah*
crossing guard	guardia del tráfico, el *or* la	*ehl / lah 'gwahr-dee·ah dehl 'trah-fee-koh*
crosswalk	cruce de peatones, el	*ehl 'kroo-seh deh peh-ah-'toh-nehs*
crutches	muletas, las	*lahs moo-'leh-tahs*
culture	cultura, la	*lah kool-'too-rah*
cup	taza, la	*lah 'tah-sah*
cupboard	armario, el	*ehl ahr-'mah-ree·oh*
curriculum	plan de estudios, el	*ehl plahn deh eh-'stoo-dee·ohs*
custom	costumbre, la	*lah koh-'stoom-breh*
cut	cortadura, la	*lah kohr-tah-'doo-rah*
dance	baile, el	*ehl 'bah·ee-leh*
danger	peligro, el	*ehl peh-'lee-groh*
dangerous	peligroso(a)	*peh-lee-'groh-soh(ah)*
dark-haired	moreno(a)	*moh-'reh-noh(ah)*
data	datos, los	*lohs 'dah-tohs*
date	fecha, la	*lah 'feh-chah*
daughter	hija, la	*lah 'ee-ha*
day	día, el	*ehl 'dee-ah*
deadbolt	pestillo, el	*ehl peh-'stee-yoh*
deaf	sordo(a)	*'sohr-doh(ah)*
death	muerte, la	*lah 'mwehr-teh*
December	diciembre	*dee-see-'ehm-bre*
deck	terraza, la	*lah teh-'rrah-sah*
deep	profundo(a)	*proh-'foon-doh(ah)*

degree (college)	licenciatura, la	*lah lee-sehn-see·ah-'too·rah*
degree (measurement)	grado, el	*ehl 'grah-doh*
delicious	delicioso(a)	*deh-lee-see-'oh-soh(ah)*
delinquent	delicuente, el *or* la	*ehl / lah deh-leen-'kwehn-teh*
dentist	dentista, el *or* la	*ehl / lah den-'tee-stah*
department	departamento, el	*ehl deh-pahr-tah-'mehn-toh*
description	descripción, la	*lah deh-skreep-see-'ohn*
desert	desierto, el	*ehl deh-see-'ehr-toh*
desk	pupitre, el; escritorio, el	*ehl poo-'pee-treh, ehl eh-skree-'toh-ree-oh*
dessert	postre, el	*ehl 'poh-streh*
detention	detención, la	*lah deh-tehn-see-'ohn*
diaper	pañal, el	*ehl pah-'nyahl*
dictionary	diccionario, el	*ehl deek-see-oh-'nah-ree·oh*
difference	diferencia, la	*lah dee-feh-'rehn-see·ah*
difficult	difícil	*dee-'fee-seel*
dinner	cena, la	*lah 'seh-nah*
director	director, el (la directora)	*ehl dee-rehk-'tohr (lah dee-rehk-'toh-rah)*
dirt	tierra, la	*lah tee-'eh-rrah*
dirty	sucio(a)	*'soo-see·oh(ah)*
disability	minusvalía, la	*lah mee-noos-vah-'lee-ah*
disaster	desastre, el	*ehl deh-'sah-streh*
discipline	disciplina, la	*lah dee-see-'plee-nah*
discovery	descubrimiento, el	*ehl deh-skoo-bree-mee-'ehn-toh*
discrimination	discriminación, la	*lah dee-skree-mee-nah-see-'ohn*
dish	traste, el	*ehl 'trah-steh*
dishwasher	lavaplatos, el	*ehl lah-vah-'plah-tohs*
disk	disco, el	*ehl 'dee-skoh*
dispenser	distribuidor, el (la distribuidora)	*ehl dee-stree-boo-ee-'dohr (lah dee-stree-boo-ee-'doh-rah)*
disrespectful	irrespetuoso(a)	*ee-reh-speh-too-'oh-soh(ah)*
distance	distancia, la	*lah dee-'stahn-see·ah*
district	distrito, el	*ehl dee-'stree-toh*
disturbance	tumulto, el	*ehl too-'mool-toh*
ditch	zanja, la	*lah' sahn-hah*
division	división, la	*lah dee-vee-see-'ohn*
divorce	divorcio, el	*ehl dee-'vohr-see·oh*
dizziness	mareos, los	*lohs mah-'reh-ohs*
doctor	doctor, el (la doctora)	*ehl dohk-'tohr (lah dohk-'toh-rah)*
dog	perro, el (la perra)	*ehl 'peh-rroh (lah 'peh-rrah)*
doll	muñeca, la	*lah moo-'nyeh-kah*
dollar	dólar, el	*ehl 'doh-lahr*

dollhouse	casa de muñecas, la	*lah 'kah-sah deh moo-'nyeh-kahs*
donation	donación, la	*lah doh-nah-see-'ohn*
door	puerta, la	*lah 'pwehr-tah*
dormitory	dormitorio, el	*ehl dohr-mee-'toh-ree·oh*
double	doble, el	*ehl 'doh-bleh*
down	abajo	*ah-'bah-hoh*
downtown	centro, el	*ehl 'sehn-troh*
dozen	docena, la	*lah doh-'seh-nah*
drama	drama, el	*ehl 'drah-mah*
drawer	cajón, el	*ehl kah-'hohn*
dream	sueño, el	*ehl 'sweh-nyoh*
dress	vestido, el	*ehl veh-'stee-doh*
drill (exercise)	simulacro, el	*ehl see-moo-'lah-kroh*
drill (tool)	taladro, el	*ehl tah-'lah-droh*
driver	chofer, el *or* la	*ehl / lah choh-'fehr*
driver's education	enseñanza de conducir, la	*lah ehn-seh-'nyahn-sah deh kohn-doo-'seer*
driveway	entrada para carros, la	*lah ehn-'trah-dah 'pah-rah 'kah-rrohs*
drug	droga, la	*lah 'droh-gah*
drug addict	drogadicto, el (la drogadicta)	*ehl drohg-ah-'deek-toh (lah drohg-ah-'deek-tah)*
drug dealer	vendedor (la vendedora) de drogas, el	*ehl vehn-deh-'dohr (lah vehn-deh-'doh-rah) deh 'droh-gahs*
drunkard	borracho, el (la borracha)	*ehl boh-'rrah-choh (lah boh-'rrah-chah)*
dry	seco(a)	*'seh-koh(ah)*
dryer	secadora, la	*lah seh-kah-'doh-rah*
duck	pato, el (la pata)	*ehl 'pah-toh (lah 'pah-tah)*
duster	limpiador, el	*ehl leem-pee-ah-'dohr*
dustpan	recogedor de basura, el	*ehl reh-koh-heh-'dohr deh bah-'soo-rah*
E-mail	correo electrónico, el	*ehl koh-'rreh-oh eh-lehk-'troh-nee-koh*
ear	oreja, la	*lah oh-'reh-hah*
early	temprano(a)	*tehm-'prah-noh(ah)*
earring	arete, el	*ehl ah-'reh-teh*
earth science	ciencia del mundo, la	*lah see-'ehn-see·ah dehl 'moon-doh*
earthquake	temblor, el	*ehl tehm-'blohr*
easel	caballete, el	*ehl kah-bah-'yeh-teh*
east	este	*'eh-steh*
easy	fácil	*'fah-seel*
economics	economía, la	*lah eh-koh-noh-'mee-ah*

educator	educador, el (la educadora)	*ehl eh-doo-kah-'dohr (lah eh-doo-kah-'doh-rah)*
egg	huevo, el	*ehl 'weh-voh*
eighth	octavo(a)	*ohk-'tah-voh(ah)*
elbow	codo, el	*ehl 'koh-doh*
election	elección, la	*lah eh-lehk-see-'ohn*
electrical outlet	enchufe, el	*ehl ehn-'choo-feh*
electricity	electricidad, la	*lah eh-lehk-tree-see-'dahd*
elevator	ascensor, el	*ehl ah-sehn-'sohr*
emergency	emergencia, la	*lah eh-mehr-'hehn-see·ah*
employee	empleado, el (la empleada)	*ehl ehm-pleh-'ah-doh (lah ehm-pleh-'ah-dah)*
encouragement	ánimo, el	*ehl 'ah-nee-moh*
encyclopedia	enciclopedia, la	*lah ehn-see-kloh-'peh-dee·ah*
engine	motor, el	*ehl moh-'tohr*
engineer	ingeniero, el (la ingeniera)	*ehl een-heh-nee-'eh-roh (lah een-heh-nee-'eh-rah)*
English as a second language	inglés como segundo idioma, el	*ehl een-'glehs 'koh-moh seh-'goon-doh ee-dee-'oh-mah*
English literature	literatura en inglés, la	*lah lee-teh-rah-'too-rah ehn een-'glehs*
enrollment	matrícula, la	*lah mah-'tree-koo-lah*
entrance	entrada, la	*lah ehn-'trah-dah*
envelope	sobre, el	*ehl 'soh-breh*
environment	ambiente, el	*ehl ahm-bee-'ehn-teh*
equipment	equipo, el	*ehl eh-'kee-poh*
eraser	borrador, el	*ehl boh-rrah-'dohr*
escalator	escalera mecánica, la	*lah eh-skah-'leh-rah meh-'kah-nee-kah*
essay	ensayo, el	*ehl ehn-'sah-yoh*
European history	historia de Europa, la	*lah ee-'stoh-ree·ah deh eh·oo-'roh-pah*
evacuation	evacuación, la	*lah eh-vah-koo-ah-see-'ohn*
evaluations	evaluaciones, las	*lahs eh-vah-loo-ah-see-'oh-nehs*
event	evento, el	*ehl eh-'vehn-toh*
evidence	evidencia, la	*lah eh-vee-'dehn-see·ah*
exam	exámen, el	*ehl ehk-'sah-meh*
example	ejemplo, el	*ehl eh-'hehm-ploh*
excellent	excelente	*ehk-seh-'lehn-teh*
exercise	ejercicio, el	*ehl eh-hehr-'see-see·oh*
exit	salida, la	*lah sah-'lee-da*
expensive	caro(a)	*'kah-roh(ah)*
explosion	explosión, la	*lah ehk-sploh-see-'ohn*
expulsion	expulsión, la	*lah ehk-spool-see-'ohn*

extension	extensión, la	*lah ehk-stehn-see-'ohn*
eye	ojo, el	*ehl 'oh-hoh*
face	cara, la	*lah 'kah-rah*
facilitator	facilitador, el (la facilitadora)	*ehl fah-see-lee-tah-'dohr (lah fah-see-lee-tah-'doh-rah)*
fact	hecho, el	*ehl 'eh-choh*
factory	fábrica, la	*lah 'fah-bree-kah*
failure	fracaso, el	*ehl frah-'kah-soh*
fair	justo(a)	*'hoo-stoh(ah)*
fall (season)	otoño, el	*ehl oh-'toh-nyoh*
family	familia, la	*lah fah-'mee-lee·ah*
fan	ventilador, el	*ehl vehn-tee-lah-'dohr*
fantastic	fantástico(a)	*fahn-'tah-stee-koh(ah)*
far	lejos	*'leh-hohs*
fat	gordo(a)	*'gohr-doh(ah)*
father	padre, el	*ehl 'pah-dreh*
faucet	grifo, el	*ehl 'gree-foh*
fax	fax, el	*ehl fahks*
feather	pluma, la	*lah 'ploo-mah*
February	febrero	*feh-'breh-roh*
feeling	sentimiento, el	*ehl sehn-tee-mee-'ehn-toh*
fence	cerca, la	*lah 'sehr-kah*
festival	festival, el	*ehl feh-stee-'vahl*
fever	fiebre, la	*lah fee-'eh-breh*
few	pocos(as)	*'poh-kohs(ahs)*
field	campo, el	*ehl 'kahm-poh*
fifth	quinto(a)	*'keen-toh(ah)*
fight	pelea, la	*lah peh-'leh-ah*
file	archivo, el	*ehl ahr-'chee-voh*
film	película, la	*lah peh-'lee-koo-lah*
finance	finanzas, las	*lahs fee-'nahn-sahs*
fine	bien	*'bee·ehn*
finger	dedo, el	*ehl 'deh-doh*
fire	incendio, el	*ehl een-'sehn-dee·oh*
fire department	departamento de bomberos, el	*ehl deh-pahr-tah-'mehn-toh deh bohm-'beh-rohs*
fire drill	simulacro de incendio, el	*ehl see-moo-'lah-kroh deh een-'sehn-dee·oh*
fire extinguisher	extintor, el	*ehl ehks-teen-'tohr*
firearm	arma de fuego, el	*ehl 'ahr-mah deh 'fweh-goh*
firefighter	bombero, el (la bombera)	*ehl bohm-'beh-roh (lah bohm-'beh-rah)*
fireworks	fuegos artificiales, los	*lohs 'fweh-gohs ahr-tee-fee-see-'ah-lehs*
first	primero(a)	*pree-'meh-roh(ah)*

fish (in water)	pez, el	*ehl pehs*
fish (out of the water)	pescado, el	*ehl peh-'skah-doh*
fishbowl	pecera, la	*lah peh-'seh-rah*
flag	bandera, la	*lah bahn-'deh-rah*
flashlight	linterna, la	*lah leen-'tehr-nah*
flood	inundación, la	*lah een-oon-dah-see-'ohn*
floor	piso, el	*ehl 'pee-soh*
flower	flor, la	*lah flohr*
flyer	hoja informativa, la	*lah 'oh-hah een-fohr-mah-'tee-vah*
folder	libreta, la	*lah lee-'breh-tah*
food	comida, la	*lah koh-'mee-dah*
foot	pie, el	*ehl pee-'eh*
football	fútbol americano, el	*ehl 'foot-bohl ah-meh-ree-'kah-noh*
for	para, por	*'pah-rah, pohr*
foreign	extranjero(a)	*ehks-trahn-'heh-roh(ah)*
forest	bosque, el	*ehl 'boh-skeh*
fork	tenedor, el	*ehl teh-neh-'dohr*
form	formulario, el	*ehl fohr-moo-'lah-ree·oh*
formula	fórmula, la	*lah 'fohr-moo-lah*
fountain	fuente, la	*lah 'fwehn-teh*
fourth	cuarto(a)	*'kwahr-toh(ah)*
fraction	fracción, la	*lah frahk-see-'ohn*
free	gratis	*'grah-tees*
freedom	libertad, la	*lah lee-behr-'tahd*
freezer	congelador, el	*ehl kohn-heh-lah-'dohr*
Friday	viernes	*vee-'ehr-nehs*
friend	amigo, el (la amiga)	*ehl ah-'mee-goh (lah ah-'mee-gah)*
friendly	amistoso(a)	*ah-mee-'stoh-soh(ah)*
friendship	amistad, la	*lah ah-mee-'stahd*
from	de	*deh*
frostbite	congelamiento, el	*ehl kohn-heh-lah-mee-'ehn-toh*
fruit	fruta, la	*lah 'froo-tah*
fun	divertido(a)	*dee-vehr-'tee-doh(ah)*
function	función, la	*lah foon-see-'ohn*
funding	fondos, los	*lohs 'fohn-dohs*
fundraising	recolección de fondos, la	*lah reh-koh-lehk-see-'ohn deh 'fohn-dohs*
funny	chistoso(a)	*chee-'stoh-soh(ah)*
furniture	muebles, los	*lohs 'mweh-blehs*
future	futuro, el	*ehl foo-'too-roh*
game	juego, el	*ehl joo·'eh-goh*
gang	pandilla, la	*lah pahn-'dee-yah*

gang member	pandillero, el (la pandillera)	*ehl pahn-dee-'yeh-roh (lah pahn-dee-'yeh-rah)*
garage	garaje, el	*ehl gah-'rah-heh*
garden	jardín, el	*ehl hahr-'deen*
gardener	jardinero, el (la jardinera)	*ehl hahr-dee-'neh-roh (lah hahr-dee-'neh-rah)*
gas station	gasolinera, la	*lah gah-soh-lee-'neh-rah*
gate	portón, el	*ehl pohr-'tohn*
geography	geografía, la	*lah heh-oh-grah-'fee-ah*
geometry	geometría, la	*lah heh-oh-meh-'tree-ah*
gift	regalo, el	*ehl reh-'gah-loh*
girdle	faja, la	*lah 'fah-hah*
girl	niña, la	*lah 'nee-nyah*
girlfriend	novia, la	*lah 'noh-vee·ah*
glass (drinking)	vaso, el	*ehl 'vah-soh*
glass (material)	vidrio, el	*ehl 'vee-dree·oh*
glasses	lentes, los	*lohs 'lehn-tehs*
globe	mundo, el	*ehl 'moon-doh*
glossary	glosario, el	*ehl gloh-'sah-ree·oh*
glove	guante, el	*ehl 'gwahn-teh*
glue	pegamento, el	*ehl peh-gah-'mehn-toh*
goal	meta, la	*lah 'meh-tah*
goat	chivo, el (la chiva)	*ehl 'chee-voh (lah 'chee-vah)*
God	Dios	*'dee-ohs*
godfather	padrino, el	*ehl pah-'dree-noh*
godmother	madrina, la	*lah mah-'dree-nah*
golf	golf, el	*ehl gohlf*
good	bueno(a)	*'bweh-noh(ah)*
good-bye	adiós	*ah-dee-'ohs*
government	gobierno, el	*ehl goh-bee-'ehr-noh*
grade (academic)	nota, la	*lah 'noh-tah*
grade (level)	grado, el	*ehl 'grah-doh*
grade school	escuela primaria, la	*lah eh-'skweh-lah pree-'mah-ree·ah*
graduation	graduación, la	*lah grah-doo-ah-see-'ohn*
graffiti	grafiti, el	*ehl grah-'fee-tee*
grammar	gramática, la	*lah grah-'mah-tee-kah*
granddaughter	nieta, la	*lah nee-'eh-tah*
grandfather	abuelo, el	*ehl ah-'bweh-loh*
grandmother	abuela, la	*lah ah-'bweh-lah*
grandson	nieto, el	*ehl nee-'eh-toh*
grape	uva, la	*lah 'oo-vah*
graph	gráfico, el	*ehl 'grah-fee-koh*
grass	pasto, el	*ehl pah-'stoh*
green	verde	*'vehr-deh*

group	grupo, el	*ehl 'groo-poh*
grove	arboleda, la	*lah ahr-boh-'leh-dah*
guest	huésped, el *or* la	*ehl / lah 'weh-spehd*
guilty	culpable	*kool-'pah-bleh*
gum	chicle, el	*ehl 'chee-kleh*
gym	gimnasio, el	*ehl heem-'nah-see·oh*
gymnastics	gimnasia, la	*lah heem-'nah-see·ah*
hair	pelo, el	*ehl 'peh-loh*
hairbrush	cepillo, el	*ehl seh-'pee-yoh*
half	mitad, la	*lah mee-'tahd*
hall	pasillo, el	*ehl pah-'see-yoh*
ham	jamón, el	*ehl hah-'mohn*
hamburger	hamburguesa, la	*lah ahm-boor-'geh-sah*
hammer	martillo, el	*ehl mahr-'tee-yoh*
hand	mano, la	*lah 'mah-noh*
handball	frontón de mano, el	*ehl frohn-'tohn deh 'mah-noh*
handcuff	esposas, las	*lahs eh-'spoh-sahs*
handicapped	incapacitado(a)	*een-kah-pah-see-'tah-doh(ah)*
handkerchief	pañuelo, el	*ehl pah-nyoo-'eh-loh*
handsome	guapo(a)	*'gwah-poh(ah)*
hanger	gancho, el	*ehl 'gahn-choh*
happy	contento(a)	*kohn-'tehn-toh(ah)*
harassment	acosamiento, el	*ehl ah-koh-sah-mee-'ehn-toh*
hard	duro(a)	*'doo-roh(ah)*
harm	daño, el	*ehl 'dah-nyoh*
hat	sombrero, el	*ehl sohm-'breh-roh*
he	él	*ehl*
head	cabeza, la	*lah kah-'beh-sah*
headache	dolor de cabeza, el	*ehl doh-'lohr deh kah-'beh-sah*
headphones	audífonos, los	*lohs ow-'dee-foh-nohs*
health	salud, la	*lah sah-'lood*
health care	cuidado de la salud, el	*ehl kwee-'dah-doh deh lah sah-'lood*
healthy	sano(a)	*'sah-noh(ah)*
hearing aids	audífonos, los	*lohs ow-'dee-foh-nohs*
heart	corazón, el	*ehl koh-rah-'sohn*
heat	calor, el	*ehl kah-'lohr*
heat stroke	prostración, la	*lah proh-strah-see-'ohn*
heater	calentador, el	*ehl kah-lehn-tah-'dohr*
heating	calefacción, la	*lah kah-leh-fahk-see-'ohn*
height	estatura, la	*lah eh-stah-'too-rah*
help	ayuda, la	*lah ah-'yoo-dah*
helper	ayudante, el (la ayudanta)	*ehl ah-yoo-'dahn-teh (lah ah-yoo-'dahn-tah)*
helpful	servicial	*sehr-vee-see-'ahl*

hen	gallina, la	*lah gah-'yee-nah*
her	su	*soo*
here	aquí; acá	*ah-'kee; ah-'kah*
hi	hola	*'oh-lah*
hiccup	hipo, el	*ehl 'ee-poh*
high school	escuela secundaria, la	*lah eh-'skweh-lah seh-koon-'dah-ree·ah*
highway	carretera, la	*lah kah-rreh-'teh-rah*
hill	cerro, el	*ehl 'seh-rroh*
hip	cadera, la	*lah kah-'deh-rah*
his	su	*soo*
hoe	azadón, el	*ehl ah-sah-'dohn*
hole	hoyo, el	*ehl 'oh-yoh*
holiday	día feriado, el	*ehl 'dee-ah feh-ree-'ah-doh*
home	casa, la	*lah 'kah-sah*
honesty	honradez, la	*lah ohn-rah-'dehs*
hope	esperanza, la	*lah eh-speh-'rahn-sah*
horn	bocina, la	*lah boh-'see-nah*
horse	caballo, el	*ehl kah-'bah-yoh*
hospital	hospital, el	*ehl oh-spee-'tahl*
hot	caliente	*kah-lee-'ehn-teh*
hot dog	perro caliente, el	*ehl 'peh-rroh kah-lee-'ehn-teh*
hour	hora, la	*lah 'oh-rah*
house	casa, la	*lah 'kah-sah*
housing	vivienda, la	*lah vee-vee-'ehn-dah*
how	cómo	*'koh-moh*
how many	cuántos	*'kwahn-tohs*
how much	cuánto	*'kwahn-toh*
humanities	humanidades, las	*lahs oo-mah-nee-'dah-dehs*
hunger	hambre, el	*ehl 'ahm-breh*
hurricane	huracán, el	*ehl oo-rah-'kahn*
husband	esposo, el	*ehl eh-'spoh-soh*
hydrant	la llave de incendios, la	*lah 'yah-veh deh een-'sehn-dee·ohs*
I	yo	*yoh*
I.D.	identificación, la	*lah ee-dehn-tee-fee-kah-see-'ohn*
ice	hielo, el	*ehl 'yeh-loh*
ice cream	helado, el	*ehl eh-'lah-doh*
ice hockey	hockey, el	*ehl 'hoh-kee*
idea	idea, la	*lah ee-'deh-ah*
if	si	*see*
illness	enfermedad, la	*lah ehn-fehr-meh-'dahd*
important	importante	*eem-pohr-'tahn-teh*
in	en	*ehn*

in front of	en frente de	*ehn 'frehn-teh deh*
inch	pulgada, la	*lah pool-'gah-dah*
incomplete	incompleto(a)	*een-kohm-'pleh-toh(ah)*
incorrect	incorrecto(a)	*een-koh-'rrehk-toh(ah)*
independence	independencia, la	*lah een-deh-pehn-'dehn-see·ah*
individualized	individualizado(a)	*een-dee-vee-doo-ah-lee-'sah-doh(ah)*
industrial arts	artes industriales, las	*lahs 'ahr-tehs een-doos-tree ah-lehs*
industry	industria, la	*lah een-'doo-stree·ah*
infection	infección, la	*lah een-fehk-see-'ohn*
information	información, la	*lah een-fohr-mah-see-'ohn*
injury	herida, la	*lah eh-'ree-dah*
inside	adentro	*ah-'dehn-troh*
institute	instituto, el	*ehl een-stee-'too-toh*
institution	institución, la	*lah een-stee-too-see-'ohn*
instruction	instrucción, la	*lah een-strook-see-'ohn*
instructor	instructor, el (la instructora)	*ehl een-strook-'tohr (lah een-strook-'toh-rah)*
instrument	instrumento, el	*ehl een-stroo-'mehn-toh*
insurance	seguro, el	*ehl seh-'goo-roh*
interesting	interesante	*een-teh-reh-'sahn-teh*
interpreter	intérprete, el *or* la	*ehl / lah een-'tehr-preh-teh*
interview	entrevista, la	*lah ehn-treh-'vee-stah*
jacket	chaqueta, la	*lah chah-'keh-tah*
jail	cárcel, la	*lah 'kahr-sehl*
janitor	conserje, el	*ehl kohn-'sehr-heh*
January	enero	*eh-'neh-roh*
jello	gelatina, la	*lah heh-lah-'tee-nah*
jewelry	joyas, las	*lahs 'hoh-yahs*
joke	chiste, el	*ehl 'chee-steh*
journalism	periodismo, el	*ehl peh-ree-oh-'dees-moh*
juice	jugo, el	*ehl 'hoo-goh*
July	julio	*'hoo-lee·oh*
jump rope	cuerda para brincar, la	*lah 'kwehr-dah 'pah-rah breen-'kahr*
June	junio	*'hoo-nee·oh*
jungle	selva, la	*lah 'sehl-vah*
just	apenas	*ah-'peh-nahs*
justice	justicia, la	*lah hoo-'stee-see·ah*
juvenile court	tribunal de menores, el	*ehl tree-boo-'nahl deh meh-'noh-rehs*
key	llave, la	*lah 'yah-veh*
keyboard	teclado, el	*ehl teh-'klah-doh*
kind	amable	*ah-'mah-bleh*

kindness	bondad, la	*lah bohn-'dahd*
kite	cometa, la	*lah koh-'meh-tah*
knee	rodilla, la	*lah roh-'dee-yah*
knife	cuchillo, el	*ehl koo-'chee-yoh*
labels	etiquetas, las	*lahs eh-tee-'keh-tahs*
laboratory	laboratorio, el	*ehl lah-boh-rah-'toh-ree·oh*
lady (Mrs.)	señora, la (Sra.)	*lah seh-'nyoh-rah*
lake	lago, el	*ehl 'lah-goh*
lamp	lámpara, la	*lah 'lahm-pah-rah*
land	terreno, el	*ehl teh-'rreh-noh*
language	lenguaje, el; idioma, el	*ehl lehn-'gwah-heh; ehl ee-dee-'oh-mah*
large room	salón, el	*ehl sah-'lohn*
latch	cerrojo, el	*ehl seh-'rroh-hoh*
late	tarde	*'tahr-deh*
later	más tarde	*'mahs 'tahr-deh*
law	ley, la	*lah leh·ee*
lawn	césped, el	*ehl 'seh-spehd*
lawnmower	cortadora de césped, la	*lah kohr-tah-'doh-rah deh 'seh-spehd*
lawyer	abogado, el (la abogada)	*ehl ah-boh-'gah-doh (lah ah-boh-'gah-dah)*
leader	líder, el *or* la	*ehl / lah 'lee-dehr*
league	liga, la	*lah 'lee-gah*
left	izquierda	*ees-kee-'ehr-dah*
leg	pierna, la	*lah pee-'ehr-nah*
legal guardian	tutor legal, el (la tutora legal)	*ehl too-'tohr leh-'gahl (lah too-'toh-rah leh-'gahl)*
lemon	limón, el	*ehl lee-'mohn*
lemonade	limonada, la	*lah lee-moh-'nah-dah*
length	largo, el	*ehl 'lahr-goh*
lens	lente, el	*ehl 'lehn-teh*
less	menos	*'meh-nohs*
lesson	lección, la	*lah lehk-see-'ohn*
letter (alphabet)	letra, la	*lah 'leh-trah*
letter (mail)	carta, la	*lah 'kahr-tah*
lettuce	lechuga, la	*lah leh-'choo-gah*
level	nivel, el	*ehl nee-'vehl*
librarian	bibliotecario, el (la bibliotecaria)	*ehl bee-blee-oh-teh-'kah-ree·oh (lah beeb-lee-oh-teh-'kah-ree·ah)*
library	biblioteca, la	*lah bee-blee-oh-'teh-kah*
license	licencia, la	*lah lee-'sehn-see·ah*
light	luz, la	*lah loos*
line	línea, la	*lah 'lee-neh-ah*

345

lip	labio, el	*ehl 'lah-bee·oh*
liquor	licor, el	*ehl lee-'kohr*
list	lista, la	*lah 'lee-stah*
little	pequeño(a)	*peh-'keh-nyoh(ah)*
liver	hígado, el	*ehl 'ee-gah-doh*
loan	préstamo, el	*ehl 'preh-stah-moh*
lobby	vestíbulo, el	*ehl veh-'stee-boo-loh*
lock	candado, el	*ehl kahn-'dah-doh*
locker	armario, el	*ehl ahr-'mah-ree·oh*
loiterer	holgazán, el (la holgazana)	*ehl ohl-gah-'sahn (lah ohl-gah-'sah-nah)*
loneliness	soledad, la	*lah soh-leh-'dahd*
long	largo(a)	*'lahr-goh(ah)*
lost	perdido(a)	*pehr-'dee-doh(ah)*
lot	lote, el	*ehl 'loh-teh*
lotion	loción, la	*lah loh-see-'ohn*
loud	ruidoso(a)	*roo-ee-'doh-soh(ah)*
loudspeaker	altoparlante, el	*ehl ahl-toh-pahr-'lahn-teh*
lounge	salón, el	*ehl sah-'lohn*
love	amor, el	*ehl ah-'mohr*
lunch	almuerzo, el	*ehl ahl-moo-'ehr-soh*
lungs	pulmones, los	*lohs pool-'moh-nehs*
machine	máquina, la	*lah 'mah-kee-nah*
machinery	maquinaria, la	*lah mah-kee-'nah-ree·ah*
magazine	revista, la	*lah reh-'vee-stah*
magnet	imán, el	*ehl ee-'mahn*
magnifying glass	lupa, la	*lah 'loo-pah*
mail carrier	cartero, el *or* la	*ehl / lah kahr-'teh-roh*
mailbox	buzón, el	*ehl boo-'sohn*
main office	oficina principal, la	*lah oh-fee-'see-nah preen-see-'pahl*
maintenance	mantenimiento, el	*ehl mahn-teh-nee-mee-'ehn-toh*
makeup	maquillaje, el	*ehl mah-kee-'yah-heh*
man	hombre, el	*ehl 'ohm-breh*
many	muchos(as)	*'moo-chohs(ahs)*
map	mapa, el	*ehl 'mah-pah*
marbles	canicas, las	*lahs kah-'nee-kahs*
March	marzo	*'mahr-soh*
mark	marca, la	*lah 'mahr-kah*
marker	marcador, el	*ehl mahr-kah-'dohr*
market	mercado, el	*ehl mehr-'kah-doh*
marvelous	maravilloso(a)	*mah-rah-vee-'yoh-soh(ah)*
mat	tapete, el	*ehl tah-'peh-teh*
match	fósforo, el	*ehl 'fohs-foh-roh*
material	materia, la	*lah mah-'teh-ree·ah*

346

mathematics	matemáticas, las	*lahs mah-teh-'mah-tee-kahs*
May	mayo	*'mah-yoh*
maybe	quizás	*kee-'sahs*
mayonnaise	mayonesa, la	*lah mah-yoh-'neh-sah*
mechanic	mecánico, el or la	*ehl / lah meh-'kah-nee-koh*
medal	medalla, la	*lah meh-'dah-yah*
media	medios de comunicación, los	*lohs 'meh-dee·ohs deh koh-moo-nee-kah-see-'ohn*
medicine	medicina, la	*lah meh-dee-'see-nah*
meeting	reunión, la	*lah reh-oo-nee-'ohn*
member	miembro, el or la	*ehl / lah mee-'ehm-broh*
memo	memorándum, el	*ehl meh-moh-'rahn-doom*
memory	memoria, la	*lah meh-'moh-ree·ah*
mentor	mentor, el (la mentora)	*ehl mehn-'tohr (lah mehn-'toh-rah)*
merry-go-round	caballitos, los	*lohs kah-bah-'yee-tohs*
message	recado, el	*ehl reh-'kah-doh*
meter (length)	metro, el	*ehl 'meh-troh*
meter (parking)	parquímetro, el	*ehl pahr-'kee-meh-troh*
method	método, el	*ehl 'meh-toh-doh*
microscope	microscopio, el	*ehl mee-kroh-'skoh-pee·oh*
microwave	horno de microonda, el	*ehl 'ohr-noh deh mee-kroh-'ohn-dah*
milk	leche, la	*lah 'leh-cheh*
mine	mío(a)	*'mee-oh(ah)*
minor	menor de edad, el or la	*ehl / lah meh-'nohr deh eh-'dahd*
mirror	espejo, el	*ehl eh-'speh-hoh*
mister (Mr.)	señor, el (Sr.)	*ehl seh-'nyohr*
mittens	mitones, los	*lohs mee-'toh-nehs*
model	modelo, el	*ehl moh-'deh-loh*
modeling clay	plastilina, la	*lah plah-stee-'lee-nah*
modified	modificado(a)	*moh-dee-fee-'kah-doh (ah)*
Monday	lunes	*'loo-nehs*
money	dinero, el	*ehl dee-'neh-roh*
monitor	monitor, el	*ehl moh-nee-'tohr*
monster	monstruo, el or la	*ehl / lah 'mohn-stroo-oh*
month	mes, el	*ehl mehs*
moon	luna, la	*lah 'loo-nah*
mop	trapeador, el	*ehl trah-peh-ah-'dohr*
moped	bicicleta motorizada, la	*lah bee-see-'kleh-tah moh-toh-ree-'sah-dah*
more	más	*mahs*
mother	madre, la	*lah 'mah-dreh*
motion	movimiento, el	*ehl moh-vee-mee-'ehn-toh*

motorcycle	motocicleta, la	*lah moh-toh-see-'kleh-tah*
mountain	montaña, la	*lah mohn-'tah-nyah*
mouth	boca, la	*lah 'boh-kah*
movie theater	cine, el	*ehl 'see-neh*
much	mucho(a)	*'moo-choh(ah)*
mud	lodo, el	*ehl 'loh-doh*
museum	museo, el	*ehl moo-'seh-oh*
music	música, la	*lah 'moo-see-kah*
mustard	mostaza, la	*lah moh-'stah-sah*
mute	mudo(a)	*'moo-doh(ah)*
my	mi	*mee*
name	nombre, el	*ehl 'nohm-breh*
napkin	servilleta, la	*lah sehr-vee-'yeh-tah*
narrow	estrecho(a)	*eh-'streh-choh(ah)*
nation	nación, la	*lah nah-see-'ohn*
nationality	nacionalidad, la	*lah nah-see·oh-nah-lee-'dahd*
nausea	náusea, la	*lah 'now-seh-ah*
near	cerca	*'sehr-kah*
necessary	necesario(a)	*neh-seh-'sah-ree·oh(ah)*
neck	cuello, el	*ehl 'kweh-yoh*
necklace	collar, el	*ehl koh-'yahr*
needs	necesidades, las	*lahs neh-seh-see-'dah-dehs*
neighbor	vecino, el	*ehl veh-'see-noh*
neighborhood	barrio, el	*ehl 'bah-rree·oh*
nephew	sobrino, el	*ehl soh-'bree-noh*
nervous	nervioso(a)	*nehr-vee-'oh-soh(ah)*
net	red, la	*lah rehd*
never	nunca	*'noon-kah*
newspaper	periódico, el	*ehl peh-ree-'oh-dee-koh*
next to	al lado de	*ahl 'lah-doh deh*
nice	simpático(a)	*seem-'pah-tee-koh(ah)*
niece	sobrina, la	*lah soh-'bree-nah*
ninth	noveno(a)	*noh-'veh-noh(ah)*
north	norte	*'nohr-teh*
nose	nariz, la	*lah nah-'rees*
note	nota, la	*lah 'noh-tah*
notebook	cuaderno, el	*ehl kwah-'dehr-noh*
notice	anuncio, el; aviso, el	*ehl ah-'noon-see·oh; ehl ah-soh*
novel	novela, la	*lah noh-'veh-lah*
November	noviembre	*noh-vee-'ehm-breh*
now	ahora	*ah-'oh-rah*
number	número, el	*ehl 'noo-meh-roh*
nurse	enfermera, la (el enfermero)	*lah ehn-fehr-'meh-rah (ehl ehn-fehr-'meh-roh)*
nursery	guardería, la	*lah gwahr-deh-'ree-ah*

nursing bottle	biberón, el	*ehl bee-beh-'rohn*
objectives	objetivos, los	*lohs ohb-heh-'tee-vohs*
occupation	ocupación, la	*lah oh-koo-pah-see-'ohn*
ocean	océano, el	*ehl oh-'seh-ah-noh*
October	octubre	*ohk-'too-breh*
of	de	*deh*
office	oficina, la	*lah oh-fee-'see-nah*
official	oficial, el *or* la	*ehl / lah oh-fee-see-'ahl*
old	viejo(a)	*vee-'eh-hoh(ah)*
older	mayor	*mah-'yohr*
on	en	*ehn*
once	una vez	*'oo-nah vehs*
onion	cebolla, la	*lah seh-'boh-yah*
operator	operario, el (la operaria)	*ehl oh-peh-'rah-ree·oh (lah oh-peh-'rah-ree·ah)*
opinion	opinión, la	*lah oh-pee-nee-'ohn*
or	o	*oh*
orange (color)	anaranjado(a)	*ah-nah-rahn-'hah-doh(ah)*
orange (fruit)	naranja, la	*lah nah-'rahn-hah*
orchard	huerta, la	*lah 'wehr-tah*
orchestra	orquesta, la	*lah ohr-'keh-stah*
organization	organización, la	*lah ohr-gah-nee-sah-see-'ohn*
organized	organizado(a)	*ohr-gah-nee-'sah-doh(ah)*
orientation	orientación, la	*lah oh-ree-ehn-tah-see-'ohn*
ounce	onza, la	*lah 'ohn-sah*
our	nuestro(a)	*'nweh-stroh(ah)*
outdoors	afueras, las	*lahs ah-'fweh-rahs*
outside	afuera	*ah-'fweh-rah*
outstanding	destacado(a); sobresaliente	*deh-stah-'kah-doh(ah); soh-breh-sah-lee-'ehn-teh*
oven	horno, el	*ehl 'ohr-noh*
overcoat	abrigo, el	*ehl ah-'bree-goh*
overdose	sobredosis, la	*lah soh-breh-'doh-sees*
overtime	sobretiempo, el	*ehl soh-breh-'tee-'ehm-poh*
owner	dueño, el (la dueña)	*ehl 'dweh-nyoh (lah 'dweh-nyah)*
pacifier	chupete, el	*ehl choo-'peh-teh*
pack	paquete, el	*ehl pah-'keh-teh*
page	página, la	*lah 'pah-hee-nah*
pain	dolor, el	*ehl doh-'lohr*
paint	pintura, la	*lah peen-'too-rah*
paintbrush	brocha, la	*lah 'broh-chah*
painter	pintor, el (la pintora)	*ehl peen-'tohr (lah peen-'toh-rah)*
painting	pintura, la	*lah peen-'too-rah*

pair	par, el	*ehl pahr*
pajamas	pijama, el	*ehl pee-'yah-mah*
pan	sartén, el	*ehl sahr-'tehn*
panties	bragas, las	*lahs 'brah-gahs*
pants	pantalones, los	*lohs pahn-tah-'loh-nehs*
paper	papel, el	*ehl pah-'pehl*
parade	desfile, el	*ehl dehs-'fee-leh*
parent	padre, el	*ehl 'pah-dreh*
park	parque, el	*ehl 'pahr-keh*
parking lot	estacionamiento, el	*ehl eh-stah-see·oh-nah-mee-'ehn-toh*
partner	socio, el (la socia)	*ehl 'soh-see·oh (lah 'soh-see·ah)*
party	fiesta, la	*lah fee-'eh-stah*
pass	permiso, el; pase, el	*ehl pehr-'mee-soh; ehl 'pah-seh*
passenger	pasajero, el (la pasajera)	*ehl pah-sah-'heh-roh (lah pah-sah-'heh-rah)*
patience	paciencia, la	*lah pah-see-'ehn-see·ah*
payment	pago, el	*ehl 'pah-goh*
peace	paz, la	*lah pahs*
peach	melocotón, el	*ehl meh-loh-koh-'tohn*
pear	pera, la	*lah 'peh-rah*
pedestrian	peatón, el (la peatona)	*ehl peh-ah-'tohn (lah peh-ah-'toh-nah)*
pen	lapicero, el; la pluma	*ehl lah-pee-'seh-roh; lah 'ploo-mah*
pencil	lápiz, el	*ehl 'lah-pees*
pencil sharpener	sacapuntas, el	*ehl sah-kah-'poon-tahs*
people	gente, la	*lah 'hehn-teh*
pepper	pimienta, la	*lah pee-mee-'ehn-tah*
percentage	porcentaje, el	*ehl pohr-sehn-'tah-heh*
performance	rendimiento, el	*ehl rehn-dee-mee-'ehn-toh*
permit	permiso, el	*ehl pehr-'mee-soh*
person	persona, la	*lah pehr-'soh-nah*
personality	personalidad, la	*lah pehr-soh-nah-lee-'dahd*
personnel	personal, el	*ehl pehr-soh-'nahl*
pet	mascota, la	*lah mah-'skoh-tah*
pharmacy	farmacia, la	*lah fahr-'mah-see·ah*
philosophy	filosofía, la	*lah fee-loh-soh-'fee-ah*
phone call	llamada, la	*lah yah-'mah-dah*
photo	foto, la	*lah 'foh-toh*
physical education	educación física, la	*lah eh-doo-kah-see-'ohn 'fee-see-kah*
physician	médico, el *or* la	*ehl / lah 'meh-dee-koh*
physics	física, la	*lah 'fee-see-kah*

pickpocket	carterista, el *or* la	*ehl / lah kahr-teh-'ree-stah*
picnic	merienda campestre, la	*lah meh-ree-'ehn-dah*
picture frame	marco, el	*ehl 'mahr-koh*
pictures	dibujos, los	*lohs dee-'boo-hohs*
pie	pastel, el	*ehl pah-'stehl*
pig	cerdo, el (la cerda)	*ehl 'sehr-doh (lah 'sehr-dah)*
pin	alfiler, el	*ehl ahl-fee-'lehr*
pipe	tubería, la	*lah too-beh-'ree-ah*
place	lugar, el	*ehl loo-'gahr*
plan	plan, el	*ehl plahn*
planet	planeta, el	*ehl plah-'neh-tah*
plant	planta, la	*lah 'plahn-tah*
plastic	plástico, el	*ehl 'plah-stee-koh*
plate	plato, el	*ehl 'plah-toh*
play (theater)	drama, el	*ehl 'drah-mah*
player	jugador, el (la jugadora)	*ehl hoo-gah-'dohr (lah hoo-gah-'doh-rah)*
playground	campo de recreo, el	*ehl 'kahm-poh deh reh-'kreh-oh*
playing cards	baraja, la	*lah bah-'rah-hah*
playpen	corral de juego, el	*ehl koh-'rrahl deh 'hweh-goh*
please	por favor	*pohr fah-'vohr*
pliers	alicate, el	*ehl ah-lee-'kah-teh*
plumber	plomero, el (la plomera)	*ehl ploh-'meh-roh (lah ploh-'meh-rah)*
plumbing	tubería, la	*lah too-beh-'ree-ah*
poetry	poesía, la	*lah poh-eh-'see-ah*
point	punto, el	*ehl 'poon-toh*
poisoning	envenenamiento, el	*ehl ehn-veh-neh-nah-mee-'ehn-toh*
pole	poste, el	*ehl 'poh-steh*
police	policía, la	*lah poh-lee-'see-ah*
police officer	agente de policía, el *or* la	*ehl / lah ah-'hehn-teh deh poh-lee-'see-ah*
police station	estación de policía, la	*lah eh-stah-see-'ohn deh poh-lee-'see-ah*
polite	cortés	*kohr-'tehs*
politics	política, la	*lah poh-'lee-tee-kah*
pollution	contaminación, la	*lah kohn-tah-mee-nah-see-'ohn*
pond	charca, la	*lah 'chahr-kah*
pool	piscina, la	*lah pee-'see-nah*
poor	pobre	*'poh-breh*
population	población, la	*lah poh-blah-see-'ohn*
porch	portal, el	*ehl pohr-'tahl*

portrait	retrato, el	*ehl reh-'trah-toh*
post office	correo, el	*ehl koh-'rreh-oh*
poster	cartel, el	*ehl kahr-'tehl*
pot	olla, la	*lah 'oh-yah*
potato	papa, la	*lah 'pah-pah*
potato chips	papitas, las	*lahs pah-'pee-tahs*
potty	vasinica, la	*lah vah-see-'nee-kah*
pound	libra, la	*lah 'lee-brah*
poverty	pobreza, la	*lah poh-'breh-sah*
powder	polvo, el	*ehl 'pohl-voh*
practice	práctica, la	*lah 'prahk-tee-kah*
pregnancy	embarazo, el	*ehl ehm-bah-'rah-soh*
prescription	receta médica, la	*lah reh-'seh-tah 'meh-dee-kah*
president	presidente, el	*ehl preh-see-'dehn-teh*
pretty	bonito(a)	*boh 'nee-toh(ah)*
principal	director, el (la directora)	*ehl dee-rehk-'tohr (lah dee-rehk-'toh-rah)*
principle	principio, el	*ehl preen-'see-pee·oh*
prism	prisma, el	*ehl 'prees-mah*
private	privado(a)	*pree-'vah-doh(ah)*
privilege	privilegio, el	*ehl pree-vee-'leh-hee·oh*
prize	premio, el	*ehl 'preh-mee·oh*
problem	problema, el	*ehl proh-'bleh-mah*
procedure	procedimiento, el	*ehl proh-seh-dee-mee-'ehn-toh*
process	proceso, el	*ehl proh-'seh-soh*
procrastination	retraso, el	*ehl reh-'trah-soh*
program	programa, el	*ehl proh-'grah-mah*
program (computer)	programación, la	*lah proh-grah-mah-see-'ohn*
programmer	programador, el (la programadora)	*ehl proh-grah-mah-'dohr (lah proh-grah-mah-'doh-rah)*
project	proyecto, el	*ehl proh-yehk-'toh*
projector	proyector, el	*ehl proh-yehk-'tohr*
promotion	promoción, la	*lah proh-moh-see-'ohn*
property	propiedad, la	*lah proh-pee-eh-'dahd*
prostitute	prostituta, la	*lah proh-stee-'too-tah*
psychiatrist	psiquiatra, el *or* la	*ehl / lah see-kee-'ah-trah*
psychologist	psicólogo, el (la psicóloga)	*ehl see-'koh-loh-goh (lah see-'koh-loh-gah)*
psychology	psicología, la	*lah see-koh-loh-'hee-ah*
public	público, el	*ehl 'poob-lee-koh*
public relations	relaciones públicas, las	*lahs reh-lah-see-'oh-nehs 'poob-lee-kahs*
punctual	puntual	*poon-too-'ahl*
punishment	castigo, el	*ehl kah-'stee-goh*
purple	morado(a)	*moh-'rah-doh(ah)*

puzzle	rompecabezas, el	*ehl rohm-peh-kah-'beh-sahs*
question	pregunta, la	*lah preh-'goon-tah*
quickly	rápidamente	*'rah-pee-dah-'mehn-teh*
quiet	quieto(a)	*kee-'eh-toh(ah)*
quiz	cuestionario, el	*ehl kweh-stee·oh-'nah-ree·oh*
rabbit	conejo, el (la coneja)	*ehl koh-'neh-hoh (lah koh-'neh-hah)*
race (competition)	carrera, la	*lah kah-'rreh-rah*
race (people)	raza, la	*lah 'rah-sah*
rack	estante, el	*ehl eh-'stahn-teh*
racket	raqueta, la	*lah rah-'keh-tah*
racquetball	frontón con raqueta, el	*ehl frohn-'tohn kohn rah-'keh-tah*
raffle	sorteo, el	*ehl sohr-'teh-oh*
raid	incursión, la	*lah een-koor-see-'ohn*
railroad track	vía del ferrocarril, la	*lah 'vee-ah dehl feh-rroh-kah-'rreel*
rain	lluvia, la	*lah 'yoo-vee·ah*
raincoat	impermeable, el	*ehl eem-pehr-meh-'ah-bleh*
rake	rastrillo, el	*ehl rah-'stree-yoh*
ramp	rampa, la	*lah 'rahm-pah*
rape	violación, la	*lah vee·oh-lah-see-'ohn*
rate	tasa, la	*lah 'tah-sah*
rattle	sonajero, el	*ehl soh-nah-'heh-roh*
reading	lectura, la	*lah lehk-'too-rah*
ready	listo(a)	*'lee-stoh(ah)*
reason	razón, la	*lah rah-'sohn*
receipt	recibo, el	*ehl reh-'see-boh*
receptionist	recepcionista, el *or* la	*ehl / lah reh-sehp-see·oh-'nee-stah*
recommendation	recomendación, la	*lah reh-koh-mehn-dah-see-'ohn*
red	rojo(a)	*'roh-hoh(ah)*
red-headed	pelirrojo(a)	*peh-lee-'rroh-hoh(ah)*
refrigerator	refrigerador, el	*ehl reh-free-heh-rah-'dohr*
region	región, la	*lah reh-hee-'ohn*
registration	inscripción, la	*lah een-skreep-see-'ohn*
relationship	relación, la	*lah reh-lah-see-'ohn*
relative	pariente, el *or* la	*ehl / lah pah-ree-'ehn-teh*
relaxed	relajado(a)	*reh-lah-'hah-doh(ah)*
religion	religión, la	*lah reh-lee-hee-'ohn*
report	reporte, el	*ehl reh-'pohr-teh*
rescue	rescate, el	*ehl reh-'skah-teh*
research	investigación, la	*lah een-veh-stee-gah-see-'ohn*
resource	recurso, el	*ehl reh-'koor-soh*

respect	respeto, el	*ehl reh-'speh-toh*
responsibility	responsabilidad, la	*lah reh-spohn-sah-bee-lee-'dahd*
restaurant	restaurante, el	*ehl reh-stah·oo-'rahn-teh*
restroom	servicio, el; baño, el	*ehl sehr-'vee-see·oh; ehl 'bah-nyoh*
result	resultado, el	*ehl reh-sool-'tah-doh*
retirement	jubilación, la	*lah hoo-bee-lah-see-'ohn*
reward	recompensa, la	*lah reh-kohm-'pehn-sah*
rhyme	rima, la	*lah 'ree-mah*
ribbon	cinta meritoria, la	*lah 'seen-tah meh-ree-'toh-ree·ah*
rice	arroz, el	*ehl ah-'rrohs*
rich	rico(a)	*'ree-koh(ah)*
right	derecha, la	*lah deh-'reh-chah*
ring	anillo, el	*ehl ah-'nee-yoh*
riot	disturbio, el	*ehl dee-'stoor-bee·oh*
risk	riesgo, el	*ehl ree-'ehs-goh*
river	río, el	*ehl 'ree-oh*
road	camino, el	*ehl kah-'mee-noh*
robbery	robo, el	*ehl 'roh-boh*
room	salón, el; cuarto, el	*ehl sah-'lohn; ehl 'kwahr-toh*
rope	soga, la	*lah 'soh-gah*
rough	áspero(a)	*'ah-speh-roh(ah)*
row	fila, la	*lah 'fee-lah*
rude	grosero(a)	*groh-'seh-roh(ah)*
rug	alfombra, la	*lah ahl-'fohm-brah*
rule; ruler	regla, la	*lah 'reh-glah*
rust	herrumbre, la	*lah eh-'rroom-breh*
sad	triste	*'tree-steh*
safe	seguro(a)	*seh-'goo-roh(ah)*
safety	seguridad, la	*lah seh-goo-ree-'dahd*
safety glasses	lentes de seguridad, los	*lohs 'lehn-tehs deh seh-goo-ree-'dahd*
salad	ensalada, la	*lah ehn-sah-'lah-dah*
salesperson	vendedor, el (la vendedora)	*ehl vehn-deh-'dohr (lah vehn-deh-'doh-rah)*
salt	sal, la	*lah sahl*
sample	muestra, la	*lah 'mweh-strah*
sand	arena, la	*lah ah-'reh-nah*
sandals	sandalias, las	*lahs sahn-'dah-lee·ahs*
sandbox	cajón de arena, el	*ehl kah-'hohn deh ah-'reh-nah*
satisfactory	satisfactorio(a)	*sah-tees-fahk-'toh-ree·oh(ah)*
Saturday	sábado	*'sah-bah-doh*
saw	serrucho, el	*ehl seh-'rroo-choh*

354

scarf	bufanda, la	*lah boo-'fahn-dah*
scene	escena, la	*lah eh-'seh-nah*
schedule	horario, el	*ehl oh-'rah-ree·oh*
scholarship	beca, la	*lah 'beh-kah*
school	escuela, la	*lah eh-'skweh-lah*
school bus	autobús escolar, el	*ehl ow-toh-'boos eh-skoh-'lahr*
science	ciencia, la	*lah see-'ehn-see·ah*
scissors	tijeras, las	*lahs tee-'heh-rahs*
score	calificación, la; cuenta, la	*lah kah-lee-fee-kah-see-'ohn; lah 'kwehn-tah*
scrape	rasguño, el	*ehl rahs-'goo-nyoh*
screen	pantalla, la	*lah pahn-'tah-yah*
screwdriver	atornillador, el	*ehl ah-tohr-nee-yah-'dohr*
sea	mar, el	*ehl mahr*
seat	asiento, el	*ehl ah-see-'ehn-toh*
second	segundo(a)	*seh-'goon-doh(ah)*
secret	secreto, el	*ehl seh-'kreh-toh*
secretary	secretario, el (la secretaria)	*ehl seh-kreh-'tah-ree·oh (lah seh-kreh-'tah-ree·ah)*
section	sección, la	*lah sehk-see-'ohn*
security	seguridad, la	*lah seh-goo-ree-'dahd*
security guard	guardia de seguridad, el *or* la	*ehl / lah 'gwahr-dee·ah deh seh-goo-ree-'dahd*
seesaw	subibaja, el	*ehl soo-bee-'bah-hah*
seminar	seminario, el	*ehl seh-mee-'nah-ree·oh*
September	septiembre	*sehp-tee-'ehm-breh*
serious	serio(a)	*'seh-ree·oh(a)*
set	juego, el	*ehl 'hweh-goh*
seventh	séptimo(a)	*'sehp-tee-moh(ah)*
sewage	desagüe, el	*ehl dehs-'ah-gweh*
sewing machine	máquina de coser, la	*lah 'mah-kee-nah deh koh-'sehr*
sex	sexo, el	*ehl 'sehk-soh*
shallow	bajo(a)	*'bah-hoh(ah)*
she	ella	*'eh-yah*
sheep	oveja, la	*lah oh-'veh-hah*
sheet	hoja, la	*lah 'oh-hah*
shelf	repisa, la	*lah reh-'pee-sah*
shelter	refugio, el; amparo, el	*ehl reh-'foo-hee·oh; ehl ahm-'pah-roh*
shirt	camisa, la	*lah kah-'mee-sah*
shock	postración, la	*lah poh-strah-see-'ohn*
shoe	zapato, el	*ehl sah-'pah-toh*
shooting	disparo, el	*ehl dee-'spah-roh*
short (in height)	bajo(a)	*'bah-hoh(ah)*

short (in length)	corto(a)	*'kohr-toh(ah)*
shorts	calzoncillos, los	*lohs kahl-sohn-'see-yohs*
shoulder	hombro, el	*ehl 'ohm-broh*
shovel	pala, la	*lah 'pah-lah*
show	espectáculo, el	*ehl eh-spehk-'tah-koo-loh*
shy	tímido(a)	*'tee-mee-doh(ah)*
sick	enfermo(a)	*ehn-'fehr-moh(ah)*
side	lado, el	*ehl 'lah-doh*
sidewalk	acera, la	*lah ah-'seh-rah*
sign	letrero, el	*ehl leh-'treh-roh*
sign language	lenguaje de sordomudos, el	*ehl lehn-'gwah-heh deh sohr-doh-'moo-dohs*
signal	señal, la	*lah seh-'nyahl*
signature	firma, la	*lah 'feer-mah*
silence	silencio, el	*ehl see-'lehn-see·oh*
silverware	cubiertos, los	*lohs koo-bee-'ehr-tohs*
sink	lavamanos, el	*ehl lah-vah-'mah-nohs*
siren	sirena, la	*lah see-'reh-nah*
sister	hermana, la	*lah ehr-'mah-nah*
site	sitio, el	*ehl 'see-tee·oh*
sixth	sexto(a)	*'sehks-toh(ah)*
skateboards	patinetas, las	*lahs pah-tee-'neh-tahs*
skates	patines, los	*lohs pah-'tee-nehs*
skill	habilidad, la	*lah ah-bee-lee-'dahd*
skin	piel, la	*lah pee-'ehl*
skirt	falda, la	*lah 'fahl-dah*
sled	trineo, el	*ehl tree-'neh-oh*
slide (microscope)	muestra en transparencia, la	*lah 'mweh-strah ehn trahns-pah-'rehn-see·ah*
slide (playground)	tobogán, el	*ehl toh-boh-'gahn*
slip	combinación, la	*lah kohm-bee-nah-see-'ohn*
slippers	zapatillas, las	*lahs sah-pah-'tee-yahs*
slowly	lentamente	*lehn-tah-'mehn-teh*
small	pequeño(a)	*peh-'keh-nyoh(ah)*
smile	sonrisa, la	*lah sohn-'ree-sah*
smog alert	alerta de smog, el *or* la	*ehl/lah ah-'lehr-tah deh 'smohg*
smoke detector	detector de humo, el	*ehl deh-tehk-'tohr deh 'oo-moh*
smooth	liso(a)	*'lee-soh(ah)*
snack	merienda, la	*lah meh-ree-'ehn-dah*
sneeze	estornudo, el	*ehl eh-stohr-'noo-doh*
snow	nieve, la	*lah nee-'eh-veh*
soap	jabón, el	*ehl hah-'bohn*
soccer	fútbol, el	*ehl 'foot-bohl*
social security	seguro social, el	*ehl seh-'goo-roh soh-see-'ahl*

social studies	estudios sociales, los	*lohs eh-'stoo-dee·ohs soh-see-'ah-lehs*
social worker	trabajador (la trabajadora) social, el	*ehl trah-bah-hah-'dohr (lah trah-bah-hah-'doh-rah) soh-see-'ahl*
socks	calcetines, los	*lohs kahl-seh-'tee-nehs*
sofa	sofá, el	*ehl soh-'fah*
soft	blando(a); suave	*'blahn-doh(ah); 'swah-veh*
soft drink	refresco, el	*ehl reh-'freh-skoh*
softball	sófbol, el	*ehl 'sohf-bohl*
software	programa, el	*ehl proh-'grah-mah*
solar system	sistema solar, el	*ehl see-'steh-mah soh-'lahr*
soldier	soldado, el *or* la	*ehl / lah sohl-'dah-doh*
solution	solución, la	*lah soh-loo-see-'ohn*
some	unos(as)	*'oo-nohs(ahs)*
sometimes	a veces	*ah-'veh-sehs*
son	hijo, el	*ehl 'ee-hoh*
song	canción, la	*lah kahn-see-'ohn*
soon	pronto	*'prohn-toh*
sound	sonido, el	*ehl soh-'nee-doh*
soup	sopa, la	*lah 'soh-pah*
sour	agrio(a)	*'ah-gree·oh(ah)*
south	sur	*soor*
space	espacio, el	*ehl eh-'spah-see·oh*
spaceship	nave espacial, la	*lah 'nah-veh eh-spah-see-'ahl*
speaker (person)	orador, el (la oradora)	*ehl oh-rah-'dohr (lah oh-rah-'doh-rah)*
speaker (stereo)	altoparlante, el	*ehl 'ahl-toh-pahr-'lahn-teh*
special education	educación especial, la	*lah eh-doo-kah-see-'ohn eh-speh-see-'ahl*
specialist	especialista, el *or* la	*ehl / lah eh-speh-see-ah-'lee-stah*
speech	discurso, el	*ehl dee-'skoor-soh*
speed	velocidad, la	*lah veh-loh-see-'dahd*
spinach	espinaca, la	*lah eh-spee-'nah-kah*
spirit	espíritu, el	*ehl eh-'spee-ree-too*
sponge	esponja, la	*lah eh-'spohn-hah*
sponsor	patrocinador, el (la patrocinadora)	*ehl pah-troh-see-nah-'dohr (lah pah-troh-see-nah-'doh-rah)*
spoon	cuchara, la	*lah koo-'chah-rah*
sport	deporte, el	*ehl deh-'pohr-teh*
sportcoat	saco, el	*ehl 'sah-koh*
sprain	torcedura, la	*lah tohr-seh-'doo-rah*
spring	primavera, la	*lah pree-mah-'veh-rah*

sprinkler	rociadora, la	*lah roh-see·ah-'doh-rah*
square	cuadrado, el	*ehl kwah-'drah-doh*
stadium	estadio, el	*ehl eh-'stah-dee·oh*
staff	funcionarios, los	*lohs foon-see·oh-'nah-ree·ohs*
stairs	escalera, la	*lah eh-skah-'leh-rah*
stand	soporte, el	*ehl soh-'pohr-teh*
stapler	engrapadora, la	*lah ehn-grah-pah-'doh-rah*
star	estrella, la	*lah eh-'streh-yah*
state	estado, el	*ehl eh-'stah-doh·oh*
stationery	objetos de escritorio, los	*lohs ohb-'heh-tohs deh eh-skree-'toh-ree·oh*
statue	estatua, la	*lah eh-'stah-too-ah*
steak	bistec, el	*ehl bee-'stehk*
step	paso, el	*ehl 'pah-soh*
stepfather	padrastro, el	*ehl pah-'drah-stroh*
stepmother	madrastra, la	*lah mah-'drah-strah*
steps	escalones, los	*lohs eh-skah-'loh-nehs*
stereo	estéreo, el	*ehl eh-'streh-reh-oh*
stick	palo, el	*ehl 'pah-loh*
sticker	etiqueta, la	*lah eh-tee-'keh-tah*
stockings	medias, las	*lahs 'meh-dee·ahs*
stomach	estómago, el	*ehl eh-'stoh-mah-goh*
stomachache	dolor de estómago, el	*ehl doh-'lohr deh eh-'stoh-mah-goh*
stone	piedra, la	*lah pee-'eh-drah*
stool	banquillo, el	*ehl bahn-'kee-yoh*
stop sign	señal de parada, la	*lah seh-'nyahl deh pah-'rah-dah*
storage	depósito, el	*ehl deh-'poh-see-toh*
store	tienda, la	*lah tee-'ehn-dah*
storm	tormenta, la	*lah tohr-'mehn-tah*
story	cuento, el	*ehl 'kwehn-toh*
storybook	libro de cuentos, el	*ehl 'lee-broh deh 'kwehn-tohs*
stove	estufa, la	*lah eh-'stoo-fah*
strange	raro(a)	*'rah-roh(ah)*
stranger	desconocido, el (la desconocida)	*ehl dehs-koh-noh-'see-doh (lah dehs-koh-noh-'see-dah)*
strategy	estrategia, la	*lah eh-strah-'teh-hee·ah*
strawberry	fresa, la	*lah 'freh-sah*
stream	arroyo, el	*ehl ah-'rroh-yoh*
street	calle, la	*lah 'kah-yeh*
streetcar	tranvía, el	*ehl trahn-'vee-ah*
strike	huelga, la	*lah 'wehl-gah*
string	hilo, el	*ehl 'ee-loh*
stroller	carrito de bebé, el	*ehl kah-'rree-toh deh beh-'beh*

strong	fuerte	*'fwehr-teh*
student	alumno, el (la alumna); el *or* la estudiante	*ehl ah-'loom-noh (lah ah-'loom-nah); ehl / lah eh-stoo-dee-'ahn-teh*
study	estudio, el	*ehl eh-'stoo-dee·oh*
stuffed animal	animal de peluche, el	*ehl ah-nee-'mahl deh peh-'loo-cheh*
subject	tema, el	*ehl 'teh-mah*
subway	metro, el	*ehl 'meh-troh*
suggestion	sugerencia, la	*lah soo-heh-'rehn-see·ah*
suit	traje, el	*ehl 'trah-heh*
sum	suma, la	*lah 'soo-mah*
summary	resumen, el	*ehl reh-'soo-mehn*
summer	verano, el	*ehl veh-'rah-noh*
sun	sol, el	*ehl sohl*
Sunday	domingo	*doh-'meen-goh*
sunglasses	lentes de sol, los	*lohs 'lehn-tehs deh sohl*
sunny	soleado(a)	*soh-leh-'ah-doh(ah)*
sunstroke	insolación, la	*lah een-soh-lah-see-'ohn*
suntan lotion	bronceador, el	*ehl broh-seh-ah-'dohr*
superintendent	superintendente, el *or* la	*ehl / lah soo-pehr-een-tehn-'dehn-teh*
supermarket	supermercado, el	*ehl soo-pehr-mehr-'kah-doh*
supervision	supervisión, la	*lah soo-pehr-vee-see-'ohn*
supervisor	supervisor, el (la supervisora)	*ehl soo-pehr-vee-'sohr (lah soo-pehr-vee-'soh-rah)*
supplies	materiales, los; provisiones, las	*lohs mah-teh-ree-'ah-lehs ; lahs proh-vee-see-'oh-nehs*
support	apoyo, el	*ehl ah-'poh-yoh*
sure	seguro(a)	*seh-'goo-roh(ah)*
surname	apellido, el	*ehl ah-peh-'yee-doh*
surprised	sorprendido(a)	*sohr-prehn-'dee-doh(ah)*
suspect	sospechoso, el (la sospechosa)	*ehl soh-speh-'choh-soh (lah soh-speh-'choh-sah)*
suspension	suspensión, la	*lah soo-spehn-see-'ohn*
sweater	suéter, el	*ehl 'sweh-tehr*
sweatsuit	sudadera, la	*lah soo-dah-'deh-rah*
sweet	dulce	*'dool-seh*
sweetheart	querido(a)	*keh-'ree-doh(ah)*
swing	columpio, el	*ehl koh-'loom-pee·oh*
switch	interruptor, el	*ehl een-teh-rroop-'tohr*
T-shirt	camiseta, la	*lah kah-mee-'seh-tah*
table	mesa, la	*lah 'meh-sah*
talcum powder	talco, el	*ehl 'tahl-koh*
tall	alto(a)	*'ahl-toh(ah)*

tape	cinta, la	*lah 'seen-tah*
tardiness	tardanza, la	*lah tahr-'dahn-sah*
tea	té, el	*ehl teh*
teacher	maestro, el (la maestra); profesor, el (la profesora)	*ehl mah-'eh-stroh (lah mah-'eh-strah); ehl proh-feh-'sohr (lah proh-feh-'soh-rah)*
teacher's aide	ayudante (la ayudanta) de maestro, el	*ehl ah-yoo-'dahn-teh (lah ah-yoo-'dahn-tah) deh mah-'eh-stroh*
team	equipo, el	*ehl eh-'kee-poh*
technician	técnico, el *or* la	*ehl / lah 'tehk-nee-koh*
technique	técnica, la	*lah 'tehk-nee-kah*
teenager	muchacho, el (la muchacha)	*ehl moo-'chah-choh (lah moo-'chah-chah)*
teeth	dientes, los	*lohs dee-'ehn-tehs*
telephone	teléfono, el	*ehl teh-'leh-foh-noh*
telescope	telescopio, el	*ehl teh-leh-'skoh-pee·oh*
television	televisor, el	*ehl teh-leh-vee-'sohr*
tennis	tenis, el	*ehl 'teh-nees*
tennis shoes	tenis, los	*lohs 'teh-nees*
tenth	décimo(a)	*'deh-see-moh(ah)*
term	período, el	*ehl peh-'ree-oh-doh*
test	prueba, la; examen, el	*lah proo-'eh-bah; ehl ehk-'sah-mehn*
test tube	tubo de ensayo, el	*ehl 'too-boh deh ehn-'sah-yoh*
textbook	libro de texto, el	*ehl 'lee-broh deh 'tehks-toh*
thanks	gracias	*'grah-see·ahs*
that	ese(a)(o)	*'eh-seh(ah)(oh)*
theater	teatro, el	*ehl teh-'ah-troh*
their	su(s)	*soo(s)*
theme	tema, el	*ehl 'teh-mah*
then	entonces	*ehn-'tohn-sehs*
theory	teoría, la	*lah teh-oh-'ree-ah*
therapist	terapeuta, el *or* la	*ehl / lah teh-rah-peh-'oo-tah*
therapy	terapia, la	*lah teh-'rah-pee·ah*
there	allá; allí	*ah-'yah; ah-'yee*
thermometer	termómetro, el	*ehl tehr-'moh-meh-troh*
thermostat	termostato, el	*ehl tehr-moh-'stah-toh*
these	estos(as)	*'eh-stohs(as)*
they	ellos(as)	*'eh-yohs(as)*
thick	grueso(a)	*groo-'eh-soh(ah)*
thief	ladrón, el (la ladrona)	*ehl lah-'drohn (lah lah-'droh-nah)*
thin	delgado(a)	*dehl-'gah-doh(ah)*
third	tercero(a)	*tehr-'seh-roh(ah)*

this	este(a)	'eh-steh(ah)
those	esos(as)	'eh-sohs(ahs)
thought	pensamiento, el	ehl pehn-sah-mee-'ehn-toh
threat	amenaza, la	lah ah-meh-'nah-sah
throat	garganta, la	lah gahr-'gahn-tah
thumbtack	tachuela, la	lah tah-choo-'eh-lah
Thursday	jueves	'hweh-vehs
ticket	boleto, el	ehl boh-'leh-toh
tie	corbata, la	lah kohr-'bah-tah
time	hora, la	lah 'oh-rah
tired	cansado(a)	kahn-'sah-doh(ah)
title	título, el	ehl 'tee-too-loh
to	a	ah
today	hoy	'oh·ee
toe	dedo, el	ehl 'deh-doh
toilet	excusado, el	ehl ehk-skoo-'sah-doh
toilet paper	papel higiénico, el	ehl pah-'pehl ee-hee-'eh-nee-koh
tomato	tomate, el	ehl toh-'mah-teh
tomato sauce	salsa de tomate, la	lah 'sahl-sah deh toh-'mah-teh
tomorrow	mañana	mah-'nyah-nah
tongue	lengua, la	lah 'lehn-gwah
tonight	esta noche	'eh-stah 'noh-cheh
tool	herramienta, la	lah eh-rrah-mee-'ehn-tah
top	trompo, el	ehl 'trohm-poh
topic	asunto, el	ehl ah-'soon-toh
tornado	tornado, el	ehl tohr-'nah-doh
tournament	torneo, el	ehl tohr-'neh-oh
tow truck	grúa, la	lah 'groo-ah
towel	toalla, la	lah toh-'ah-yah
tower	torre, la	lah 'toh-rreh
toy	juguete, el	ehl hoo-'geh-teh
track and field	atletismo, el	ehl aht-leh-'tees-moh
tractor	tractor, el	ehl trahk-'tohr
trade union	sindicato, el	ehl seen-dee-'kah-toh
traffic signal	semáforo, el	ehl seh-'mah-foh-roh
tragedy	tragedia, la	lah trah-'heh-dee·ah
train	tren, el	ehl trehn
trainer	entrenador, el (la entrenadora)	ehl ehn-treh-nah-'dohr (lah ehn-treh-nah-'doh-rah)
training	entrenamiento, el	ehl ehn-treh-nah-mee-'ehn-toh
transfer	transferencia, la	lah trahns-feh-'rehn-see·ah
translator	traductor, el (la traductora)	ehl trah-dook-'tohr (lah trah-dook-'toh-rah)
transparency	diapositiva, la	lah dee-ah-poh-see-'tee-vah

transportation	transporte, el	*ehl trahns-'pohr-teh*
trash	basura, la	*lah bah-'soo-rah*
trash can	bote para basura, el	*ehl 'boh-teh 'pah-rah bah-'soo-rah*
tray	bandeja, la	*lah bahn-'deh-hah*
treadmill	molino, el	*ehl moh-'lee-noh*
tree	árbol, el	*ehl 'ahr-bohl*
trespasser	intruso, el (la intrusa)	*ehl een-'troo-soh (lah een-'troo-sah)*
trespassing	intrusión, la	*lah een-'troo-see 'ohn*
trick	truco, el	*ehl 'troo-koh*
tricycle	triciclo, el	*ehl tree-'see-kloh*
trigonometry	trigonometría, la	*lah tree-goh-noh-meh-'tree-ah*
trip	viaje, el	*ehl vee-'ah-heh*
trophy	trofeo, el	*ehl troh-'feh-oh*
truck	camión, el	*ehl kah-mee-'ohn*
trust	confianza, la	*lah kohn-fee-'ahn-sah*
tube	tubo, el	*ehl 'too-boh*
Tuesday	martes	*'mahr-tehs*
tuna	atún, el	*ehl ah-'toon*
tune	tono, el	*ehl 'toh-noh*
tunnel	túnel, el	*ehl 'too-nehl*
turkey	pavo, el (la pava)	*ehl 'pah-voh (lah 'pah-vah)*
turtle	tortuga, la	*lah tohr-'too-gah*
tutor	tutor, el (la tutora)	*ehl too-'tohr (lah too-'toh-rah)*
typewriter	máquina de escribir, la	*lah 'mah-kee-nah deh eh-skree-'beer*
typing	escribir a máquina, el	*ehl eh-skree-'beer ah 'mah-kee-nah*
typist	mecanógrafo, el (la mecanógrafa)	*ehl meh-kah-'noh-grah-foh (lah meh-kah-'noh-grah-fah)*
U.S. history	historia de los Estados Unidos, la	*lah ee-'stoh-ree·ah deh lohs eh-'stah-dohs oo-'nee-dohs*
ugly	feo(a)	*'feh-oh(ah)*
umbrella	paraguas, el	*ehl pah-'rah-gwahs*
uncle	tío, el	*ehl 'tee-oh*
underground	subterráneo(a)	*soob-teh-'rrah-neh-oh(ah)*
underwear	ropa interior, la	*lah 'roh-pah een-teh-ree-'ohr*
unemployment	desempleo, el	*ehl dehs-ehm-'pleh-oh*
uniform	uniforme, el	*ehl oo-nee-'fohr-meh*
unit	unidad, la	*lah oo-nee-'dahd*
universe	universo, el	*ehl oo-nee-'vehr-soh*
university	universidad, la	*lah oo-nee-vehr-see-'dahd*
up	arriba	*ah-'rree-bah*
upset	enojado(a)	*eh-noh-'hah-doh(ah)*

urgent	urgente	*oor-'hehn-teh*
urinal	orinal, el	*ehl oh-ree-'nahl*
vacations	vacaciones, las	*lahs vah-kah-see-'oh-nehs*
vaccination	vacunación, la	*lah vah-koo-nah-see-'ohn*
valley	valle, el	*ehl 'vah-yeh*
value	valor, el	*ehl vah-'lohr*
vase	florero, el	*ehl floh-'reh-roh*
VCR	videocasetera, la	*lah vee-deh-oh-kah-seh-'teh-rah*
vegetables	vegetales, los	*lohs veh-heh-'tah-lehs*
vest	chaleco, el	*ehl chah-'leh-koh*
vice-principal	subdirector, el (la subdirectora)	*ehl soob-dee-rehk-'tohr (lah soob-dee-rehk-'toh-rah)*
victim	víctima, la	*lah 'veek-tee-mah*
video	vídeo, el	*ehl 'vee-deh-oh*
violation	violación, la	*lah vee-oh-lah-see-'ohn*
violence	violencia, la	*lah vee-oh-'lehn-see·ah*
visitor	visitante, el *or* la	*ehl / lah vee-see-'tahn-teh*
vitamins	vitaminas, las	*lahs vee-tah-'mee-nahs*
vocabulary	vocabulario, el	*ehl voh-kah-boo-'lah-ree·oh*
voice	voz, la	*lah vohs*
volleyball	vóleibol, el	*ehl 'voh-leh·ee-bohl*
volunteer	voluntario, el (la voluntaria)	*ehl voh-loon-'tah-ree·oh (lah voh-loon-'tah-ree·ah)*
wages	sueldo, el	*ehl 'swehl-doh*
wagon	vagón, el	*ehl vah-'gohn*
wall	pared, la	*lah pah-'rehd*
war	guerra, la	*lah 'geh-rrah*
warehouse	almacén, el	*ehl ahl-mah-'sehn*
warm	tibio(a)	*'tee-bee·oh(ah)*
warning	advertencia, la	*lah ahd-vehr-'tehn-see·ah*
washer	lavadora, la	*lah lah-vah-'doh-rah*
waste	desperdicios, los	*lohs dehs-pehr-'dee-see·ohs*
wastebasket	cesto de basura, el	*ehl 'seh-stoh deh bah-'soo-rah*
watch	reloj, el	*ehl reh-'loh*
water	agua, el	*ehl 'ah-gwah*
water fountain	bebedero, el	*ehl beh-beh-'deh-roh*
water polo	polo acuático, el	*ehl 'poh-loh ah-'kwah-tee-koh*
we	nosotros(as)	*noh-'soh-trohs(as)*
weak	débil	*'deh-beel*
wealth	riqueza, la	*lah ree-'keh-sah*
weather	tiempo, el	*ehl tee-'ehm-poh*
Wednesday	miércoles	*mee-'ehr-koh-lehs*
weed	hierba, la	*lah 'yehr-bah*
week	semana, la	*lah seh-'mah-nah*

weight	peso, el	*ehl 'peh-soh*
weights	pesas, las	*lahs 'peh-sahs*
welcome	bienvenidos(as)	*bee·ehn-veh-'nee-dohs(ahs)*
welfare	bienestar social, el	*ehl bee·ehn-eh-'stahr soh-see-'ahl*
west	oeste	*oh-'eh-steh*
wet	mojado(a)	*moh-'hah-doh(ah)*
what	qué	*keh*
wheelbarrow	carretilla, la	*lah kah-rreh-'tee-yah*
wheelchair	silla de ruedas, la	*lah 'see-yah deh 'rweh-dahs*
when	cuándo	*'kwahn-doh*
where	dónde	*'dohn-deh*
which	cuál	*kwahl*
whistle	silbato, el	*ehl seel-'bah-toh*
white	blanco(a)	*'blahn-koh(ah)*
who	quién	*kee-'ehn*
whose	de quién	*deh kee-'ehn*
why	por qué	*pohr keh*
wide	ancho(a)	*'ahn-choh(ah)*
wife	esposa, la	*lah eh-'spoh-sah*
wind	viento, el	*ehl vee-'ehn-toh*
window	ventana, la	*lah vehn-'tah-nah*
winter	invierno, el	*ehl een-vee-'ehr-noh*
wire	alambre, el	*ehl ah-'lahm-breh*
with	con	*kohn*
without	sin	*seen*
witness	testigo, el *or* la	*ehl / lah teh-'stee-goh*
woman	mujer, la	*lah moo-'hehr*
wood	madera, la	*lah mah-'deh-rah*
word	palabra, la	*lah pah-'lah-brah*
work	trabajo, el	*ehl trah-'bah-hoh*
workshop	taller, el	*ehl tah-'yehr*
world	mundo, el	*ehl 'moon-doh*
worried	preocupado(a)	*preh-oh-koo-'pah-doh(ah)*
worse	peor	*peh-'ohr*
wrench	llave inglesa, la	*lah 'yah-veh een-'gleh-sah*
wrestling	lucha libre, la	*lah 'loo-chah 'lee-breh*
wrist	muñeca, la	*lah moo-'neyh-kah*
writing	escritura, la	*lah eh-skree-'too-rah*
wrong	equivocado(a)	*eh-kee-voh-'kah-doh(ah)*
year	año, el	*ehl 'ah-nyoh*
yearbook	anuario, el	*ehl ah-noo-'ah-ree·oh*
yellow	amarillo(a)	*ah-mah-'ree-yoh(ah)*
yes	sí	*see*
yesterday	ayer	*ah-'yehr*

yet	todavía	*toh-dah-'vee-ah*
you (singular, informal)	tú	*too*
you (plural, formal and informal)	ustedes	*oo-'steh-dehs*
you (singular, formal)	usted	*oo-'stehd*
young	joven	*'hoh-vehn*
younger	menor	*meh-'nohr*
your	su(s)	*soo(s)*
zip code	zona postal, la	*lah 'soh-nah poh-'stahl*
zipper	cierre, el	*ehl see-'eh-rreh*
zone	zona, la	*lah 'soh-nah*
zoo	zoológico, el	*ehl soh-oh-'loh-hee-koh*

SPANISH-ENGLISH DICTIONARY

➤ The gender of Spanish nouns is indicated by the article (**el** or **la**).
➤ When a noun can be either masculine or feminine, it is shown in the masculine form and then in the feminine form: **adulto, el (la adulta)**
➤ All adjectives are shown in the masculine form. An **(a)** is added to remind you of the feminine ending.

a	to	*ah*
a veces	sometimes	*ah-'veh-sehs*
abajo	down	*ah-'bah-hoh*
abogado, el (la abogada)	lawyer	*ehl ah-boh-'gah-doh (lah ah-boh-'gah-dah)*
aborto, el	abortion	*ehl ah-'bohr-toh*
abrigo, el	overcoat	*ehl ah-'bree-goh*
abril	April	*ah-'breel*
abuela, la	grandmother	*lah ah-'bweh-lah*
abuelo, el	grandfather	*ehl ah-'bweh-loh*
aburrido(a)	bored	*ah-boo-rree-doh(ah)*
abuso, el	abuse	*ehl ah-'boo-soh*
academia, la	academy	*lah ah-kah-'deh-mee·ah*
accidente, el	accident	*ehl ahk-see-'dehn-teh*
acción, la	action	*lah ahk-see-'ohn*
acera, la	sidewalk	*lah ah-'seh-rah*
acné, el	acne	*ehl ahk-'neh*
acondicionador de aire, el	air conditioner	*ehl ah-kohn-dee-see·oh-nah-'dohr deh 'ah·ee-reh*
acosamiento, el	harassment	*ehl ah-koh-sah-mee-'ehn-toh*
actitud, la	attitude	*lah ahk-tee-'tood*
actividad, la	activity	*lah ahk-tee-vee-'dahd*
acuario, el	aquarium	*ehl ah-'kwah-ree·oh*
adelante	ahead	*ah-deh-'lahn-teh*
adentro	inside	*ah-'dehn-troh*
adicción, la	addiction	*lah ah-deek-see-'ohn*
adiós	good-bye	*ah-dee-'ohns*
administración, la	administration	*lah ahd-mee-nee-strah-see-'ohn*
administrador, el (la administradora)	administrator	*ehl ahd-mee-nee-strah-'dohr (lah ahd-mee-nee-strah-'doh-rah)*
admisiones, las	admissions	*lahs ahd-mee-see-'oh-nehs*
adulto, el (la adulta)	adult	*ehl ah-'dool-toh (lah ah-'dool-tah)*
advertencia, la	warning	*lah ahd-vehr-'tehn-see·ah*
aeropuerto, el	airport	*ehl ah-eh-roh-'pwehr-toh*

afuera	outside	*ah-'fweh-rah*
afueras, las	outdoors	*lahs ah-'fweh-rahs*
agencia, la	agency	*lah ah-'hehn-see·ah*
agente de polica, el *or* la	police officer	*ehl/lah ah-'hehn-teh deh poh-lee 'see·ah*
agosto	August	*ah-'goh-stoh*
agrio(a)	sour	*'ah-gree·oh(ah)*
agua, el	water	*ehl 'ah-gwah*
ahora	now	*ah-'oh-rah*
ajedrez, el	chess	*ehl ah-heh-'drehs*
al lado de	next to	*ahl 'lah-doh deh*
alambre, el	wire	*ehl ah-'lahm-breh*
alarma, la	alarm	*lah ah-'lahr-mah*
alcohol, el	alcohol	*ehl ahl-koh-'ohl*
alergias, las	allergies	*lahs ah-'lehr-hee-ahs*
alerta de smog, el *or* la	smog alert	*ehl/lah ah-'lehr-tah deh 'smohg*
alfabeto, el	alphabet	*ehl ahl-fah-'beh-toh*
alfiler, el	pin	*ehl ahl-fee-'lehr*
alfombra, la	rug	*lah ahl-'fohm-brah*
álgebra, el	algebra	*ehl 'ahl-heh-'brah*
algodón, el	cotton	*ehl ahl-goh-'dohn*
alicate, el	pliers	*ehl ah-lee-'kah-teh*
aliento, el	breath	*ehl ah-lee-'ehn-toh*
allá; allí	there	*ah-'yah; ah-'yee*
almacén, el	warehouse	*ehl ahl-mah-'sehn*
almuerzo, el	lunch	*ehl ahl-moo-'ehr-soh*
altavoz, el	bullhorn	*ehl ahl-tah-'vohs*
alternativa, la	alternative	*lah ahl-tehr-nah-'tee-vah*
alto(a)	tall	*'ahl-toh(ah)*
altoparlante, el	speaker (stereo); loudspeaker	*ehl ahl-toh-pahr-'lahn-teh*
alumno, el (la alumna); el *or* la estudiante	student	*ehl ah-'loom-noh (lah ah-'loom-nah); ehl/lah eh-stoo-dee-'ahn-teh*
amable	kind	*ah-'mah-bleh*
amarillo(a)	yellow	*ah-mah-'ree-yoh(ah)*
ambiente, el	environment	*ehl ahm-bee-'ehn-teh*
ambulancia, la	ambulance	*lah ahm-boo-'lahn-see·ah*
amenaza, la	threat	*lah ah-meh-'nah-sah*
amigo, el (la amiga)	friend	*ehl ah-'mee-goh (lah ah-'mee-gah)*
amistad	friendship	*ah-mee-'stahd*
amistoso(a)	friendly	*ah-mee-'stoh-soh(ah)*
amor, el	love	*ehl ah-'mohr*

amparo, el	shelter	*ehl ahm-'pah-roh*
ampolla, la	blister	*lah ahm-'poh-yah*
anaranjado(a)	orange (color)	*ah-nah-rahn-'hah-doh(ah)*
ancho(a)	wide	*'ahn-choh(ah)*
anfiteatro, el	arena	*ehl ah-fee-teh-'ah-troh*
anillo, el	ring	*ehl ah-'nee-yoh*
animal de peluche, el	stuffed animal	*ehl ah-nee-'mahl deh peh-'loo-cheh*
animal, el	animal	*ehl ah-nee-'mahl*
ánimo, el	encouragement	*ehl 'ah-nee-moh*
año, el	year	*ehl 'ah-nyoh*
antes	before	*'ahn-tehs*
anuario, el	yearbook	*ehl ah-noo-'ah-ree·oh*
anuncio, el	announcement; bulletin; notice	*ehl ah-'noon-see-oh*
apartamento, el	apartment	*ehl ah-pahr-tah-'mehn-toh*
apellido, el	surname	*ehl ah-peh-'yee-doh*
apenas	just	*ah-'peh-nahs*
apoyo, el	support	*ehl ah-'poh-yoh*
aquí; acá	here	*ah-'kee; ah-'kah*
árbol, el	tree	*ehl 'ahr-bohl*
arboleda, la	grove	*lah ahr-boh-'leh-dah*
archivo, el	file	*ehl ahr-'chee-voh*
área, el	area	*ehl 'ah-reh-ah*
arena, la	sand	*lah ah-'reh-nah*
arete, el	earring	*ehl ah-'reh-teh*
argumento, el	argument	*ehl ahr-goo-'mehn-toh*
arma de fuego, el	firearm	*ehl 'ahr-mah deh 'fweh-goh*
armario, el	cupboard; locker	*ehl ahr-'mah-ree·oh*
arquitecto, el *or* la	architect	*ehl ahr-kee-'tehk-toh*
arriba	up	*ah-'rree-bah*
arroyo, el	stream	*ehl ah-'rroh-yoh*
arroz, el	rice	*ehl ah-'rrohs*
arte, el	art	*ehl 'ahr-teh*
artes industriales, las	industrial arts	*lahs 'ahr-tehs een-doos-tree-'ah-lehs*
artículo, el	article	*ehl ahr-'tee-koo-loh*
asamblea, la	assembly	*lah ah-sahm-'bleh-ah*
ascensor, el	elevator	*ehl ah-sehn-'sohr*
asiento, el	seat	*ehl ah-see-'ehn-toh*
asistencia, la	attendance	*lah ah-see-'stehn-see·ah*
asistente, el (la asistenta)	assistant	*ehl ah-see-'stehn-teh (lah ah-see-'stehn-tah)*
asociado, el (la asociada)	associate	*ehl ah-soh-see-'ah-doh (lah ah-soh-see-'ah-dah)*

áspero(a)	rough	*'ah-speh-roh(ah)*
aspirina, la	aspirin	*lah ah-spee-'ree-nah*
astronomía, la	astronomy	*lah ah-stroh-noh-'mee-ah*
asunto, el	topic	*ehl ah-'soon-toh*
asustado(a)	afraid	*ah-soo-'stah-doh(ah)*
atlas, el	atlas	*ehl 'aht-lahs*
atletismo, el	track and field	*ehl aht-leh-'tees-moh*
atornillador, el	screwdriver	*ehl ah-tohr-nee-yah-'dohr*
atún, el	tuna	*ehl ah-'toon*
audiencia, la	audience	*lah ow-dee-'ehn-see·ah*
audífonos, los	headphones; hearing aids	*lohs ow-'dee-foh-nohs*
auditorio, el	auditorium	*ehl ow-dee-'toh-ree·oh*
ausencia, la	absence	*lah ow-'sehn-see·ah*
autobús, el	bus	*ehl ow-toh-'boos*
autobús escolar, el	school bus	*ehl ow-toh-'boos eh-skoh-'lahr*
autor, el (la autora)	author	*ehl ow-'tohr, lah ow-'toh-rah*
avanzado(a)	advanced	*ah-vahn-'sah-doh(ah)*
avenida, la	avenue	*lah ah-veh-'nee-dah*
avión, el	airplane	*ehl ah-vee-'ohn*
aviso, el	notice	*ehl ah 'vee-soh*
ayer	yesterday	*ah-'yehr*
ayuda, la	assistance; help	*lah ah-'yoo-dah*
ayudante, el (la ayudanta)	aide; helper	*ehl ah-yoo-'dahn-teh (lah ah-yoo-'dahn-tah)*
ayudante (la ayudanta) de maestro, el	teacher's aide	*ehl ah-yoo-'dahn-teh (lah ah-yoo-'dahn-tah) deh mah-'eh-stroh*
azadón, el	hoe	*ehl ah-sah-'dohn*
azul	blue	*ah-'sool*
babero, el	bib	*ehl bah-'beh-roh*
bacinete, el	bassinet	*ehl bah-see-'neh-teh*
bádminton, el	badminton	*ehl 'bahd-meen-tohn*
baile, el	dance	*ehl 'bah-ee-leh*
bajo(a)	short (in height); shallow	*'bah-hoh(ah)*
balcón, el	balcony	*ehl bahl-'kohn*
balde, el	bucket	*ehl 'bahl-deh*
bancas, las	benches	*lahs 'bahn-kahs*
banco, el	bank	*ehl 'bahn-koh*
banda, la	band	*lah 'bahn-da*
bandeja, la	tray	*lah bahn-'deh-hah*
bandera, la	flag	*lah bahn-'deh-rah*
baño, el	restroom; bathroom	*ehl 'bah-nyoh*
banquete, el	banquet	*ehl bahn-'keh-teh*
banquillo, el	stool	*ehl bahn-'kee-yoh*

baraja de juguete, la	playing cards	*lah bah-'rah-hah deh hoo-'geh-teh*
barato(a)	cheap	*bah-'rah-toh(ah)*
barbilla, la	chin	*lah bahr-'bee-yah*
barco, el	boat	*ehl 'bahr-koh*
barrio, el	neighborhood	*ehl 'bah-rree·oh*
básquetbol, el	basketball	*ehl 'bah-skeht-bohl*
basura, la	trash	*lah bah-'soo-rah*
bata de bano, la	bathrobe	*lah 'bah-tah deh 'bahn-yoh*
batalla, la	battle	*lah bah-'tah-yah*
bate, el	bat	*ehl 'bah-teh*
baúl, el	chest (trunk)	*ehl bah-'ool*
bebé, el *or* la	baby	*ehl/lah beh-'beh*
bebedero, el	water fountain	*ehl beh-beh-'deh-roh*
beca, la	scholarship	*lah 'beh-kah*
béisbol, el	baseball	*ehl 'beh·ees-bohl*
bello(a)	beautiful	*'beh-yoh(ah)*
beneficios, los	benefits	*lohs beh-neh-'fee·see·ohs*
biberón, el	nursing bottle	*ehl bee-beh-'rohn*
biblioteca, la	library	*lah bee-blee-oh-'teh-kah*
bibliotecario, el (la bibliotecaria)	librarian	*ehl bee-blee-oh-teh-'kah-ree·oh (lah beeb-lee-oh-teh-'kah-ree·ah)*
bicicleta, la	bicycle	*lah bee-see-'kleh-tah*
bicicleta motorizada, la	moped	*lah bee-see-'kleh-tah moh-toh-ree-'sah-dah*
bien	fine	*'bee·ehn*
bienestar social, el	welfare	*ehl bee·ehn-eh-'stahr soh-see-'ahl*
bienvenidos(as)	welcome	*bee·ehn-veh-'nee-dohs(ahs)*
bilingüe	bilingual	*bee-'leen-gweh*
biografía, la	biography	*lah bee-oh-grah-'fee-ah*
biología, la	biology	*lah bee-oh-loh-'hee-ah*
bistec, el	steak	*ehl bee-'stehk*
blanco(a)	white	*'blahn-koh (ah)*
blando(a); suave	soft	*'blahn-doh(ah); 'swah-veh*
blusa, la	blouse	*lah 'bloo-sa*
boca, la	mouth	*lah 'boh-kah*
bocina, la	horn	*lah boh-'see-nah*
boleto, el	ticket	*ehl boh-'leh-toh*
bolsa, la	bag	*lah 'bohl-sah*
bomba, la	bomb	*lah 'bohm-bah*
bombero, el (la bombera)	firefighter	*ehl bohm-'beh-roh (lah bohm-'beh-rah)*
bondad, la	kindness	*lah bohn-'dahd*

bonito(a)	pretty	*boh-'nee-toh(ah)*
borracho, el	drunkard	*ehl boh-'rrah-choh (lah*
(la borracha)		*boh-'rrah-chah)*
borrador, el	eraser	*ehl boh-rrah-'dohr*
bosque, el	forest	*ehl 'boh-skeh*
bota, la	boot	*lah 'boh-tah*
bote para basura, el	trash can	*ehl 'boh-teh 'pah-rah bah-'soo-rah*
boxeo, el	boxing	*ehl bohk-'seh-oh*
bragas, las	panties	*lahs 'brah-gahs*
brazalete, el	bracelet	*ehl brah-sah-'leh-teh*
brazo, el	arm	*ehl 'brah-soh*
brocha, la	brush; paintbrush	*lah 'broh-chah*
bronceador, el	suntan lotion	*ehl broh-seh-ah-'dohr*
bueno(a)	good	*'bweh-noh(ah)*
bufanda, la	scarf	*lah boo-'fahn-dah*
buzón, el	mailbox	*ehl boo-'sohn*
caballete, el	easel	*ehl kah-bah-'yeh-teh*
caballitos, los	merry-go-round	*lohs kah-bah-'yee-tohs*
caballo, el	horse	*ehl kah-'bah-yoh*
cabeza, la	head	*lah kah-'beh-sah*
cable, el	cable	*ehl 'kah-bleh*
cadena, la	chain	*lah kah-'deh-nah*
cadera, la	hip	*lah kah-'deh-rah*
café	brown	*kah-'feh*
café, el	coffee	*ehl kah-'feh*
cafetería, la	cafeteria	*lah kah-feh-teh-'ree-ah*
caja, la	box	*lah 'kah-hah*
cajero, el (la cajera)	cashier	*ehl kah-'heh-roh (lah kah-'heh-rah)*
cajón de arena, el	sandbox	*ehl kah-'hohn deh ah-'reh-nah*
cajón, el	drawer	*ehl kah-'hohn*
calcetines, los	socks	*lohs kahl-seh-'tee-nehs*
calculadora, la	calculator	*lah kahl-koo-lah-'doh-rah*
cálculo, el	calculus; calculation	*ehl 'kahl-koo-loh*
calefacción, la	heating	*lah kah-leh-fahk-see-'ohn*
calendario, el	calendar	*ehl kah-lehn-'dah-ree·oh*
calentador, el	heater	*ehl kah-lehn-tah-'dohr*
caliente	hot	*kah-lee-'ehn-teh*
calificación, la	score	*lah kah-lee-fee-kah-see-'ohn*
calle, la	street	*lah 'kah-yeh*
callejón, el	alley	*ehl kah-yeh-'hohn*
calor, el	heat	*ehl kah-'lohr*
calvo(a)	bald	*'kahl-voh(ah)*
calzoncillos, los	shorts	*lohs kahl-sohn-'see-yohs*

cama, la	bed	*lah 'kah-mah*
cambio, el	change	*ehl 'kahm-bee·oh*
camino, el	road	*ehl kah-'mee-noh*
camión, el	truck	*ehl kah-mee-'ohn*
camisa, la	shirt	*lah kah-'mee-sah*
camiseta, la	T-shirt	*lah kah-mee-'seh-tah*
campamento, el	camp	*ehl kahm-pah-'mehn-toh*
campana, la	bell	*lah kahm-'pah-nah*
campo de recreo, el	playground	*ehl 'kahm-poh deh reh-'kreh-oh*
campo, el	campus; field	*ehl 'kahm-poh*
canasta, la	basket	*lah kah-'nah-stah*
cancha, la	court (tennis)	*lah 'kahn-chah*
canción, la	song	*lah kahn-see-'ohn*
candado, el	lock	*ehl kahn-'dah-doh*
canicas, las	marbles	*lahs kah-'nee-kahs*
cansado(a)	tired	*kahn-'sah-doh(ah)*
capacidad, la	capacity	*lah kah-pah-see-'dahd*
capitán, el (la capitana)	captain	*ehl kah-pee-'tahn (lah kah-pee-'tah-nah)*
capítulo, el	chapter	*ehl kah-'pee-too-loh*
cara, la	face	*lah 'kah-rah*
cárcel, la	jail	*lah 'kahr-sehl*
carnaval, el	carnival	*ehl kahr-nah-'vahl*
carne, la	beef	*lah 'kahr-neh*
caro(a)	expensive	*'kah-roh(ah)*
carpintero, el (la carpintera)	carpenter	*ehl kahr-peen-'teh-roh (lah kahr-peen-'teh-rah)*
carrera, la	race (competition)	*lah kah-'rreh-rah*
carreta, la	cart	*lah kah-'rreh-tah*
carretera, la	highway	*lah kah-rreh-'teh-rah*
carretilla, la	wheelbarrow	*lah kah-rreh-'tee-yah*
carrito de bebé, el	stroller	*ehl kah-'rree-toh deh beh-'beh*
carro, el	car	*ehl 'kah-rroh*
carta, la	letter (mail)	*lah 'kahr-tah*
cartel, el	poster	*ehl kahr-'tehl*
carterista, el (la carterista)	pickpocket	*ehl kahr-teh-'ree-stah (lah kahr-teh-'ree-stah)*
cartero, el *or* la	mail carrier	*ehl / lah kahr-'teh-roh*
cartón, el	cardboard	*ehl kahr-'tohn*
casa de muñecas, la	dollhouse	*lah 'kah-sah deh moo-'nyeh-kahs*
casa, la	house; home	*lah 'kah-sah*
casete, el	cassette	*ehl kah-'seh-teh*

castigo corporal, el	corporal punishment	*ehl kah-'stee-goh kohr-poh-'rahl*
castigo, el	punishment	*ehl kah-'stee-goh*
cebolla, la	onion	*lah seh-'boh-yah*
cementerio, el	cemetery	*ehl seh-mehn-'teh-ree·oh*
cena, la	dinner	*lah 'seh-nah*
centavo, el	cent	*ehl sehn-'tah-voh*
centro, el	center; downtown	*ehl 'sehn-troh*
cepillo, el	hairbrush	*ehl seh-'pee-yoh*
cerca	near	*'sehr-kah*
cerca, la	fence	*lah 'sehr-kah*
cerdo, el (la cerda)	pig	*ehl 'sehr-doh (lah 'sehr-dah)*
cerebro, el	brain	*ehl seh-'reh-broh*
ceremonia, la	ceremony	*lah seh-reh-'moh-nee·ah*
cerro, el	hill	*ehl 'seh-rroh*
cerrojo, el	latch	*ehl seh-'rroh-hoh*
certificado, el	certificate	*ehl sehr-tee-fee-'kah-doh*
césped, el	lawn	*ehl 'seh-spehd*
cesto de basura, el	wastebasket	*ehl 'seh-stoh deh bah-'soo-rah*
chaleco, el	vest	*ehl chah-'leh-koh*
chaqueta, la	jacket	*lah chah-'keh-tah*
charca, la	pond	*lah 'chahr-kah*
cheque, el	check	*ehl 'cheh-keh*
chicle, el	gum	*ehl 'chee-kleh*
chiste, el	joke	*ehl 'chee-steh*
chistoso(a)	funny	*chee-'stoh-soh(ah)*
chivo, el (la chiva)	goat	*ehl 'chee-voh (lah 'chee-vah)*
chocolate, el	chocolate	*ehl choh-koh-'lah-teh*
chofer de autobús, el *or* la	bus driver	*ehl / lah choh-'fehr deh ow-toh-'boos*
chofer, el *or* la	driver	*ehl / lah choh-'fehr*
chupete, el	pacifier	*ehl choo-'peh-teh*
ciego(a)	blind	*see-'eh-goh(ah)*
ciencia del mundo, la	earth science	*lah see-'ehn-see·ah dehl 'moon-doh*
ciencia, la	science	*lah see-'ehn-see·ah*
cierre, el	zipper	*ehl see-'eh-rreh*
cigarrillos, los	cigarettes	*lohs see-gah-'rree-yohs*
cine, el	movie theater	*ehl 'see-neh*
cinta, la	tape	*lah 'seen-tah*
cinta meritoria, la	ribbon (of merit)	*lah 'seen-tah meh-ree-'toh-ree·ah*
cinturón, el	belt	*ehl seen-too-'rohn*
cita, la	appointment	*lah 'see-tah*
ciudad, la	city	*lah see-oo-'dahd*

clase, la	class; classroom	*lah 'klah-seh*
clima, el	climate	*ehl 'klee-mah*
clínica, la	clinic	*lah 'klee-nee-kah*
club, el	club	*ehl kloob*
cobija, la	blanket	*lah koh-'bee-hah*
cocinero, el (la cocinera)	cook	*ehl koh-see-'neh-roh (lah koh-see-'neh-rah)*
código, el	code	*ehl 'koh-dee-goh*
codo, el	elbow	*ehl 'koh-doh*
collar, el	necklace	*ehl koh-'yahr*
color, el	color	*ehl koh-'lohr*
colores, los	colors	*lohs koh-'loh-rehs*
columpio, el	swing	*ehl koh-'loom-pee·oh*
combinación, la	slip	*lah kohm-bee-nah-see-'ohn*
comentario, el	comment	*ehl koh-mehn-'tah-ree·oh*
cometa, la	kite	*lah koh-'meh-tah*
comida, la	food	*lah koh-'mee-dah*
comité, el	committee	*ehl koh-mee-'teh*
cómo	how	*'koh-moh*
cómodo(a)	comfortable	*'koh-moh-doh(ah)*
compañero, el (la compañera)	companion, acquaintance	*ehl kohm-pah-'nyeh-roh (lah kohm-pah-'nyeh-rah)*
comportamiento, el	behavior; conduct	*ehl kohm-pohr-tah-mee-'ehn-toh*
computadora, la	computer	*lah kohm-poo-tah-'doh-rah*
comunicación, la	communication	*lah koh-moo-nee-kah-see-'ohn*
con	with	*kohn*
concepto, el	concept	*ehl kohn-'sehp-toh*
concurso, el	contest	*ehl kohn-'koor-soh*
condado, el	county	*ehl kohn-'dah-doh*
conejo, el (la coneja)	rabbit	*ehl koh-'neh-hoh (lah koh-'neh-hah)*
conferencia, la	conference	*lah kohn-feh-'rehn-see·ah*
confianza, la	trust	*lah kohn-fee-'ahn-sah*
conflicto, el	conflict	*ehl kohn-'fleek-toh*
confundido(a)	confused	*kohn-foon-'dee-doh(ah)*
congelador, el	freezer	*ehl kohn-heh-lah-'dohr*
congelamiento, el	frostbite	*ehl kohn-heh-lah-mee-'ehn-toh*
cono, el	cone	*ehl 'koh-noh*
consejero, el (la consejera)	counselor	*eh kohn-seh-'heh-roh (lah kohn-seh-'heh-rah)*
consejo, el	counseling	*ehl koh-'seh-hoh*
consentimiento, el	consent	*ehl kohn-sehn-tee-mee-'ehn-toh*
conserje, el	janitor	*ehl kohn-'sehr-heh*

consultor, el **(la consultora)**	consultant	*ehl kohn-sool-'tohr (lah kohn- sool-'toh-rah)*
contaminación, la	pollution	*lah kohn-tah-mee-nah-see- 'ohn*
contenido, el	content	*ehl kohn-teh-'nee-doh*
contento(a)	happy	*kohn-'tehn-toh(ah)*
contrato, el	contract	*ehl kohn-'trah-toh*
contusión, la	bruise	*lah kohn-too-see-'ohn*
convención, la	convention	*lah kohn-vehn-see-'ohn*
copiadora, la	copier	*lah koh-pee-ah-'doh-rah*
corazón, el	heart	*ehl koh-rah-'sohn*
corbata, la	tie	*lah kohr-'bah-tah*
coro, el	choir	*ehl 'koh-roh*
corral de juego, el	playpen	*ehl koh-'rrahl deh 'hweh-goh*
correcto(a)	correct	*koh-'rrehk-toh(ah)*
correo, el	post office	*ehl koh-'rreh-oh*
correo electrónico, el	E-mail	*ehl koh-'rreh-oh eh-lehk-'troh- nee-koh*
correr a campo traviesa, el	cross country	*ehl koh-'rrehr ah 'kahm-poh trah-vee-'eh-sah*
cortadora de césped, la	lawnmower	*lah kohr-tah-'doh-rah deh 'seh-spehd*
cortadura, la	cut	*lah kohr-tah-'doo-rah*
corte, la	court (law); courthouse	*lah 'kohr-teh*
cortés	polite	*kohr-'tehs*
corto(a)	short (in length)	*'kohr-toh(ah)*
costa, la	coast	*lah 'koh-stah*
costo, el	cost	*ehl 'koh-stoh*
costumbre, la	custom	*lah koh-'stoom-breh*
creativo(a)	creative	*kreh-ah-'tee-voh(ah)*
crédito, el	credit	*ehl 'kreh-dee-toh*
creencia, la	belief	*lah kreh-'ehn-see·ah*
crema, la	cream	*lah 'kreh-mah*
criadero, el	nursey	*ehl kree-ah-'deh-roh*
crimen, el	crime	*ehl 'kree-mehn*
criminal, el *or* la	criminal	*ehl / lah kree-mee-'nahl*
cruce de peatones, el	crosswalk	*ehl 'kroo-seh deh peh-ah-'toh- nehs*
cuaderno, el	notebook	*ehl kwah-'dehr-noh*
cuadrado, el	square	*ehl kwah-'drah-doh*
cuál	which	*kwahl*
cuándo	when	*'kwahn-doh*
cuánto	how much	*'kwahn-toh*
cuántos	how many	*'kwahn-tohs*
cuarto(a)	fourth	*'kwahr-toh(ah)*

cuarto, el	room	*ehl 'kwahr-toh*
cubiertos, los	silverware	*lohs koo-bee-'ehr-tohs*
cubito, el	(play) block	*ehl koo-'bee-toh*
cuchara, la	spoon	*lah koo-'chah-rah*
cuchillo, el	knife	*ehl koo-'chee-yoh*
cuello, el	neck	*ehl 'kweh-yoh*
cuenta, la	bill; score	*lah 'kwehn-tah*
cuento, el	story	*ehl 'kwehn-toh*
cuerda para brincar, la	jump rope	*lah 'kwehr-dah 'pah-rah breen-'kahr*
cuerpo, el	body	*ehl 'kwehr-poh*
cuestionario, el	quiz	*ehl kweh-stee·oh-'nah-ree·oh*
cueva, la	cave	*lah 'kweh-vah*
cuidado de la salud, el	health care	*ehl kwee-'dah-doh deh lah sah-'lood*
cuidado, el	care	*ehl kwee-'dah-doh*
culpable	guilty	*kool-'pah-bleh*
cultura, la	culture	*lah kool-'too-rah*
cuna, la	crib	*lah 'koo-nah*
cuna mecedora, la	cradle	*lah 'ko-nah meh-seh-'doh-rah*
cupón, el	coupon	*ehl koo-'pohn*
curita, la	Band Aid®	*lah koo-'ree-tah*
curso, el	course	*ehl 'koor-soh*
daño, el	harm	*ehl 'dah-nyoh*
datos, los	data	*lohs 'dah-tohs*
de	from; of	*deh*
de quién	whose	*deh kee-'ehn*
débil	weak	*'deh-beel*
décimo(a)	tenth	*'deh-see-moh(ah)*
dedo, el	finger; toe	*ehl 'deh-doh*
delantal, el	apron	*ehl deh-lahn-'tahl*
delgado(a)	thin	*dehl-'gah-doh(ah)*
delicioso(a)	delicious	*deh-lee-see-'oh-soh(ah)*
delicuente, el *or* la	delinquent	*ehl/lah deh-leen-'kwehn-teh*
dentista, el (la dentista)	dentist	*ehl dehn-'tee-stah (lah dehn-'tee-stah)*
departamento de bomberos, el	fire department	*ehl deh-pahr-tah-'mehn-toh deh bohm-'beh-rohs*
departamento, el	department	*ehl deh-pahr-tah-'mehn-toh*
dependiente, el (la dependienta)	clerk	*ehl deh-pehn-dee-'ehn-teh (lah deh-pehn-dee-'ehn-tah)*
deporte, el	sport	*ehl deh-'pohr-teh*
deportes competitivos, los	competitive athletics	*lohs deh-'pohr-tehs kohm-peh-tee-'tee-vohs*
depósito, el	bin; storage	*ehl deh-'poh-see-toh*

derecho(a)	right	*lah deh-'reh-choh(ah)*
derechos civiles, los	civil rights	*lohs deh-'reh-chohs see-'vee-lehs*
desagüe, el	sewage	*ehl dehs-'ah-gweh*
desastre, el	disaster	*ehl deh-'sah-streh*
desayuno, el	breakfast	*ehl deh-sah-'yoo-noh*
descanso, el	break	*ehl deh-'skahn-soh*
desconocido, el (la desconocida)	stranger	*ehl dehs-koh-noh-'see-doh (lah dehs-koh-noh-'see-dah)*
descripción, la	description	*lah deh-skreep-see-'ohn*
descubrimiento, el	discovery	*ehl deh-skoo-bree-mee-'ehn-toh*
descuidado(a)	careless	*dehs-kwee-'dah-doh(ah)*
desempleo, el	unemployment	*ehl dehs-ehm-'pleh-oh*
desfile, el	parade	*ehl dehs-'fee-leh*
desierto, el	desert	*ehl deh-see-'ehr-toh*
desperdicios, los	waste	*lohs dehs-pehr-'dee-see·ohs*
después	afterward	*deh-'spwehs*
destacado(a); sobresaliente	outstanding	*deh-stah-'kah-doh(ah); soh-breh-sah-lee-'ehn-teh*
detector de humo, el	smoke detector	*ehl deh-tehk-'tohr deh 'oo-moh*
detención, la	detention	*lah deh-tehn-see-'ohn*
detrás	behind	*deh-'trahs*
día, el	day	*ehl 'dee-ah*
día feriado, el	holiday	*ehl 'dee-ah feh-ree-'ah-doh*
diagrama, el	chart	*ehl dee-ah-'grah-mah*
diapositiva, la	transparency	*lah dee-ah-poh-see-'tee-vah*
dibujos animados, los	cartoons	*lohs dee-'boo-hohs ah-nee-'mah-dohs*
dibujos, los	pictures	*lohs dee-'boo-hohs*
diccionario, el	dictionary	*ehl deek-see-oh-'nah-ree·oh*
diciembre	December	*dee-see-'ehm-bre*
dientes, los	teeth	*lohs dee-'ehn-tehs*
diferencia, la	difference	*lah dee-feh-'rehn-see·ah*
difícil	difficult	*dee-'fee-seel*
dinero, el	money	*ehl dee-'neh-roh*
Dios	God	*dee-'ohs*
dirección, la	address	*lah dee-rehk-see-'ohn*
director (la directora) del departamento, el	chairperson	*ehl dee-rehk-'tohr (lah dee-rehk-'toh-rah) dehl deh-pahr-tah-'mehn-toh*
director, el (la directora)	director; principal	*ehl dee-rehk-'tohr (lah dee-rehk-'toh-rah)*
disciplina, la	discipline	*lah dee-see-'plee-nah*
disco, el	disk	*ehl 'dee-skoh*

discos compactos, los	CDs	*lohs 'dee-skohs kohm-'pahk-tohs*
discriminación, la	discrimination	*lah dee-skree-mee-nah-see-'ohn*
discurso, el	speech	*ehl dee-'skoor-soh*
discusión, la	argument	*lah dees-koo-see-'ohn*
disparo, el	shooting	*ehl dee-'spah-roh*
disponible	available	*dee-spoh-'nee-bleh*
dispuesto(a)	cooperative	*dee-'spweh-stoh(ah)*
distancia, la	distance	*lah dee-'stahn-see·ah*
distribuidor, el (la distribuidora)	dispenser	*ehl dee-stree-boo-ee-'dohr (lah dee-stree-boo-ee-'doh-rah)*
distrito, el	district	*ehl dee-'stree-toh*
disturbio, el	disturbance; riot	*ehl dee-'stoor-bee·oh*
divertido(a)	fun	*dee-vehr-'tee-doh(ah)*
división, la	division	*lah dee-vee-see-'ohn*
divorcio, el	divorce	*ehl dee-'vohr-see·oh*
doble, el	double	*ehl 'doh-bleh*
docena, la	dozen	*lah doh-'seh-nah*
doctor, el (la doctora)	doctor	*ehl dohk-'tohr (lah dohk-'toh-rah)*
dólar, el	dollar	*ehl 'doh-lahr*
dolor de cabeza, el	headache	*ehl doh-'lohr deh kah-'beh-sah*
dolor de espalda, el	backache	*ehl doh-'lohr deh eh-'spahl-dah*
dolor de estómago, el	stomachache	*ehl doh-'lohr deh eh-'stoh-mah-goh*
dolor, el	pain	*ehl doh-'lohr*
domingo	Sunday	*doh-'meen-goh*
donación, la	donation	*lah doh-nah-see-'ohn*
dónde	where	*'dohn-deh*
dormitorio, el	bedroom; dormitory	*ehl dohr-mee-'toh-ree·oh*
drama, el	drama; play (theater)	*ehl 'drah-mah*
droga, la	drug	*lah 'droh-gah*
drogadicto, el (la drogadicta)	drug addict	*ehl drohg-ah-'deek-toh (lah drohg-ah-'deek-tah)*
dueño, el (la dueña)	owner	*ehl 'dweh-nyoh (lah 'dweh-nyah)*
dulce	sweet	*'dool-seh*
dulces, los	candy	*lohs 'dool-sehs*
duro(a)	hard	*'doo-roh(ah)*
economía, la	economics	*lah eh-koh-noh-'mee-ah*
edad, la	age	*lah eh-'dahd*
edificio, el	building	*ehl eh-dee-'fee-see·oh*

educación especial, la	special education	*lah eh-doo-kah-see-'ohn eh-speh-see-'ahl*
educación física, la	physical education	*lah eh-doo-kah-see-'ohn 'fee-see-kah*
educador, el (la educadora)	educator	*ehl eh-doo-kah-'dohr (lah eh-doo-kah-'doh-rah)*
ejemplo, el	example	*ehl eh-'hehm-ploh*
ejercicio, el	exercise	*ehl eh-hehr-'see-see·oh*
él	he	*ehl*
agente de policía, el *or* **la**	police officer	*ehl / lah ah-'hehn-teh deh poh-lee-'see-ah*
elección, la	election	*lah eh-lehk-see-'ohn*
electricidad, la	electricity	*lah eh-lehk-tree-see-'dahd*
electrodoméstico, el	appliance	*ehl eh-lehk-troh-doh-'meh-stee-koh*
ella	she	*'eh-yah*
ellos(as)	they	*'eh-yohs(as)*
embarazo, el	pregnancy	*ehl ehm-bah-'rah-soh*
emblema, el	badge	*ehl ehm-'bleh-mah*
emergencia, la	emergency	*lah eh-mehr-'hehn-see·ah*
empleado, el (la empleada)	employee	*ehl ehm-pleh-'ah-doh (lah ehm-pleh-'ah-dah)*
en	at; in; on	*ehn*
en frente de	in front of	*ehn 'frehn-teh deh*
enchufe, el	electrical outlet	*ehl ehn-'choo-feh*
enciclopedia, la	encyclopedia	*lah ehn-see-kloh-'peh-dee·ah*
encima	above	*ehn-'see-mah*
encuadernador, el	binder	*ehl ehn-kwah-dehr-nah-'dohr*
enero	January	*eh-'neh-roh*
enfermedad, la	illness	*lah ehn-fehr-meh-'dahd*
enfermera, la (el enfermero)	nurse	*lah ehn-fehr-'meh-rah (ehl ehn-fehr-'meh-roh)*
enfermo(a)	sick	*ehn-'fehr-moh*
enfoque, el	approach	*ehl ehn-'foh-keh*
engrapadora, la	stapler	*lah ehn-grah-pah-'doh-rah*
enojado(a)	angry; upset	*eh-noh-'hah-doh(ah)*
ensalada, la	salad	*lah ehn-sah-'lah-dah*
ensayo, el	essay	*ehl ehn-'sah-yoh*
enseñanza de conducir, la	driver's education	*lah ehn-seh-'nyahn-sah deh kohn-doo-'seer*
entonces	then	*ehn-'tohn-sehs*
entrada, la	entrance	*lah ehn-'trah-dah*
entrada para carros, la	driveway	*lah ehn-'trah-dah 'pah-rah 'kah-rrohs*

entrenador, el (la entrenadora)	trainer; coach	*ehl ehn-treh-nah-'dohr (lah ehn-treh-nah-'doh-rah)*
entrenamiento, el	training	*ehl ehn-treh-nah-mee-'ehn-toh*
entrevista, la	interview	*lah ehn-treh-'vee-stah*
envenenamiento, el	poisoning	*ehl ehn-veh-neh-nah-mee-'ehn-toh*
equilibrio, el	balance	*ehl eh-kee-'lee-bree·oh*
equipo, el	team; equipment	*ehl eh-'kee-poh*
equivocado(a)	wrong	*eh-kee-voh-'kah-doh(ah)*
eructo, el	burp	*ehl eh-'rook-toh*
escalera, la	stairs	*lah eh-skah-'leh-rah*
escalera mecánica, la	escalator	*lah eh-skah-'leh-rah meh-'kah-nee-kah*
escalones, los	steps	*lohs eh-skah-'loh-nehs*
escena, la	scene	*lah eh-'seh-nah*
escoba, la	broom	*lah eh-'skoh-bah*
escribir a máquina, el	typing	*ehl eh-skree-'beer ah 'mah-kee-nah*
escritorio, el	desk	*ehl ehs-kree-'toh-ree·oh*
escritura, la	writing	*lah eh-skree-'too-rah*
escuela, la	school	*lah eh-'skweh-lah*
escuela primaria, la	grade school	*lah eh-'skweh-lah pree-'mah-ree·ah*
escuela secundaria, la	high school	*lah eh-'skweh-lah seh-koon-'dah-ree·ah*
ese(a)(o)	that	*'eh-seh(ah)(oh)*
esos(as)	those	*'eh-sohs(ahs)*
espacio, el	space	*ehl eh-'spah-see·oh*
espalda, la	back	*lah eh-'spahl-dah*
especialista, el *or* la	specialist	*ehl / lah eh-speh-see-ah-'lee-stah*
espectáculo, el	show	*ehl eh-spehk-'tah-koo-loh*
espejo, el	mirror	*ehl eh-'speh-hoh*
esperanza, la	hope	*lah eh-speh-'rahn-sah*
espinaca, la	spinach	*lah eh-spee-'nah-kah*
espíritu, el	spirit	*ehl eh-'spee-ree-too*
esponja, la	sponge	*lah eh-'spohn-hah*
esposa, la	wife	*lah eh-'spoh-sah*
esposas, las	handcuffs	*lahs eh-'spoh-sahs*
esposo, el	husband	*ehl eh-'spoh-soh*
esquina, la	corner	*lah eh-'skee-nah*
esta noche	tonight	*'eh-stah 'noh-cheh*
estación de autobús, la	bus station	*lah eh-stah-see-'ohn deh ow-toh-'boos*

estación de policía, la	police station	*lah eh-stah-see-'ohn deh poh-lee-'see-ah*
estacionamiento, el	parking lot	*ehl eh-stah-see·oh-nah-mee-'ehn-toh*
estadio, el	stadium	*ehl eh-'stah-dee·oh*
estado, el	state	*ehl eh-'stah-doh*
estante, el	rack	*ehl eh-'stahn-teh*
estatua, la	statue	*lah eh-'stah-too-ah*
estatura, la	height	*lah eh-stah-'too-rah*
este	east	*'eh-steh*
este(a)	this	*'eh-steh(ah)*
estéreo, el	stereo	*ehl eh-'steh-reh-oh*
estómago, el	stomach	*ehl eh-'stoh-mah-goh*
estornudo, el	sneeze	*ehl eh-stohr-'noo-doh*
estos(as)	these	*'eh-stohs(ahs)*
estrategia, la	strategy	*lah eh-strah-'teh-hee·ah*
estrecho(a)	narrow	*eh-'streh-choh(ah)*
estrella, la	star	*lah eh-'streh-yah*
estudiante, el *or* la	student	*ehl / lah eh-stoo-dee-'ahn-teh*
estudio, el	study	*ehl eh-'stoo-dee·oh*
estudios sociales, los	social studies	*lohs eh-'stoo-dee·ohs soh-see-'ah-lehs*
estufa, la	stove	*lah eh-'stoo-fah*
etiqueta, la	sticker; label	*lah eh-tee-'keh-tah*
evacuación, la	evacuation	*lah eh-vah-koo-ah-see-'ohn*
evaluación, la	assessment; evaluation	*lah eh-vah-loo-ah-see-'ohn*
evento, el	event	*ehl eh-'vehn-toh*
evidencia, la	evidence	*lah eh-vee-'dehn-see·ah*
examen, el	test; exam	*ehl ehk-'sah-meh*
excelente	excellent	*ehk-seh-'lehn-teh*
excusado, el	toilet	*ehl ehk-skoo-'sah-doh*
explosión, la	explosion	*lah ehk-sploh-see-'ohn*
expulsión, la	expulsion	*lah ehk-spool-see-'ohn*
extensión, la	extension	*lah ehk-stehn-see-'ohn*
extintor, el	fire extinguisher	*ehl ehks-teen-'tohr*
extranjero(a)	foreign	*ehks-trahn-'heh-roh(ah)*
fábrica, la	factory	*lah 'fah-bree-kah*
fácil	easy	*'fah-seel*
facilitador, el (la facilitadora)	facilitator	*ehl fah-see-lee-tah-'dohr (lah fah-see-lee-tah-'doh-rah*
faja, la	girdle	*lah 'fah-hah*
falda, la	skirt	*lah 'fahl-dah*
familia, la	family	*lah fah-'mee-lee·ah*
fantástico(a)	fantastic	*fahn-'tah-stee-koh(ah)*
farmacia, la	pharmacy	*lah fahr-'mah-see·ah*

fax, el	fax	*ehl fahks*
febrero	February	*feh-'breh-roh*
fecha, la	date	*lah 'feh-chah*
felicitaciones, las	congratulations	*lahs feh-lee-see-tah-see-'oh-nehs*
feo(a)	ugly	*'feh-oh(ah)*
festival, el	festival	*ehl feh-stee-'vahl*
fiebre, la	fever	*lah fee-'eh-breh*
fiesta, la	party	*lah fee-'eh-stah*
fila, la	row	*lah 'fee-lah*
filosofía, la	philosophy	*lah fee-loh-soh-'fee-ah*
finanzas, las	finance	*lahs fee-'nahn-sahs*
firma, la	signature	*lah 'feer-mah*
física, la	physics	*lah 'fee-see-kah*
flecha, la	arrow	*lah 'fleh-chah*
flor, la	flower	*lah flohr*
florero, el	vase	*ehl floh-'reh-roh*
folleto, el	brochure	*ehl foh-'yeh-toh*
fondos, los	funding	*lohs 'fohn-dohs*
fórmula, la	formula	*lah 'fohr-moo-lah*
formulario, el	form	*ehl fohr-moo-'lah-ree·oh*
fósforo, el	match	*ehl 'fohs-foh-roh*
foto, la	photo	*lah 'foh-toh*
fracaso, el	failure	*ehl frah-'kah-soh*
fracción, la	fraction	*lah frahk-see-'ohn*
fraude, el	cheating	*ehl 'frow-deh*
fresa, la	strawberry	*lah 'freh-sah*
frijoles, los	beans	*lohs free-'hoh-lehs*
frío(a)	cold	*'free-oh(ah)*
frontón con raqueta, el	racquetball	*ehl frohn-'tohn kohn rah-'keh-tah*
frontón de mano, el	handball	*ehl frohn-'tohn deh 'mah-noh*
fruta, la	fruit	*lah 'froo-tah*
fuegos artificiales, los	fireworks	*lohs 'fweh-gohs ahr-tee-fee-see-'ah-lehs*
fuente, la	fountain	*lah 'fwehn-teh*
fuerte	strong	*'fwehr-teh*
fuerzas armadas, las	armed forces	*lahs 'fwehr-sahs ahr-'mah-dahs*
función, la	function	*lah foon-see-'ohn*
funcionarios, los	staff	*lohs foon-see-oh-'nah-ree·ohs*
fútbol americano, el	football	*ehl 'foot-bohl ah-meh-ree-'kah-noh*
fútbol, el	soccer	*ehl 'foot-bohl*
futuro, el	future	*ehl foo-'too-roh*

gabinete, el	cabinet	*ehl gah-bee-'neh-teh*
galardón, el	award	*ehl gah-lahr-'dohn*
galleta, la	cookie	*lah gah-'yeh-tah*
gallina, la	hen	*lah gah-'yee-nah*
gancho, el	hanger	*ehl 'gahn-choh*
garaje, el	garage	*ehl gah-'rah-heh*
garganta, la	throat	*lah gahr-'gahn-tah*
gasolinera, la	gas station	*lah gah-soh-lee-'neh-rah*
gato, el (la gata)	cat	*ehl 'gah-toh (lah 'gah-tah)*
gelatina, la	jello	*lah heh-lah-'tee-nah*
gente, la	people	*lah 'hehn-teh*
geografía, la	geography	*lah heh-oh-grah-'fee-ah*
geometría, la	geometry	*lah heh-oh-meh-'tree-ah*
gimnasia, la	gymnastics	*lah heem-'nah-see·ah*
gimnasio, el	gym	*ehl heem-'nah-see·oh*
gis, el	crayon	*ehl hees*
globo, el	balloon	*ehl 'gloh-boh*
glosario, el	glossary	*ehl gloh-'sah-ree·oh*
gobierno, el	government	*ehl goh-bee-'ehr-noh*
golf, el	golf	*ehl gohlf*
gordo(a)	fat	*'gohr-doh(ah)*
gorra, la	cap	*lah 'goh-rrah*
gracias	thanks	*'grah-see·ahs*
grado, el	degree (measurement); grade (level)	*ehl 'grah-doh*
graduación, la	graduation	*lah grah-doo-ah-see-'ohn*
gráfico, el	graph	*ehl 'grah-fee-koh*
grafiti, el	graffiti	*ehl grah-'fee-tee*
gramática, la	grammar	*lah grah-'mah-tee-kah*
grande	big	*'grahn-de*
gratis	free	*'grah-tees*
grifo, el	faucet	*ehl 'gree-foh*
grosero(a)	rude	*groh-'seh-roh(ah)*
grúa, la	tow truck	*lah 'groo-ah*
grueso(a)	thick	*groo-'eh-soh(ah)*
grupo, el	group	*ehl 'groo-poh*
guante, el	glove	*ehl 'gwahn-teh*
guapo(a)	handsome	*'gwah-poh(ah)*
guardería, la	nursery	*lah gwahr-deh-'ree-ah*
guardia de seguridad, el *or* la	security guard	*ehl / lah 'gwahr-dee·ah deh seh-goo-ree-'dahd*
guardia del tráfico, el *or* la	crossing guard	*ehl / lah 'gwahr-dee·ah dehl 'trah-fee-koh*
guerra, la	war	*lah 'geh-rrah*
habilidad, la	skill	*lah ah-bee-lee-'dahd*

hacha, el	ax	*ehl 'ah-chah*
hambre, el	hunger	*ehl 'ahm-breh*
hamburguesa, la	hamburger	*lah ahm-boor-'geh-sah*
hecho, el	fact	*ehl 'eh-choh*
helado, el	ice cream	*ehl eh-'lah-doh*
herida, la	injury	*lah eh-'ree-dah*
hermana, la	sister	*lah ehr-'mah-nah*
hermano, el	brother	*ehl ehr-'mah-noh*
herramienta, la	tool	*lah eh-rrah-mee-'ehn-tah*
herrumbre, la	rust	*lah eh-'rroom-breh*
hielo, el	ice	*ehl 'yeh-loh*
hierba, la	weed	*lah 'yehr-bah*
hígado, el	liver	*ehl 'ee-gah-doh*
hija, la	daughter	*lah 'ee-ha*
hijo, el	son	*ehl 'ee-hoh*
hilo, el	string	*ehl 'ee-loh*
hipo, el	hiccup	*ehl 'ee-poh*
historia de Europa, la	European history	*lah ee-'stoh-ree·ah deh eh·oo-'roh-pah*
historia de los Estados Unidos, la	U.S. history	*lah ee-'stoh-ree·ah deh lohs eh-'stah-dohs oo-'nee-dohs*
hockey, el	ice hockey	*ehl 'hoh-kee*
hoja informativa, la	flyer	*lah 'oh-hah een-fohr-mah-'tee-vah*
hoja, la	sheet	*lah 'oh-hah*
hola	hi	*'oh·lah*
holgazán, el (la holgazana)	loiterer	*ehl ohl-gah-'sahn (lah ohl-gah-'sah-nah)*
hombre, el	man	*ehl 'ohm-breh*
hombro, el	shoulder	*ehl 'ohm-broh*
honradez, la	honesty	*lah ohn-rah-'dehs*
hora, la	hour; time	*lah 'oh-rah*
horario, el	schedule	*ehl oh-'rah-ree·oh*
horno de microonda, el	microwave	*ehl 'ohr-noh deh mee-kroh-'ohn-dah*
horno, el	oven	*ehl 'ohr-noh*
hospital, el	hospital	*ehl oh-spee-'tahl*
hoy	today	*'oh·ee*
hoyo, el	hole	*ehl 'oh-yoh*
huelga, la	strike	*lah 'wehl-gah*
huerta, la	orchard	*lah 'wehr-tah*
huésped, el *or* la	guest	*ehl / lah 'weh-spehd*
huevo, el	egg	*ehl 'weh-voh*
humanidades, las	humanities	*lahs oo-mah-nee-'dah-dehs*
huracán, el	hurricane	*ehl oo-rah-'kahn*

idea, la	idea	*lah ee-'deh-ah*
identificación, la	I.D.	*lah ee-dehn-tee-fee-kah-see-'ohn*
idioma, el	language	*ehl ee-dee-'oh-mah*
iglesia, la	church	*lah ee-'gleh-see·ah*
imán, el	magnet	*ehl ee-'mahn*
impermeable, el	raincoat	*ehl eem-pehr-meh-'ah-bleh*
importante	important	*eem-pohr-'tahn-teh*
incapacitado(a)	handicapped	*een-kah-pah-see-'tah-doh(ah)*
incendio, el	fire	*ehl een-'sehn-dee·oh*
incompleto(a)	incomplete	*een-kohm-'pleh-toh(ah)*
incorrecto(a)	incorrect	*een-koh-'rrehk-toh(ah)*
incursión, la	raid	*lah een-koor-see-'ohn*
independencia, la	independence	*lah een-deh-pehn-'dehn-see·ah*
individualizado(a)	individualized	*een-dee-vee-doo-ah-lee-'sah-doh(ah)*
industria, la	industry	*lah een-'doo-stree·ah*
infección, la	infection	*lah een-fehk-see-'ohn*
información, la	information	*lah een-fohr-mah-see-'ohn*
ingeniero, el (la ingeniera)	engineer	*ehl een-heh-nee-'eh-roh (lah een-heh-nee-'eh-rah)*
inglés como segundo idioma, el	English as a second language	*ehl een-'glehs 'koh-moh seh-'goon-doh ee-dee-'oh-mah*
inscripción, la	registration	*lah een-skreep-see-'ohn*
insolación, la	sunstroke	*lah een-soh-lah-see-'ohn*
institución, la	institution	*lah een-stee-too-see-'ohn*
instituto, el	institute	*ehl een-stee-'too-toh*
instrucción, la	instruction	*lah een-strook-see-'ohn*
instructor, el (la instructora)	instructor	*ehl een-strook-'tohr (lah een-strook-'toh-rah)*
instrumento, el	instrument	*ehl een-stroo-'mehn-toh*
interesante	interesting	*een-teh-reh-'sahn-teh*
intérprete, el *or* la	interpreter	*ehl / lah een-'tehr-preh-teh*
interruptor, el	switch	*ehl een-teh-rroop-'tohr*
intruso, el (la intrusa)	trespassing	*ehl een-'troo-soh (lah een-'troo-sah)*
inundación, la	flood	*lah een-oon-dah-see-'ohn*
investigación, la	research	*lah een-veh-stee-gah-see-'ohn*
invierno, el	winter	*ehl een-vee-'ehr-noh*
irrespetuoso(a)	disrespectful	*ee-reh-speh-too-'oh-soh(ah)*
izquierdo(a)	left	*ees-kee-'ehr-doh(ah)*
jabón, el	soap	*ehl hah-'bohn*
jamón, el	ham	*ehl hah-'mohn*
jardín, el	garden	*ehl hahr-'deen*

jardinero, el (la jardinera)	gardener	*ehl hahr-dee-'neh-roh (lah hahr-dee-'neh-rah)*
joven	young	*'hoh-vehn*
joyas, las	jewelry	*lahs 'hoh-yahs*
jubilación, la	retirement	*lah hoo-bee-lah-see-'ohn*
juego de damas, el	checkers	*ehl 'hoo·ee-goh deh 'dah-mahs*
juego, el	game; set	*ehl 'joo·eh-goh*
jueves	Thursday	*'hweh-vehs*
jugador, el (la jugadora)	player	*ehl hoo-gah-'dohr (lah hoo-gah-'doh-rah)*
jugo, el	juice	*ehl 'hoo-goh*
juguete, el	toy	*ehl hoo-'geh-teh*
julio	July	*'hoo-lee·oh*
junio	June	*'hoo-nee·oh*
junta de educación	Board of Education	*lah 'hoon-tah deh eh-doo-kah-see-'ohn*
junta, la	council	*lah 'hoon-tah*
justicia, la	justice	*lah hoo-'stee-see·ah*
justo(a)	fair	*'hoo-stoh(ah)*
la llave de incendios, la	hydrant	*lah 'yah-veh deh een-'sehn-dee·ohs*
labio, el	lip	*ehl 'lah-bee·oh*
laboratorio, el	laboratory	*ehl lah-boh-rah-'toh-ree·oh*
lado, el	side	*ehl 'lah-doh*
ladrón, el (la ladrona)	thief	*ehl lah-'drohn (lah lah-'droh-nah)*
lago, el	lake	*ehl 'lah-goh*
lámpara, la	lamp	*lah 'lahm-pah-rah*
lapicero, el; pluma, la	pen	*ehl lah-pee-'seh-roh; lah 'ploo-mah*
lápiz, el	pencil	*ehl 'lah-pees*
largo(a)	long	*'lahr-goh(ah)*
largo, el	length	*ehl 'lahr-goh*
lavadora, la	washer	*lah lah-vah-'doh-rah*
lavamanos, el	sink	*ehl lah-vah-'mah-nohs*
lavaplatos, el	dishwasher	*ehl lah-vah-'plah-tohs*
lección, la	lesson	*lah lehk-see-'ohn*
leche, la	milk	*lah 'leh-cheh*
lechuga, la	lettuce	*lah leh-'choo-gah*
lectura, la	reading	*lah lehk-'too-rah*
lejos	far	*'leh-hohs*
lengua, la	tongue	*lah 'lehn-gwah*
lenguaje de sordomudos, el	sign language	*ehl lehn-'gwah-heh deh sohr-doh-'moo-dohs*

lenguaje, el; idioma, el	language	*ehl lehn-'gwah-heh; ehl ee-dee-'oh-mah*
lentamente	slowly	*lehn-tah-'mehn-teh*
lente, el	lens	*ehl 'lehn-teh*
lentes de seguridad, los	safety glasses	*lohs 'lehn-tehs deh seh-goo-ree-'dahd*
lentes de sol, los	sunglasses	*lohs 'lehn-tehs deh sohl*
lentes, los	glasses	*lohs 'lehn-tehs*
letra, la	letter (alphabet)	*lah 'leh-trah*
letrero, el	billboard; sign	*ehl leh-'treh-roh*
ley, la	law	*lah leh·ee*
libertad, la	freedom	*lah lee-behr-'tahd*
libra, la	pound	*lah 'lee-brah*
librería, la	bookstore	*lah lee-breh-'ree-ah*
libreta, la	folder	*lah lee-'breh-tah*
libro de cuentos, el	storybook	*ehl 'lee-broh deh 'kwehn-tohs*
libro de texto, el	textbook	*ehl 'lee-broh deh 'tehks-toh*
libro, el	book	*ehl 'lee-broh*
licencia, la	license	*lah lee-'sehn-see·ah*
licenciatura, la	degree (college)	*lah lee-sehn-see·ah-'too-rah*
licor, el	liquor	*ehl lee-'kohr*
líder, el *or* la	leader	*ehl / lah 'lee-dehr*
liga, la	league	*lah 'lee·gah*
limón, el	lemon	*ehl lee-'mohn*
limonada, la	lemonade	*lah lee-moh-'nah-dah*
limosnero, el (la limosnera)	beggar	*ehl lee-mohs-'neh-roh (lah lee-mohs-'neh-rah)*
limpiador, el	duster	*ehl leem-pee-ah-'dohr*
limpio(a)	clean	*'leem-pee·oh(ah)*
línea, la	line	*lah 'lee-neh-ah*
linterna, la	flashlight	*lah leen-'tehr-nah*
liso(a)	smooth	*'lee-soh(ah)*
lista, la	list	*lah 'lee-stah*
listo(a)	clever; ready	*'lee-stoh(ah)*
literatura en inglés, la	English literature	*lah lee-teh-rah-'too-rah ehn een-'glehs*
llamada, la	phone call	*lah yah-'mah-dah*
llave inglesa, la	wrench	*lah 'yah-veh een-'gleh-sah*
llave, la	key	*lah 'yah-veh*
lluvia, la	rain	*lah 'yoo-vee·ah*
loción, la	lotion	*lah loh-see-'ohn*
lodo, el	mud	*ehl 'loh-doh*
lote, el	lot	*ehl 'loh-teh*
lucha libre, la	wrestling	*lah 'loo-chah 'lee-breh*
lugar, el	place	*ehl loo-'gahr*

luna, la	moon	*lah 'loo-nah*
lunes	Monday	*'loo-nehs*
lupa, la	magnifying glass	*lah 'loo-pah*
luz, la	light	*lah loos*
madera, la	wood	*lah mah-'deh-rah*
madrastra, la	stepmother	*lah mah-'drah-strah*
madre, la	mother	*lah 'mah-dreh*
madrina, la	godmother	*lah mah-'dree-nah*
maestro, el (la maestra); el profesor (la profesora)	teacher	*'ehl mah-'eh-stroh (lah mah-'eh-strah); ehl proh-feh-'sohr (lah proh-feh-'soh-rah)*
maíz, el	corn	*ehl mah-'ees*
malo(a)	bad	*'mah-loh(ah)*
mañana	tomorrow	*mah-'nyah-nah*
mano, la	hand	*lah 'mah-noh*
mantenimiento, el	maintenance	*ehl mahn-teh-nee-mee-'ehn-toh*
manzana, la	apple	*lah mahn-'sah-nah*
mapa, el	map	*ehl 'mah-pah*
maquillaje, el	makeup	*ehl mah-kee-'yah-heh*
máquina de coser, la	sewing machine	*lah 'mah-kee-nah deh koh-'sehr*
máquina, la	machine	*lah 'mah-kee-nah*
máquina de escribir, la	typewriter	*lah 'mah-kee-nah 'deh eh-skree-'beer*
maquinaria, la	machinery	*lah mah-kee-'nah-ree·ah*
mar, el	sea	*ehl mahr*
maravilloso(a)	marvelous	*mah-rah-vee-'yoh-soh(ah)*
marca, la	mark	*lah 'mahr-kah*
marcador, el	marker	*ehl mahr-kah-'dohr*
marco, el	picture frame	*ehl 'mahr-koh*
mareos, los	dizziness	*lohs mah-'reh-ohs*
martes	Tuesday	*'mahr-tehs*
martillo, el	hammer	*ehl mahr-'tee-yoh*
marzo	March	*'mahr-soh*
más	more	*mahs*
más tarde	later	*'mahs tahr-deh*
mascota, la	pet	*lah mah-'skoh-tah*
matemáticas, las	mathematics	*lahs mah-teh-'mah-tee-kahs*
materia, la	material	*lah mah-'teh-ree·ah*
materiales, los; provisiones, las	supplies	*lohs mah-teh-ree-'ah-lehs; lahs proh-vee-see-'oh-nehs*
matrícula, la	enrollment	*lah mah-'tree-koo-lah*
mayo	May	*'mah-yoh*
mayonesa, la	mayonnaise	*lah mah-yoh-'neh-sah*

mayor	older	*mah-'yohr*
mecánico, el *or* **la**	mechanic	*ehl / lah meh-'kah-nee-koh*
mecanógrafo, el (la mecanógrafa)	typist	*ehl meh-kah-'noh-grah-foh (lah meh-kah-'noh-grah-fah)*
medalla, la	medal	*lah meh-'dah-yah*
medias, las	stockings	*lahs 'meh-dee·ahs*
medicina, la	medicine	*lah meh-dee-'see-nah*
médico, el *or* **la**	physician	*ehl / lah 'meh-dee-koh*
medios de comunicación, los	media	*lohs 'meh-dee·ohs deh koh-moo-nee-kah-see-'ohn*
mejilla, la	cheek	*lah meh-'hee-yah*
mejor	better	*meh-'hohr*
melocotón, el	peach	*ehl meh-loh-koh-'tohn*
memorándum, el	memo	*ehl meh-moh-'rahn-doom*
memoria, la	memory	*lah meh-'moh-ree·ah*
menor	younger	*meh-'nohr*
menor de edad, el *or* **la**	minor	*ehl / lah meh-'nohr deh eh-'dahd*
menos	less	*'meh-nohs*
mentor, el (la mentora)	mentor	*ehl mehn-'tohr (lah mehn-'toh-rah)*
mercado, el	market	*ehl mehr-'kah-doh*
merienda, la	snack	*lah meh-ree-'ehn-dah*
merienda campestre, la	picnic	*lah meh-ree-'ehn dah kahm-'peh-streh*
mes, el	month	*ehl mehs*
mesa, la	table	*lah 'meh-sah*
meta, la	goal	*lah 'meh-tah*
método, el	method	*ehl 'meh-toh-doh*
metro, el	meter (length); subway	*ehl 'meh-troh*
mi(s)	my	*mee(s)*
microscopio, el	microscope	*ehl mee-kroh-'skoh-pee·oh*
miembro, el *or* **la**	member	*ehl / lah mee-'ehm-broh*
miércoles	Wednesday	*mee-'ehr-koh-lehs*
minusvalía, la	disability	*lah mee-noos-vah-'lee-ah*
mío(a)	mine	*'mee-oh(ah)*
mitad, la	half	*lah mee-'tahd*
mitones, los	mittens	*lohs mee-'toh-nehs*
mochila, la	backpack	*lah moh-'chee-lah*
modelo, el	model	*ehl moh-'deh-loh*
modificado(a)	modified	*moh-dee-fee-'kah-doh(ah)*
mojado(a)	wet	*moh-'hah-doh(ah)*
molino, el	treadmill	*ehl moh-'lee-noh*
monitor, el	monitor	*ehl moh-nee-'tohr*
monstruo, el *or* **la**	monster	*ehl / lah 'mohn-stroo-oh*

montaña, la	mountain	*lah mohn-'tah-nyah*
morado(a)	purple	*moh-'rah-doh(ah)*
moreno(a)	brunette; dark-haired	*moh-'reh-noh(ah)*
mostaza, la	mustard	*lah moh-'stah-sah*
motocicleta, la	motorcycle	*lah moh-toh-see-'kleh-tah*
motor, el	engine	*ehl moh-'tohr*
movimiento, el	motion	*ehl moh-vee-mee-'ehn-toh*
muchacho, el (la muchacha)	teenager	*ehl moo-'chah-choh (lah moo-'chah-chah)*
mucho(a)	much	*'moo-choh(ah)*
muchos(as)	many	*'moo-chohs(ahs)*
mudo(a)	mute	*'moo-doh(ah)*
muebles, los	furniture	*lohs 'mweh-blehs*
muerte, la	death	*lah 'mwehr-teh*
muestra en transparencia, la	slide (microscope)	*lah 'mweh-strah ehn trahns-pah-'rehn-see·ah*
muestra, la	sample	*lah 'mweh-strah*
mujer, la	woman	*lah moo-'hehr*
muletas, las	crutches	*lahs moo-'leh-tahs*
mundo, el	world; globe	*ehl 'mon-doh*
muñeca, la	doll; wrist	*lah moo-'nyeh-kah*
municipio, el	city hall	*ehl moo-nee-'see-pee·oh*
museo, el	museum	*ehl moo-'seh-oh*
música, la	music	*lah 'moo-see-kah*
nacimiento, el	birth	*ehl nah-see-mee-'ehn-toh*
nación, la	nation	*lah nah-see-'ohn*
nacionalidad, la	nationality	*lah nah-see·oh-nah-lee-'dahd*
naranja, la	orange (fruit)	*lah nah-'rahn-hah*
nariz, la	nose	*lah nah-'rees*
náusea, la	nausea	*lah 'now-seh-ah*
nave espacial, la	rocket	*lah 'nah-veh eh-spah-see-'ahl*
Navidad, la	Christmas	*lah nah-vee-'dahd*
necesario(a)	necessary	*neh-seh-'sah-ree·oh(ah)*
necesidades, las	needs	*lahs neh-seh-see-'dah-dehs*
negro(a)	black	*'neh-groh(ah)*
nervioso(a)	nervous	*nehr-vee-'oh-soh(ah)*
nieta, la	granddaughter	*lah nee-'eh-tah*
nieto, el	grandson	*ehl nee-'eh-toh*
nieve, la	snow	*lah nee-'eh-veh*
niña, la	girl	*lah 'nee-nyah*
niño, el	boy	*ehl 'nee-nyoh*
nivel, el	level	*ehl nee-'vehl*
nombre, el	name	*ehl 'nohm-breh*
norte	north	*'nohr-teh*
nosotros(as)	we	*noh-'soh-trohs(as)*

nota, la	grade (academic); note	*lah 'noh-tah*
noticia, la	notice	*lah noh-'tee-see·ah*
novela, la	novel	*lah noh-'veh-lah*
noveno(a)	ninth	*noh-'veh-noh(ah)*
novia, la	girlfriend; bride	*lah 'noh-vee·ah*
noviembre	November	*noh-vee-'ehm-breh*
novio, el	boyfriend; groom	*ehl 'noh-vee·oh*
nuestro(a)	our	*'nweh-stroh(ah)*
número, el	number	*ehl 'noo-meh-roh*
nunca	never	*'noon-kah*
o	or	*oh*
objetivo, el	objective	*ehl ohb-heh-'tee-voh*
objetos de escritorio, los	stationery	*lohs ohb-'heh-tohs deh eh-skree-'toh-ree·oh*
océano, el	ocean	*ehl oh-'seh-ah-noh*
octavo(a)	eighth	*ohk-'tah-voh (ah)*
octubre	October	*ohk-'too-breh*
ocupación, la	occupation	*lah oh-koo-pah-see-'ohn*
ocupado(a)	busy	*oh-koo-'pah-doh(ah)*
oeste	west	*oh-'eh-steh*
oficial, el *or* la	official	*ehl / lah oh-fee-see-'ahl*
oficina, la	office	*lah oh-fee-'see-nah*
oficina principal, la	main office	*lah oh-fee-'see-nah preen-see-'pahl*
ojo, el	eye	*ehl 'oh-hoh*
olla, la	pot	*lah 'oh-yah*
onza, la	ounce	*lah 'ohn-sah*
operario, el (la operaria)	operator	*ehl oh-peh-'rah-ree·oh (lah oh-peh-'rah-ree·ah)*
opinión, la	opinion	*lah oh-pee-nee-'ohn*
orador, el (la oradora)	speaker (person)	*ehl oh-rah-'dohr (lah oh-rah-'doh-rah)*
oreja, la	ear	*lah oh-'reh-hah*
organización, la	organization	*lah ohr-gah-nee-sah-see-'ohn*
organizado(a)	organized	*ohr-gah-nee-'sah-doh(ah)*
orientación, la	orientation	*lah oh-ree-ehn-tah-see-'ohn*
orinal, el	urinal	*ehl oh-ree-'nahl*
orquesta, la	orchestra	*lah ohr-'keh-stah*
otoño, el	fall (season)	*ehl oh-'toh-nyoh*
oveja, la	sheep	*lah oh-'veh-hah*
paciencia, la	patience	*lah pah-see-'ehn-see·ah*
padrastro, el	stepfather	*ehl pah-'drah-stroh*
padre, el	father; parent	*ehl 'pah-dreh*
padrino, el	godfather	*ehl pah-'dree-noh*
página, la	page	*lah 'pah-hee-nah*

pago, el	payment	*ehl 'pah-goh*
país, el	country	*ehl pah-'ees*
pájaro, el	bird	*ehl 'pah-hah-roh*
pala, la	shovel	*lah 'pah-lah*
palabra, la	word	*lah pah-'lah-brah*
palo, el	stick	*ehl 'pah-loh*
pañal, el	diaper	*ehl pah-'nyahl*
pandilla, la	gang	*lah pahn-'dee-yah*
pandillero, el	gang member	*ehl pahn-dee-'yeh-roh (lah*
(la pandillera)		*pahn-dee-'yeh-rah)*
pantalla, la	screen	*lah pahn-'tah-yah*
pantalones, los	pants	*lohs pahn-tah-'loh-nehs*
pañuelo, el	handkerchief	*ehl pah-nyoo-'eh-loh*
papa, la	potato	*lah 'pah-pah*
papel, el	paper	*ehl pah-'pehl*
papel higiénico, el	toilet paper	*ehl pah-'pehl ee-hee-'eh-nee-koh*
papitas, las	potato chips	*lahs pah-'pee-tahs*
paquete, el	pack	*ehl pah-'keh-teh*
par, el	pair	*ehl pahr*
para	for	*'pah-rah,*
parada de autobús, la	bus stop	*lah pah-'rah-dah deh ow-toh-'boos*
paraguas, el	umbrella	*ehl pah-'rah-gwahs*
pared, la	wall	*lah pah-'rehd*
pariente, el *or* la	relative	*ehl / lah pah-ree-'ehn-teh*
parque, el	park	*ehl 'pahr-keh*
parquímetro, el	meter (parking)	*ehl pahr-'kee-meh-troh*
pasajero, el (la pasajera)	passenger	*ehl pah-sah-'heh-roh (lah pah-sah-'heh-rah)*
pase, el	pass	*ehl 'pah-seh*
pasillo, el	aisle; hall	*ehl pah-'see-yoh*
paso, el	step	*ehl 'pah-soh*
pastel, el	pie	*ehl pah-'stehl*
pasto, el	grass	*ehl pah-'stoh*
patines, los	skates	*lohs pah-'tee-nehs*
patinetas, las	skateboards	*lahs pah-tee-'neh-tahs*
pato, el (la pata)	duck	*ehl 'pah-toh (lah 'pah-tah)*
patrocinador, el	sponsor	*ehl pah-troh-see-nah-'dohr*
(la patrocinadora)		*(lah pah-troh-see-nah-'doh-rah)*
pavo, el (la pava)	turkey	*ehl 'pah-voh (lah 'pah-vah)*
paz, la	peace	*lah pahs*
peatón, el (la peatona)	pedestrian	*ehl peh-ah-'tohn (lah peh-ah-'toh-nah)*

392

pecera, la	fishbowl	*lah peh-'seh-rah*
pecho, el	chest (body)	*ehl 'peh-choh*
pegamento, el	glue	*ehl peh-gah-'mehn-toh*
peine, el	comb	*ehl 'peh·ee-neh*
pelea, la	fight	*lah peh-'leh-ah*
película, la	film	*lah peh-'lee-koo-lah*
peligro, el	danger	*ehl peh-'lee-groh*
peligroso(a)	dangerous	*peh-lee-'groh-soh(ah)*
pelirrojo(a)	red-headed	*peh-lee-'rroh-hoh(ah)*
pelo, el	hair	*ehl 'peh-loh*
pelota, la	ball	*lah peh-'loh-tah*
pensamiento, el	thought	*ehl pehn-sah-mee-'ehn-toh*
peor	worse	*peh-'ohr*
pequeño(a)	little; small	*peh-'keh-nyoh(ah)*
pera, la	pear	*lah 'peh-rah*
perdido(a)	lost	*pehr-'dee-doh(ah)*
periódico, el	newspaper	*ehl peh-ree-'oh-dee-koh*
periodismo, el	journalism	*ehl peh-ree-oh-'dees-moh*
período, el	term	*ehl peh-'ree-oh-doh*
permiso, el	permit; pass	*ehl pehr-'mee-soh*
pero	but	*'peh-roh*
perro caliente, el	hot dog	*ehl 'peh-rroh kah-lee-'ehn-teh*
perro, el (la perra)	dog	*ehl 'peh-rroh (lah 'peh-rrah)*
persona, la	person	*lah pehr-'soh-nah*
personal, el	personnel	*ehl pehr-soh-'nahl*
personalidad, la	personality	*lah pehr-soh-nah-lee-'dahd*
pesas, las	weights	*lahs 'peh-sahs*
pescado, el	fish (out of the water)	*ehl peh-'skah-doh*
peso, el	weight	*ehl 'peh-soh*
pestillo, el	deadbolt	*ehl peh-'stee-yoh*
pez, el	fish (in water)	*ehl pehs*
pie, el	foot	*ehl 'pee-eh*
piedra, la	stone	*lah pee-'eh-drah*
piel, la	skin	*lah pee-'ehl*
pierna, la	leg	*lah pee-'ehr-nah*
pijama, el	pajamas	*ehl pee-'yah-mah*
pimienta, la	pepper	*lah pee-mee-'ehn-tah*
pintor, el (la pintora)	painter	*ehl peen-'tohr (lah peen-'toh-rah)*
pintura, la	paint; painting	*lah peen-'too-rah*
piscina, la	pool	*lah pee-'see-nah*
piso, el	floor	*ehl 'pee-soh*
pizarrón, el	chalkboard	*ehl pee-sah-'rrohn*
plan de estudios, el	curriculum	*ehl plahn deh eh-'stoo-dee·ohs*
plan, el	plan	*ehl plahn*

planeta, el	planet	*ehl plah-'neh-tah*
planta, la	plant	*lah 'plahn-tah*
plástico, el	plastic	*ehl 'plah-stee-koh*
plastilina, la	modeling clay	*lah plah-stee-'lee-nah*
plátano, el	banana	*ehl 'plah-tah-noh*
plato, el	plate	*ehl 'plah-toh*
plato hondo, el	bowl	*ehl 'plah-toh 'ohn-doh*
playa, la	beach	*lah 'plah-yah*
plaza, la	courtyard	*lah 'plah-sah*
plomero, el (la plomera)	plumber	*ehl ploh-'meh-roh (lah ploh-'meh-rah)*
pluma, la	feather; pen	*lah 'ploo-mah*
población, la	population	*lah poh-blah-see-'ohn*
pobre	poor	*'poh-breh*
pobreza, la	poverty	*lah poh-'breh-sah*
pocos(as)	few	*'poh-kohs(ahs)*
poesía, la	poetry	*lah poh-eh-'see-ah*
policía, la	police	*lah poh-lee-'see-ah*
política, la	politics	*lah poh-'lee-tee-kah*
pollo, el	chicken	*ehl 'poh yoh*
polo acuático, el	water polo	*ehl 'poh-loh ah-'kwah-tee-koh*
polvo, el	powder	*ehl 'pohl-voh*
por	for	*pohr*
por favor	please	*pohr fah-'vohr*
por qué	why	*pohr keh*
porcentaje, el	percentage	*ehl pohr-sehn-'tah-heh*
portal, el	porch	*ehl pohr-'tahl*
portón, el	gate	*ehl pohr-'tohn*
poste, el	pole	*ehl 'poh-steh*
postre, el	dessert	*ehl 'poh-streh*
práctica, la	practice	*lah 'prahk-tee-kah*
pregunta, la	question	*lah preh-'goon-tah*
premio, el	prize	*ehl 'preh-mee·oh*
preocupado(a)	worried	*preh-oh-koo-'pah-doh(ah)*
presidente, el (la presidenta)	president	*ehl preh-see-'dehn-teh (lah preh-see-'dehn-tah)*
préstamo, el	loan	*ehl 'preh-stah-moh*
presupuesto, el	budget	*ehl preh-soo-'pweh-stoh*
primavera, la	spring	*lah pree-mah-'veh-rah*
primero(a)	first	*pree-'meh-roh(ah)*
primo, el (la prima)	cousin	*ehl 'pree-moh (lah 'pree-mah)*
principio, el	principle	*ehl preen-'see-pee·oh*
prisma, el	prism	*ehl 'prees-mah*
privado(a)	private	*pree-'vah-doh(ah)*
privilegio, el	privilege	*ehl pree-vee-'leh-hee·oh*

problema, el	problem	*ehl proh-'bleh-mah*
procedimiento, el	procedure	*ehl proh-seh-dee-mee-'ehn-toh*
proceso, el	process	*ehl proh-'seh-soh*
producto químico, el	chemical	*ehl proh-'dook-toh 'kee-mee-koh*
profundo(a)	deep	*proh-'foon-doh(ah)*
programa, el	program; software	*ehl proh-'grah-mah*
programación, la	program (computer)	*lah proh-grah-mah-see-'ohn*
programador, el (la programadora)	programmer	*ehl proh-grah-mah-'dohr (lah proh-grah-mah-'doh-rah)*
promedio, el	average	*ehl proh-'meh-dee·oh*
promoción, la	promotion	*lah proh-moh-see-'ohn*
pronto	soon	*'prohn-toh*
propiedad, la	property	*lah proh-pee-eh-'dahd*
prostituta, la	prostitute	*lah proh-stee-'too-tah*
postración, la	heat stroke; shock	*lah poh-strah-see-'ohn*
provisiones, las	supplies	*lahs proh-vee-see-'oh-nehs*
proyecto, el	project	*ehl proh-yehk-'toh*
proyector, el	projector	*ehl proh-yehk-'tohr*
prueba, la	test	*lah proo-'eh-bah;*
psicología, la	psychology	*lah see-koh-loh-'hee-ah*
psicólogo, el (la psicóloga)	psychologist	*ehl see-'koh-loh-goh (lah see-'koh-loh-gah)*
psiquiatra, el *or* la	psychiatrist	*ehl / lah see-kee-'ah-trah*
público, el	public	*ehl 'poob-lee-koh*
puente, el	bridge	*ehl 'pwehn-teh*
puerta, la	door	*lah 'pwehr-tah*
pulgada, la	inch	*lah pool-'gah-dah*
pulmones, los	lungs	*lohs pool-'moh-nehs*
punto, el	point	*ehl 'poon-toh*
puntual	punctual	*poon-too-'ahl*
pupitre, el	desk	*ehl poo-'pee-treh*
qué	what	*keh*
quemadura, la	burn	*lah keh-mah-'doo-rah*
querido, el	sweetheart	*ehl keh-'ree-doh*
quién	who	*kee-'ehn*
quieto(a)	quiet	*kee-'eh-toh(ah)*
química, la	chemistry	*lah 'kee-mee-kah*
quinto(a)	fifth	*'keen-toh(ah)*
quizás	maybe	*kee-'sahs*
rama, la	branch	*lah 'rah-mah*
rampa, la	ramp	*lah 'rahm-pah*
rápidamente	quickly	*'rah-pee-dah-mehn-teh*
raqueta, la	racket	*lah rah-'keh-tah*
raro(a)	strange	*'rah-roh(ah)*

rasguño, el	scrape	*ehl rahs-'goo-nyoh*
rastrillo, el	rake	*ehl rah-'stree-yoh*
raza, la	race (people)	*lah 'rah-sah*
razón, la	reason	*lah rah-'sohn*
recado, el	message	*ehl reh-'kah-doh*
recepcionista, el *or* la	receptionist	*ehl / lah reh-sehp-see·oh-'nee-stah*
receta médica, la	prescription	*lah reh-'seh-tah 'meh-dee-kah*
recibo, el	receipt	*ehl reh-'see-boh*
recogedor de basura, el	dustpan	*ehl reh-koh-heh-'dohr deh bah-'soo-rah*
recolección de fondos, la	fundraising	*lah reh-koh-lehk-see-'ohn deh 'fohn-dohs*
recomendación, la	recommendation	*lah reh-koh-mehn-dah-see-'ohn*
recompensa, la	reward	*lah reh-kohm-'pehn-sah*
recurso, el	resource	*ehl reh-'koor-soh*
red, la	net	*lah rehd*
rendimiento, el	performance	*ehl rehn-dee-mee-'ehn-toh*
refresco, el	soft drink	*ehl reh-'freh-skoh*
refrigerador, el	refrigerator	*ehl reh-free-heh-rah-'dohr*
refugio, el	shelter	*ehl reh-'foo-hee·oh*
regalo, el	gift	*ehl reh-'gah-loh*
región, la	region	*lah reh-hee-'ohn*
regla, la	rule; ruler	*lah 'reh-glah*
relación, la	relationship	*lah reh-lah-see-'ohn*
relaciones públicas, las	public relations	*lahs reh-lah-see-'oh-nehs 'poob-lee-kahs*
relajado(a)	relaxed	*reh-lah-'hah-doh(ah)*
religión, la	religion	*lah reh-lee-hee-'ohn*
reloj, el	clock; watch	*ehl reh-'loh*
repisa, la	shelf	*lah reh-'pee-sah*
reporte, el	report	*ehl reh-'pohr-teh*
rescate, el	rescue	*ehl reh-'skah-teh*
respeto, el	respect	*ehl reh-'speh-toh*
responsabilidad, la	responsibility	*lah reh-spohn-sah-bee-lee-'dahd*
respuesta, la	answer	*lah reh-'spweh-stah*
restaurante, el	restaurant	*ehl reh-stah·oo-'rahn-teh*
resultado, el	result	*ehl reh-sool-'tah-doh*
resumen, el	summary	*ehl reh-'soo-mehn*
retraso, el	delay; procrastination	*ehl reh-'trah-soh*
retrato, el	portrait	*ehl reh-'trah-toh*
reunión, la	meeting	*lah reh-oo-nee-'ohn*
revés, al	backwards	*ahl reh-'vehs*

revista, la	magazine	*lah reh-'vee-stah*
rico(a)	rich	*'ree-koh(ah)*
riesgo, el	risk	*ehl ree-'ehs-goh*
rima, la	rhyme	*lah 'ree-mah*
río, el	river	*ehl 'ree-oh*
riqueza, la	wealth	*lah ree-'keh-sah*
robo, el	robbery	*ehl 'roh-boh*
rociadora, la	sprinkler	*lah roh-see·ah-'doh-rah*
rodilla, la	knee	*lah roh-'dee-yah*
rojo(a)	red	*'roh-hoh(ah)*
rompecabezas, el	puzzle	*ehl rohm-peh-kah-'beh-sahs*
ropa interior, la	underwear	*lah 'roh-pah een-teh-ree-'ohr*
ropa, la	clothing	*lah 'roh-pah*
rubio(a)	blond	*'roo-bee·oh(ah)*
ruidoso(a)	loud	*roo-ee-'doh-soh(ah)*
sábado	Saturday	*'sah-bah-doh*
sacapuntas, el	pencil sharpener	*ehl sah-kah-'poon-tahs*
saco, el	sportcoat	*ehl 'sah-koh*
sal, la	salt	*lah sahl*
salida, la	exit	*lah sah-'lee-da*
salón, el	large room; lounge	*ehl sah-'lohn*
salsa de tomate, la	tomato sauce	*lah 'sahl-sah deh toh-'mah-teh*
salud, la	health	*lah sah-'lood*
sandalias, las	sandals	*lahs sahn-'dah-lee·ahs*
sangre, la	blood	*lah 'sahn-greh*
sano(a)	healthy	*'sah-noh(ah)*
sartén, el	pan	*ehl sahr-'tehn*
satisfactorio	satisfactory	*sah-tees-fahk-'toh-ree·oh*
secadora, la	dryer	*lah seh-kah-'doh-rah*
sección, la	section	*lah sehk-see-'ohn*
seco(a)	dry	*'seh-koh (ah)*
secretario, el (la secretaria)	secretary	*ehl seh-kreh-'tah-ree·oh (lah seh-kreh-'tah-ree·ah)*
secreto, el	secret	*ehl seh-'kreh-toh*
segundo(a)	second	*seh-'goon-doh(ah)*
seguridad, la	safety; security	*lah seh-goo-ree-'dahd*
seguro(a)	safe; sure	*seh-'goo-roh(ah)*
seguro, el	insurance	*ehl seh-'goo-roh*
seguro social, el	social security	*ehl seh-'goo-roh soh-see-'ahl*
selva, la	jungle	*lah 'sehl-vah*
semáforo, el	traffic signal	*ehl seh-'mah-foh-roh*
semana, la	week	*lah seh-'mah-nah*
seminario, el	seminar	*ehl seh-mee-'nah-ree·oh*
señal de parada, la	stop sign	*lah seh-'nyahl deh pah-'rah-dah*

señal, la	signal	*lah seh-'nyahl*
señor, el (Sr.)	mister (Mr.)	*ehl seh-'nyohr*
señora, la (Sra.)	lady (Mrs.)	*lah seh-'nyoh-rah*
sentimiento, el	feeling	*ehl sehn-tee-mee-'ehn-toh*
septiembre	September	*sehp-tee-'ehm-breh*
séptimo(a)	seventh	*'sehp-tee-moh(ah)*
serio(a)	serious	*'seh-ree·oh(ah)*
serrucho, el	saw	*ehl seh-'rroo-choh*
servicial	helpful	*sehr-vee-see-'ahl*
servicio, el	restroom	*ehl sehr-'vee-see·oh*
servilleta, la	napkin	*lah sehr-vee-'yeh-tah*
sexo, el	sex	*ehl 'sehk-soh*
sexto(a)	sixth	*'sehks-toh(ah)*
si	if	*see*
sí	yes	*see*
siempre	always	*see-'ehm-preh*
silbato, el	whistle	*ehl seel-'bah-toh*
silencio, el	silence	*ehl see-'lehn-see·oh*
silla de ruedas, la	wheelchair	*lah 'see-yah deh 'rweh-dahs*
silla, la	chair	*lah 'see-yah*
sillón, el	armchair	*ehl see-'yohn*
simpático	nice	*seem-'pah-tee-koh*
simulacro de incendio, el	fire drill	*ehl see-moo-'lah-kroh deh een-'sehn-dee·oh*
simulacro, el	drill (exercise)	*ehl see-moo-'lah-kroh*
sin	without	*seen*
sindicato, el	trade union	*ehl seen-dee-'kah-toh*
sirena, la	siren	*lah see-'reh-nah*
sistema solar, el	solar system	*ehl see-'steh-mah soh-'lahr*
sitio, el	site	*ehl 'see-tee·oh*
sobre, el	envelope	*ehl 'soh-breh*
sobredosis, la	overdose	*lah soh-breh-'doh-sees*
sobresaliente	outstanding	*soh-breh-sah-lee-'ehn-'teh*
sobretiempo, el	overtime	*ehl soh-breh-tee-'ehm-poh*
sobrina, la	niece	*lah soh-'bree-nah*
sobrino, el	nephew	*ehl soh-'bree-noh*
socio, el (la socia)	partner	*ehl 'soh-see·oh (lah 'soh-see·ah)*
sofá, el	sofa	*ehl soh-'fah*
sófbol, el	softball	*ehl 'sohf-bohl*
soga, la	rope	*lah 'soh-gah*
sol, el	sun	*ehl sohl*
soldado, el *or* la	soldier	*ehl / lah sohl-'dah-doh*
soleado(a)	sunny	*soh-leh-'ah-doh(ah)*
soledad, la	loneliness	*lah soh-leh-'dahd*

solicitud, la	application	*lah soh-lee-see-'tood*
solución, la	solution	*lah soh-loo-see-'ohn*
sombrero, el	hat	*ehl sohm-'breh-roh*
sonajero, el	rattle	*ehl soh-nah-'heh-roh*
sonido, el	sound	*ehl soh-'nee-doh*
sonrisa, la	smile	*lah sohn-'ree-sah*
sopa, la	soup	*lah 'soh-pah*
soporte, el	stand	*ehl soh-'pohr-teh*
sordo(a)	deaf	*'sohr-doh(ah)*
sorprendido(a)	surprised	*sohr-prehn-'dee-doh(ah)*
sorteo, el	raffle	*ehl sohr-'teh-oh*
sospechoso, el	suspect	*ehl soh-speh-'choh-soh (lah*
(la sospechosa)		*soh-speh-'choh-sah)*
sostén, el	brassiere	*ehl soh-'stehn*
su	her; his	*soo*
su(s)	their; your	*soo(s)*
subdirector, el	vice-principal	*ehl soob-dee-rehk-'tohr (lah*
(la subdirectora)		*soob-dee-rehk-'toh-rah)*
subibaja, el	seesaw	*ehl soo-bee-'bah-hah*
subterráneo(a)	underground	*soob-teh-'rrah-neh-oh(ah)*
sucio(a)	dirty	*'soo-see·oh(ah)*
sudadera, la	sweatsuit	*lah soo-dah-'deh-rah*
sueldo, el	wages	*ehl 'swehl-doh*
sueño, el	dream	*ehl 'sweh-nyoh*
suéter, el	sweater	*ehl 'sweh-tehr*
sugerencia, la	suggestion	*lah soo-heh-'rehn-see·ah*
suma, la	sum	*lah 'soo-mah*
superintendente, el *or* la	superintendent	*ehl / lah soo-pehr-een-tehn-*
		'dehn-teh
supermercado, el	supermarket	*ehl soo-pehr-mehr-'kah-doh*
supervisión, la	supervision	*lah soo-pehr-vee-see-'ohn*
supervisor, el	supervisor	*ehl soo-pehr-vee-'sohr (lah soo-*
(la supervisora)		*pehr-vee-'soh-rah)*
sur	south	*soor*
suspensión, la	suspension	*lah soo-spehn-see-'ohn*
tablero de anuncios, el	bulletin board	*ehl tah-'bleh-roh deh ah-*
		'noon-see·ohs
tachuela, la	thumbtack	*lah tah-choo-'eh-lah*
taladro, el	drill (tool)	*ehl tah-'lah-droh*
talco, el	talcum powder	*ehl 'tahl-koh*
taller, el	workshop	*ehl tah-'yehr*
tapete, el	mat	*ehl tah-'peh-teh*
tardanza, la	tardiness	*lah tahr-'dahn-sah*
tarde	late	*'tahr-deh*
tarea, la	assignment	*lah tah-'reh-ah*

tarjeta, la	card	*lah tahr-'heh-tah*
tasa, la	rate	*lah 'tah-sah*
taza, la	cup	*lah 'tah-sah*
tazón, el	beaker	*ehl tah-'sohn*
té, el	tea	*ehl teh*
teatro, el	theater	*ehl teh-'ah-troh*
teclado, el	keyboard	*ehl teh-'klah-doh*
técnica, la	technique	*lah 'tehk-nee-kah*
técnico, el *or* la	technician	*ehl / lah 'tehk-nee-koh*
tela, la	cloth	*lah 'teh-lah*
teléfono, el	telephone	*ehl teh-'leh-foh-noh*
teléfono celular, el	cellular phone	*ehl teh-'leh-foh-noh seh-loo-'lahr*
telescopio, el	telescope	*ehl teh-leh-'skoh-pee·oh*
televisor, el	television (set)	*ehl teh-leh-vee-'sohr*
tema, el	subject; theme	*ehl 'teh-mah*
temblor, el	earthquake	*ehl tehm-'blohr*
temprano(a)	early	*tehm-'prah-noh(ah)*
tenedor, el	fork	*ehl teh-neh-'dohr*
tenis, el	tennis	*ehl 'teh-nees*
tenis, los	tennis shoes	*lohs 'teh-nees*
teoría, la	theory	*lah teh-oh-'ree-ah*
terapeuta, el *or* la	therapist	*ehl / lah teh-rah-peh-'oo-tah*
terapia, la	therapy	*lah teh-'rah-pee·ah*
tercero(a)	third	*tehr-'seh-roh(ah)*
termómetro, el	thermometer	*ehl tehr-'moh-meh-troh*
termostato, el	thermostat	*ehl tehr-moh-'stah-toh*
terraza, la	deck	*lah teh-'rrah-sah*
terreno, el	land	*ehl teh-'rreh-noh*
testigo, el *or* la	witness	*ehl / lah teh-'stee-goh*
tía, la	aunt	*lah 'tee-ah*
tibio(a)	warm	*'tee-bee·oh(ah)*
tiempo, el	weather	*ehl tee-'ehmpoh*
tienda, la	store	*lah tee-'ehn-dah*
tierra, la	dirt	*lah tee-'eh-rrah*
tijeras, las	scissors	*lahs tee-'heh-rahs*
timbre, el	buzzer	*ehl 'teem-breh*
tímido(a)	shy	*'tee-mee-doh(ah)*
tía, la	aunt	*lah 'tee-ah*
tío, el	uncle	*ehl 'tee-oh*
título, el	title	*ehl 'tee-too-loh*
tiza, la	chalk	*lah 'tee-sah*
toalla, la	towel	*lah toh-'ah-yah*
tobillo, el	ankle	*ehl toh-'bee-yoh*
tobogán, el	slide (playground)	*ehl toh-boh-'gahn*

tocador de casetes, el	cassette player	*ehl toh-kah-'dohr deh kah-'seh-tehs*
todavía	yet	*toh-dah-'vee-ah*
todo(a) (os) (as)	all	*'toh-doh(ah) (ohs) (ahs)*
tomate, el	tomato	*ehl toh-'mah-teh*
tono, el	tune	*ehl 'toh-noh*
torcedura, la	sprain	*lah tohr-seh-'doo-rah*
tormenta, la	storm	*lah tohr-'mehn-tah*
tornado, el	tornado	*ehl tohr-'nah-doh*
torneo, el	tournament	*ehl tohr-'neh-oh*
torre, la	tower	*lah 'toh-rreh*
torta, la	cake	*lah 'tohr-tah*
tortuga, la	turtle	*lah tohr-'too-gah*
tos, la	cough	*lah tohs*
trabajador (la trabajadora) social, el	social worker	*ehl trah-bah-hah-'dohr (lah trah-bah-hah-'doh-rah) soh-see-'ahl*
trabajo, el	work	*ehl trah-'bah-hoh*
tractor, el	tractor	*ehl trahk-'tohr*
traductor, el (la traductora)	translator	*ehl trah-dook-'tohr (lah trah-dook-'toh-rah)*
tragedia, la	tragedy	*lah trah-'heh-dee·ah*
traje, el	suit	*ehl 'trah-heh*
transferencia, la	transfer	*lah trahns-feh-'rehn-see·ah*
transporte, el	transportation	*ehl trahns-'pohr-teh*
tranvía, el	streetcar	*ehl trahn-'vee-ah*
trapeador, el	mop	*ehl trah-peh-ah-'dohr*
traste, el	dish	*ehl 'trah-steh*
tren, el	train	*ehl trehn*
tribunal de menores, el	juvenile court	*ehl tree-boo-'nahl deh meh-'noh-rehs*
triciclo, el	tricycle	*ehl tree-'see-kloh*
trigonometría, la	trigonometry	*lah tree-goh-noh-meh-'tree-ah*
trineo, el	sled	*ehl tree-'neh-oh*
triste	sad	*'tree-steh*
trofeo, el	trophy	*ehl troh-'feh-oh*
trompo, el	top	*ehl 'trohm-poh*
truco, el	trick	*ehl 'troo-koh*
trusa, la	bathing suit	*lah 'troo-sah*
tú	you (singular, informal)	*too*
tubería, la	pipe; plumbing	*lah too-beh-'ree-ah*
tubo de ensayo, el	test tube	*ehl 'too-boh deh ehn-'sah-yoh*
tubo, el	tube	*ehl 'too-boh*
tumulto, el	disturbance	*ehl too-'mool-toh*

túnel, el	tunnel	*ehl 'too-nehl*
tutor, el (la tutora)	tutor	*ehl too-'tohr (lah too-'toh-rah)*
tutor (la tutora) legal, el	legal guardian	*ehl too-'tohr leh-'gahl (lah too-'toh-rah leh-'gahl)*
una vez	once	*'oo-nah vehs*
unidad, la	unit	*lah oo-nee-'dahd*
uniforme, el	uniform	*ehl oo-nee-'fohr-meh*
universidad, la	university; college	*lah oo-nee-vehr-see-'dahd*
universo, el	universe	*ehl oo-nee-'vehr-soh*
unos(as)	some	*'oo-nohs(ahs)*
urgente	urgent	*oor-'hehn-teh*
usted	you (singular, formal)	*oo-'stehd*
ustedes	you (plural, formal and informal)	*oo-'steh-dehs*
uva, la	grape	*lah 'oo-vah*
vaca, la	cow	*lah 'vah-kah*
vacaciones, las	vacation	*lahs vah-kah-see-'oh-nehs*
vacunación, la	vaccination	*lah vah-koo-nah-see-'ohn*
vagón, el	wagon	*ehl vah-'gohn*
valle, el	valley	*ehl 'vah-yeh*
valor, el	value	*ehl vah-'lohr*
vasinica, la	potty	*lah vah-see-'nee-kah*
vaso, el	glass (drinking)	*ehl 'vah-soh*
vecino, el (la vecina)	neighbor	*ehl veh-'see-noh (lah veh-'see-nah)*
vegetales, los	vegetables	*lohs veh-heh-'tah-lehs*
vela, la	candle	*lah 'veh-lah*
velocidad, la	speed	*lah veh-loh-see-'dahd*
vendaje, el	bandage	*ehl vehn-'dah-heh*
vendedor, el (la vendedora)	salesperson	*ehl vehn-deh-'dohr (lah vehn-deh-'doh-rah)*
vendedor (la vendedora) de drogas, el	drug dealer	*ehl vehn-deh-'dohr (lah ven-deh-'doh-rah) deh 'droh-gahs*
ventana, la	window	*lah vehn-'tah-nah*
ventilador, el	fan	*ehl vehn-tee-lah-'dohr*
verano, el	summer	*ehl veh-'rah-noh*
verde	green	*'vehr-deh*
vestíbulo, el	lobby	*ehl veh-'stee-boo-loh*
vestido, el	dress	*ehl veh-'stee-doh*
vía del ferrocarril, la	railroad track	*lah 'vee-ah dehl feh-rroh-kah-'rreel*
viaje, el	trip	*ehl vee-'ah-heh*
víctima, la	victim	*lah 'veek-tee-mah*
vídeo, el	video	*ehl 'vee-deh-oh*
videocasetera, la	VCR	*lah vee-deh-oh-kah-seh-'teh-rah*

vidrio, el	glass (material)	*ehl 'vee-dree·oh*
viejo(a)	old	*vee-'eh-hoh(ah)*
viento, el	wind	*ehl vee-'ehn-toh*
viernes	Friday	*vee-'ehr-nehs*
violación, la	rape; violation	*lah vee·oh-lah-see-'ohn*
violencia, la	violence	*lah vee-oh-'lehn-see·ah*
visitante, el *or* la	visitor	*ehl / lah vee-see-'tahn-teh*
vitaminas, las	vitamins	*lahs vee-tah-'mee-nahs*
vivienda, la	housing	*lah vee-vee-'ehn-dah*
vocabulario, el	vocabulary	*ehl voh-kah-boo-'lah-ree·oh*
vóleibol, el	volleyball	*ehl voh-'leh·ee-bohl*
voluntario, el	volunteer	*ehl voh-loon-'tah-ree·oh (lah*
(la voluntaria)		*voh-loon-'tah-ree·ah)*
voz, la	voice	*lah vohs*
y	and	*ee*
ya	already	*yah*
yo	I	*yoh*
zanahoria, la	carrot	*lah sah-nah-'oh-ree·ah*
zanja, la	ditch	*lah 'sahn-hah*
zapatillas, las	slippers	*lahs sah-pah-'tee-yahs*
zapato, el	shoe	*ehl sah-'pah-toh*
zona, la	zone	*lah 'soh-nah*
zona postal, la	zip code	*lah 'soh-nah poh-'stahl*
zoológico, el	zoo	*ehl soh-oh-'loh-hee-koh*

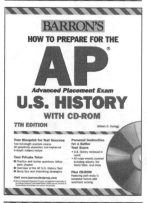
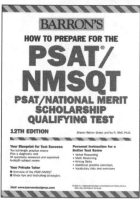

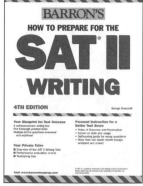

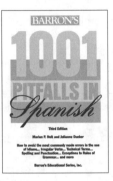